# Machine Learning

**Special Issues of Artificial Intelligence: An International Journal**

The titles in this series are paperback, readily accessible editions of the Special Volumes of *Artificial Intelligence: An International Journal*, edited by Daniel G. Bobrow and produced by special agreement with Elsevier Science Publishers B.V.

*Qualitative Reasoning about Physical Systems*, edited by Daniel G. Bobrow, 1985.

*Geometric Reasoning*, edited by Deepak Kapur and Joseph L. Mundy, 1989.

*Machine Learning: Paradigms and Methods*, edited by Jaime G. Carbonell, 1990.

# Machine Learning
## Paradigms and Methods

*edited by*
**J. G. Carbonell**

**A Bradford Book**
The MIT Press
Cambridge, Massachusetts
London, England

Second printing, 1992

First MIT Press edition, 1990

Reprinted from *Artificial Intelligence: An International Journal*, Volume 40,
Number 1–3 (1989). The MIT Press has exclusive license to sell this
English-language book edition throughout the world.

Printed and bound in the United States of America.

Library of Congress Cataloging-in-Publication Data

Machine learning : paradigms and methods / edited by J.G. Carbonell.
     p.    cm.
"A Bradford book"
Published also as: Artificial intelligence : an international journal, v. 40 (1989), no.
1-3, Sept. 1989.
    Includes bibliographical references.
    ISBN 0-262-53088-0
    1. Machine learning. 2. Artificial intelligence. I. Carbonell, Jaime G. (Jaime
Guillermo)
    Q325.5.M33    1990                        89-13641
    006.3′ 1--dc20                                    CIP

# Contents

# Introduction:
# Paradigms for Machine Learning

**Jaime G. Carbonell**

*School of Computer Science, Carnegie-Mellon University,
Pittsburgh, PA 15213, U.S.A.*

## 1. Historical Perspectives

Machine learning (ML) played a central role in artificial intelligence at its very beginning. Although the AI limelight has wandered away from machine learning in the advent of other significant developments, such as problem solving, theorem proving, planning, natural language processing, robotics, and expert systems, ML has returned cast in multiple guises, playing increasingly more significant roles. For instance, early work in linear perceptrons faded away in light of theoretical limitations, but resurged this decade with much fanfare as connectionist networks with hidden units able to compute and learn nonlinear functions. In the interim, many symbolic machine learning paradigms flourished, and several have evolved into powerful computational methods, including inductive concept acquisition, classifier systems, and explanation-based learning. Today, there are many active research projects spanning the gamut of machine learning methods, several focusing on the theory of learning and others on improving problem solving performance in complex domains. In the 1980s, the field of machine learning has re-emerged one of the major areas of artificial intelligence, with an annual ML conference, an established 1,000-subscriber journal, dozens of books, and ample representation in all major AI conferences.

Perhaps the tenacity of ML researchers in light of the undisputed difficulty of their ultimate objectives, and in light of early disappointments, is best explained by the very nature of the learning process. The ability to learn, to adapt, to modify behavior is an inalienable component of human intelligence. How can we build truly artificially intelligent machines that are not capable of self-improvement? Can an expert system be labeled "intelligent," any more than the *Encyclopedia Britanica* be labeled intelligent, merely because it contains useful knowledge in quantity? An underlying conviction of many ML researchers is that learning is a prerequisite to any form of true intelligence—

therefore it must be investigated in depth, no matter how formidable the challenge. Philosophical considerations aside, machine learning, like knowledge representation and reasoning, cuts across all problem areas of AI: problem solving, theorem proving, analogical and nonmonotonic reasoning, natural language processing, speech recognition, vision, robotics, planning, game playing, pattern recognition, expert systems, and so on. In principle, progress in ML can be leveraged in all these areas; it is truly at the core of artificial intelligence.

Recently, machine learning research has begun to pay off in various ways: solid theoretical foundations are being established; machine learning methods are being successfully integrated with powerful performance systems; and practical applications based on the more established techniques have already made their presence felt. Recent successes in machine learning include decision tree induction applied to industrial process control (based on Quinlan's ID3 [14] and its successors), the integration of explanation-based learning into general knowledge-intensive reasoning systems (such as SOAR [9], PRODIGY [11] and THEO), and extended forms of neural network learning to produce phonemic-level speech recognition at an accuracy surpassing conventional methods (such as hidden Markoff models) in modular time delay neural networks.

To date one can identify four major ML paradigms and multiple sub-paradigms under active investigation: inductive learning (e.g., acquiring concepts from sets of positive and negative examples), analytic learning (e.g., explanation-based learning and certain forms of analogical and case-based learning methods), genetic algorithms (e.g., classifier systems) [7]), and connectionist learning methods (e.g., nonrecurrent "*backprop*" hidden layer neural networks). These machine learning paradigms emerged from quite different scientific roots, employ different computational methods, and often rely on subtly different ways of evaluating success, although all share the common goal of building machines that can learn in significant ways for a wide variety of task domains. In all cases, learning can be defined operationally to mean the ability to perform new tasks that could not be performed before or perform old tasks better (faster, more accurately, etc.) as a result of changes produced by the learning process. Except for this basic consensus on what it means to learn, there are precious few assumptions shared by all four paradigms.

The central purpose of this special volume is to acquaint the reader with each machine learning paradigm, and do so directly from the proverbial horse's mouth—that is, as presented by one or more prominent researchers who practice each respective ML approach. Each author was asked to write a self-contained article with explicit historical and cross-paradigmatic perspectives for a reader well informed in artificial intelligence, but not necessarily an expert in machine learning.[1] Most authors complied and produced comprehen-

---

[1] The articles solicited were submitted to formal review, resulting in significant filtering and in substantial improvements to most of the accepted manuscripts.

sive articles setting forth explicitly many of the assumptions inherent in their machine learning paradigm, the basic computational methods, and the evolution of these methods up to and including reports on the authors' latest research results. If this special volume also serves the role of improving communication between practitioners of different paradigms of machine learning by encouraging cross-comparisons and providing better comprehension of different means to achieve common aims, so much the better.

## 2. The Inductive Paradigm

The most widely studied method for symbolic learning is one of inducing a general concept description from a sequence of instances of the concept and (usually) known counterexamples of the concept. The task is to build a concept description from which all the previous positive instances can be rederived by universal instantiation but none of the previous negative instance (the counterexamples) can be rederived by the same process. At this level of abstraction, the problem may sound simple, but it is not even well posed. The design space of potential inductive systems is determined by many important dimensions, such as:

– *Description language.* The language in which input instances and output concepts are expressed can vary in representational power (e.g., propositional calculus, first-order logic, or beyond), in whether the domain of variables in the description language is discrete, continuous or mixed, and in whether individual values are points in the domain or probability distributions among the possible domain values. Most early concept acquisition systems handled only certain classes of propositional representations (attribute-value lists) with single-valued variables drawn from a finite nominal domain. Continuous variables were arbitrarily partitioned into discrete intervals. Present systems explore the full range of possibilities. However, most systems make a fixed vocabulary assumption in that all the relevant descriptors must be present at the outset. Lately, some researchers are starting to consider the implications of description languages that grow during the learning cycle, labeling the process *representational shift.*

– *Noise and instance classification.* Most early learning-from-examples systems assumed that every instance was correctly classified as positive or negative with respect to the desired concept; that is, they assumed a benign and accurate teacher providing a stream of well-formed data [16]. Since such an assumption is much too restrictive for real-world applications, new systems explore the possibility of inaccurately labeled and unlabeled instances, of partially specified instances (where some attributes may be unknown), of measurement errors in the values of the attributes, and of differential relevance among the attributes. So long as the signal-to-noise ratio is acceptable, and the number of instances is sufficiently high, statistical techniques integrated into the learning method come to the rescue.

– *Concept type*. Some learning systems strive for *discriminant concepts*, where the concept description is a set of tests which separate all instances of the concept apart from all instances of every other concept known to the system. Often discriminant concept descriptions are encoded as paths from the root to the leaves of incrementally acquired decision trees. Other learning systems acquire *characteristic concepts*, which strive for compactness and elegance in the concept descriptions. Such concepts are far easier to communicate to human users and often prove more usable when they must be interpreted by some other part of the performance system. However, the tradeoff for simplicity of description is often loss of complete accuracy; characteristic concepts do not necessarily comply with the strict discrimination criterion. Characteristic concept descriptions are often encoded as frames or logical formulae. The *inductive bias* of a learning system is often expressed as preferences in the type of concept to be acquired, and simplicity of the concept description is the most prevalent form of domain-independent inductive bias.

– *Source of instances*. The initial learning-from-examples model called for an external teacher to supply a stream of classified examples for a single concept to be acquired at one time. In addition to considering the possibility of noise in the data (discussed above), one can remove the teacher entirely and use the external world as a source of data. In such cases, the learner must be proactive in seeking examples, must cope with multiple concepts at one time, and must seek its own classification of instances by appealing to an external oracle (if available), by performing experiments (if possible), or by conceptual clustering techniques [10]. Current work also addresses the judicious selection of instances to reduce maximally the uncertainty in partially formed concepts (a complex form of multi-dimensional binary search).

– *Incremental versus one-shot induction*. One-shot inductive learning systems consider all the positive and negative instances that will ever be seen as training data at one time and produce a concept description not open to further modification [4]. Incremental techniques produce the best-guess concept [16] or the range of concepts consistent with the data so far (as in version spaces [12]), and can interleave learning and performance. As the latter reflect more accurately real-world situations in which learning is an ongoing process, they are currently the ones more heavily investigated.

### 3. The Analytic Paradigm

A more recent but very widely studied paradigm for learning is based on analytical learning from few exemplars (often a single one) plus a rich underlying domain theory. The methods involved are deductive rather than inductive, utilizing past problem solving experience (the exemplars) to guide which deductive chains to perform when solving new problems, or to formulate search control rules that enable more efficient application of domain knowledge. Thus, analytic methods focus on improving the efficiency of a system without sacrificing accuracy or generality, rather than extending its library of concept descriptions. The precursors of modern analytic learning methods are macro-operators [5], and formal methods such as weakest precondition analysis. Presently, analytic learning methods focus on explanation-based learning [3, 13], multi-level chunking [9], iterative macro-operators [2] and derivational analogy [1]. Some fundamental issues cut across all analytic methods:

– *Representation of instances*. In analytic methods an instance corresponds to a portion of a problem solving trace, and learning uses that single instance plus background knowledge (often called a *domain theory*). In the simplest case an instance is just a sequence of operators, which can be grouped into macro-operators, modified in analogical transfer, or viewed as steps in a "proof" of the problem solution for explanation-based learning. More recently, problem solving traces carry with them the justification structure (i.e., the goal-subgoal tree, annotations on why each operator was selected, and a trace of failed solution attempts, all interconnected with dependency links). These traces permit richer learning processes such as generalized chunking, derivational analogy (applied by Mostow in this volume) and explanation-based specialization (discussed by Minton et al. in this volume).

– *Learning from success or failure*. The earliest analytic techniques acquired only the ability to replicate success more efficiently (e.g., macro-operators, early EBL, and early chunking). However, much can be learned from failure in order to avoid similar pitfalls in future situations sharing the same underlying failure causes. Recent EBL techniques, analogical methods, and to some extent chunking in systems like SOAR [9] learn both from success and from failure.

– *Degree of generalization*. The control knowledge acquired in analytical learning can be specific to the situation in the exemplar or generalized as permitted by the domain theory. Generalization strategies range from the elimination of irrelevant information (in virtually all analytical methods) to the application of general meta-reasoning strategies to elevate control knowledge to the provably most general form in the presence of a strong domain and architectural theory (as discussed by Minton et al. in this volume).

– *Closed versus open loop learning*. Open loop learning implies one-pass acquisition of new knowledge, regardless of later evidence questioning its correctness or utility. In contrast, closed loop learning permits future evaluation of the new knowledge for modification or even elimination should it not improve system performance as desired. Performance measures of newly

acquired knowledge are often empirical in nature; only the acquisition of the
control knowledge is purely analytical.

## 4. The Genetic Paradigm

Genetic algorithms (also called "classifier systems") represent the extreme
empirical position among the machine learning paradigms. They have been
inspired by a direct analogy to mutations in biological reproduction (cross-
overs, point mutations, etc.) and Darwinian natural selection (survival of the
fittest in each ecological niche). Variants of a concept description correspond to
individuals of a species, and induced changes and recombinations of these
concepts are tested against an objective function (the natural selection criterion) to see which to preserve in the gene pool. In principle, genetic algorithms
encode a parallel search through concept space, with each process attempting
coarse-grain hill climbing.

Stemming from the work of Holland [7], the genetic algorithm community
has grown largely independent of other machine learning approaches, and has
developed its own analysis tools, applications, and workshops. However, many
of the underlying problems and techniques are shared with the mainline
inductive methods and with the connectionist paradigm. For instance, as in all
empirical learning, assigning credit (or blame) for changes in performance as
measured by the objective function is difficult and indirect. There are a
multiplicity of methods to address this problem in the inductive approaches,
dating back to Samuel [15]. For genetic algorithms, Holland developed the
*bucket brigade* algorithm [8]. And, credit/blame assignment is positively
central to all connectionist learning methods, as exemplified by the backpropagation technique.

## 5. The Connectionist Paradigm

Connectionist learning systems, also called "neural networks" (NNets) or
"parallel distributed systems" (PDPs), have received much attention of late.
They have overcome the theoretical limitations of perceptrons and early linear
networks by the introduction of "hidden layers" to represent intermediate
processing and compute nonlinear recognition functions. There are two basic
types of connectionist systems: those that use distributed representations—
where a concept corresponds to an activation pattern spanning, potentially, the
entire network—and those that use localized representations where physical
portions of the network correspond to individual concepts. The former is the
more prevalent, although hierarchical modularization for complex systems
limits the physical extent of concept representations.

Connectionist systems learn to discriminate among equivalence classes of
patterns from an input domain in a holistic manner. They are presented with
training sets of representative instances of each class, correctly labeled (with

some noise tolerance), and they learn to recognize these and other instances of each representative class. Learning consists of readjusting weights in a fixed-topology network via different learning algorithms such as *Boltzmann* [6] or *backpropagation*. These algorithms, in essence, calculate credit assignment from the final discrimination back to the individual weights on all the active links in the network. There are, of course, much more complexity and many subtle variations involved, as reported in Hinton's article in this volume.

Amidst structural diversity, one can find strong functional similarities between connectionist learning systems and their symbolic counterparts, namely discriminant learning in inductive systems and genetic algorithms. Induced symbolic decision trees and NNets both are trained on a number of pre-classified instance patterns, both are noise-tolerant, and after training both are given the task of classifying new instances correctly. In order to evaluate the appropriateness of each technique to the task at hand, one must ask some detailed quantitative questions, such as comparing the ease of casting training data into acceptable representations, the amount of training data required for sufficiently accurate performance, the relative computational burden of each technique in both training and performance phases, and other such metrics.

### 6. Cross-Paradigmatic Observations

Consider the larger picture, contrasting the three symbolic paradigms and connectionist systems in general. But, rather than engaging in the perennial sectarian debate of supporting one paradigm at the expense of the other, let us summarize the properties of a domain problem that favor the selection of each basic approach:

– *Signal-symbol mapping*. From continuous signals such as wave forms into meaningful discrete symbols such as phonemes in speech recognition. Best approach: Connectionism (or traditional statistical learning methods such as dynamic programming or hidden Markoff models).

– *Continuous pattern recognition*. From analog signals to a small discrete set of equivalence classes. Best approach: Connectionism. Inductive or genetic approaches require that the signal-symbol map be solved first, or that a predefined feature set with numerical ranges be given a priori.

– *Discrete pattern recognition*. From collections of features to membership in a predefined equivalence class (e.g., noninteractive medical diagnosis). Best approach: Inductive learning of decision trees. Other inductive approaches, genetic algorithms, and even connectionist methods can apply.

– *Acquiring new concept descriptions*. From examples to general descriptions. Best approach: Induction with characteristic concept descriptions, permitting explanation to human users or manipulation by other system modules. Genetic algorithms and connectionist approaches do not produce characteristic concept descriptions.

– *Acquiring rules for expert systems.* From behavioral traces to general rules. If a strong domain theory is present, analogical or EBL approaches are best. If not inductive or genetic approaches prevail. Connectionist systems do not preserve memory of earlier states and therefore cannot emulate well multi-step inferences or deductive chains.

– *Enhancing the efficiency of rule-based systems.* From search guided only by weak methods to domain-dependent focused behavior. Best approach: Analytic techniques ranging from macro-operators and chunking to EBL and analogy. Here is where background knowledge can be used most effectively to reformulate control decisions for efficient behavior by analytic means.

– *Instruction and symbiotic reasoning.* From stand-alone system to collaborative problem solving. When user and system must pool resources and reason jointly, or when either attempts to instruct the other, knowledge must be encoded in an explicit manner comprehensible to both. Best approaches: Inductive (with characteristic concept descriptions) or analytic (often case-based analogical) reasoning. Neither genetic systems nor (especially) connectionist ones represent the knowledge gained in a manner directly communicable to the user or other system modules. Imagine attempting to understand the external significance of a huge matrix of numerical connection strengths.

– *Integrated reasoning architectures.* From general reasoning principles to focused behavior in selected domains. In principle all methods of learning should apply, although the analytic ones have been most successful thus far.

At the risk of oversimplification, one may make a general observation: Connectionist approaches are superior for single-step gestalt recognition in unstructured continuous domains, if very many training examples are present. At the opposite end of the spectrum, analytic methods are best for well-structured knowledge-rich domains that require deep reasoning and multi-step inference, even if few training examples are available. Inductive and genetic techniques are best in the center of the wide gulf between these two extreme points. Clearly there are many tasks that can be approached by more than one method, and evaluating which might be the best approach requires detailed quantitative analysis. Perhaps more significantly, there are complex tasks where multiple forms of learning should co-exist, with connectionist approaches at the sensor interface, inductive ones for formulating empirical rules of behavior, and analytic ones to improve performance when the domain model is well enough understood.

## REFERENCES

1. Carbonell, J.G., Derivational analogy: A theory of reconstructive problem solving and expertise acquisition, in: R.S. Michalski, J.G. Carbonell and T.M. Mitchell (Eds.), *Machine Learning: An Artificial Intelligence Approach* 2 (Morgan Kaufmann, Los Altos, CA, 1986).
2. Cheng, P.W. and Carbonnel, J.G., Inducing iterative rules from experience: The FERMI experiment, in: *Proceedings AAAI-86*, Philadelphia, PA (1986) 490–495.
3. DeJong, G.F. and Mooney, R., Explanation-based learning: An alternative view, *Mach. Learning* 1 (1986) 145–176.
4. Dietterich, T.G. and Michalski, R.S., A comparative review of selected methods for learning structural descriptions, in: R.S. Michalski, J.G. Carbonell and T.M. Mitchell (Eds.), *Machine Learning: An Artificial Intelligence Approach* (Tioga, Palo Alto, CA, 1983).
5. Fikes, R.E. and Nilsson, N.J., STRIPS: A new approach to the application of theorem proving to problem solving, *Artificial Intelligence* 2 (1971) 189–208.
6. Hinton, G.E., Sejnowski, T.J. and Ackley, D.H., Boltzmann machines: Constraint satisfaction networks that learn, Tech. Rept. CMU-CS-84-119, Computer Science Department, Carnegie-Mellon University, Pittsburgh, PA (1984).
7. Holland, J., *Adaptation in Natural and Artificial Systems* (University of Michigan Press, Ann Arbor, MI, 1975).
8. Holland, J.H., Escaping brittleness: The possibilities of general-purpose learning algorithms applied to parallel rule-based systems, in: R.S. Michalski, J.G. Carbonell and T.M. Mitchell (Eds.), *Machine Learning: An Artificial Intelligence Approach* 2 (Morgan Kaufmann, Los Altos, CA, 1986) 593–624.
9. Laird, J.E., Rosenbloom, P.S. and Newell, A., Chunking in Soar: The anatomy of a general learning mechanism, *Mach. Learning* 1 (1986) 11–46.
10. Michalski, R.S. and Stepp R.E., Learning from observation: Conceptual clustering, in: R.S. Michalski, J.G. Carbonell and T.M. Mitchell (Eds.), *Machine Learning: An Artificial Intelligence Approach* (Tioga, Palo Alto, CA, 1983).
11. Minton, S., Carbonell, J.G., Etzioni, O., Knoblock, C.A. and Kuokka, D.R., Acquiring effective search control rules: Explanation-based learning in the PRODIGY system, in: *Proceedings Fourth International Workshop on Machine Learning*, Irvine, CA (1987) 122–133.
12. Mitchell, T.M., Version spaces: An approach to concept learning, Ph.D. Dissertation, Stanford University, Stanford, CA (1978).
13. Mitchell, T., Keller, R. and Kedar-Cabelli, S., Explanation-based generalization: A unifying view, *Mach. Learning* 1 (1986) 47–80.
14. Quinlan, J.R., Learning efficient classification procedures and their application to chess end games, in: R.S. Michalski, J.G. Carbonell and T.M. Mitchell (Eds.), *Machine Learning: An Artificial Intelligence Approach* (Tioga, Palo Alto, CA, 1983).
15. Samuel, A.L., Some studies in machine learning using the game of checkers, in: E.A. Feigenbaum and J. Feldman (Eds.), *Computers and Thought* (McGraw-Hill, New York, 1963) 71–105.
16. Winston, P., Learning structural descriptions from examples, in: P. Winston (Ed.), *The Psychology of Computer Vision* (McGraw-Hill, New York, 1975).

# Models of Incremental Concept Formation

## John H. Gennari, Pat Langley and Doug Fisher*

*Irvine Computational Intelligence Project,
Department of Information and Computer Science,
University of California, Irvine, CA 92717, U.S.A.*

ABSTRACT

*Given a set of observations, humans acquire concepts that organize those observations and use them in classifying future experiences. This type of concept formation can occur in the absence of a tutor and it can take place despite irrelevant and incomplete information. A reasonable model of such human concept learning should be both incremental and capable of handling the type of complex experiences that people encounter in the real world. In this paper, we review three previous models of incremental concept formation and then present CLASSIT, a model that extends these earlier systems. All of the models integrate the process of recognition and learning, and all can be viewed as carrying out search through the space of possible concept hierarchies. In an attempt to show that CLASSIT is a robust concept formation system, we also present some empirical studies of its behavior under a variety of conditions.*

## 1. Introduction

Much of human learning can be viewed as a gradual process of *concept formation*. In this view, the agent observes a succession of objects or events from which he induces a hierarchy of concepts that summarize and organize his experience. This task is very similar to the problem of *conceptual clustering* as defined by Michalski and Stepp [30], with the added constraint that learning be incremental. More formally:

- *Given*: a sequential presentation of instances and their associated descriptions;
- *Find*: clusterings that group those instances in categories;
- *Find*: an intensional definition for each category that summarizes its instances;
- *Find*: a hierarchical organization for those categories.

---

* Current address: Department of Computer Science, Vanderbilt University, Nashville, TN, U.S.A.

The goals of conceptual clustering are straightforward: to help one better understand the world and to make predictions about its future behavior. Concept formation has essentially the same goals, and differs mainly in the constraints it places on achieving them.

In this paper, we focus on the concept formation task and examine some methods for incrementally forming clusters, concept descriptions, and concept hierarchies. We begin by attempting to abstract the features that are common to the existing work on concept formation and that set it apart from other approaches. After this, we review in some detail three models of the concept formation process—Feigenbaum's [9] EPAM, Lebowitz's [24, 26] UNIMEM, and Fisher's [12] COBWEB. Next we describe CLASSIT, an extension of Fisher's system, and report some experimental studies of the program's learning behavior. We close with some suggestions for future research and a summary of our main observations.

## 2. Methods for Concept Formation

The majority of machine learning research has focused on the broad area of concept learning. To many readers, the work on concept formation may seem a minor variation on better-known approaches, and it certainly has close ties to other work. However, methods for concept formation share a number of important features that, taken together, distinguish them from other efforts. In this section we identify those features that are common to the approach and that serve to separate it from alternative paradigms, particularly other methods for conceptual clustering. In some sense, one can also view these features as "defining" the term *concept formation*.

### 2.1. Representing knowledge in a concept hierarchy

The most obvious common feature of concept formation methods is their organization of knowledge into a *concept hierarchy*. This type of data structure contains a set of nodes partially ordered by generality, and thus is similar to the *is-a* hierarchies used by some machine learning systems (Michalski [29], Mitchell, Utgoff and Banerji [32]). Each node in a concept hierarchy represents a concept, but unlike most *is-a* hierarchies, each node also contains an intensional description of that concept.

The hierarchical organization of acquired concepts is one distinctive feature of methods for concept formation (and conceptual clustering). In contrast, most work on learning from examples (Mitchell [31], Michalski [29]) focuses on learning one or a few concepts at a single level of abstraction. Methods for constructing decision trees (Quinlan [34]) are closer in spirit, but lack any explicit descriptions on the nodes themselves.

## 2.2. Top-down classification of instances

The presence of a concept hierarchy suggests a natural approach for classifying new instances that is shared by all concept formation systems. One simply begins at the most general (top) node and sorts the instance down through the hierarchy. This classification method is very similar to that used by decision-tree systems. However, the scheme for determining which branch to follow need not be based on the result of a single attribute's value, and some concept formation systems allow the instance to follow more than one branch. Nor must the instance always be sorted to a terminal node; in principle, the sorting process may stop at a node higher in the hierarchy.

Once the instance has finished its descent, one can use the concept description at the selected node to make predictions about unseen aspects of the instance. Decision-tree systems typically make predictions about the class of the instance, but concept formation systems can make predictions about a wider range of features. This suggests measuring the performance of an acquired hierarchy in terms of its ability to make predictions about unseen attributes.[1] In principle, other methods for conceptual clustering could be evaluated along the same dimension, but few researchers have taken this approach.

## 2.3. Unsupervised nature of the learning task

The unsupervised nature of the learning task leads to another common feature of concept formation systems—they must cluster instances without advice from a teacher. In other words, they must decide not only which instances each class should contain, but also the number of such classes. This is the most important feature separating work on concept formation (and conceptual clustering) from research on learning conjunctive concepts from examples (Winston [44], Mitchell [31]).

Techniques for inducing decision trees (e.g., Quinlan [34]) come much closer to concept formation methods on this dimension. Although supervised in the sense that they are given teacher-specified class information, these systems must determine their own subclasses, which equates to forming instance clusters. Rendell, Seshu and Tcheng's [35] work on probabilistic concept learning has a similar flavor.

## 2.4. Integrating learning and performance

We have defined the concept formation task to be incremental in nature. By *incremental*, we mean not only that the agent accepts instances one at a time,

---

[1] Although all of the concept formation systems we will examine assume attribute-value representations, the framework we outline can handle relational or structural descriptions as well. See Levinson [27] for some initial work along these lines.

but also that it does not extensively reprocess previously encountered instances while incorporating the new one. Without this constraint, one could make any nonincremental method "incremental" simply by adding the new instance to an existing set and reapplying the nonincremental method to the extended set. Note that our definition of incremental does *not* forbid retaining all instances in memory, only the extensive reprocessing of those instances. In fact, most existing methods for concept formation retain at least some instances as terminal nodes in the concept hierarchy.

This focus on incremental learning leads naturally to the integration of learning with performance. In any incremental system (Winston [44], Mitchell [31], Schlimmer and Fisher [38]), action by the performance component (e.g., classifying an instance) drives the learning element (e.g., modifying a concept hierarchy). In contrast, nonincremental schemes (Michalski [29], Quinlan [34]) isolate the processes of learning and performance. Most research on both numerical taxonomy (Everitt [8]) and conceptual clustering (Michalski and Stepp [30], Fisher [11]) has taken a nonincremental approach. Thus, this dimension constitutes one major distinction between earlier approaches to clustering and concept formation as we have defined it.

The role of classification in concept formation systems exerts a strong influence on the nature of learning. We noted above that the performance component of these methods sort instances down through a concept hierarchy. As a result, it seems natural to acquire the concept hierarchies in a top-down fashion as well. Thus, concept formation methods typically construct their hierarchies in a *divisive* manner, rather than using the *agglomerative* approach more common within the statistical clustering community.[2]

## 2.5. Learning as incremental hill climbing

The features described above seem almost to follow from the task of concept formation itself, but the final commonality has a different flavor. The models we describe in the following pages can all be characterized as *incremental hill-climbing learners*. We have elaborated on this notion elsewhere (Langley, Gennari and Iba [21], Fisher [12]), and Schlimmer and Fisher [38] described the basic idea (without using this term) even earlier. One can view concept formation as a search through a space of concept hierarchies, and hill climbing is one possible method for controlling that search.

Hill climbing is a classic AI search method in which one applies all operator instantiations, compares the resulting states using an evaluation function, selects the best state, and iterates until no more progress can be made. There are many variants on the basic algorithm, but these do not concern us here. The main advantage of hill climbing is its low memory requirement; since there

---

[2] For one exception, see Hanson and Bauer's work on WITT [16], an agglomerative clustering system that can operate incrementally.

are never more than a few states in memory, it sidesteps the combinatorial memory requirements associated with search-intensive methods. However, it also suffers from well-known drawbacks, such as the tendency to halt at local optima and a dependence on step size.

We are using the term *hill climbing* in a nontraditional sense, focusing on some features and ignoring others. For instance, we do not require an incremental hill-climbing learner to have an explicit evaluation function, or even that it carry out a one-step lookahead. One can replace this approach with a strong generator that computes the successor state from new input, such as an observed instance. For our purposes, the main feature of a hill-climbing system is its limited memory. At each point in learning, the system may retain only one knowledge structure, even though this structure may itself be quite complex. Thus, hill-climbing learners cannot carry out a breadth-first search (Mitchell [3]) or a beam search (Michalski [29]) through the space of hypotheses, nor can they carry out explicit backtracking (Winston [44]). They can only move "forward," revising their single knowledge structure in the light of new experience.[3]

The most important difference between incremental hill-climbing learners and their traditional cousins lies in the role of input. As we have seen, incremental learning methods are driven by new instances, and in the case of incremental hill-climbing systems, this means that each step through the hypothesis space occurs in response to (and takes into account) some new experience. More generally, each instance may lead to a number of learning steps (e.g., one for each level in the concept hierarchy). In other words, the learner does not move through the space of hypotheses until it obtains a new datum, and this alters the nature of the hill-climbing task.

Recall that hill-climbing methods search an $n$-dimensional space over which some function $f$ is defined. This function determines the shape of an $n$-dimensional surface, and the agent attempts to find that point with the highest $f$ score. In traditional hill-climbing approaches, the shape of the surface is constant. In contrast, for systems that learn through incremental hill climbing, each new instance modifies the contours of the surface. Like Simon's [41] wandering ant, the learner's behavior is controlled by the shape of its world. However, the hills and valleys of the hill-climbing learner's space are constantly changing as it gathers more information, altering the path it follows.[4] This

---

[3] Some "strength-based" methods retain competing hypotheses in memory, gradually deleting some and adding others on the basis of their performance. Genetic algorithms (Holland [17], Grefenstette [15]) follow this approach, as do Anderson and Kline's [2] and Langley's [20] work on production system learning. One could view these methods as incremental hill-climbing learners, provided one treats the entire set of rules as a single "state." However, we believe this violates the spirit of our limited memory assumption.

[4] Note that this feature does *not* hold for nonincremental learners that use hill-climbing methods (Michalski and Stepp [30]) or greedy algorithms (Quinlan [34]); the shape of the surface over which these systems travel remains constant throughout the learning process.

feature of incremental hill climbing is novel enough that it becomes unclear whether the limitations of traditional hill-climbing methods still hold. It also gives the potential for dealing with *concept drift* (Schlimmer and Granger [39]), in which the environment actually changes over time.

However, this dependence on new instances to control the search process can make memory-limited incremental learning methods sensitive to the order of instance presentation. Initial nonrepresentative data may lead a learning system astray, and one would like it to recover when later data point the way to the correct knowledge structure. Thus, Schlimmer and Fisher [38] have argued for including *bidirectional* learning operators that can reverse the effects of previous learning should new instances suggest the need. In the context of concept formation, one might include an operator not only for creating new subcategories, but also for deleting them should they not prove useful. Similarly, one might desire an operator not only for creating new disjunctive classes, but also one for combining classes if the distinction fares poorly. Such bidirectional operators can give incremental hill-climbing learners the *effect* of backtracking search without the memory required by true backtracking. Whether this approach works or not is an empirical question, but in Section 5 we will see evidence that it can help significantly.

## 2.6. Summary

In this section we identified some common threads that run through a number of research efforts, and we borrowed the term *concept formation* to refer to this research area. The basic approach can be viewed as a form of conceptual clustering, but it also differs from "traditional" work in this area. The common features of concept formation methods include the hierarchical organization of concepts, top-down classification, and an unsupervised, incremental, hill-climbing approach to learning.

We should emphasize that none of these features by itself makes work on concept formation unique. It shares many of these features with other methods for conceptual clustering, and there exist many supervised learning methods that process instances incrementally. Even the incremental hill-climbing approach has been widely used within the machine learning community, though it has not been labeled as such.[5] However, when one takes all these features together, what emerges is a distinctive and promising approach to concept learning.

---

[5] For example, recent work on supervised concept learning (Schlimmer and Fisher [38], Iba, Wogulis and Langley [18]) has been within this paradigm, as has recent work on theory formation (Shrager [40], Rose and Langley [36]). Much of the work on grammar acquisition (Anderson [1], Berwick [3]) has also occurred within the incremental hill-climbing framework. Even such diverse paradigms as neural networks and explanation-based learning share incremental hill climbing as an unstated assumption.

## 3. Earlier Research on Concept Formation

Before describing our own research on concept formation, we should review previous work on the problem. In this section we review three models of this process—Feigenbaum's EPAM, Lebowitz's UNIMEM, and Fisher's COBWEB. We will see that, with minor exceptions, each system operates within the common framework described in the previous section. We will also see that each system addresses issues that its predecessor ignored. This does not mean later systems are superior to earlier ones, since they also ignore some issues addressed by their precursors. However, there has been clear progress on certain fronts, and we will focus on these. We describe each model in terms of its representation and organization of knowledge, its classification and learning methods, and its metric for evaluating the resulting concepts and hierarchies.

### 3.1. Feigenbaum's EPAM

Feigenbaum's EPAM [9] can be viewed as an early model of incremental concept formation.[6] The system was intended as a psychological model of human learning on verbal memorization tasks, and it successfully explained a variety of well-established learning phenomena. These included the serial position effect, the conditions for multi-trial versus one-trial learning, forgetting through oscillation and retroactive inhibition, and a number of other empirical generalizations.

### 3.1.1. *Representation and organization in EPAM*

EPAM represents each instance as a conjunction of attribute-value pairs, along with an optional ordered list of component objects. Each component is in turn described as a conjunction of attribute-value pairs, with its own optional components, and so forth. For instance, the system might represent the nonsense syllable GAK as a list of three component objects—the first letter, the second letter, and the third letter. Each letter might itself be described in terms of lower-level components (e.g., the lines making it up), or it might be viewed as a primitive object having only attributes and no components. For simplicity, we will avoid examples that involve components and focus on single-level instances that can be described purely in terms of attribute-value pairs.

EPAM represents and organizes its acquired knowledge in a *discrimination network*. Each nonterminal node in this network specifies some *test*, and each link emanating from this node corresponds to one possible result of that test. Some tests involve examining the value of an attribute, whereas others involve examining the category of a subobject, which can itself be learned. Each

---

[6] For a more comprehensive treatment of EPAM and its extensions, see Feigenbaum and Simon [10].

nonterminal node also includes a branch marked OTHER, which lets EPAM avoid specifying all possible results of the test at the outset. Each terminal node contains an *image*—a partial set of attribute values (and component categories) expected to hold for instances sorted to that node.

Consider the example discrimination network in Fig. 1, which includes only attribute tests. This domain assumes instances composed of a single cell with three attributes—surface color, number of nuclei, and number of tails. The root node in Fig. 1(a) contains a test on the attribute NUCLEI, and the two links emanating from this node are labeled ONE and OTHER. The leftmost successor is a terminal node and thus has an associated image; this contains the partial description NUCLEI = ONE ∧ TAILS = ONE. (Note that color is unspecified.) The rightmost successor is nonterminal and thus has an associated test, this one involving the attribute COLOR. One link (labeled LIGHT) points to a successor node with image COLOR = LIGHT ∧ NUCLEI = TWO. The other (labeled OTHER) leads to a successor node with image COLOR = DARK.

### 3.1.2. *Classification and learning in* EPAM

As with all the concept formation systems we will examine, EPAM's classification process is completely integrated with its learning method. Table 1 presents the top-level EPAM algorithm, which focuses on performance. As the system encounters each instance, it sorts that instance through the discrimination network, starting at the top (root) node and proceeding until it reaches a

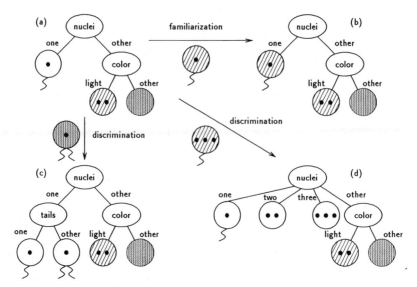

Fig. 1. Examples of EPAM's learning methods.

Table 1
The top-level EPAM algorithm

---

Input: The current node $N$ in the discrimination network.
      An unclassified (attribute-value) instance $I$.
Results: A discrimination net that classifies the instance.
Top-level call: EPAM(Top-node, $I$).
Variables: $N$ and $S$ are nodes in the hierarchy.
          $M$ is an image associated with a terminal node.
          $A$ is an attribute test.
          $V$ is the value of an attribute.
          $D$ is a set of attributes.

EPAM($N$, $I$)
  **If** $N$ is a terminal node,
    **Then** let $M$ be the image associated with $N$.
      Let $D$ be the set of tests on which $I$ and $M$ differ.
      **If** $D$ is the empty set,
        **Then** Familiarize($M$, $I$).
      **Else** Discriminate(Top-node, $I$, $M$, $D$, empty set).
  **Else** let $A$ be the test associated with $N$.
    Let $V$ be the value of instance $I$ on test $A$.
    **If** $N$ has a branch labeled $V$,
      **Then** let $S$ be the successor of $N$ by branch $V$.
    **Else** let $S$ be the successor of $N$ by branch OTHER.
    EPAM($S$, $I$)

---

terminal node. At each node, EPAM examines the instance's value on the test specified for that node. In the case of tests examining the category of a subobject, the model calls on itself recursively to determine the appropriate category; we have omitted this option from the table for the sake of clarity. If the category or attribute value equals that on one of the emanating branches, EPAM sends the instance down that branch; otherwise it goes down the OTHER branch. Eventually, the instance reaches a terminal node. For example, in Fig. 1(a) a dark cell with one nucleus and two tails would reach the leftmost terminal node, whereas a dark cell with two nuclei and two tails would reach the rightmost one.

Once EPAM has "recognized" an object as an instance of a terminal node, it "recalls" the image associated with that node. At this point, the algorithm invokes one of two learning mechanisms. If the image matches the instance (i.e., if no attribute-value pairs differ), then *familiarization* occurs. As summarized in Table 2, this process selects an attribute that occurs in the instance but not in the image, and then adds the attribute (along with the instance's value) to the image. In this way, EPAM gradually makes its images more specific as it encounters more instances. Eventually, a given image may become so detailed that it effectively becomes equivalent to a particular instance. Given the

Table 2
Familiarization and discrimination in EPAM

---

Variables: $I$ is an (attribute-value) instance.
$N$ and $S$ are nodes in the hierarchy.
$M$ is an image associated with a terminal node.
$A$ is an attribute test.
$U$ and $V$ are the values of attributes.
$D$ and $L$ are sets of attributes.
$T$ is a set of attribute-values $((A, V), \ldots)$.

Familiarize$(M, I)$
Let $L$ be those attributes in instance $I$ not in image $M$.
Select an attribute $A$ from $L$.
Let $V$ be the value of $A$ for $I$.
Add the attribute-value pair $(A, V)$ to the image $M$.

Discriminate$(N, I, M, D, T)$
**If** $N$ is a terminal node,
  **Then** Deepen$(N, I, M, D, T)$.
**Else** let $A$ be the attribute associated with node $N$.
  Let $U$ be the value of $A$ for instance $I$.
  Let $V$ be the value of $A$ for image $M$.
  **If** $U$ does not equal $V$,
    **Then** Add-branch$(N, U, \text{Union}(T, (A, U)))$.
        Add-branch$(N, V, \text{Union}(T, (A, V)))$.
  **Else if** $N$ has a branch labeled $V$,
      **Then** let $S$ be the successor of $N$ by branch $V$.
      **Else** let $S$ be the successor of $N$ by branch OTHER.
      Discriminate$(S, I, M, D, \text{Union}(T, (A, U)))$.

Deepen$(N, I, M, D, T)$
Select an attribute $A$ from $D$.
Remove the image $M$ from node $N$.
Associate the attribute $A$ with node $N$.
Let $U$ be the value of $A$ for instance $I$.
Let $V$ be the value of $A$ for image $M$.
Add-branch$(N, U, \text{Union}(T, (A, U)))$.
Add-branch$(N, \text{OTHER}, \text{Union}(M, (A, U)))$.

Add-branch$(N, V, I)$
Create a successor node of $N$ called $S$.
Connect $N$ to $S$ with a branch having value $V$.
Store the image $I$ on $S$.

---

network in Fig. 1(a) and the instance COLOR = DARK $\wedge$ NUCLEI = ONE $\wedge$ TAILS = ONE, familiarization would produce the network shown in Fig. 1(b).

If the image fails to match the instance (i.e., if any attribute-value pairs differ), then *discrimination* occurs instead. This process sorts the instance through the discrimination network a second time, looking for the first node at which the image and instance differ on a stored test. This can occur at a nonterminal node only if the instance was sorted down the OTHER branch leading from that node. If EPAM finds such a node, it creates two new branches, one based on the instance's value for the test and the other based on the image's value.[7] Each branch points to a new terminal node, and each image consists of the results of tests that lead to the node. In this way, EPAM gradually increases the breadth of its discrimination network. The transition between Fig. 1(a) and (d) gives an example of this type of discrimination, in this case invoked by the instance COLOR = LIGHT ∧ NUCLEI = THREE ∧ TAILS = ONE.

If no such node exists, the system eventually sorts the instance back down to the terminal node where the mismatch originally occurred. EPAM creates two new branches in this case as well, along with corresponding terminal nodes. The discrimination process selects a test on which the image and instance differ and which has not yet been examined. This test's value for the instance becomes the label on one branch and OTHER becomes the label for the other. The image for the instance-based node contains the results of all tests leading to that node; the image for the image-based node contains the original image plus the value for the discriminating test. In this way, EPAM gradually increases the depth of its discrimination network. The transition between Fig. 1(a) and (c) shows this type of learning in action, this time produced by the instance COLOR = DARK ∧ NUCLEI = ONE ∧ TAILS = TWO. Table 2 summarizes the overall discrimination process.

### 3.1.3. Search control in EPAM

In line with our discussion in Section 2, we can summarize EPAM's learning method in terms of search through a space of discrimination networks. Three basic operators make up this search:

- adding features to an image through familiarization;
- creating new disjunctive branches through discrimination;
- extending the network downward through discrimination.

Although the search-based view has its advantages, it provides little insight when one examines EPAM's control scheme. The classification method is completely deterministic, and the learning algorithm has only two choice points. One of these occurs during familiarization, when EPAM must decide which attribute to add to the image. The other occurs when discrimination must deepen the network to avoid a mismatch, when it must decide which attribute to select. One version of EPAM [9] preferred tests that had proven useful in previous discriminations. Other versions simply selected tests in a prespecified order. However, these decisions are minor in comparison to the choice between familiarization and discrimination, and between the branching

---

[7] The reason for this second branch is not clear, since the branch based on the instance's value is enough to avoid repeating the misclassification. However, we have attempted to faithfully reconstruct Feigenbaum's model as he describes it.

and deepening variants of discrimination. These are completely determined by the data and the existing network.

### 3.1.4. *Comments on* EPAM

The EPAM model introduced some very important ideas into the machine learning literature. First, it set forth the notion of a discrimination network, and it specified an incremental method that integrated classification and learning. Second, it introduced the distinction between tests (for use in sorting) and images (for use in making predictions). One can view discrimination networks as precursors of the concept hierarchies used in later work, and images as the precursors of concept descriptions. EPAM's distinction between the process of recognition (classification) and recall (prediction) was also an important insight. Finally, it introduced the two learning mechanisms of discrimination and familiarization, which it successfully used to explain aspects of human learning and memory.

Despite its successes, EPAM also had some significant shortcomings. For instance, the system's method for selecting among attributes during discrimination and familiarization was somewhat ad hoc. Moreover, the model retained concept descriptions (images) only at terminal nodes, and so lacked a true concept hierarchy. Finally, it assumed that concepts (images) were "all or none" entities, rather than the more fluid structures suggested by recent psychological studies (Rosch [37]). The last two criticisms are not really appropriate, since EPAM's goal was to model human memorization and not the broader area of concept formation. However, our concern here is with models of the latter process, and so we have evaluated Feigenbaum's work in those terms.

### 3.2. Lebowitz's UNIMEM

One can view Lebowitz's UNIMEM [24, 25] as a successor to EPAM,[8] since it shares many features with the earlier model, but also introduces some novel ideas. The motivation behind the two systems was also quite different. EPAM modeled empirical results from verbal learning experiments, whereas Lebowitz focused on the acquisition and use of concepts for more complex tasks such as natural language understanding and inference. In addition, UNIMEM was cast within a broader framework called *generalization-based memory*. Another system that independently incorporated many of the same advances as UNIMEM, is Kolodner's [19] CYRUS. We will highlight similarities and differences between these systems as they become relevant. Our stress on UNIMEM is due primarily to Lebowitz's [26] treatment of his system as conceptual clustering, a topic of primary interest for this paper.

---

[8] Actually, UNIMEM is a direct descendant of Lebowitz's [22, 23] IPP system. For a discussion of the differences between these two models, see Lebowitz [26].

### 3.2.1. *Representation and organization in* UNIMEM

UNIMEM represents instances in the same manner as EPAM—as a conjunction of features or attribute-value pairs. In one sense, it is less general than the earlier model, since it cannot handle objects with components, though Wasserman [43] has addressed this issue within the UNIMEM framewok. However, Lebowitz's system is more general than Feigenbaum's in that it can handle numeric attributes in addition to nominal (symbolic) ones. Thus, an instance that describes a university would have some nominal attributes (e.g., location, academic-emphasis) and some numeric attributes (e.g., male/female ratio, average SAT score). In addition, nominal attributes can take on more than one value, letting the system represent sets.

Lebowitz's approach diverges even more from Feigenbaum's in its representation and organization of concepts. In EPAM's network, only terminal nodes have associated images, but in UNIMEM both terminal and nonterminal nodes have concept descriptions. Each description consists of a conjunction of attribute-value pairs, with each value having an associated integer. This number measures what Lebowitz refers to as the *confidence* in that feature. Later, we will see that this corresponds to the idea of *predictability*, i.e., how well the feature can be predicted given an instance of the concept. In order to use consistent terminology, we refer to this count as the "predictability score" for a feature.[9]

Like its precursor, UNIMEM organizes knowledge into a concept hierarchy through which it sorts new instances. However, the details of this hierarchy differ from EPAM's discrimination network. We have mentioned that Lebowitz's system stores concept descriptions with each node in the hierarchy. Nodes high in the hierarchy represent general concepts, with their children representing more specific variants, their children still more specific concepts, and so on. Each concept has an associated set of instances stored with it; these can be viewed as terminal nodes in the hierarchy, though Lebowitz does not describe them in this fashion. Thus UNIMEM's terminal nodes are quite specific from the outset;[10] this contrasts with EPAM's images, which converge on completely specified instances only after considerable learning. Another difference is that, unlike EPAM, each instance may be stored with multiple nodes, so that categories need not be disjoint.

As in Feigenbaum's system, UNIMEM's network consists of nodes and links, with each of a node's links leading to a different child. However, in EPAM each link was labeled with the result of a single test. In contrast, UNIMEM allows

---

[9] Kolodner's [19] CYRUS uses a similar concept representation scheme, but maintains a probability rather than an integer with each attribute value. We argue in the context of our COBWEB discussion that this is an important distinction.

[10] Actually, the system stores only those features not inherited from nodes higher in the hierarchy, but the effect is the same as storing completely specified instances.

each link to specify the results of multiple tests (i.e., to specify multiple features). This redundant indexing lets the system handle instances with missing attributes and, as we describe below, it allows a very flexible sorting strategy. In addition, each feature on a link has an associated integer score, specifying the number of links on which that feature occurs. This second score measures the *predictiveness* of the feature, i.e., how well it can be used to predict instances of the various children.

Figure 2 presents a simple UNIMEM hierarchy after the system has created three concept nodes from six instances. For each node, we have shown its feature list and associated predictability scores. (For simplicity, we have omitted the predictiveness scores.) These scores represent the number of times a feature has been reinforced by successive instances. Note that one instance is indexed into both top-level nodes. This instance affects the predictability scores for both level-one nodes, although it is only incorporated into one of them.

### 3.2.2. *Classification and learning in* UNIMEM

Like other concept formation systems, UNIMEM integrates the processes of classification and learning. It sorts each instance through its concept hierarchy, modifying this hierarchy in the process. Table 3 summarizes the main steps in the algorithm.

As UNIMEM descends through its hierarchy, it uses the features (i.e., the attribute-value pairs) on each node and its emanating links to sort the instance. If the instance matches the description on the node closely enough, then it sends the instance down those links that contain features in the instance, and it continues the process with the relevant children. Both the number of features

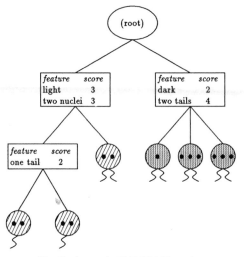

Fig. 2. A sample UNIMEM hierarchy.

Table 3
The basic UNIMEM algorithm

---

Input: The current node $N$ of the concept hierarchy.
   The name of an unclassified instance $I$.
   The set of $I$'s unaccounted features $F$.
Results: The concept hierarchy that classifies the instance.
Top-level call: Unimem(Top-node, $I$, $F$).
Variables: $N$ and $C$ are nodes in the hierarchy.
      $G$, $H$, and $K$ are sets of features (attribute values).
      $J$ is an instance stored on a node.
      $S$ is a list of nodes.

Unimem($N$, $I$, $F$).
   Let $G$ be the set of features stored on $N$.
   Let $H$ be the features in $F$ that match features in $G$.
   Let $K$ be the features in $F$ that do not match features in $G$.
   **If** $N$ is not the root node,
      **Then If** Evaluate($N$, $H$, $K$) returns TRUE or there are too few features in $H$,
         **Then** return the empty list.
   Let $S$ be the empty list.
   **For** each child $C$ of node $N$,
      **If** $C$ is indexed by a feature in $K$,
         **Then** let $S$ be Union($S$, Unimem($C$, $I$, $K$)).
   **If** $S$ is the empty list,
      **Then** for each instance $J$ of node $N$,
         Let $S$ be Union($S$, Generalize($N$, $J$, $I$, $F$)).
   **If** $S$ is the empty list,
      **Then** store $I$ as an instance of node $N$ with features $K$,
         **For** each feature $J$ in $F$ serving as in index to $N$,
            Increment the predictiveness score $R$ of $J$ by 1.
            **If** $R$ is high enough,
               **Then** remove $J$ as an index leading to $N$.
   Return $N$.

---

necessary for this match and the closeness of each value (for numeric attributes) are system parameters.[11] Whether or not the instance successfully
matches, UNIMEM calls on EVALUATE (which we discuss in Section 3.2.3) to
modify the node's scores. Note that, in some cases, the system may sort an
instance down multiple paths in the hierarchy.

Eventually UNIMEM reaches a node that matches the instance but none of
whose children match. In this case, the system examines all instances currently
stored with the node, comparing each of them in turn to the new instance. If an
old instance shares enough features with a new one (another system
parameter), the model creates a new, more general node based on these
features and stores both instances as its children. When this occurs, the system
increments the predictiveness count for each feature indexing the new node.

---

[11] UNIMEM uses a distance metric to determine the degree of match between two numeric
values. This is an important issue, to which we will return in Section 4.

Table 4
UNIMEM's update and evaluation processes

Variables: $N$ and $C$ are nodes in the hierarchy.
$F$, $G$, $H$, and $K$ are sets of features (attribute values).
$I$ and $J$ are the names of instances.
$S$ and $T$ are predictability scores of nodes' features.
$R$ is the predictiveness score of a node's feature.

Generalize($N$, $J$, $I$, $F$)
Let $G$ be the features in instance $J$.
Let $H$ be the features in $F$ that match features in $G$.
**If** $H$ contains enough features,
  **Then** create a new child $C$ of node $N$.
    Index and describe $C$ by the features in $H$.
    **For** each feature $K$ serving as index to $C$,
      Increment the predictiveness score $R$ of $K$ by 1.
      **If** $R$ is high enough,
        **Then** remove $K$ as an index.
    Remove $J$ as an instance of $N$.
    Let $G'$ be the features in $G$ that are not in $H$.
    Let $F'$ be the features in $F$ that are not in $H$.
    Store $J$ as an instance of $C$ with features $G'$.
    Store $I$ as an instance of $C$ with features $F'$.
    Return $C$.

Evaluate($N$, $H$, $K$)
**For** each nonpermanent feature $F$ in $H$,
  Raise the predictability score $S$ for $F$ on $N$.
  **If** $S$ is high enough,
    **Then** make $F$ a permanent feature of $N$.
**For** each nonpermanent feature $G$ in $K$,
  Lower the predictability score $T$ for $G$ on $N$.
  **If** $T$ is low enough,
    **Then** remove the feature $G$ from $N$.
      **If** $N$ has too few features,
        **Then** remove $N$ from its parent's list of children.
          Remove all indices serving $N$.
          Return TRUE
Return FALSE

Since UNIMEM compares the new instance to each of the stored instances, it can form multiple nodes in this manner. Table 4 summarizes the steps in this GENERALIZE process.[12] If none of the existing instances are similar enough to the new one, the system simply stores it with the current node, effectively creating a new disjunct.

---

[12] Our description of the UNIMEM algorithm (Tables 3 and 4) differs syntactically from that given by Lebowitz [24, 26]. Our somewhat different view of his algorithm produced a different organization to the specification. We believe that our description is clearer and functionally equivalent to Lebowitz's.

Note that when UNIMEM places an instance into more than one category, these categories overlap: they do not form disjoint partitions over the instances. In the literature on cluster analysis (Everitt [8]), this approach has been called *clumping*. Lebowitz [26] has argued that in some domains, overlapping concepts may describe the data more accurately than disjoint partitions. In addition, clumping introduces flexibility into the search for useful categories. UNIMEM may initially decide to retain multiple categories and later decide to remove one or more of them. This gives the effect of a beam search while still working within the hill-climbing metaphor described in Section 2. The clumping strategy and its associated advantages are shared by CYRUS.

### 3.2.3. *Evaluation and pruning in UNIMEM*

We have noted that UNIMEM retains two counts on nodes' features. The EVALUATE procedure shown in Table 4 updates these scores each time the system attempts to match an instance to a node's description. If a given feature in the instance matches a feature on the node, UNIMEM increments the predictability score for that feature. The increment for nominal attributes is one; the increment for numeric attributes is a function of the distance between the stored and observed values. If a given instance feature fails to match a node feature, the system decrements that feature's predictability score in a similar fashion.

When the predictability score for a feature exceeds a (user-specified) threshold, UNIMEM permanently fixes that feature as part of the node's description, so that future instances no longer affect it. More important, when a feature's score drops below another (user-specified) threshold, the system removes that feature from the concept description. In this way, an initially specific concept may gradually become more and more general. However, it may also become so general that it has little usefulness in making predictions. Thus, when the number of features stored on a node becomes low enough (another parameter), UNIMEM removes the node from memory along with all links to its children.

When the predictiveness score for a node's feature becomes too high (i.e., when the feature indexes too many children), UNIMEM removes that feature from links emanating from the node. In this way, concepts that were originally retrieved often may become accessed more selectively. However, if the system removes all indices to a child, that node is effectively forgotten, since there is no longer any way to sort instances to it. This is another way in which UNIMEM prunes its concept hierarchy.

### 3.2.4. *Comments on UNIMEM*

To summarize, UNIMEM can be viewed as carrying out a hill-climbing search through a space of concept hierarchies. This search process involves six basic operators:

- storing a new instance with a node (creating a new disjunct);
- creating a more general node based on the features shared by two instances;
- permanently fixing a feature in a node's description;
- deleting an unreliable feature from a node's description;
- deleting an overly general node (and its children);
- deleting a nonpredictive index to a node's children.

Lebowitz's approach to concept formation introduces a number of advances over EPAM. Each node in the UNIMEM hierarchy has an associated concept description, rather than just the terminal nodes. Moreover, each feature in these descriptions has associated weights; thus concepts are less "all or none." There is a clear evaluation of concepts and their components, and the notions of predictiveness and predictability further clarify the distinction between recognition (classification) and recall (prediction). The system also introduced the possibility of multiple indices to a given concept, and provided one method for constructing nondisjoint hierarchies. Each of these general advances is also true of CYRUS, although their realization differs in some important respects from UNIMEM.

However, UNIMEM also has significant drawbacks as a model of concept formation. The measures of predictiveness and predictability are informal and have no clear semantics. The system also lacks a principled method for deciding between learning operators, being dependent on user-specified parameters to make such decisions. Lebowitz [26] has carried out initial studies on how these parameters affect the system's behavior, but much work remains before their full impact becomes clear.

### 3.3. Fisher's COBWEB

Fisher's [12, 13] COBWEB constitutes another algorithm for incremental concept formation. As we will see below, this research builds heavily on Lebowitz's earlier approach, and it also borrows from Kolodner's [19] work on CYRUS. Although Fisher does not present COBWEB itself as a psychological model, it has been heavily influenced by research in cognitive psychology on basic-level and typicality effects (Rosch [37]). Briefly, experiments with humans suggest that some categories are more "basic" than others, being retrieved more rapidly and named more frequently. In addition, there is evidence that for a given category, some members are more "typical" than others, being retrieved more quickly and rated as better examples. Fisher [13] describes COBWEB/2, a related system that models these effects, but we will focus on the simpler COBWEB instead.

#### 3.3.1. *Representation and organization in COBWEB*

Like its predecessors, Fisher's system represents each instance as a set of attribute-value pairs. The mapping is closest to EPAM, since each attribute takes on only one value and since only nominal attributes are allowed.[13] As in UNIMEM, each concept node is described in terms of attributes, values, and associated weights, but here the similarity ends. One difference is that COBWEB stores the probability of each concept's occurrence. Another is that each node, from the most specific to the most general, includes every attribute observed in the instances. Moreover, associated with each attribute is every possible value for that attribute. Each such value has two associated numbers, which roughly correspond to Lebowitz's predictiveness and predictability scores. However, in COBWEB these scores have a formal grounding in probability theory.

Fisher defines the *predictiveness* of a value $v$ for category $c$ as the conditional probability that an instance $i$ will be a member of $c$, given that $i$ has value $v$, or $P(c|a = v)$. Similarly, he defines the *predictability* of a value $v$ for category $c$ as the conditional probability that an instance $i$ will have value $v$, given that $i$ is a member of $c$, or $P(a = v|c)$. Actually, COBWEB does not explicitly store predictiveness scores, since it can derive them from predictability and node probability using Bayes' rule. Smith and Medin [42] have used the term *probabilistic concepts* to refer to concept representations that incorporate such conditional probabilities.

Figure 3 presents a sample concept hierarchy, including the probabilities associated with each concept and with its attribute values. For instance, the top node $(N_1)$ has an associated probability of 1.0. It also states that its members have an equal chance of having one or two tails and an even chance of being light or dark. Concept $N_3$ has a 50% chance of occurring, and its members so far have always had one tail and two nuclei, but have been evenly split among light and dark colors. The terminal nodes in the hierarchy—$N_2$, $N_4$, $N_5$, and $N_6$—have less interesting probabilistic descriptions, since each is based on a single instance. However, note that the probability of each node's occurrence is specified relative to its parent, rather than with respect to the entire distribution.

COBWEB's concept hierarchy is similar to UNIMEM's in that each node has an associated "image," with more general nodes higher in the hierarchy and more specific ones below their parents. However, the system's terminal nodes are always specific instances that it has encountered; unlike UNIMEM, it never deletes instances. In addition, the hierarchy divides instances into disjoint classes. More important, COBWEB links parents to their children only through *is-a* links. The system differs from both EPAM and UNIMEM in that it avoids explicit indices stated as tests on attribute values. Thus, the sample hierarchy shown in Fig. 3 has a different semantics than those we have seen earlier. This assumption leads to a novel method for sorting instances through the concept hierarchy.

---

[13] In Section 4, we will see how COBWEB can be extended to handle both numeric attributes and instances involving multiple components.

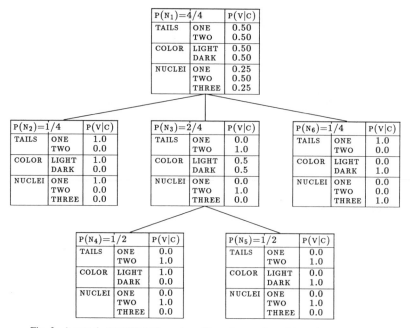

| P(N₁)=4/4 |        | P(v\|c) |
|-----------|--------|---------|
| TAILS     | ONE    | 0.50    |
|           | TWO    | 0.50    |
| COLOR     | LIGHT  | 0.50    |
|           | DARK   | 0.50    |
| NUCLEI    | ONE    | 0.25    |
|           | TWO    | 0.50    |
|           | THREE  | 0.25    |

| P(N₂)=1/4 |        | P(v\|c) |
|-----------|--------|---------|
| TAILS     | ONE    | 1.0     |
|           | TWO    | 0.0     |
| COLOR     | LIGHT  | 1.0     |
|           | DARK   | 0.0     |
| NUCLEI    | ONE    | 1.0     |
|           | TWO    | 0.0     |
|           | THREE  | 0.0     |

| P(N₃)=2/4 |        | P(v\|c) |
|-----------|--------|---------|
| TAILS     | ONE    | 0.0     |
|           | TWO    | 1.0     |
| COLOR     | LIGHT  | 0.5     |
|           | DARK   | 0.5     |
| NUCLEI    | ONE    | 0.0     |
|           | TWO    | 1.0     |
|           | THREE  | 0.0     |

| P(N₆)=1/4 |        | P(v\|c) |
|-----------|--------|---------|
| TAILS     | ONE    | 1.0     |
|           | TWO    | 0.0     |
| COLOR     | LIGHT  | 0.0     |
|           | DARK   | 1.0     |
| NUCLEI    | ONE    | 0.0     |
|           | TWO    | 0.0     |
|           | THREE  | 1.0     |

| P(N₄)=1/2 |        | P(v\|c) |
|-----------|--------|---------|
| TAILS     | ONE    | 0.0     |
|           | TWO    | 1.0     |
| COLOR     | LIGHT  | 1.0     |
|           | DARK   | 0.0     |
| NUCLEI    | ONE    | 0.0     |
|           | TWO    | 1.0     |
|           | THREE  | 0.0     |

| P(N₅)=1/2 |        | P(v\|c) |
|-----------|--------|---------|
| TAILS     | ONE    | 0.0     |
|           | TWO    | 1.0     |
| COLOR     | LIGHT  | 0.0     |
|           | DARK   | 1.0     |
| NUCLEI    | ONE    | 0.0     |
|           | TWO    | 1.0     |
|           | THREE  | 0.0     |

Fig. 3. A sample COBWEB hierarchy with nodes numbered in order of creation.

### 3.3.2. *Classification and learning in* COBWEB

The basic COBWEB algorithm is quite simple, as can be seen from the summaries in Tables 5 and 6. Again classification and learning are intertwined, with each instance being sorted down through a concept hierarchy and altering that hierarchy in its passage. The system initializes its hierarchy to a single node, basing the values of this concept's attributes on the first instance. Upon encountering a second instance, COBWEB averages its values into those of the concept and creates two children, one based on the first instance and another based on the second.

Unlike EPAM and UNIMEM, Fisher's model does not use explicit tests or indices to retrieve potential categories. Instead, at each node COBWEB retrieves all children and considers placing the instance in each of these categories. Each of these constitutes an alternative *clustering* (a set of clusters with a common parent) that incorporates the new instance. Using an evaluation function that we describe in Section 3.3.3, it then selects the best such clustering. COBWEB also considers creating a new category that contains only the new instance, and compares this clustering to the best clustering that uses only existing categories.

If the clustering based on existing classes wins the competition, COBWEB modifies the probability of the selected category and the conditional prob-

Table 5
The COBWEB algorithm

---

Input: The current node $N$ of the concept hierarchy.
         An unclassified (attribute-value) instance $I$.
Results: A concept hierarchy that classifies the instance.
Top-level call: Cobweb(Top-node, $I$).
Variables: $C$, $P$, $Q$, and $R$ are nodes in the hierarchy.
            $U$, $V$, $W$, and $X$ are clustering (partition) scores.

Cobweb($N$, $I$)
   **If** $N$ is a terminal node,
      **Then** Create-new-terminals($N$, $I$)
              Incorporate $(N, I)$.
   **Else** Incorporate($N$, $I$).
           **For** each child $C$ of node $N$,
               Compute the score for placing $I$ in $C$.
           Let $P$ be the node with the highest score $W$.
           Let $R$ be the node with the second highest score.
           Let $X$ be the score for placing $I$ in a new node $Q$.
           Let $Y$ be the score for merging $P$ and $R$ into one node.
           Let $Z$ be the score for splitting $P$ into its children.
           **If** $W$ is the best score,
               **Then** Cobweb($P$, $I$) (place $I$ in category $P$).
           **Else if** $X$ is the best score,
                   **Then** initialize $Q$'s probabilities using $I$'s values
                           (place $I$ by itself in the new category $Q$).
           **Else if** $Y$ is the best score,
                   **Then** let $O$ be Merge($P$, $R$, $N$).
                           Cobweb($O$, $I$).
           **Else if** $Z$ is the best score,
                   **Then** Split($P$, $N$).
                           Cobweb($N$, $I$).

---

abilities for its attribute values. Thus, predictability scores for values occurring in the instance will increase, whereas those for values not occurring will decrease. Predictiveness scores change as well, but since the system does not actually store these, it does not update them explicitly. In addition, COBWEB continues to sort the instance down through the hierarchy, recursively considering the children of the selected category. Node $N_3$ in Fig. 3 shows the result of incorporating a new instance into an existing node. At an earlier stage, this had been a terminal node based on a single instance. However, the act of hosting a new instance has left its COLOR probabilities evenly divided and given it two children.

If the clustering with the singleton class emerges as the winner, COBWEB creates this new category and makes it a child of the current parent node. The system bases the values for this new concept's attributes on those found in the instance, giving them each predictability scores of one. In this case, classification halts at this step, since the new concept is a terminal node. Node $N_6$ in

Table 6
Auxiliary COBWEB operations

---

Variables: $N$, $O$, $P$, and $R$ are nodes in the hierarchy.
$I$ is an unclassified instance
$A$ is a nominal attribute.
$V$ is a value of an attribute.

Incorporate($N$, $I$)
Update the probability of category $N$.
**For** each attribute $A$ in instance $I$,
**For** each value $V$ of $A$,
Update the probability of $V$ given category $N$.

Create-new-terminals($N$, $I$)
Create a new child $M$ of node $N$.
Initialize $M$'s probabilities to those for $N$.
Create a new child $O$ of node $N$.
Initialize $O$'s probabilities using $I$'s values.

Merge($P$, $R$, $N$)
Make $O$ a new child of $N$.
Set $O$'s probabilities to be $P$ and $R$'s average.
Remove $P$ and $R$ as children of node $N$.
Add $P$ and $R$ as children of node $O$.
Return $O$.

Split($P$, $N$)
Remove the child $P$ of node $N$.
Promote the children of $P$ to be children of $N$.

---

Fig. 3 was created in this fashion, since the instance it summarizes was sufficiently different from node $N_2$ and $N_3$.

Although in principle the above method provides everything needed to construct hierarchies of probabilistic concepts, it can be sensitive to the order of instance presentation, creating different hierarchies from different orders of the same data. In particular, if the initial instances are nonrepresentative of the entire population, one may get hierarchies with poor predictive ability. For example, if the first instances are all conservative congressmen, the algorithm would create subcategories of these at the top level. When it finally encountered instances of liberal congressmen, it would create one category for them at the top level. However, it would still have all the conservative instances at this same level, when one would prefer them grouped under a separate category.

COBWEB includes two additional operators to help it recover from such nonoptimal hierarchies. At each level of the classification process, the system considers *merging* the two[14] nodes that best classify the new instance. If the

---

[14] Although one could consider merging all possible node pairs, such a strategy would be costly and unlikely to improve the resulting hierarchy.

resulting clustering is better (according to the function described in Section 3.3.3) than the original, it combines the two nodes into a single category, though still retaining the original nodes as its children. This transforms a clustering of $N$ nodes into one having $N - 1$ nodes, as in the transition shown by Fig. 4.

The system also incorporates the inverse operation of *splitting* nodes. At each level, if COBWEB decides to classify an instance as a member of an existing category, it also considers removing this category and elevating its children. If this action leads to an improved clustering, the system changes the structure of its hierarchy accordingly. Thus, if one of $N$ nodes at a given level has $M$ children, splitting this node would give $N + M - 1$ nodes at this level, as depicted by the transition in Fig. 5.

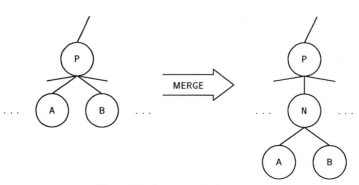

Fig. 4. Merging categories in COBWEB.

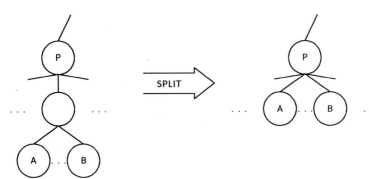

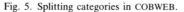

Fig. 5. Splitting categories in COBWEB.

### 3.3.3. *Evaluation in* COBWEB

We have made numerous references to COBWEB's evaluation function, but we have yet to define this metric. We have also mentioned Fisher's concern with the basic-level phenomena, but we have yet to show how the system has been influenced by these phenomena. The key to both issues involves *category utility*, a measure that Gluck and Corter [14] have shown predicts the basic level found in psychological experiments. They derive this function by two paths, one using information theory and the other using game theory.

COBWEB uses a slightly generalized version of Gluck and Corter's function to control its classification and learning behavior. Category utility favors clusterings that maximize the potential for inferring information (Fisher [13]). In doing this, it attempts to maximize intra-class similarity and inter-class differences, and it also provides a principled tradeoff between predictiveness and predictability. The basic measure assumes that concept descriptions are probabilistic in nature. We do not have space to rederive this metric, but we can consider some of its characteristics.

For any set of instances, any attribute-value pair, $A_i = V_{ij}$, and any class, $C_k$, one can compute $P(A_i = V_{ij}|C_k)$, the conditional probability of the value given membership in the class, or its predictability. One can also compute $P(C_k|A_i = V_{ij})$, the conditional probability of membership in the class given this value, or its predictiveness. One can combine these measures of individual attributes and values into an overall measure of clustering quality. Specifically,

$$\sum_k \sum_i \sum_j P(A_i = V_{ij})P(C_k|A_i = V_{ij})P(A_i = V_{ij}|C_k) \qquad (1)$$

represents a tradeoff between predictability $P(A_i = V_{ij}|C_k)$ and predictiveness $P(C_k|A_i = V_{ij})$ that has been summed across all classes $(k)$, attributes $(i)$, and values $(j)$. The probability $P(A_i = V_{ij})$ weights the individual values, so that frequently occurring values play a more important role than those occurring less frequently.

Using Bayes' rule, we have $P(A_i = V_{ij})P(C_k|A_i = V_{ij}) = P(C_k)P(A_i = V_{ij}|C_k)$, letting us transform expression (1) into the alternative form

$$\sum_k P(C_k) \sum_i \sum_j P(A_i = V_{ij}|C_k)^2 . \qquad (2)$$

Gluck and Corter have shown that the subexpression $\sum_i \sum_j P(A_i = V_{ij}|C_k)^2$ is the *expected* number of attribute values that one can correctly guess for an arbitrary member of class $C_k$. This expectation assumes a *probability matching* strategy, in which one guesses an attribute value with a probability equal to its probability of occurring. Thus, it assumes that one guesses a value with probability $P(A_i = V_{ij}|C_k)$ and that this guess is correct with the same probability.

Gluck and Corter build on expression (2) in their derivation. They define category utility as the *increase* in the expected number of attribute values that can be correctly guessed, given a set of $n$ categories, over the expected number of correct guesses without such knowledge. The latter term is simply $(\Sigma_i \Sigma_j P(A_i = V_{ij})^2)$, so one must subtract this from expression (2). The complete expression for category utility is thus

$$\frac{\sum_{k=1}^{K} P(C_k) \sum_i \sum_j P(A_i = V_{ij} | C_k)^2 - \sum_i \sum_j P(A_i = V_{ij})^2}{K}. \qquad (3)$$

Note that the difference between the two expected numbers is divided by $K$, the number of categories. This division lets one compare different size clusterings, which must occur whenever one considers merging, splitting, or creating a new category.

Since category utility is based on expected numbers of correct guesses about attribute values, it suggests predictive ability as the natural measure of behavior. Fisher has tested COBWEB on both natural and artificial domains, measuring its performance by asking it to predict missing attribute values on test instances. This approach is similar to Quinlan's [34] methodology for evaluating supervised learning systems, except that one averages across many attributes rather than predicting a single one (the class name). In Section 4, we will extend this notion of prediction (and category utility) to domains involving numeric attributes.

COBWEB is not the first inductive learning system that has employed an evaluation function based on information theory. The best-known work of this type is Quinlan's [34] ID3 method for constructing decision trees. Machine learning researchers have explored many extensions and variations of the basic technique, including incremental versions (Schlimmer and Fisher [38]). Rendell et al.'s [35] PLS system also uses an information-theoretic metric to direct its divisive construction of disjunctive concept descriptions. In addition, Hanson and Bauer [16] have used an information-based function in their WITT clustering system, Cheeseman et al. [6] have used a Bayesian approach in their nonincremental clustering system AUTOCLASS, and Anderson (personal communication) has used conditional probabilities in his recent work on incremental clustering.

### 3.3.4. *Comments on COBWEB*

Like its predecessors, one can view COBWEB as carrying out a hill-climbing search through a space of concept hierarchies. In this case, there are four main operators:

– classifying the object into an existing class;
– creating a new class (a new disjunct);

– combining two classes into a single class (merging);
– dividing a class into several classes (splitting).

The system employs an evaluation function—category utility—to determine which operator (and which instantiation) to employ at each point in the classification process.

The use of a well-defined evaluation function constitutes an advance over previous work on concept formation, as does Fisher's reformulation of predictiveness and predictability in terms of conditional probabilities. The explicit inclusion of merging and splitting also seems desirable, since they should let COBWEB recover from nonrepresentative samples without losing its incremental, memory-limited flavor.

However, Fisher's work also has some limitations. As implemented, COB-WEB can handle only nominal attributes, whereas UNIMEM dealt with both symbolic and numeric data. The system also assumes that each instance consists of a single "object," and thus avoids issues of finding mappings between analogous components. Finally, COBWEB retains all instances ever encountered as terminal nodes in its concept hierarchy. Although this approach works well in noise-free, symbolic domains, it can lead to "overfitting the data" in noisy or numeric domains. In these cases, some form of pruning or cutoff seems in order. These and other concerns led us to carry out the research described in the following section.

## 4. Modeling the Formation of Object Concepts

With these systems as background, we can turn to CLASSIT, a model of concept formation that attempts to improve upon earlier work. This system has been most strongly influenced by COBWEB, differing mainly in its representation of instances, its representation of concepts, and its evaluation function. However, CLASSIT uses the same basic operators and the same control strategy that Fisher's system employs. Below we describe the new model, stressing its differences from earlier systems, and explaining our motivations for introducing these differences.

### 4.1. Representation and organization in CLASSIT

Although symbolic or nominal attributes occupy an important role in natural language, they are less useful for describing the physical world. When describing a stick in English, one might say that stick is short or long, but our perceptual system can also distinguish two sticks that differ only slightly in length. This latter capability suggests that humans' representation of real-world objects can include detailed information about the quantitative features of those objects. A variety of real-world attributes can be described using real numbers, including features such as color, which are usually treated symbolically. Since we are concerned with the formation of physical object concepts, CLASSIT currently only accepts real-valued attributes as input.[15] In Section 6, we will discuss combining real-valued and symbolic attributes.

Physical objects can be represented with numeric attributes by describing each object as a set of components, each with a list of attributes such as height and width. Although this approach represents some relation information implicitly (such as the adjacency of components), it does not restrict the types of objects that can be described. Furthermore, this form of numeric representation seems a more plausible output from a perception system.

The introduction of real-valued data requires an analogous extension in one's representation of concepts. There are two obvious approaches to this problem. First, one can divide each numeric attribute into ranges; by "discretizing" the continuous values, one can retain the symbolic concept representation used in COBWEB. Lebowitz [24] has taken this approach in one version of UNIMEM. Alternatively, one can represent concepts directly in terms of real-valued attributes.

CLASSIT takes the second approach, retaining COBWEB's notion of storing a probability distribution with each attribute occurring in a concept. However, instead of storing a probability for each attribute value (e.g., for a given concept $C$, $P(small|C) = 0.3$; $P(large|C) = 0.7$), our model stores a continuous normal distribution (bell-shaped curve) for each attribute. CLASSIT expresses each distribution in terms of a mean (average) value and a standard deviation.[16] For instance, it might believe that the average length of a dog's tail is 1.1 feet and that its standard deviation is 0.65 feet. Attributes with low standard deviations have narrow, tall distributions, whereas those with high standard deviations have wide, shallow distributions.

CLASSIT organizes concepts into a hierarchy in the same manner as do UNIMEM and COBWEB. General concepts representing many instances are near the top of the tree, with more specific concepts below them. In general, concepts lower in the hierarchy will have attributes with lower standard deviations, since they represent more specific classes with greater within-group regularity.

### 4.2. Classification and learning in CLASSIT

This new representation scheme requires no modification to COBWEB's learning operators or basic control structure. Thus, CLASSIT includes the same four

---

[15] Statisticians have developed methods for clustering objects described in terms of real-valued attributes; these are known as *cluster analysis* and *numerical taxonomy* (Everitt [8]). Unfortunately, these methods are usually nonincremental.

[16] Standard deviation is defined as the square root of $\Sigma_{i=1}^{N} (x_i - \bar{x})^2/N$. Note that this equation as written cannot be computed incrementally; all $x_i$ values need to be present. However, one can transform this expression for incremental computation by expanding the squared term and storing the sum of squares. Specifically, each concept contains a count, a sum of values, and a sum of squares. From these, we compute the mean and the standard deviation when needed.

basic operators as its predecessor—one for incorporating an instance into an existing concept, another for creating a new disjunctive concept, a third operator for merging two classes, and a final one for splitting classes. As described in Tables 5 and 6, for every new instance, the algorithm considers all four operators, computes the score of the evaluation function in each case, and selects that choice with the highest score. In Section 4.4, we will step through a detailed example of this procedure.

However, CLASSIT makes a few important additions to the basic algorithm. For example, rather than always descending to the leaves of the hierarchy as it classifies an instance, our system may decide to halt at some higher-level node. When this occurs, the system has decided that the instance is similar enough to an existing concept that further descent is unnecessary and that it should throw away specific information about that instance. We define "similar enough" with a system parameter, *cutoff*, that is based on our evaluation function.

There are two advantages of this modification. First, Quinlan [34] has shown that methods for building exhaustive decision trees tend to "overfit" the data in noisy domains, leading to decreased performance. The same effect should occur with concept formation systems, unless they employ some form of cutoff. Second, a system that retains every instance builds too large a data structure for real applications. Forgetting certain instances should lead to both better performance and to greater efficiency.

The representation of objects that CLASSIT uses requires another addition to the COBWEB algorithm. If instances are described as a set of components, how can the system correctly match instance components to concept components? For example, how can it know that the right front leg in the instance corresponds to the right front leg in the "dog" concept? In general terms, this problem is that of finding an optimal match in a weighted bipartite graph.

The brute force solution to this problem is far too expensive for practical use: to calculate the worth of every possible correspondence for $n$ components has an $O(n!)$ time cost. Instead we have used a cheaper $O(n^2)$ time complexity heuristic algorithm. Using the variances for each attribute in the concept description, CLASSIT finds a match for that component with the least associated variation. Using this as a constraint, the system then finds a match for the next most constrained component and so forth, continuing this process until all components in the concept description have been matched against components in the instance. This "greedy" approach is not assured of finding the best match, but it is likely to find an acceptable one with minimal cost.[17]

We have chosen to retain COBWEB's learning operators because we believe they provide a good framework for concept formation. The hill-climbing search organization provides a robust method for learning while making minimal demands on memory. Rather than formulating new algorithms, our goal has

---

[17] There also exists an $O(n^3)$ guaranteed algorithm for this problem, which we will describe in Section 6.

been to extend the existing program to work in new domains and with a more general representational scheme.

## 4.3. CLASSIT's evaluation function

CLASSIT's use of real-valued attributes in both instances and concepts requires a generalization of category utility, COBWEB's evaluation function. In particular, the two innermost summations in category utility (equation (3)) need to be generalized for real-valued attributes:

$$\sum_{j}^{values} P(A_i = V_{ij}|C_k)^2 \quad \text{and} \quad \sum_{j}^{values} P(A_i = V_{ij})^2 .$$

Both of these terms are a sum of squares of the probabilities of all values of an attribute. The former uses probabilities given membership in a particular class, $C_k$, while the latter is without any class information. The second term is equivalent to the probability at the parent, since that node includes all instances for the clustering and therefore has no information about class membership.

In order for these terms to be applied to a continuous domain, summation must be changed to integration, and some assumption must be made about the distribution of values. Without any prior knowledge about the distribution of an attribute, the best assumption is that the distribution of values for each attribute follows a normal curve. Thus, the probability of a particular attribute value is the height of the curve at that value and the summation of the square of all probabilities becomes the integral of the normal distribution squared. For the first summation, the distribution is for a particular class, while the second must use the distribution at the parent. In either case, the integral evaluates to a simple expression:

$$\sum_{j}^{values} P(A_i = V_{ij})^2 \Leftrightarrow \int \frac{1}{\sigma^2 2\pi} \exp\left(\frac{x-\mu}{\sigma}\right)^2 dx = \frac{1}{\sigma} \frac{1}{2\sqrt{\pi}} ,$$

where $\mu$ is the mean and $\sigma$ is the standard deviation. Finally, since the expression is used for comparison only (see the COBWEB algorithm), the constant term $1/2\sqrt{\pi}$ can be discarded.

In summary, one can replace the innermost summations from category utility with the term $1/\sigma$. The revised evaluation function used by CLASSIT is:

$$\frac{\sum_{k}^{K} P(C_k) \sum_{i}^{I} 1/\sigma_{ik} - \sum_{i}^{I} 1/\sigma_{ip}}{K} ,$$

where $I$ is the number of attributes, $K$ is the number of classes in the partition, $\sigma_{ik}$ is the standard deviation for a given attribute in a given class, and $\sigma_{ip}$ is the standard deviation for a given attribute in the parent node.[18]

---

[18] In our implementation, the attribute summations are divided by $I$. This is necessary because CLASSIT allows instances to have some missing attributes.

This evaluation function is equivalent to the function used by COBWEB; it is a transformation of category utility. Unfortunately, this transformation introduces a problem when the standard deviation is zero for a concept. For any concept based on a single instance, the value of $1/\sigma$ is therefore infinite.

In order to resolve this problem, we have introduced the notion of *acuity*, a system parameter that specifies the minimum value for $\sigma$. This limit corresponds to the notion of a "just noticeable difference" in psychophysics—the lower limit on our perception ability. Because acuity strongly affects the score of new disjuncts, it indirectly controls the breadth, or branching factor of the concept hierarchy produced, just as the cutoff parameter controls the depth of the hierarchy.

### 4.4. A detailed example

Now that we have examined CLASSIT's representation, control structure, and evaluation function, we will demonstrate the system's behavior in more detail by stepping through a sample execution. For this example, we have constructed a very simple input domain. Imagine a set of rectangles that naturally divides into three classes: small, medium, and large. Each instance has only one component and is described with only three attributes; height, width, and a texture attribute. For this domain, the texture attribute is irrelevant to classification. Small rectangles have a mean height of 12.5 and width of 6.5; medium rectangles average 30 by 14 and large rectangles average 41 by 35. The texture attribute is allowed to vary over the range 5 to 40, independent of class. Note that the system is not given any class information—it is not told whether a given instance is small, medium, or large. Instead, these concepts must be induced from regularity in the data. This is precisely the task of unsupervised concept formation.

We will now step through an execution as CLASSIT encounters the first six rectangles. The system begins with an empty concept hierarchy. Suppose the first instance is a small rectangle with values of 14 for height, 7 for width and 8 for texture. This instance is used to create the root node of the hierarchy, as shown in Fig. 6(a). Since this initial concept is based on a single instance, it has the minimum value for its $\sigma$ values. For this execution the acuity parameter specifies this minimum to be 1.0 for all attributes.

For each concept created by the system, we have shown the mean and standard deviation ($\sigma$) for all attributes, as well as $P(C_k)$, the probability of that concept within the clustering. As noted earlier, concepts store cumulative sums and sum of squares in order to recompute the standard deviation incrementally. Similarly, $P(C_k)$ is computed on demand by using counts stored at each concept. In order to make clear the semantics of our concepts, we have not shown these computational values in our figures.

Figure 6(b) shows the entire concept hierarchy after the system classifies the

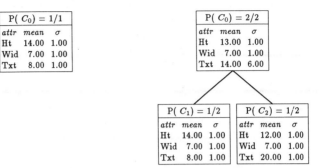

Fig. 6. Extending the CLASSIT hierarchy downward.

second instance. Since every instance encountered is incorporated into the root node, there is only one decision point as the system classifies this instance: is it different enough from the first to warrant extending the hierarchy down a level and creating separate concepts for each instance? In this case, although the second instance is also a "small" rectangle, the texture attribute is different enough from the first instance that CLASSIT creates a new level. Note that the $\sigma$ scores for height and width at the root node are unchanged; this is because the standard deviations of these attributes remain lower than acuity.

Figure 7 shows the concept hierarchy after the system observes a third instance. After incorporating the instance into the root, the system must decide whether to add the instance into an existing child concept, or to make a new disjunct at level one. In this case, the choice with the highest category quality score is to create a new disjunct. Intuitively, this occurs because the instance is

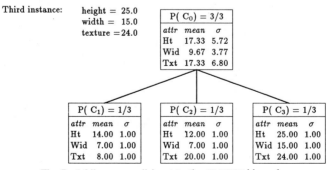

Fig. 7. Adding a new disjunct to the CLASSIT hierarchy.

a medium-sized rectangle; attributes height and width are sufficiently different from the existing classes to cause the creation of a new concept.

Figure 8 shows the hierarchy after the system classifies a second medium-sized rectangle. In this case, adding to an existing concept has a higher score than creating a new disjunct. This instance is therefore added to the existing "medium rectangle" concept ($C_3$) at level one. The system also decides that the new instance is different enough from concept $C_3$ to continue and extend the hierarchy to level two, creating a concept for each instance at that level.

The fifth instance is a large rectangle, and the system chooses to create another disjunct at level one. Figure 9 presents the hierarchy at this stage in the learning process. Remember that CLASSIT does not label this node as "large" nor does it know that the fifth instance belongs to the large class. The system incorporates each instance into its hierarchy without the benefit of class information.

Figure 10 shows the hierarchy after CLASSIT incorporates the final instance, a third "small" rectangle. This instance allows the system to merge two level-one concepts into a more general concept describing all three "small" rectangles. In more detail, the system proceeds as follows: It first considers adding the new instance to each of the four existing classes. In this case, the concept $C_1$ in Fig. 9 is the best candidate. CLASSIT then compares this score to that of making another level-one disjunct. Finally the system considers merging the best and

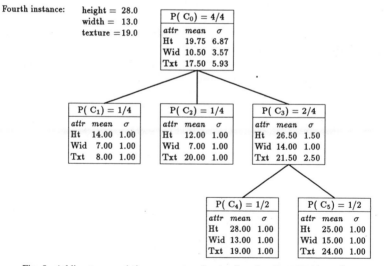

Fig. 8. Adding to an existing concept and extending the CLASSIT hierarchy.

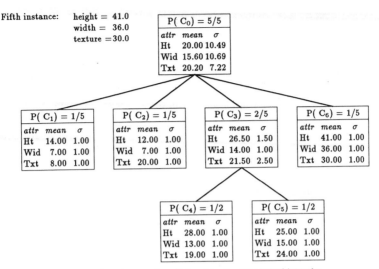

Fig. 9. Creating another disjunct in the CLASSIT hierarchy.

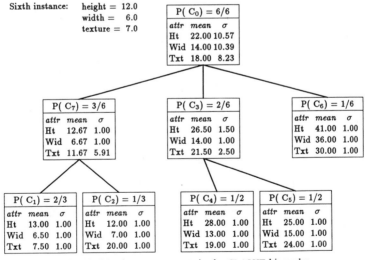

Fig. 10. Merging two concepts in the CLASSIT hierarchy.

the second-best concepts into a new node; in our example, this last option has the best score.[19]

The merge operator merely pushes existing categories down a level. CLASSIT must also consider what to do with the new instance at level two. In this execution, the system decides to incorporate it into an existing child concept, $C_1$. At this point the cutoff parameter comes into play and the system decides that the new instance does not warrant its own concept at level three. This is hardly surprising, since the new instance is so close to the existing concept description that the standard deviations do not rise above acuity. In fact, the match among the three small rectangles is close enough so that the standard deviations for attributes height and width remain at acuity even for the new level-one concept, $C_7$.

CLASSIT continues processing new instances in this manner, incrementally modifying both its concept descriptions and the structure of its concept hierarchy as it encounters new data. Unlike some incremental learning systems—such as Mitchell's [31] version space method—CLASSIT never achieves a final knowledge state; the system continues to learn as long as new instances are available. This behavior is the strength of an incremental model. For example, it allows a system to recover from *concept drift*; if the environment changes over time, the learner must continue to modify his conceptual structures in response to new data.

### 4.5. A summary of CLASSIT

A principle motivation for the CLASSIT system was to model concept formation in the domain of real-valued inputs. This has affected our representation and our evaluation function. As yet, we have worked only with real-valued attributes since we feel that this type of input more closely models the output of the human perceptual system.

Since the same algorithm and four learning operators are used, CLASSIT retains the advantages of COBWEB. Both are incremental systems that integrate learning (concept formation and modification) and performance (classification), while carrying out a hill-climbing search for an optimal concept hierarchy.

## 5. Experimental Studies of CLASSIT's Behavior

One important approach to evaluating any AI system involves experimentation—studying the system's behavior under a variety of conditions. In this section, we present some experimental results that demonstrate CLASSIT's learning ability. We begin by introducing the domain we have used in most of

---

[19] The split operator is only considered when CLASSIT is about to add to a concept that already has children.

these studies. After this, we report three experiments in which we vary aspects of CLASSIT, followed by another study in which we vary the regularity in the domain. In each case, we describe the independent and dependent variables used in the experiment, summarizing the results in graphs. We close by reporting the system's behavior on a real-world domain that involves numeric attributes.

## 5.1. The domain of quadruped mammals

For our initial experiments, we designed an artificial domain involving four-legged mammals, each described as a set of eight cylinders. This approach let us control the environment while still retaining a reasonable approximation of physical objects. One can view our representation of objects as a simplification of Binford's [5] generalized cylinders, which have received wide attention within the machine vision community. Also, Marr [28] has argued that such representations are reasonable approximations of the output of the human visual system.[20]

As discussed earlier, CLASSIT assumes that each instance consists of a set of component objects, each described by a set of real-valued attributes. In the domain of quadruped mammals, each instance consists of eight cylindrical components: a head, a neck, a torso, a tail, and four legs. Each cylinder includes attributes such as height, radius, and location; there are a total of nine attributes per component, hence 72 attribute-value pairs per instance. We believe that real-world objects have at least this order of complexity and that a robust concept formation system should be able to handle instances of this form.[21]

In the runs described below, we assumed four basic categories that differed systematically only in the sizes of their cylinders. We will refer to these classes as *cats*, *dogs*, *horses*, and *giraffes*, since their relative sizes are roughly the same as those occurring for these real-world categories. Figure 11 shows a typical instance for each of these classes. One can view the prototype for a class as the "Platonic form" or ideal for that class. To generate instances from a particular class, we use a template that defines the prototypical value for each attribute

---

[20] We have developed CLASSIT within the context of the World Modeler's Project, a joint research effort between the University of California, Irvine, and Carnegie Mellon University. This project incorporates a simulated three-dimensional world, representing physical objects in terms of cylinders, spheres, circles, and polygons. Agents that interact with this environment perceive their surroundings directly in terms of such primitive shapes, along with their size, location, and orientation. Of course, CLASSIT need not assume such representations; it can be applied to any domain that one can express using numeric attributes.

[21] A more realistic description would represent physical objects at different levels of aggregation, as Marr [28] has proposed. Thus, an animal might have four legs, with each leg having three components, etc. However, such multi-level representations introduce some difficult problems, which we discuss in Section 6.

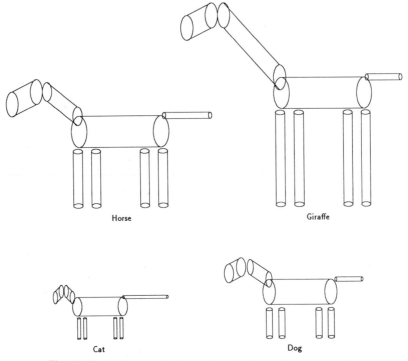

Fig. 11. Typical instances for four categories of quadruped mammals.

and a variance, specifying the degree to which that attribute will vary in the actual distribution of instances. Finally, each category has a probability that it will occur; some classes can be more common than others.

In producing data for our experiments, we used the prototype for each basic category to generate each instance according to the following procedure:

> Randomly select a template $C$ with probability $P(C)$.
> **For** each component $O$ in the prototype for $C$,
>> **For** each attribute $A$ of component $O$,
>>> Let $M$ be the typical value of $A$ for $O$ in template $C$.
>>> Let $S$ be the variance of $A$ for $O$ in template $C$.
>>> Randomly select a value $V$ for $A$ according to a
>>> normal distribution with mean $M$ and variance $S$.

Thus, every instance is a member of one of the four categories, although CLASSIT is told neither the class name nor the number of classes. Each instance diverges from the ideal for that category, though some diverge more from this ideal than others and some attributes tend to vary more than others. Later we will examine CLASSIT's behavior on another artificial domain, but we will use the same basic method for generating data.

## 5.2. Learning and component matching

We have claimed that CLASSIT is a learning system, and learning is usually defined as some improvement in performance. Following Fisher [12], our first experiment examined the incremental improvement in the system's ability to make predictions. The dashed line in Fig. 12 presents CLASSIT's learning curve as it incorporates instances from the domain of quadruped mammals into its concept hierarchy.

The independent variable here is simply the number of instances seen. The dependent variable is the system's ability to predict a single missing attribute from all the other attributes in an instance. We measured this variable after every five instances by "turning off" the learning component and presenting CLASSIT with five randomly selected test instances, each missing a single attribute. After classifying each instance, the system uses the selected category to predict the value of the missing attribute. The graph measures the percentage error between the predicted value and the ideal value for the instance's actual class.[22] The percentage error describes the absolute prediction error relative to the other categories present in the hierarchy. One hundred percent indicates that the system has confused the instance with the wrong category.

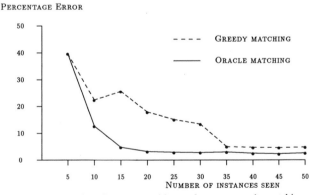

Fig. 12. CLASSIT learning curves with greedy versus oracle matching.

[22] Obviously, this measurement of error only makes sense for attributes that are relevant to classification; those attributes whose values differ across different classes. One cannot expect the system to correctly predict the value of an attribute that is irrelevant with respect to classification. Thus, we omitted only relevant attributes in measuring CLASSIT's improvement in predictive ability.

Clearly, the system's performance improves with experience, starting at 40% error and moving down to less than 5% error after 35 instances.

As described earlier, incremental algorithms tend to be sensitive to instance ordering. Although CLASSIT's split and merge operators allow some recovery from initial nonrepresentative orderings, learning curves still vary with different orderings. In order to minimize this effect, the measures in Fig. 12 have been averaged over 15 runs involving different random orderings. Also, since the data are produced randomly from templates, different instances are used for each ordering. We have followed this procedure in all our experiments.

In Section 4.2 we discussed CLASSIT's use of a greedy algorithm to match components in an instance to components in its concept descriptions, and it is this version that is summarized by the dashed line in Fig. 12. Given the heuristic nature of this matching scheme, we were interested in how it would fare against a version that had the optimal match available. The solid line in the figure shows the learning curve for such a system, in which we supplied CLASSIT with the correct correspondence between concept and instance components. This "oracle"-based variant improves its performance more quickly than the greedy version, reaching an asymptotic level after only 20 instances. However, despite some major errors early on (due to mismatched components), the greedy algorithm gradually narrows the gap, converging on nearly the same performance as the oracle version after 35 instances. This is a fairly impressive result for objects involving eight distinct components. In the remaining experiments, we report results only for the oracle version of CLASSIT, in order to factor out errors due to mismatches.

## 5.3. The effect of system parameters

We introduce the parameters for acuity and cutoff into CLASSIT only reluctantly, since such parameters encourage fine-tuning to achieve desirable behavior. To determine the effect of such tuning, we carried out the second experiment summarized in Fig. 13. As in the previous study, the horizontal axis specifies the number of instances and the vertical (dependent) axis shows the average percentage error. However, this time there are four learning curves, one for each setting of the acuity and cutoff parameters. We have repeated the oracle curve from Fig. 12, which was based on an acuity setting of 1.0 and cutoff setting of 0.2.

In this experiment we examined two levels of the cutoff parameter—0.2 and zero. The latter is the lowest possible setting, and effectively forces CLASSIT to retain all instances it has ever seen as terminal nodes in the hierarchy. Since the system always sorts a new instance as far down the hierarchy as possible, it will base its predictions on the values for a singleton concept. Unless each instance actually represents a distinct category, this strategy should lead to an

PERCENTAGE ERROR

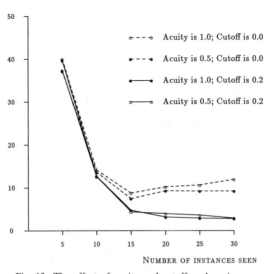

Fig. 13. The effect of acuity and cutoff on learning.

*overfitting* effect, similar to that Quinlan [34] has observed with decision trees in noisy domains.

Since we designed our quadruped data set to have only four generic categories, we would expect such overfitting on this domain as well. Indeed, the curves in Fig. 13 confirm this prediction. Both learning curves for the no-cutoff condition appear to asymptote at a higher error rate than the curves in the cutoff condition. With a higher setting for this parameter (i.e., with cutoff in operation), the system constructs simpler hierarchies with more general concepts as terminal nodes, and thus is able to make better predictions.

We also examined the effect of acuity, using two settings in this case as well. Unfortunately, the role of acuity is not as clear. In principle, one would expect overfitting to occur for low values of this parameter since this encourages CLASSIT to form many disjuncts. This should lead to a larger number of singleton classes, and thus to idiosyncratic predictions. However, this seems to occur only for extreme settings of the acuity parameter. Modifying the breadth of the hierarchy slightly does not have as strong an effect on prediction as does changing the depth of the tree with the cutoff parameter. Clearly, we need to carry out further studies to clarify the effect of this parameter.

In principle, one can get underfitting as well as overfitting effects. This should result in cases where CLASSIT constructs too shallow a hierarchy or creates too few disjunctive categories. However, the former can occur only if the "true" hierarchy contains multiple levels, and our quadruped data contains only one level of categories. For both parameters, one would expect a U-shaped curve, with high error from overfitting at one end of the spectrum and high error from underfitting at the other end, but we have not yet tested this prediction.

### 5.4. The effect of merging

We have discussed both COBWEB's and CLASSIT's potential sensitivity to the ordering of instances, and their use of merging and splitting operators to alleviate this effect. Our third experiment verifies that the merge operator has this predicted beneficial effect. Our technique was to "lesion" the system: that is, create a version of CLASSIT that cannot apply the merge operator, and compare its performance to the complete system. Recall that these "backtrack-ing" operators are most useful when the system initially receives nonrepresen-tative instances. Therefore, for this experiment we arranged the order of instances by hand.

Figure 14 shows the results of an experiment in which two versions of CLASSIT—one with merging and the other without—were given a very skewed ordering of instances from the quadruped domain. First we presented five instances of the "horse" category, then five "giraffes," then five "cats," then five "dogs," then five more "horses," and finally five more "giraffes." Given such data, CLASSIT splits the initial horses into several classes at the top level, then creates new categories upon seeing the giraffes, cats, and dogs. The result is a skewed hierarchy, in which different types of horses are given the same status as the general classes of giraffes, cats, and dogs. The merge operator is designed to restructure such a hierarchy, creating a new category for horses and bringing particular horses down to an appropriate (lower) level.

Since CLASSIT sorts an instance as far down the hierarchy as possible, the internal structure of the hierarchy will have little if any effect on prediction. For this reason, we have used a different dependent measure in Fig. 14—the

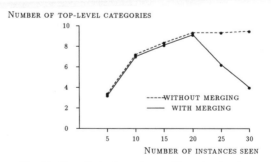

Fig. 14. The effect of merging on hierarchy structure.

number of top-level categories. This measure demonstrated precisely what one would expect. The number of categories at the top level continues to increase through instance 20. At this point, the new instances of "horse" lead the merging version of CLASSIT to combine the horse nodes at the top level into a single category. By instance 25, the number of top-level classes has decreased to around six, and by instance 30 it has reached four, the "correct" number. Note that merging combines only two nodes at a time, so this decrease is due to a sequence of merge operations. In contrast, the nonmerging version of CLASSIT incorporates the new horses into its existing categories, but retains the same top-level classes that the initially skewed data led it to create.

### 5.5. The effect of overlap and redundancy

Having considered the effect of varying CLASSIT's components on its learning behavior, let us examine the influence of two interesting domain characteristics. The first involves the number of attributes that are *relevant* in the sense that their values vary systematically with category membership. Intuitively, the more relevant attributes, the more *redundant* the data. The second variable involves the degree to which there is overlap between categories' values on an attribute; this corresponds to the percentage area that an attribute's probability distribution shares with the distribution from a neighboring class. Intuitively, the less overlap between two categories' values on an attribute, the more *distinguishable* those classes are on that attribute.

One would expect CLASSIT to have more difficulty in forming useful categories in the presence of highly overlapping attributes. The overlap between two distributions determines the probability that, on any given instance, the attribute value will fall in the region shared by both categories. In such cases, the attribute cannot be effectively used to determine the category to which the instance should be assigned. However, one would also expect highly redundant data to mitigate this effect. The more relevant attributes, the more attributes are likely to have values falling outside the area of overlap. Thus, we can predict an interaction effect, with CLASSIT's learning behavior worsening with increased overlap between categories, but with increased numbers of relevant attributes lessening this effect.

We tested this prediction in a fourth experiment. In this case we used a somewhat simpler artificial domain that let us independently control the two domain variables. Each instance consisted of five components with six attributes each, giving a total of 30 attributes, and instances were generated from only three category templates. (Hence, we assume there should be only three top-level categories). We varied the number of relevant attributes from two to ten. This represents a large amount of irrelevant information; two thirds or more of the attributes are irrelevant to predicting an instance's class. In contrast, an instance from the quadruped domain had two thirds of its attributes relevant. We also varied the amount of overlap between zero and fifty percent.

Figure 15 presents the results of this experiment. For simplicity, we have not reported learning curves in this case. Instead, the dependent variable shows predictive ability (average percentage error) after CLASSIT has viewed 30 instances. In all runs, we set acuity at 1.0 and cutoff at 0.2. As before, we averaged each point over 15 different random orderings.

The results are surprising. For higher numbers of relevant attributes, we see the expected interaction: increasing the number of relevant features helps more for higher levels of overlap, since they are worse to begin with. However, unexpected effects occur for lower redundancy settings, where even data with zero overlap leads to high error rates. Closer inspection suggests an explanation for this phenomenon. When there are only two relevant attributes (only one of which can be used on test instances), there are some 28 irrelevant ones that vary independently of category. Even when the relevant attributes never fall into the overlap areas, the irrelevant ones almost certainly do; despite their small individual contributions to category utility, their numbers overwhelm the small set of relevant features.

Unfortunately, this experiment confounds the total number of relevant attributes with the *percentage* of relevant attributes. To test our explanation, we must carry out further experiments in which we vary these two factors

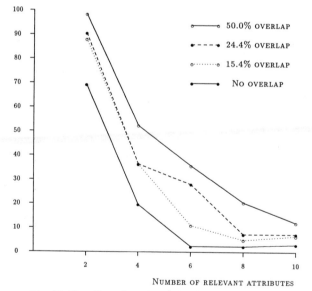

Fig. 15. The effect of overlap and redundancy.

independently. This is an important direction for future work, and it may ultimately let us predict CLASSIT's behavior from domain characteristics.

### 5.6. CLASSIT in a natural domain

Our final study examined CLASSIT's behavior on a real-world domain, using data on cardiology patients (Detrano [7]). In this data set, each patient has 13 measured or derived numeric attributes, along with a "class" attribute— whether or not the patient has heart disease. Unfortunately, Detrano indicates that this class information does not have a high accuracy; he estimates a 20% error rate.

Since CLASSIT is an unsupervised learning system, we discarded the class name and presented the system only with the numeric attributes for each instance. We then measured performance in terms of whether the system created concepts that corresponded to the prespecified classes. In effect, we asked the system to rediscover the class information from regularity in the numeric data. After seeing only ten of the total 303 instances, CLASSIT created three top-level concepts, and it retained this structure for the entire learning run.

Upon inspection, we found that one of these categories clearly corresponded to patients without heart disease; some 86.1% of its members had this label in the original data. The other two classes corresponded to patients with heart disease, one more consistently than the other; the accuracy was 79.7% and 66.6% for these groups. Overall, this represents a weighted average of 78.9% accuracy, which matches very well with the expected error rate of 20%. This is impressive, given that CLASSIT arrived at these categories without benefit of the class information.

### 6. Directions for Future Research

We believe that CLASSIT constitutes a promising framework for concept formation, and that it incorporates significant advances of earlier models. However, the existing system has a number of limitations that should be remedied in future efforts, and we discuss these below. We divide our treatment into issues of representation, matching, and learning.

### 6.1. Extending CLASSIT's representation

CLASSIT is designed to operate on numeric attributes, and we feel this is appropriate for domains based on visual input. However, symbolic or nominal attributes also have their uses, and we need to extend the system to handle this form of data. Recall that Fisher designed COBWEB to operate on nominal representations, and that CLASSIT uses a nearly identical algorithm for classification and learning. Moreover, our system's evaluation function is equivalent to Fisher's category utility metric, though we have modified it to work with numeric attributes. Thus, we hope to use a mixed evaluation function that includes discrete conditional probabilities for symbolic attributes and variances for numeric ones.[23] This should result in an integrated system that supports mixed forms of data.

In our work to date, we have used a simple set of primitives for describing objects, including cylinders and polygons. Clearly, we need to extend our framework to more realistic representations of the physical world. One approach would employ arbitrary polygons, which can be used to describe the surface characteristics on any three-dimensional object in arbitrary detail. However, this approach quickly leads to an unmanageable number of components for moderately complex objects. Alternatively, one might use Binford's [5] generalized cylinders to describe the volumetric aspects of objects. These require fewer components, but they introduce complex functional expressions to describe variations from a simple cylinder, and it would be difficult to extend CLASSIT to handle this scheme.

A more promising approach involves Biederman's [4] theory of *geons*, a set of 36 primitive shapes that can represent a wide range of complex objects. We see no difficulty in replacing our cylinders and polygons with geons, combining them to form more complex structures just as we currently do with simpler shapes. As before, each primitive component would be described in terms of its basic shape, along with numeric parameters specifying its size, location, and orientation. Some geons would require additional attributes to specify relative lengths of edges, but this would not be a problem for CLASSIT. Biederman has presented evidence that humans use geons in recognizing physical objects, and we hope that our revised system would make predictions about the human classification process.

### 6.2. Improving the matching process

The process of matching components between instance and concept is central to CLASSIT's behavior. Although the "oracle" approach was useful for experimental studies, it is not appropriate for normal operation. The greedy algorithm works reasonably well, but it leads to slower learning than the oracle method. We need additional studies to determine the robustness of the greedy scheme but we should also look for improvements on this method.

One approach involves making the greedy technique more heuristic in nature. The current version selects a component from the concept at random, finds the best matching component from the instance, selects another concept component at random, and so on. However, some components may have more diagnostic attributes than others, and matching against these components first

---

[23] This means that the $1/2\sqrt{\pi}$ term from Section 4.3 must be retained.

should improve the greedy method's chances for finding the optimal correspondences.

We also plan to examine the Hungarian algorithm (Papademetriou and Steiglitz [33]), a more expensive matching process that is guaranteed to find the optimal match. Given a bipartite graph with $2n$ nodes, along with some function for evaluating the quality of a match, the Hungarian method finds the best match in $O(n^3)$ time, as compared with $O(n^2)$ time for the greedy method. The algorithm works by creating an $n \times n$ cost matrix for all possible pairs of components and then solving an "$n$ rooks" problem over this matrix. In general, we would expect this approach to perform better than the greedy algorithm. However, although it is guaranteed to find the optimal match according to CLASSIT's evaluation function, this need not agree with the "correct" match. Thus, we expect the resulting learning curve for this algorithm to fall somewhere between the two curves of Fig. 12. Whether the $n^3$ cost is prohibitive is an empirical question, but we guess that it is not, since $n$ (the number of components) should seldom exceed ten for physical objects.

### 6.3. Handling missing attributes and components

Another aspect of matching involves dealing with instances having missing attributes. The current version of CLASSIT already takes this possibility into account, dividing the summed $1/\sigma$ scores by the number of attributes present. We used this scheme in classifying instances with a single missing attribute in our experiments, but we need further studies of its behavior when many attributes have been omitted.

In addition, entire components may be missing from an instance description. If we assume that CLASSIT's input is generated by a vision system, then components may be omitted because they are not visible. We may be able to use the same evaluation function in this case, simply treating the missing components as a set of missing attributes. However, we must still modify the component matching process to find a *partial* match between components in the instance and the concept. Although we do not have a complete specification, this modification seems feasible for either the greedy matching algorithm or the Hungarian algorithm.

### 6.4. Multiple levels of aggregation

Another research issue relates to the organization of complex objects with multiple components. Marr [28] has argued that the human visual system can generate descriptions of physical objects at different levels of aggregation. Thus, a dog might be viewed as a single cylinder at one level, as eight connected cylinders for (torso, neck, head, tail, and legs) at a lower level, with each leg described as three cylinders (thigh, calf, and foot) at a still lower level.

One difficulty with such a *part-of* hierarchy of objects lies in specifying the relation between different levels. We need to specify algorithms for moving from lower to higher levels that minimize information loss.

Once we have extended CLASSIT's representation in this direction, we will also need to alter its evaluation function and its matcher. CLASSIT can deal with two levels (a composite object and its components), but it cannot handle the general *n*-level case. Although EPAM was designed to handle composite, multi-level instances, neither UNIMEN nor COBWEB retained this ability. Wasserman [43] has described an extension to UNIMEM that takes a similar approach to EPAM, recursively sorting each component (and its components) through the concept hierarchy. However, EPAM does not address the problem of matching components at all (i.e., each component fills a unique slot), and Wasserman's extension uses a "greedy" matching strategy, the performance characteristics of which are not systematically evaluated.

Adding multiple levels of description to the CLASSIT framework raises a number of questions. Should the system use all levels in classification or only some? EPAM preferred to use attributes of composite objects when these were sufficient for avoiding errors. If we represent different levels in the same language, how can CLASSIT determine analogous levels between an instance and a concept description? How can one adapt the component matching process to work at multiple levels? Finally, how can one match a complex instance to a complex concept when its components are structurally different (e.g., a cylinder versus a block), and how should one alter the concept description in such cases? We must find at least tentative answers to these questions before we can extend CLASSIT in this direction.

## 6.5. Matching and normalization

We have designed CLASSIT with the domain of physical objects in mind, and this has led to our focus on composite instances and numeric attributes. In our experiments with the system, we have assumed that instances have the same location, orientation, and scale, but we must clearly abandon this simplification in future versions. Upon seeing a cat from a different angle than normal, one still recognizes it as a cat. Similarly, if one sees a cat in a different location, or even a cat of unusually large or small size, there is no recognition problem. Apparently, recognition focuses not on the absolute values of attributes, but on their *relative* values.

One might store in a concept description all pairwise relations between component objects, but this is neither space-efficient nor very plausible. A better approach involves selecting some scale, origin, and set of axes for the overall object concept, and then specify the scale, origin, and axes for each component relative to them. However, this raises a new issue: how can one determine these parameters for a new complex instance before it has been classified? We have not been able to devise a general algorithm that generates a canonical representation regardless of viewing angle, location, and size.

Instead, we hope to solve this *normalization* problem during the act of matching concept to instance. Upon observing an instance with multiple components, an extended CLASSIT would first match one of these components and use it to hypothesize the scale, origin, and axes for the composite object. This will lead to predictions about the locations of other components, which may or may not be correct. Hypothesized coordinate systems would be rejected, and those with better predictive ability would be extended, eventually leading to a completely normalized match. We plan to implement this normalization process in future versions of CLASSIT, though many details must still be specified.

### 6.6. Abstract descriptions and selective attention

Like Fisher's COBWEB, our system stores all known attributes on every concept description, even when they are neither predictive nor predictable. Earlier models of concept formation were more selective. Feigenbaum's EPAM starts with very general descriptions and gradually makes its images more specific through a process of familiarization. Lebowitz's UNIMEM and Kolodner's CYRUS gradually make their descriptions less specific through a generalization process. We need to explore variants on our basic algorithm that let it generate more abstract concept summaries, though the exact method is an open question.

A closely related problem is that CLASSIT inspects every attribute during the classification process, even if they have no predictive value. An improved system would incorporate the idea of selective attention, in which one focuses only on some features, presumably the useful ones. Earlier models of concept formation have this ability, including EPAM, UNIMEM, and CYRUS, as well as Fisher's COBWEB/2. The latter is encouraging, since it gives one path for incorporating attention into COBWEB, and thus into CLASSIT.

Ideally, the modified system would learn to prefer some attributes over others. In the early stages this selection would be random, since it would not know a priori which features would be diagnostic. However, as the system gained experience, it would come to prefer some attributes to others. Actually, CLASSIT already keeps statistics that would support this process. Using Bayes' rule, one can compute the predictiveness of each attribute from the existing scores. For example, the attribute "height" in Fig. 10 is clearly more predictive than "texture" at the first level. This is reflected by the fact that the difference between the average $1/\sigma$ score and the parent's $1/\sigma$ score is much larger for height than for texture.

In other words, CLASSIT's learning mechanism already supports such a focusing mechanism, and we need modify only the performance algorithm. The revised system would select only those attributes necessary to determine category membership with high probability. We could make this selection a deterministic function of predictiveness scores, but there is danger in this approach. If the initial instances are nonrepresentative or if the environment changes, the system might come to ignore attributes that later proved relevant. For this reason we prefer a probabilistic scheme, with more predictive attributes being selected more often, but even those with very low scores occasionally being sampled. We believe the addition of selective attention will make CLASSIT a more accurate model of human categorization and concept formation.

## 7. Summary

In this paper, we proposed a unifying framework for concept formation. We identified five features common to work on this task: that knowledge is represented in a concept hierarchy, that classification occurs in a top-down manner, that learning is unsupervised, integrated with performance, and employs an incremental hill-climbing search. We feel the search metaphor is especially important in understanding concept formation; it suggests both operators for learning and heuristics for controlling those operators.

We reviewed three concept formation systems (EPAM, UNIMEM, and COB-WEB) that fit within our framework, along with a new system (CLASSIT) that builds on the earlier work. We have tried to emphasize the close relation between the systems, as well as the additions each makes over its predecessor. In particular, CLASSIT extends Fisher's approach to numeric attributes, can handle instances with multiple (unordered) components, and retains only some of the instances it encounters.

Finally, we presented some experimental studies of CLASSIT's behavior. We found that for the artificial domain of quadruped mammals, the system significantly improved its performance with experience, and that the greedy matching algorithm slowed down learning but did not seem to affect asymptotic performance. CLASSIT showed some sensitivity to its parameter settings, with low values for cutoff giving overfitting effects. We also presented evidence that the merge operator leads to more balanced hierarchies when the initial data is nonrepresentative. In examining the effects of domain characteristics, we found that more overlap between categories led to reduced improvement, and that more redundancy alleviated this effect. However, the relationship was more complex than we expected, and we need further experiments along these lines. Finally, we showed that when given real-world data on heart disease, CLASSIT was able to formulate diagnostically useful categories even without class information.

The representation, use, and acquisition of concepts is a complex, inter-connected set of problems, and we cannot claim to have solved these problems in any absolute sense. However, we believe the basic approach we have described, and which is reflected in EPAM, UNIMEM, CYRUS, COBWEB, and CLASSIT, constitutes a promising thrust towards the computational understanding of categorization. We encourage other researchers to join in the effort, and to construct incremental models of concept formation that extend the initial results that have been achieved to date.

## ACKNOWLEDGMENT

The ideas in this paper have resulted from many fruitful discussions with members of the UCI World Modelers Group. We would like to particularly acknowledge the criticism and encouragement provided by our work with Wayne Iba, Kevin Thompson, Patrick Young, and David Benjamin. Dennis Kibler, David Nicholas, Rick Granger and Jaime Carbonell also contributed important ideas. This research was supported by Contract MDA 903-85-C-0324 from the Army Research Institute.

## REFERENCES

1. Anderson, J.R., Induction of augmented transition networks, *Cognitive Sci.* 1 (1977) 125–157.
2. Anderson, J.R. and Kline, P.J., A learning system and its psychological implications, in: *Proceedings IJCAI-79*, Tokyo (1979) 16–21.
3. Berwick, R., Learning structural descriptions of grammar rules from examples, in: *Proceedings IJCAI-79*, Tokyo (1979) 56–58.
4. Biederman, I., Matching image edges to object memory, in: *Proceedings IEEE First International Conference on Computer Vision*, London (1987) 384–392.
5. Binford, T.O., Visual perception by computer, Presented at IEEE Conference on Systems and Control, Miami, FL (1971).
6. Cheeseman, P., Kelly, J., Self, M., Taylor, W. and Freeman, D., Autoclass: A Bayesian classification system, in: *Proceedings Fifth International Conference on Machine Learning*, Ann Arbor, MI (1988) 65–64.
7. Detrano, R., International application of a new probability algorithm for the diagnosis of coronary artery disease, VA Medical Center, Long Beach, CA.
8. Everitt, B., *Cluster Analysis* (Heinemann Educational, London, 1974).
9. Feigenbaum, E.A., The simulation of verbal learning behavior, in: E.A. Feigenbaum and J. Feldman (Eds.), *Computers and Thought* (McGraw-Hill, New York, 1963).
10. Feigenbaum, E.A. and Simon, H., EPAM-like models of recognition and learning, *Cognitive Sci.* 8 (1984) 305–336.
11. Fisher, D., A hierarchical conceptual clustering algorithm, Tech. Rept. No. 85-21, Department of Information and Computer Science, University of California, Irvine, CA (1984).
12. Fisher, D., Knowledge acquisition via incremental conceptual clustering, *Mach. Learning* 2 (1987) 139–172.
13. Fisher, D., Knowledge acquisition via incremental conceptual clustering, Tech. Rept. No. 87-22 (Doctoral Dissertation), Department of Information and Computer Science, University of California, Irvine, CA (1987).
14. Gluck, M. and Corter, J., Information, uncertainty and the utility of categories, in: *Proceedings Seventh Annual Conference of the Cognitive Science Society*, Irvine, CA (1985) 283–287.
15. Grefenstette, J., Multilevel credit assignment in a genetic learning system, in: *Proceedings Second International Conference on Genetic Algorithms* (1987) 202–209.
16. Hanson, S.J. and Bauer, M., Conceptual clustering, categorization, and polymorphy, *Mach. Learning* 3 (1989) 343–372.
17. Holland, J., Escaping brittleness: The possibilities of general purpose algorithms applied to parallel rule-based systems, in: R.S. Michalski, J.G. Carbonell and T.M. Mitchell (Eds.),

*Machine Learning: An Artificial Intelligence Approach* **2** (Morgan Kaufmann, Los Altos, CA, 1986).

18. Iba, W., Wogulis, J. and Langley, P., Trading off simplicity and coverage in incremental learning, in: *Proceedings Fifth International Conference on Machine Learning*, Ann Arbor, MI (1988) 73–79.

19. Kolodner, J., Maintaining organization in a dynamic long-term memory, *Cognitive Sci.* **7** (1983) 243–280.

20. Langley, P., A general theory of discrimination learning, in: D. Klahr, P. Langley and R. Neches (Eds.), *Production System Models of Learning and Development* (MIT Press, Cambridge, MA, 1987).

21. Langley, P., Gennari, J. and Iba, W., Hill climbing theories of learning, in: *Proceedings Fourth International Workshop on Machine Learning*, Irvine, CA (1987) 312–323.

22. Lebowitz, M., Generalization and memory in an integrated understanding system, Tech. Rept. No. 186 (Doctoral Dissertation), Department of Computer Science, Yale University, New Haven, CT (1980).

23. Lebowitz, M., Generalization from natural language text, *Cognitive Sci.* **7** (1983) 1–40.

24. Lebowitz, M., Categorizing numeric information for generalization, *Cognitive Sci.* **9** (1985) 285–309.

25. Lebowitz, M., Concept learning in a rich input domain: Generalization based memory, in: R.S. Michalski, J.G. Carbonell and T.M. Mitchell (Eds.), *Machine Learning: An Artificial Intelligence Approach* **2** (Morgan Kaufmann, Los Altos, CA, 1986).

26. Lebowitz, M., Experiments with incremental concept formation: UNIMEM, *Mach. Learning* **2** (1987) 103–138.

27. Levinson, R., A self-organizing retrieval system for graphs, in: *Proceedings AAAI-84*, Austin, TX (1984) 203–206.

28. Marr, D., *Vision: A Computational Investigation into the Human Representation and Processing of Visual Information* (Freeman, San Francisco, CA, 1982).

29. Michalski, R.S., A theory and methodology of inductive learning, in: R.S. Michalski, J.G. Carbonell and T.M. Mithcell (Eds.), *Machine Learning: An Artificial Intelligence Approach* (Tioga, Palo Alto, CA, 1983).

30. Michalski, R.S. and Stepp, R., Learning from observation: Conceptual clustering, in: R.S. Michalski, J.G. Carbonell and T.M. Mitchell (Eds.), *Machine Learning: An Artificial Intelligence Approach* (Tioga, Palo Alto, CA, 1983).

31. Mitchell, T.M., Generalization as search, *Artificial Intelligence* **18** (1982) 203–226.

32. Mitchell, T.M., Utgoff, P. and Banerji, R., Learning by experimentation: Acquiring and refining problem-solving heuristics, in: R.S. Michalski, J.G. Carbonell and T.M. Mitchell (Eds.), *Machine Learning: An Artificial Intelligence Approach* (Tioga, Palo Alto, CA, 1983) 163–190.

33. Papademetriou, C. and Steiglitz, K., *Combinatorial Optimization* (Prentice-Hall, Englewood Cliffs, NJ, 1982).

34. Quinlan, J.R., Induction of decision trees, *Mach. Learning* **1** (1986) 81–106.

35. Rendell, L., Seshu, R. and Tcheng, D., More robust concept learning using dynamically-variable bias, in: *Proceedings Fourth International Workshop on Machine Learning*, Irvine, CA (1987) 66–78.

36. Rose, D. and Langley, P., A hill-climbing approach to machine discovery, in: *Proceedings Fifth International Conference on Machine Learning*, Ann Arbor, MI (1988) 367–373.

37. Rosch, E., *The principles of categorization, in: E. Rosch and B.B. Lloyd (Eds.), Cognition and Categorization* (Erlbaum, Hillsdale, NJ, 1978).

38. Schlimmer, J. and Fisher, D., A case study of incremental concept induction, in: *Proceedings AAAI-86*, Philadelphia, PA (1986) 496–501.

39. Schlimmer, J. and Granger, R., Beyond incremental processing: Tracking concept drift, in: *Proceedings AAAI-86*, Philadelphia, PA (1986) 502–507.
40. Shrager, J., Theory change via application in instructionless learning, *Mach. Learning* **2** (1987) 247–276.
41. Simon, H.A., *The Sciences of the Artificial* (MIT Press, Cambridge, MA, 1969).
42. Smith, E.E. and Medin, D.L., *Categories and Concepts* (Harvard University Press, Cambridge, MA, 1981).
43. Wasserman, K., Unifying representation and generalization: Understanding hierarchically structured objects, Doctoral Dissertation, Columbia University, New York (1985).
44. Winston, P.H., Learning structural descriptions from examples, in: P.H. Winston (Ed.), *The Psychology of Computer Vision* (McGraw-Hill, New York, 1975).

# Explanation-Based Learning:
# A Problem Solving Perspective

**Steven Minton\*, Jaime G. Carbonell,**
**Craig A. Knoblock, Daniel R. Kuokka,**
**Oren Etzioni and Yolanda Gil**
*Computer Science Department, Carnegie Mellon University,*
*Pittsburgh, PA 15213, U.S.A.*

ABSTRACT

*This article outlines explanation-based learning (EBL) and its role in improving problem solving performance through experience. Unlike inductive systems, which learn by abstracting common properties from multiple examples, EBL systems explain why a particular example is an instance of a concept. The explanations are then converted into operational recognition rules. In essence, the EBL approach is analytical and knowledge-intensive, whereas inductive methods are empirical and knowledge-poor. This article focuses on extensions of the basic EBL method and their integration with the PRODIGY problem solving system. PRODIGY's EBL method is specifically designed to acquire search control rules that are effective in reducing total search time for complex task domains. Domain-specific search control rules are learned from successful problem solving decisions, costly failures, and unforeseen goal interactions. The ability to specify multiple learning strategies in a declarative manner enables EBL to serve as a general technique for performance improvement. PRODIGY's EBL method is analyzed, illustrated with several examples and performance results, and compared with other methods for integrating EBL and problem solving.*

## 1. Introduction

Learning from examples has long been a focus of machine learning research. Early work in this area focused primarily on inductive methods, which compare many positive and negative instances of the desired concept in order to extract a general concept description [43]. However, in recent years many researchers have focused their attention on analytical methods, which view instances of concepts as more than independent collections of features; they consider each example in the context of background knowledge. Some of the analytical methods most intensively investigated fall under the label of explanation-based learning (EBL) [20, 26, 46, 48, 56, 63, 64, 69, 76]. EBL methods can generalize

---

\* Present address: Artificial Intelligence Research Branch, NASA Ames Research Center, Sterling Federal Systems, Mail Stop 244-17, Moffett Field, CA 94035, U.S.A.

from a single example by analyzing *why* that example is an instance of the concept. The explanation identifies the relevant features of the example, which constitute *sufficient conditions* for describing the concept. Typically, the purpose of EBL is to produce a description of the concept that enables instances of the concept to be recognized efficiently. The power of EBL stems from its use of a domain theory to drive the analysis process. Thus, while inductive learning is data-intensive, EBL is knowledge-intensive. As such, EBL represents part of a more general trend in AI towards knowledge-based systems.

In this article we describe the general EBL approach to learning, and discuss issues that arise when using EBL to improve problem solving performance. In particular, we explore one method, implemented in the PRODIGY problem solving system, for learning search control knowledge from problem solving experience. By providing PRODIGY's learning component with axiomatized knowledge about the architecture of the problem solver itself, as well as the application domain, we can use EBL to implement strategies for optimizing problem solving performance. This knowledge-based approach gives PRODIGY the capability to improve its performance rapidly as it solves problems in a particular domain. In the late 1950s John McCarthy declared that, "Our ultimate objective is to make programs that learn from their experience as effectively as humans do" [15, p. 360]. The EBL paradigm takes a major step towards effective learning by using a domain theory to guide the learning process. PRODIGY takes the next step in that direction by employing EBL as a general method for improving problem solving performance.

In the next section, we review the EBL paradigm and present several examples from the literature. Next, we discuss the issues that arise when employing EBL to improve problem solving performance. We then describe in detail how PRODIGY learns control knowledge to improve its problem solving efficiency, and conclude by comparing PRODIGY with other EBL problem solving systems.

## 2. The EBL Paradigm

The development of explanation-based learning has been a collaborative, evolutionary effort, marked by a gradual transition from exploratory research to more general and well-defined methods. The roots of EBL can be traced back to early analytical learning programs, such as STRIPS [29], HACKER [79] and Waterman's poker player [86], that improved their performance on the basis of experience. These EBL precursors, developed before the phrase was coined, did not investigate the method systematically. Thus the "modern" EBL era did not start until the early 1980s, when a number of researchers including DeJong [19], Silver [75], Mitchell [54], Carbonell [10], and others [2, 71, 87], were independently working on projects in a variety of different domains where learning depended on analyzing why observed examples had some significant property. These projects all emphasized knowledge-based learning from a single example, in contrast to much of the research on inductive learning which was being conducted at the time. Eventually a series of comparison papers [20, 48, 56, 58, 69] were written that attempted to unify these approaches in a single paradigm. The term *explanation-based learning*, which was suggested by DeJong, has come to be identified with the paradigm. To illustrate EBL and its progression we will describe four examples demonstrating different approaches to EBL, as well as some of the applications that have been proposed.

## 2.1. The STRIPS approach

The STRIPS macro-operator formation technique [29] is perhaps the most influential precursor of present EBL techniques. After the STRIPS planner solves a problem, the plan can be turned into a set of macro-operators for solving similar problems in the future. In the STRIPS task domain a robot can move from room to room and push boxes together. Consider the problem of achieving (NEXT-TO BOX1 BOX2) when the robot is in ROOM1 and BOX1 and BOX2 are in an adjacent room, ROOM2. One plan that STRIPS might construct to solve this problem is:

> (GOTO-DOOR ROOM1 ROOM2)
> (GOTHRU-DOOR ROOM1 ROOM2)
> (GOTO-BOX BOX1)
> (PUSH-BOX BOX1 BOX2)

By analyzing why the plan solved the problem, the STRIPS macro-operator learning method produces a general plan for achieving any goal matching (NEXT-TO box-x box-y):

> (GOTO-DOOR rm-w rm-v)
> (GOTHRU-DOOR rm-w rm-v)
> (GOTO-BOX box-x)
> (PUSH-BOX box-x box-y)

The procedure for generalizing the plan involves more than simply replacing constants by variables. STRIPS analyzes why each step in the plan is necessary so that, for example, two identical constants can be replaced by distinct variables if doing so does not disturb the structural integrity of the plan. Once the plan is generalized, the preconditions of the resulting macro-operator describe conditions under which the goal (NEXT-TO box-x box-y) is solvable.

The EBL perspective on this process is that the successful plan explains why the goal (NEXT-TO BOX1 BOX2) is achievable. The general concept of interest is the class of situations in which (NEXT-TO box-x box-y) is achievable. Macro-operator formation computes sufficient conditions for membership in this class, represented by the preconditions of the macro-operator. Thus, in contrast to inductive techniques, the planner learns from single examples.

## 2.2. Explanatory schema acquisition

More recently, DeJong and his students have experimented with a series of EBL programs that learn schemata for tasks such as problem solving and natural language understanding [19–21, 57, 63, 72, 74]. For instance, the GENESIS system [57, 59] is a schema-based natural language understanding system that learns new schemata in the normal course of processing narratives. Consider the first kidnapping story in Fig. 1. Although GENESIS may not know anything about kidnappings per se, the story is detailed enough so that GENESIS can understand the important events in the story in terms of pre-existing low-level schemata such as CAPTURE and BARGAIN. Thus the system can build up a causal explanation that relates the goals of the characters and the actions in the story. The explanation can then be generalized by eliminating details incidental to the explanation, such as the names of the particular characters involved. The resulting schema reflects only the constraints necessary to preserve the causal structure of the explanation, and serves as a general schema for understanding kidnappings.

Using the learned schema, GENESIS is able to understand sketchy stories such as the second story shown in Fig. 1. This sketchy story could not have been understood by the system had it not seen the first, causally complete, kidnapping story. Notice that the sketchy story leaves out information such as why Bob imprisoned Alice. Without the learned schema, the inferencing necessary to understand the sketchy story is combinatorially explosive. The

---

**Story1:**
Fred is the father of Mary and is a millionaire. John approached Mary. She was wearing blue jeans. John pointed a gun at her and told her he wanted her to get into his car. He drove her to his hotel and locked her in his room. John called Fred and told him John was holding Mary captive. John told Fred if Fred gave him $250,000 at Treno then John would release Mary. Fred gave him the money and John released Mary.

**Story2:**
Ted is the husband of Alice. He won $100,000 in the lottery. Bob imprisoned Alice in his basement. Bob got $75,000 and released Alice.

---

Fig. 1. Two kidnapping stories.

learned schema thus enables GENESIS to connect the events in the sketchy story without incurring the cost of the combinatorial explosion.

## 2.3. Constraint-based generalization

A third example of EBL is due to Minton [48], who describes a game playing program that learns by analyzing why its opponent was able to force it into a trap. Game playing offers a fertile domain for EBL because games are well-defined, so that clear-cut explanations of why a move was appropriate can often be found [3, 80, 83]. Consider the chess diagram in Fig. 2, which illustrates a simple chess combination called a "skewer." The black bishop has the white king in check. After the king moves out of check, as it must, the bishop can take the queen.

Minton's program can learn about tactical combinations of this type, where one opponent forces the other into an outright loss, a capture, or some other undesirable state. After falling into a trap, the program analyzes why the trap succeeded, and learns a rule that enables it to avoid the trap, or spring it on an opponent. The analysis operates by reconstructing the causal chain of events that forced the program into an undesirable state. In conducting this causal analysis, the program identifies a sequence of rules that explain why the trap succeeded. By computing the *weakest preconditions* of that sequence of rules the program can identify the general constraints that enable the trap to succeed. In our example, such an analysis can establish that while the pawns were irrelevant, the queen had to be "behind" the king for the plan to succeed. Ultimately, a general set of preconditions for applying this combination can be found. In future games this knowledge can be used to the system's advantage, both to avoid falling into traps of this type and to recognize when they can be employed against an opponent.

Fig. 2. A skewer position in chess.

## 2.4. The EBG approach

Mitchell, Keller and Kedar-Cabelli describe a unified approach to EBL, called explanation-based generalization (EBG) [56], which clarifies many of the common aspects of the various systems developed since STRIPS. One of the major contributions of the EBG approach is that explanations are identified with proofs, thus giving a precise meaning to the term "explanation" (as discussed by Minton [52]). Furthermore, Mitchell et al. suggest a clear specification of the input and output of EBL, as shown in Fig. 3. The input consists of a target concept,[1] a theory for constructing explanations, an example, and an operationality criterion that defines what it means for a description to be useful. Here *concepts* are viewed as predicates over instances, and therefore denote sets of instances. Thus a concept such as "BOX" refers to the set of objects that are identified as boxes. An *explanation* is a proof that the instance is a valid example of the concept. After generalizing the explanation, EBG produces an operational description that constitutes *sufficient conditions* for recognizing the target concept.

As an example, Mitchell et al. consider the target concept SAFE-TO-STACK$(x, y)$, that is, the set of object pairs $\langle x, y \rangle$ such that $x$ can be safely stacked on $y$. The target concept definition, training instance, theory, and operationality criterion are given in Fig. 4.

---

Given:
- *Target concept definition*: A concept definition describing the concept to be learned. (It is assumed that this concept definition fails to satisfy the operationality criterion.)
- *Training example*: An example of the target concept.
- *Domain theory*: A set of rules and facts to be used in explaining how the training example is an example of the target concept.
- *Operationality criterion*: A predicate over concept definitions, specifying the form in which the learned concept definition must be expressed.

Determine:
- A generalization of the training example that is a sufficient concept description for the target concept and that satisfies the operationality criterion.

---

Fig. 3. Mitchell et al.'s specification of EBL.

[1] We have slightly modified Mitchell et al.'s terminology for consistency with the remainder of this paper. In particular, we use the term *target concept* rather than *goal concept*, since the latter could be confused with the goals of the problem solver.

*Target concept definition*:
  SAFE-TO-STACK($x$, $y$) iff NOT(FRAGILE($y$)) or LIGHTER($x$, $y$)

*Training example*:
  ON(OBJ1, OBJ2)
  ISA(OBJ1, BOX)
  ISA(OBJ2, ENDTABLE)
  COLOR(OBJ1, RED)
  COLOR(OBJ2, BLUE)
  VOLUME(OBJ1, 1)
  DENSITY(OBJ1, 0.1)

*Domain theory*:
  VOLUME($p_1, v_1$) and DENSITY($p_1, d_1$) $\rightarrow$ WEIGHT($p_1, v_1 * d_1$)
  WEIGHT($p_1, w_1$) and WEIGHT($p_2, w_2$) and LESS($w_1, w_2$)
    $\rightarrow$ LIGHTER($p1, p2$)
  ISA($p_1$, ENDTABLE) $\rightarrow$ WEIGHT($p_1$, 5) [default]
  LESS(1, 5)

*Operationality criterion*:
  The learned concept description must be expressed in terms of the
  predicates used to describe examples (e.g., VOLUME, COLOR,
  DENSITY) or other selected, easily evaluated predicates from the
  domain theory (e.g., LESS).

Fig. 4. The SAFE-TO-STACK example for EBG.

The definition of SAFE-TO-STACK specifies that an object can be safely
stacked on a second object if the second object is not fragile or the first object
is lighter than the second. The domain theory encapsulates the system's
knowledge about objects, weight, etc. The training example illustrates an
instance of two objects, OBJ1 and OBJ2, that can be safely stacked on top of
each other. Finally, the system's operationality criterion specifies that the
explanation must be expressed in terms of easily evaluated predicates.

Now we are in a position to describe how EBG learns from this example.
EBG proves that OBJ1 is SAFE-TO-STACK on OBJ2 (see Fig. 5). The proof is
then generalized by *regressing* the target concept through the proof structure.
The regression process replaces constants with variables while preserving the
structure of the proof. The purpose of regression is to find the weakest
conditions under which the proof structure will hold. In this manner EBG
produces the following sufficient conditions for describing the concept SAFE-
TO-STACK:

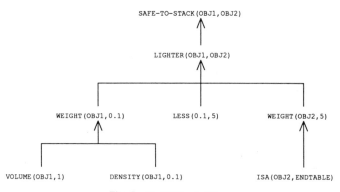

Fig. 5. An EBG proof tree.

VOLUME($x$, $v_1$) and
DENSITY($x$, $d_1$) and
LESS($v_1 * d_1$, 5) and
ISA($y$, ENDTABLE)

These conditions specify that $x$ can be safely stacked on $y$ if $y$ is an endtable and the volume times the density of $x$ is less than 5. (Notice that the domain theory specifies that all endtables weigh 5 lbs by default.) This description satisfies the operationality criterion and is justified by the proof.

## 2.5. Discussion

The four examples of EBL that we have reviewed share a common, fundamental theme. In each case, there was a general target concept that the system attempted to learn: STRIPS learned conditions under which two boxes could be placed NEXT-TO each other, GENESIS learned how a kidnapping could succeed in meeting a character's goals, Minton's game playing program learned how a skewer could succeed, and the EBG method was used to learn the conditions under which an object could be safely stacked on another object. As we have seen, the power of these programs stems from their ability to construct an explanation after observing a single example. The explanation answers the question: Why is the training example an instance of the target concept? Thus, computing the weakest conditions under which the explanation holds produces sufficient conditions for recognizing the target concept.

   A question commonly asked about EBL is: In what sense does the system learn if it starts with a definition of the concept? Simon has defined learning as "any change in a system that allows it to perform better the second time on repetition of the same task or on another task drawn from the same population" [77]. The definition of the concept that the system receives as input is nonoperational, which means that it is expensive (if not impossible) to use it to recognize instances of the concept. EBL can be viewed as operationalizing the definition—transforming it to a definition that can be used as an efficient recognizer for the concept. The operationality criterion enforces the efficiency requirement on the sufficient conditions that are the output of EBL.

Another important question is: What role does the example play in EBL? In principle, given a complete domain theory the concept's definition could be operationalized without the example [39, 61]. However, the example serves two functions. First, the example guides the search for an operational definition thereby making the search more tractable. Second, to the extent that the example is representative of the instances of the concept that the system will be asked to recognize, the example leads to recognizers (sufficient conditions) that are likely to be applicable.

### 2.6. Current issues

EBL is still a rather new paradigm and an area of very active research in machine learning [22]. The specification of EBL described previously is only an initial specification of the EBL problem. Several attempts have been made to refine EBL's formalization. Furthermore, in extending the use of EBL a host of new issues arise. The following is a brief survey of some of the important issues currently being explored.

#### 2.6.1. Formalizing EBL

Work on domain-independent EBL algorithms [20, 56] and on EBL in logic environments [34, 36] has pointed to the intimate relation between EBL on the one hand, and logic programming and theorem proving on the other [6, 53]. Indeed, recent papers by van Harmelen and Bundy [84] and Prieditis [67] argue that EBL algorithms are essentially equivalent to partial evaluation algorithms. However, van Harmelen and Bundy discount the importance of training examples for EBL. In doing so they largely overlook the fact that EBL is intended as a technique for learning from experience. The example plays an essential role in EBL by allowing a domain-independent problem solver to adapt to the particular environment it finds itself in. An analysis that attempts to clarify the role of examples in EBL, and the utility of EBL for improving problem solving performance appears in [47].

#### 2.6.2. The domain theory

Making explicit the role of the domain theory in the generalization process led Mitchell et al. [56] to consider how EBL would perform given an imperfect domain theory. They described three types of imperfect theories that have since received considerable attention [68]:

– When the theory is *incomplete* it may be impossible to construct an explanation due to a lack of information. However, generating partial or plausible explanations may suggest experiments or hypotheses useful for strengthening the theory [12, 32, 68].

– When the theory is *intractable*, an explanation may exist in principle, but finding it would take too long in practice. For example, the rules of chess form a complete theory of the game, but trying to prove that P-K4 belongs to the class of winning moves might take longer than the lifetime of the universe. Methods for moving from an intractable theory to a tractable, but approximate theory are being explored by a number of researchers, including Tadepalli [80] Bennett [4], Chien [14], Ellman [27], and Braverman and Russell [7].

– When the theory is *inconsistent* a desired assertion may be provable, but its negation will also be provable. This problem can arise when a theory has default rules that allow two inconsistent explanations to be formulated. In general, default or nonmonotonic logics are useful for generating explanations in the presence of uncertainty, but may necessitate retracting learned information. This problem may also arise if the theory is simply wrong, in which case experiments may help to resolve the inconsistency. Doyle [25] reports on a failure-driven approach for refining explanations constructed from an inconsistent theory.

The role of the domain theory in justifying explanation-based generalizations is another important issue. Mitchell et. al. argued that the domain theory enables EBL to produce generalizations that are deductively justified in terms of the learner's domain knowledge, whereas an inductive learner inevitably relies on some form of inductive bias to guide its generalization. Consequently, Mitchell et al. suggest that EBL techniques "provide a more reliable means of generalization" than inductive techniques [56, p. 48]. In response, Etzioni [28] argues that inductively formed generalizations may be justified by testing them on small samples. The test may be crafted to guarantee arbitrarily reliable generalization. Consequently, although the domain theory provides EBL with a measure of justification (a measure that is only as dependable as the theory), inductive learning may be *test-justified* to guarantee reliable generalization as well.

Furthermore, although EBL systems make no inductive leaps, bias plays a role in EBL as well. A learning system's bias determines which of the generalizations consistent with its training data is chosen [55]. Since an EBL system learns from a single example using a domain theory, the bias is encoded in the domain theory; the axioms that are used to construct a proof determine the generality of the concept description that results from the proof. Therefore, it is important to have a theory that will produce descriptions that are both general and useful (e.g., efficient for recognition). One important open question is how to build programs that can reason about and modify their own biases. Utgoff [83] has considered automatic methods for adjusting the bias in LEX, an inductive learning program. Related methods may also be useful for EBL.

### 2.6.3. *The explanation*

Significant effort has gone into crafting EBL's proofs or explanations to achieve superior generalizations. For example, several researchers [13, 16, 66, 74] have shown that, in some domains, producing descriptions at a useful level of generality may require explanations specifically suited to repetitive events. In the blocks world, for instance, to explain how to build towers of arbitrary height, it is useful to capitalize on the repetitive nature of the task by generalizing the number of blocks that appear in any given example. This is referred to as "generalization-to-$N$" [74]. One can view this body of work as investigating alternative *generalization* algorithms for EBL. However, we view this research and related efforts as investigating alternative *explanation* algorithms for EBL. This perspective was suggested by Minton [52, 53], who argued that the generalization process in EBL can always be described as computing the weakest preconditions (or equivalently, weakest premises) of an explanation. This provides a simple formal model of EBL, in which the semantics of the generalization process is fixed and only the explanation process varies.

### 2.6.4. *The example*

Although this notion has yet to be made precise, it appears intuitively clear that the example used in EBL focuses the learning mechanism by constraining the explanation process. However, Keller [38] and Mostow [61] have considered EBL-like systems that can search for operational concept descriptions without the benefit of examples to constrain the search. Another possibility that has received considerable attention is combining EBL with inductive techniques that make use of *many* examples. Utilizing both a domain theory and multiple examples appears to be a promising approach to addressing the problems raised by imperfect theories. For example, Lebowitz has explored combining inductive methods and explanation-based methods in the context of his UNIMEM system [44, 45]. Flann and Dietterich [30] have explored using explanations as input to an inductive component. Distinct approaches to this problem have been taken in [5, 16, 17, 65].

### 2.6.5. *The operationality criterion*

As pointed out by DeJong and Mooney [20], the EBG paper [56] suggests some very simple operationality criteria that are not necessarily realistic. In practice, it is difficult to guarantee that the knowledge learned by EBL will be useful. In some cases, the benefits of applying the knowledge may compare unfavorably with the costs of testing whether the knowledge is applicable [51]. Both Minton [52] and DeJong and Mooney [20] describe techniques for reformulating explanations to increase the utility of learned knowledge. In some cases it may be necessary to trade efficiency for generality, as pointed out by Segre [73], because knowledge that is expressed in a very general way may be more expensive to employ. Keller [40] considers the operationality question in depth, comparing several different operationality criteria that have been used in EBL systems. Finally, Hirsh [34, 35] suggests explicitly reasoning about operationality.

### 2.6.6. *The target concept*

The question of "what to learn" has only just begun to be addressed in EBL applications [37, 39]. For example, EBL problem solvers have primarily been used to learn from successful operator sequences. Recently, however, EBL was demonstrated to be useful for learning from problem solving failures as well [14, 31, 33, 50, 62]. In Section 5 of this paper we explore this issue further and describe how PRODIGY uses multiple target concepts, each of which corresponds to a distinct strategy for improving problem solving performance (i.e., replicating success, avoiding failure, coping with goal interactions). This approach achieves much better results than if the system is confined to a single strategy, such as learning from successful operator sequences.

## 3. EBL as a Method for Improving Problem Solving Performance

Let us now consider in greater depth the issues involved in using EBL to improve problem solving performance. In the past, EBL problem solvers learned primarily by observing solutions to problems, and ignoring failure paths or other problematical impasses. However, learning from successful solutions is only one stategy for improving performance, and EBL can be used to learn a general class of optimization strategies.

First, let us be precise about our terminology. An optimization strategy is simply a method for improving a program with respect to some performance metric. Optimization strategies may be heuristic, in that they may typically improve performance, but not be guaranteed to do so in every instance. We note that, theoretically, the problem of improving a general problem solver so that it is optimal with respect to efficiency (or some other arbitrary performance metric) is undecidable. In any event our emphasis is on *improved* performance, not necessarily optimal performance.

A *dynamic* optimization strategy modifies a program based on its observed behavior, in contrast to a *static* optimization strategy, which modifies a program in isolation. For example, an optimizing compiler typically performs only static optimizations, such as constant folding, loop unrolling, and extraction of loop invariants [1]. In contrast, STRIPS' macro-operator learning technique is a dynamic optimization strategy, because each macro-operator is acquired by observing the solution to a problem. Here the problem solver operating in a particular domain constitutes the program, and the addition of the macro-operator to the set of operators constitutes an optimization for that domain.

EBL is well-suited for implementing dynamic optimization strategies because it provides a mechanism for improving problem solving behavior on the basis of observed examples. In this paper we focus on optimizations that can be expressed as control knowledge. Specifically, our optimization strategies will be represented by rules of the form IF TEST($st$) THEN DO ACTION($st$) where $st$ is a state of the problem solver, TEST($st$) is true if TEST matches state $st$, and ACTION($st$) is some modification of the program's normal behavior in state $st$. By letting the TEST be a target concept, EBL can produce a specialization of the TEST that is efficient to evaluate, whereas the original TEST is presumably very inefficient to evaluate.

To illustrate our approach, we have implemented a variety of optimization strategies in the PRODIGY problem solving system. Currently the system can learn by observing problem solving failures, successes, and interfering goals, each of which corresponds to a target concept. Furthermore, the set of target concepts is specified declaratively so that additional optimization strategies can be implemented.

Before describing our approach in detail, let us consider the issues that arise when using EBL to implement dynamic optimization strategies. For clarity, the following list is organized according to Mitchell et al.'s description of EBL's inputs:

– *Target concept coverage*. The learning component's target concepts describe the conditions under which each optimization strategy is applicable. Thus the coverage of the target concepts determines the situations where performance can be improved.

– *Scope of the theory*. The theory provides the means for proving that an optimization strategy applies in a given problem solving episode. The scope of the theory delimits the types of explanations that the system can construct. To implement dynamic optimization strategies, the theory must be capable of explaining relevant aspects of the system's problem solving behavior.

– *Method of constructing explanations from examples*. To learn by observing a problem solver, the system must be able to identify examples of the target concepts from the problem solving trace, and efficiently explain why the examples are subsumed by the target concepts. This requires a means for mapping from the trace to an explanation.

– *Operationality criterion*. The system's operationality criterion must reflect the computational costs and benefits of the transformations that are learned. In particular, the operationality criterion must insure that the time cost of testing whether a transformation is appropriate does not outweigh the benefits provided by the transformation.[2]

Learning does not happen in a vacuum. In practice, the design of the problem solving architecture will greatly affect the design of the learning system, and the optimization strategies that can be implemented. Therefore, when designing the problem solving architecture, the following issues also need to be considered:

– *Flexibility*. Learning control knowledge is useful only if the problem solver is sufficiently flexible to take advantage of the learned knowledge. The language used to encode the problem solver's control knowledge will determine what the EBL component can express to the problem solver.

– *Parsimony*: The problem solver must be relatively simple. In general, the simpler the problem solver, the easier it is to formulate a theory describing its behavior.

There is a synergistic relationship between the problem solver and the EBL subsystem in PRODIGY. The problem solver provides problem solving episodes for the EBL component to analyze, and is a testbed for measuring the utility of the learned control knowledge. In turn the EBL component provides the problem solver with control knowledge.[3] Due to the power of EBL, sophisticated general search control strategies such as least commitment to not necessarily need to be built into the problem solver. Instead, appropriate domain-specific search control knowledge can be acquired via learning.

## 4. The PRODIGY System

PRODIGY is a domain-independent problem solver that acquires new knowledge by analyzing its experiences and interacting with an expert. In addition to the EBL method which this paper focuses on, there are several other learning components (described below). In essence, the PRODIGY architecture is inspired by observation of how human students transition gradually from novice to increasingly more expert performance by being taught through problem solving practice and much trial and error. Although not a fine-grain cognitive model, PRODIGY nevertheless strives to retain the human flexibility of applying focused expertise when available, and relying on less focused general problem solving behavior when domain knowledge fails to produce an adequate answer.

---

[2] Learning is typically used to improve performance by reducing search time, but other performance benefits might additionally be realized. For example, qualitatively better plans can be produced. We assume that there is a single metric for comparing the costs and benefits of learned knowledge.

[3] The EBL component may also direct the problem solver to explore alternative solutions so that EBL can generate a proof of some conjecture.

Thus, the learning components acquire either factual domain knowledge or domain-specific control knowledge, both necessary components for search-limited, knowledge-intensive, expert behavior. This new knowledge is then used by the problem solver (whose structure does not change) when encountering new, progressively more difficult problems in the same domain.

PRODIGY consists of a general means-ends problem solver connected to a set of learning modules: EBL, derivational analogy, plan abstraction, and experimentation. These modules augment the domain-specific knowledge bases, including operators and control rules, through incremental problem solving experience. The PRODIGY architecture is diagrammed and discussed further in Appendix A and the reader is referred to the references cited therein for in-depth discussion of the various learning modules. This article, however, focuses only on EBL and the necessary support to EBL provided by the problem solving engine.

## 4.1. The problem solver

In order to solve problems in a particular domain, PRODIGY must first be given a specification of that domain, which consists of a set of operators and inference rules. Operators correspond to external actions with consequences in the world. Each operator has a precondition expression that must be satisfied before the operator can be applied, and a list of effects that describes how the application of the operator changes the current state of the world. The effects can either directly or conditionally add or delete atomic formulas from the state description.

Inference rules, unlike operators, do not correspond to external actions; they simply increase PRODIGY's explicit knowledge about the current state. Even so, inference rules are specified much in the same way that operators are. Each inference rule has a precondition expression that must be true for the rule to be applicable. Each inference rule also has a list of effects. However, inference rules only add formulas to the state description; they never delete formulas. Because inference rules are treated similarly to operators, PRODIGY can use a homogeneous control structure, enabling the search control knowledge to guide the application of operators and inference rules alike. The homogeneous control structure makes for a parsimonious problem solver.

There are two types of predicates used in the system: primitive predicates and defined predicates. Primitive predicates are directly observable, or *closed-world* [15, p. 115], and they may be added to and deleted from the state by operators. Defined predicates are inferred (on demand) using inference rules. They represent useful abstractions in the domain, allowing operator preconditions to be expressed more concisely.

PRODIGY's description language (PDL), is a form of predicate logic that allows negation, conjunction, disjunction and existential quantification, as well as universal quantification over sets.[4] Preconditions of operators, inference rules, and also search control rules (see Section 4.3) are expressed in PDL.

## 4.2. The problem solving process

To facilitate our discussion, we will describe PRODIGY in terms of a simple machine-shop scheduling task. The shop contains several machines, including a lathe and a roller that are used to reshape objects, and a polisher. We assume that each machining operation takes one time unit. Given a set of objects to be polished, shaped, etc., and a finite amount of time, the task is to schedule the objects on the machines so as to meet these requirements. (Note that we are considering a satisficing rather than an optimizing task.) The specifications for the LATHE, ROLL, and POLISH operators are shown in Appendix B. (A complete specification of the domain can be found in [52].)

Consider the LATHE operator:

```
(LATHE (obj time)
 (PRECONDITIONS
  (AND
    (LAST-SCHEDULED obj prev-time)
    (LATER time prev-time)
    (NOT (EXISTS other-obj SUCH-THAT
            (SCHEDULED other-obj LATHE time)))))
 (EFFECTS
    (DELETE (SHAPE obj old-shape))
    (DELETE (LAST-SCHEDULED obj prev-time))
    (IF (POLISHED obj)
        (DELETE (POLISHED obj)))
    (ADD (LAST-SCHEDULED obj time))
    (ADD (SHAPE obj CYLINDRICAL))
    (ADD (SCHEDULED obj LATHE time))))
```

The LAST-SCHEDULED relation indicates the time period at which an object was last scheduled to be operated on. Thus, the first two preconditions force the problem solver to schedule operations chronologically; once an object has been scheduled for a machine at time $t$, it cannot be scheduled for another operation at an earlier time period. (Initially, all objects are LAST-SCHEDULED at TIME-0.) This restriction will make our examples easier to understand, and will enable us to represent properties of objects in a straightforward manner. (Inefficiencies due to this restriction can be largely compensated for by control knowledge.)

---

[4] Constants are shown in upper case and variables are in italics. To enhance readability, quantifiers are omitted when they are obvious. The reader may note that PDL is more expressive than Horn clauses in PROLOG that permit neither disjunction nor explicit quantification over sets.

The last precondition of LATHE states that there cannot be another object scheduled to be lathed during the same time period. The effects of the operator include scheduling the object on the LATHE, and updating the LAST-SCHEDULED relation. Furthermore, the effects indicate that lathing changes the object's shape, and removes the polish from its surface (if it is polished).

The ROLL and POLISH operators have similar preconditions and effects. Notice, however, that polishing an object requires that the object must either be rectangular, or clampable to the polisher. The CLAMPABLE predicate is a defined predicate; the domain specification in Appendix B includes an inference rule for determining whether an object is clampable to a given machine. All other predicates referred to in this paper are primitives (i.e., closed-world).

Once the domain has been specified, problems are presented to the problem solver by describing an initial state and a goal expression to be satisfied. The goal expression for our example problem is:

> (AND (SHAPE OBJECT-A CYLINDRICAL)
>      (POLISHED OBJECT-A))

This expression is satisfied if there is an object named OBJECT-A that is polished and has a cylindrical shape.[5]

The initial state for our example is illustrated in Fig. 6. OBJECT-B and OBJECT-C have already been scheduled, while OBJECT-A has yet to be scheduled. Let us suppose that the schedule consists of 20 time slots, and that OBJECT-A is initially unpolished, oblong-shaped, and cool.

The search tree for this example is shown in Fig. 7. The left side of each node shows the goal stack and the pending operators at that point. The right side shows a subset of the state that is relevant to our discussion. For example, at Node 3, the current goal is to make the object CLAMPABLE, a precondition

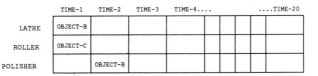

Fig. 6. The initial state provided to PRODIGY.

---

[5] We have simplified our representation so that attributes such as shape and temperature take ordinal values such as RECTANGULAR and COOL. Normally, a richer representation would be used to reflect real-world complexities. For example, a shape might be represented by the list [CYLINDRICAL 1 3], describing a cylindrical shape with diameter 1 and length 3. When necessary, predicates such as IS-LENGTH can then be used to extract particular fields of lists. For example the following formula would be true, only if $x$ equals 3: (IS-LENGTH $x$ [CYLINDRICAL 1 3]). This is easy to implement because PRODIGY allows *static* predicates (those whose truth value is not dependent on the state), such as IS-LENGTH and LESS-THAN, to be computed by user-defined functions.

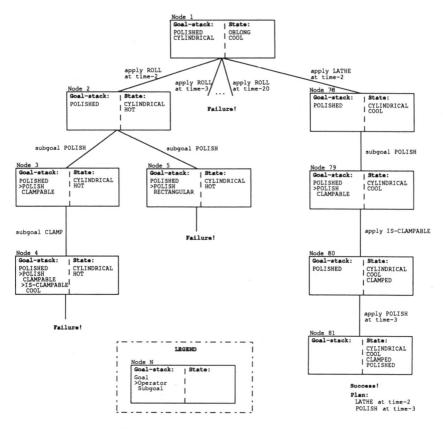

Fig. 7. PRODIGY's search tree prior to learning.

of the POLISH operator that is being considered to achieve the higher goal of being polished. The predicates like CYLINDRICAL and HOT in the figure are shorthand for the actual formulas, such as (SHAPE OBJECT-A CYLINDRICAL) and (TEMPERATURE OBJECT-A HOT).

By default, PRODIGY achieves goals from left to right in an expression, unless control knowledge indicates a more appropriate ordering. For each goal the system selects a relevant operator (or inference rule), matches the preconditions against the database, and subgoals if the match does not succeed. If the match does succeed, the operator (or inference rule) is applied to the current state, and then the system returns its focus to goals that remain to be achieved. In our example, (SHAPE OBJECT-A CYLINDRICAL) is not true in the initial state, therefore PRODIGY considers the operators LATHE and ROLL, since only these operators add effects that unify with this goal. At this point

PRODIGY arbitrarily decides to try ROLL first, as there are no control rules that indicate otherwise.

In order to satisfy the preconditions of ROLL, PRODIGY must select a time slot later than the last time slot for which OBJECT-A has last been scheduled (i.e., TIME-0). Furthermore, the machine must be idle at this time. Let us assume that previously acquired control knowledge indicates a preference for the earliest time slot that satisfies these constraints, TIME-2. After rolling the object at TIME-2, PRODIGY attempts to polish the object, but the preconditions of POLISH specify that the object must either be rectangular, or clampable to the polisher. Unfortunately, the object is not clampable because rolling the object has raised its temperature so that it is too hot to clamp. Furthermore, there is no way to make the object clampable, because there is no operator that will cool the object. And finally, since there is no way to make the object rectangular, the attempt to apply POLISH fails.

Backtracking, PRODIGY then tries rolling the object at TIME-3, and then TIME-4, and so on, until the end of the schedule is reached at TIME-20.[6] Each of these attempts fails to produce a solution, because rolling the object always makes it hot, and therefore unclampable. As we will see, when learning is interleaved with problem solving, PRODIGY can reason about the failures and therefore backtrack more intelligently. In any event, the problem solver finally succeeds when it eventually backs up and tries LATHING rather than ROLLING.

As our example illustrates, the problem solving process can be extremely expensive without control knowledge. The next section describes how control knowledge is represented in the PRODIGY architecture.

## 4.3. Control rules

The PRODIGY architecture separates domain knowledge, which specifies *what* operators and inference rules are available, from control knowledge, which describes *how* to solve problems in the domain. PRODIGY's control rules constrain the possible choices that the problem solver makes as it searches. The search is conducted by repeating the following decision cycle:

*Step* 1. A node in the search tree is chosen. A node consists of a set of goals and a state of the world.

*Step* 2. One of the goals at that node is chosen as the immediate focus. (The other goals will be addressed later, at subsequent nodes.)

*Step* 3. An operator relevant to fulfilling the goal is chosen.

*Step* 4. Bindings for the variables in the operator are selected. If the instantiated operator is applicable, then it is applied, otherwise PRODIGY subgoals on the operator's unmatched preconditions. In either case, a new node is created.

---

[6] PRODIGY does not have to consider alternative time slots for POLISH, because it has not yet selected one when it subgoals on CLAMPABLE.

At each of these choice points there is always a default set of candidates and a simple default decision strategy. For example, depth-first search is the default strategy for choosing a new node. There is a set of control rules for each of the four decisions (nodes, goals, operators, and variable bindings). Control rules modify the default behavior by specifying either that a particular candidate should be selected (over all others), rejected (from any future consideration), or that it should be preferred over another candidate or candidates (all else being equal).

Each control rule has left-hand side conditions testing applicability and a right-hand side indicating whether to SELECT, REJECT, or PREFER a candidate. To make a control decision, PRODIGY first applies the applicable selection rules to select a set of candidates. (If no selection rules are applicable, all the default candidates are selected.) Next, rejection rules further filter this set, and finally, preference rules are used to order the remaining alternatives.[7] If backtracking is necessary, the next most preferred is attempted, and so on, until all candidates are exhausted. (In effect, PRODIGY backtracks when it returns to a previously chosen node in order to explore a different goal, operator, and/or bindings.)

The control rule depicted in Fig. 8 is an operator rejection rule. Notice that the rule uses meta-level predicates such as ADJUNCT-GOAL and CURRENT-NODE in addition to domain-level predicates such as SHAPE. (An adjunct goal at a node will be achieved after the current goal.) The rule states that if the current goal at a node is to make an object cylindrical and the object must subsequently be polished, then the ROLL operator should be rejected.

The example problem from the previous section illustrates why this rule is appropriate: polishing OBJECT-A after rolling it turned out to be impossible. Had the problem solver previously learned this rule, the problem would have been solved directly, without the costly backtracking at Node 1. In general, control rules can serve the following purposes:

(1) *To increase the efficiency of the problem solver's search.* Control rules

---

```
IF (AND (CURRENT-NODE node)
        (CURRENT-GOAL node (SHAPE obj CYLINDRICAL))
        (CANDIDATE-OPERATOR node ROLL)
        (ADJUNCT-GOAL node (POLISH obj)))
THEN (REJECT OPERATOR ROLL)
```

---

Fig. 8. An operator rejection rule.

[7] Preferences are transitive. If there is a cycle in the preference graph, then those preferences in the cycle are disregarded. A candidate is "most preferred" if there is no candidate that is preferred over it.

guide the problem solver down the correct path so that solutions are found faster.

(2) *To improve the quality of the solutions that are found.* There is usually more than one solution to a problem, but only the first one that is found will be returned. By directing the problem solver's attention along a particular path, control rules can express preferences for solutions that are qualitatively better (e.g., more reliable, less costly to execute, etc.).

(3) *To direct the problem solver along paths that it would not explore otherwise.* As with most planners, for efficiency PRODIGY normally explores only a portion of the complete search space. This is accomplished through this use of default control rules. For example, PRODIGY will not normally explore all permutations of conjunctive sets of subgoals. However, when these default heuristics prove too restrictive, they can be overridden by additional selection rules.

PRODIGY's reliance on explicit control rules, which are typically learned for specific domains (e.g., by the EBL process), distinguishes it from most domain-independent problem solvers. Instead of using a least-commitment search strategy, for example, PRODIGY expects that any important decisions will be guided by appropriate domain-specific control rules. If no control rules are relevant to a decision, then PRODIGY makes an arbitrary choice. If in fact the wrong choice was made, and costly backtracking is necessary, an attempt will be made to learn the control knowledge that must be missing. However, should the choice prove immaterial no effort will have been wasted on the decision-making process. Thus, the rationale for PRODIGY's "casual commitment" strategy is that control rules are expected to guide any decision with significant ramifications. Instead of relying on sophisticated, but potentially very weak, domain-independent problem solving strategies, PRODIGY relies on learning to generate clever behavior. In fact, the more clever the underlying problem solver is, the more difficult the job will be for the learning component. For instance, the inclusion of complex domain-independent conflict resolution criteria [8] would make it difficult to add far more useful and constraining domain-specific control knowledge. In the next section, we describe in detail how the EBL learning component acquires control rules.

## 5. The EBL Component

In this section we discuss in detail PRODIGY's explanation-based learning component. As mentioned in Section 3, four basic design issues need to be addressed in integrating an explanation-based learning system with a problem solver. First, there is the question of *target concept coverage.* What are the system's target concepts? The second issue in the *scope of the theory,* which determines the space of explanations that the system can generate for a given target concept. The third is the *method for mapping from an example to an explanation.* Is the explanation process expensive, or can the explanation be constructed directly from a problem solving trace? Finally, the last issue concerns the *operationality criterion.* What makes an explanation useful? How does the system determine whether a particular explanation satisfies this criterion? In the next four sections we discuss how PRODIGY addresses these issues, and in the following section we present several detailed examples of learning in PRODIGY.

## 5.1. Target concept coverage

Currently, for each of the four types of search control decisions that PRODIGY makes (i.e., choosing a node, goal, operator, or bindings, as described in Section 4.3), there are four types of target concepts: SUCCEEDS, FAILS, SOLE-ALTERNATIVE, and GOAL-INTERFERENCE. A control choice is said to *succeed* if it leads to a solution. Similarly, a choice *fails* if there is no solution to be found along that path. A choice is a *sole alternative* if all other alternatives fail. Finally, a choice results in *goal interference* if either a previously achieved goal is undone, or a precondition of a subsequent action in the plan is undone, even if (suboptimal) success is eventually achieved. Each type of target concept is associated with a control rule type, as given by Fig. 9.

The target concepts that we have selected for PRODIGY are useful and effective (as demonstrated below), but do not represent the complete range of potential target concepts. The language provided for specifying target concepts makes it easy to add target concepts as they are needed. For example, in some planning domains we believe it would be worthwhile to learn from advantageous goal interactions; thus far PRODIGY only learns to optimize against harmful interactions.

## 5.2. The scope of the theory

PRODIGY constructs search control rules by explaining why a target concept was satisfied by a training example—e.g., why a problem solving attempt failed, or why a goal interaction yielded a suboptimal plan. In order to construct explanations, we require a theory describing the relevant aspects of the problem solver, as well as a theory that describes the task domain (such as

| Target concept type | Control rule type |
|---|---|
| Succeeds | Preference rule |
| Fails | Rejection rule |
| Sole alternative | Selection rule |
| Goal interference | Preference rule |

Fig. 9. Correspondence of target concept type to control rule type.

our machine-shop world). Therefore, PRODIGY employs a set of *architecture-level* axioms that serve as its theory of the problem solver, and a set of *domain-level* axioms that are automatically derived from the domain specification.[8] Each axiom is a conditional statement written in PDL that describes when a concept (i.e., an atomic formula) is true. Figure 10 shows two architecture-level axioms and Fig. 11 shows two domain-level axioms.

The domain-level axioms state the domain operators' effects and preconditions. The architecture-level axioms describe how the problem solver operates. For example, the axioms for OPERATOR-SUCCEEDS shown in Fig. 10 state that an operator succeeds in solving a goal at a node if the operator directly solves the goal (i.e., the operator has an effect that unifies with the goal), or applying another operator results in a node at which the operator succeeds in solving the goal.

## 5.3. The mapping method

Mapping from a problem solving trace into an explanation involves first selecting an example of a target concept that is to be learned and then constructing an explanation of that particular example. We will first describe how examples are selected and then describe PRODIGY's explanation method.

### 5.3.1. *Selecting an example*

The EBL process can be either initiated after problem solving has terminated, or interleaved with problem solving. In either case, the learning component

---

Axiom-S1: An operator succeeds if it directly solves the goal.
(OPERATOR-SUCCEEDS *op goal node*)
if (AND (IS-EFFECT *goal op params*)
          (APPLICABLE *op params node*))

Axiom-S2: An operator succeeds if it succeeds after precursor operator is applied
(OPERATOR-SUCCEEDS *op goal node*)
if (AND (APPLICABLE *next-op params node*)
          (OPERATOR-SUCCEEDS *op goal child-node*)
          (CHILD-NODE-AFTER-APPLYING-OP *child-node next-op node*))

---

Fig. 10. Architecture-level axioms describing OPERATOR-SUCCEEDS.

[8] The architecture-level axioms are domain-independent but must be hand-coded. In contrast, the domain-level axioms are created automatically for each domain by a simple conversion procedure that examines the operators, inference rules and control rules for the domain.

Axiom-D1: POLISH is applicable if its preconditions are satisfied.
(APPLICABLE *op params node*)
if (AND (MATCHES *op* POLISH)
        (MATCHES *params* (*obj time*))
        (KNOWN *node* (AND (OR (SHAPE *obj* RECTANGULAR)
                               (CLAMPABLE *obj* POLISHER))
                           (LAST-SCHEDULED *obj prev-time*)
                           (LATER *time prev-time*)
                           (NOT (EXISTS *other-obj* SUCH-THAT
                                       (SCHEDULED *other-obj*
                                        POLISHER *time*)))))))


Axiom-D2: After applying the operator POLISH to an object it is polished.
(IS-EFFECT *effect op params*)
if (AND (MATCHES *op* POLISH)
        (MATCHES *params* (*obj time*))
        (MATCHES *effect* (POLISHED *obj*)))

Fig. 11. Examples of domain-level axioms for machine-shop scheduling.

begins by examining the explored portion of the search tree in order to find examples of its target concepts. After each suitable training example is selected, PRODIGY constructs an explanation, and from this explanation creates a search control rule. The system continues its examination until a fixed time limit is exceeded or the search tree has been fully analyzed.

PRODIGY conducts its examination of the tree in postorder: children are analyzed before parents, from left to right in the search tree. This bottom-up style of processing is preferred because, due to the fixed time limit, PRODIGY may not have the opportunity to analyze the entire tree. (The search tree may consist of thousands of nodes.) Beginning the analysis at the farthest limbs of the tree insures that some learning will take place even if the learning process must be aborted early due to time constraints. Thus the EBL process is incremental, similar in spirit to an "anytime algorithm" as defined by Dean and Boddy [18].

When PRODIGY examines a node in the tree, *training example selection heuristics* are used to select the examples that appear worth learning about. There is a set of selection heuristics associated with each target concept. For example, one selection heuristic for OPERATOR-SUCCEEDS, called "others-have-failed," states that a successful operator is interesting only if the problem solver previously tried an operator that failed. (If the problem solver immediately found the correct operator, there is no reason to learn additional control knowledge.) To illustrate this, consider the search tree from our machine-shop problem described in Section 4.2. In solving this problem, PRODIGY first tried the ROLL operator, and only after ROLL failed did it try LATHE. Once LATHE was chosen, the system had no other difficulties with subsequent decisions and, for instance, chose the POLISH operator without incident. Thus, the success of LATHE is deemed interesting, but the subsequent success of POLISH is not.

However, even if an example is not interesting in its own right, it may be selected for explanation because the result can be used as a "lemma" in explaining a higher-level example. This is, in fact, the case with POLISH. The success of POLISH is not considered worth learning about. However, it is necessary to explain the success of POLISH in order to explain why LATHE was the appropriate choice higher up in the search tree. The explanation of POLISH's success will *not* be converted into a control rule.

It can also be the case that an example is both interesting in its own right, and useful for explaining higher-level examples. For instance, in order to explain why the ROLL operator failed at Node 1 it is necessary to explain the failure of Node 2, a child of Node 1. But this lower-level failure is also considered worth learning for its own sake. PRODIGY uses a selection heuristic for failure, called "highest-failure-per-node," which always considers node failures to be worth learning about. (Other failures, such as operator failures, are considered interesting only if the entire node did not fail.)

### 5.3.2. *Constructing an explanation*

PRODIGY constructs explanations using a method that we refer to as *explanation-based specialization* (EBS). A target concept is specialized by retrieving an axiom that describes the concept and recursively specializing the axiom, as described in Fig. 12. The recursion terminates upon encountering primitive formulas. The sequence of specializations proves that the example is a valid instance of the target concept.

When there is more than one axiom available to specialize a concept, as is the case with OPERATOR-SUCCEEDS, the system must select the axiom that corresponds to the training example. To find the appropriate axiom we allow each concept (i.e., each predicate) to be associated with a *discriminator* function that examines the search tree and selects an axiom corresponding to the example. Each discriminator function is a piece of code that takes the concept to be specialized and its example and returns the appropriate axiom with which to specialize the concept. (It also updates bookkeeping information associating the formulas in the axiom body with their corresponding examples in the search tree, so that the EBS algorithm can correctly specialize the axiom body.)

To illustrate how the EBS process operates, let us return to our machine-shop problem. As described in the previous section, the success of POLISH at Node 80 constitutes an example of OPERATOR-SUCCEEDS. Below we outline how the explanation for this example is constructed. (In Section 6.1 we show how this explanation is extended to explain why the LATHE operator preceding POLISH succeeded.)

To specialize a formula:
  – If the formula is a conjunctive formula, (AND $F_1$ $F_2$...), then specialize each conjunct, and return the result: (AND (specialize $F_1$) (specialize $F_2$)...).
  – If the formula is a disjunctive formula, (OR $F_1$ $F_2$...), then specialize the first disjunct consistent with the example, e.g. $F_2$, and return the result: (specialize $F_2$).
  – If the formula is a universal formula, (FORALL ($x_1$...) SUCH-THAT $F_1$, $F_2$), then there will be a set of examples for $F_2$ in the search tree. For each of these subexamples, specialize $F_2$. Return the result:

    (FORALL ($x_1$...) SUCH-THAT $F_1$
      (OR (specialize $F_2$)$_1$
        (specialize $F_2$)$_2$...))

  – If the formula is negated, (NOT $F$), then return the formula unchanged: (NOT $F$).
  – If the formula is atomic, ($P$ $x_1$ $x_2$...), and primitive (i.e., there are no axioms that define $P$) then return the formula unchanged: ($P$ $x_1$ $x_2$...).
  – If the formula is atomic, ($P$ $x_1$ $x_2$...), and not primitive, then
    (1) Call the discriminator function associated with the concept $P$ to retrieve an axiom that corresponds to the training example. The axiom will be a conditional of the form: ($P$ $y_1$ $y_2$...) if axiom-body, where $y_1$, $y_2$, ... are distinct variables.
    (2) Replace the variables $y_1$, $y_2$, ... in the axiom with the corresponding values in the formula $x_1$, $x_2$, ....
    (3) Uniquely rename all other variables in the axiom body.
    Return the result: (specialize axiom-body).

Fig. 12. The EBS algorithm.

Target concept:   (OPERATOR-SUCCEEDS *op goal node*)

Training example:
    (OPERATOR-SUCCEEDS POLISH (POLISHED OBJECT-A) Node80)

To explain why the POLISH operator was successful, PRODIGY will specialize the concept OPERATOR-SUCCEEDS. In this case, since POLISH directly solved the goal, the system begins by specializing OPERATOR-SUCCEEDS with Axiom-S1 in Fig. 10, the axiom that corresponds to the training example. The system then recursively specializes the subconcepts APPLICABLE, and IS-EFFECT as shown below. The specializations performed at each step are indicated in bold face.

Target concept: (OPERATOR-SUCCEEDS *op goal node*)

Specialize (OPERATOR-SUCCEEDS *op goal node*) using Axiom-S1:
   **(AND (IS-EFFECT *goal op params*)**
         **(APPLICABLE *op params node*))**

Specialize (IS-EFFECT *goal op params*) using Axiom-D2:
   (AND **(AND (MATCHES *op* POLISH)**
              **(MATCHES *params* (*obj-x time-x*))**
         **(MATCHES *goal* (POLISHED *obj-x*)))**
         (APPLICABLE *op params node*))

Specialize (APPLICABLE *op params node*) using Axiom-D1:
   (AND (AND (MATCHES *op* POLISH)
             (MATCHES *params* (*obj-x time-x*))
             (MATCHES *goal* (POLISHED *obj-x*)))
         **(AND (MATCHES *op* POLISH)**
              **(MATCHES *params* (*obj-y time-y*))**
              **(KNOWN *node* (AND (OR (SHAPE *obj-y* RECTANGULAR)**
                                      **(CLAMPABLE *obj-y* POLISHER))**
                          **(LAST-SCHEDULED *obj-y time-z*)**
                          **(LATER *time-y time-z*)**
                          **(NOT (EXISTS *obj-w* SUCH-THAT**
                                      **(SCHEDULED *obj-w* POLISHER**
                                      *time-y*))))))**

Both APPLICABLE and IS-EFFECT can be specialized by more than one axiom. The appropriate specializations are determined by discriminator functions that retrieve the axioms corresponding to the training example.

As specialization proceeds, the system also simplifies the result in order to reduce its match cost. (This process, called *compression*, is described in [52].) Thus, after some trivial simplifications performed by the system, our specialized concept is re-expressed as follows:

(OPERATOR-SUCCEEDS *op goal node*)
if (AND (MATCHES *op* POLISH)
        (MATCHES *goal* (POLISHED *obj*))
        (KNOWN *node* (AND (OR (SHAPE *obj* RECTANGULAR)
                               (CLAMPABLE *obj* POLISHER))
                    (LAST-SCHEDULED *obj time-z*)
                    (LATER *time-x time-z*)
                    (NOT (EXISTS *obj-w* SUCH-THAT
                                (SCHEDULED *obj-w* POLISHER *time-x*))))))

The expression simply states that an operator succeeds in solving a goal at a node if the operator is POLISH, the goal is to have the object POLISHED, and the preconditions of POLISH are known to be satisfied at the node. (An expression is KNOWN at a node if it matches the state at that node.)

When the EBS process terminates we are left with a learned description that is a specialization of the target concept. The explanation that was used to arrive at this description is simply the sequence of specializations (and simplifications) employed by the EBS process; the learned description represents the weakest conditions under which the explanation holds. Many other EBL systems use a two-phase algorithm that first constructs the explanation and then finds its weakest preconditions (e.g., [48, 56, 58]). The EBS method computes the weakest preconditions in a single pass.

To improve the efficiency of the learning process, PRODIGY caches learned descriptions so that they can be used as lemmas in subsequent analyses. For example, in our machine-shop example the result describing why POLISH succeeded is cached and used to explain the success of LATHE. Similarly, the explanation of why Node 2 failed can not only be converted into a control rule, but also used as part of the explanation of why ROLL failed at Node 1. Moreover, cached results can prevent duplication of effort when two or more nodes fail for the same reason, since only one explanation has to be generated. This is described further in Section 6.2.

Once a description is returned by EBS, a search control rule can be constructed by filling in the *rule construction template* associated with the target concept. (Figure 13 shows the rule construction templates for OPERATOR-SUCCEEDS and OPERATOR-FAILS). This is simply a matter of replacing the target concept in the template with the learned description, and simplifying.

### 5.4. The operationality criterion

Learned control knowledge should not just be *usable*, but *useful* as well. Therefore PRODIGY extends the standard motion of operationality to include utility [61]. In other words, PRODIGY not only requires that learned control rules be executable, it also requires that they actually improve the system's performance. Specifically, the utility of a control rule is defined as the cumulative improvement in *search time* attributable to the rule. Utility is given by the cost-benefit formula:

$$\text{Utility} = (\text{AvrSavings} \times \text{ApplicFreq}) - \text{AvrMatchCost}$$

where

AvrMatchCost = is the average cost of matching the rule,
AvrSavings = the average savings when the rule is applicable,
ApplicFreq = the fraction of times that the rule is
                  applicable when it is tested.

Target Concept: (OPERATOR-FAILS *op goal node*)

Training example selection heuristics: Highest-failure-per-node, . . .

Rule construction template:
```
IF (AND (CURRENT-NODE node)
        (CURRENT-GOAL node goal)
        (CANDIDATE-OPERATOR node op)
        (OPERATOR-FAILS op goal node))
THEN (REJECT OPERATOR op)
```

Target concept: (OPERATOR-SUCCEEDS *op goal node*)

Training example selection heuristics: Others-have-failed, . . .

Rule construction template:
```
IF (AND (CURRENT-NODE node)
        (CURRENT-GOAL node goal)
        (CANDIDATE-OPERATOR node op)
        (CANDIDATE-OPERATOR node other-op)
        (OPERATOR-SUCCEEDS op goal node))
THEN (PREFER OPERATOR op OVER other-op)
```

Fig. 13. Two target concept specifications.

After learning a control rule, PRODIGY maintains statistics on the rule's use during subsequent problem solving, in order to determine its utility. If the rule has negative utility, it is discarded.[9]

Because the representation of the left-hand side of a control rule significantly affects its match cost, the simplification process that occurs in conjunction with EBS can greatly increase the utility of the resulting rule. PRODIGY's utility evaluation process and the effect of simplification on utility are discussed by Minton [51, 52].

## 5.5. Results

Figure 14 summarizes the system's performance on one hundred randomly generated problems from the machine-shop domain. Three conditions are

[9] Unfortunately, although match cost and application frequency can be directly measured during subsequent problem solving, it is more difficult to measure the savings. Doing so would require running the problem solver with and without the rule on each problem. (This would have to be done for all rules.) Instead, PRODIGY uses an estimate of the rule's average savings based on the savings that the rule would have produced on the training example for which it was learned.

shown: the problem solver running without any control rules, the problem solver running with learned control rules, and problem solver running with hand-coded control rules. The learned control rules were acquired during a separate training phase consisting of approximately one hundred problems. The hand-coded control rules were written by the authors. (They took about eight hours to code.) The graph shows how the cumulative problem solving time grows as the number of problems solved increases. The cumulative time is the total problem solving time *over all problems* up to that point. Thus, the slopes of the curves are positive because the $y$-axis represents cumulative time. Because the problems were ordered according to size (i.e., number of objects to be scheduled, etc.), and therefore progressively more difficult, the second derivatives of the curves are also positive.

As the graph shows, PRODIGY performed approximately fifty percent worse with the learned rules than with the hand-coded rules, but much better than without control rules. Similar results were obtained in other domains as well. In other experiments, PRODIGY's EBL methods were also shown to perform better than standard macro-operator methods. A detailed discussion of these experimental results can be found in [52]. Overall, we have concluded that EBL appears to be a promising approach to performance optimization. However, we believe that methods for generating even better explanations must be found before PRODIGY's learned control rules equal hand-coded control rules in performance.

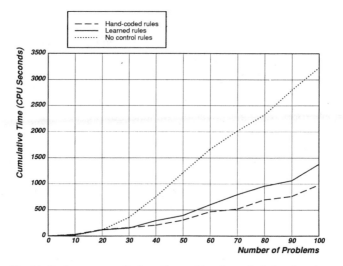

Fig. 14. Performance results from the machine-shop scheduling domain.

## 6. Examples of Learning in PRODIGY

Having described PRODIGY's EBL method, we now focus on concrete examples of learning from success, failure and goal interference. In each case, we present the relevant fragment of the pre-learning search tree and the steps in the subsequent analysis that yields new control rules.

### 6.1. Learning from success

Returning to the machine-shop domain, let us illustrate how PRODIGY learns from success. Figure 15 shows the nodes along the solution path (the right

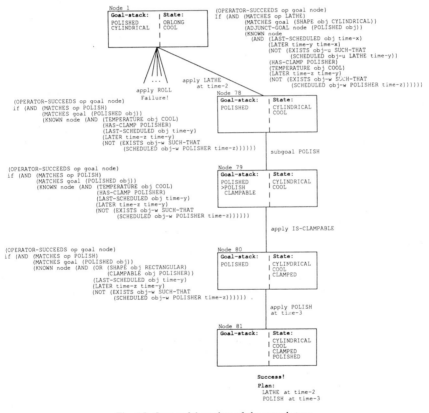

Fig. 15. Successful section of the search tree.

branch of the search tree). As we described in the last section, the only interesting example of success occurs at Node 1, where the problem solver chooses LATHE after having unsuccessfully tried ROLL. To explain LATHE's success, PRODIGY first explains why POLISH succeeded at Node 80 (as illustrated in the last section). Then this result is propagated up the tree as PRODIGY analyzes each node in turn. The result at each step of the analysis is shown next to each node in Fig. 15.

Let us briefly consider how the explanation process unfolds. The result from Node 80, which describes why POLISH was applicable at that node, is used as a lemma when explaining how the application of IS-CLAMPABLE at Node 79 enables the success of POLISH. The target concept and training example at Node 79 are shown below:

Target concept:
(OPERATOR-SUCCEEDS *op goal node*),

Training example:
(OPERATOR-SUCCEEDS POLISH (POLISHED OBJECT-A) Node 79)

As is evident from the problem solving trace, applying IS-CLAMPABLE at Node 79 was necessary to achieve the CLAMPABLE precondition of POLISHED. Therefore, when the system specializes OPERATOR-SUCCEEDS, Axiom-S2 (the recursive axiom for OPERATOR-SUCCEEDS) is retrieved:

(AND (APPLICABLE *next-op params node*)
        (OPERATOR-SUCCEEDS *op goal child-node*)
        (CHILD-NODE-AFTER-APPLYING-OP *child-node next-op node*))

First, APPLICABLE is specialized by a domain-level axiom specifying that the preconditions of IS-CLAMPABLE must be known to be true at *node*. Next, OPERATOR-SUCCEEDS is specialized by replacing it with the cached result from Node 80 with appropriate variable substitutions. Finally, specializing CHILD-NODE-AFTER-APPLYING-OP enables the simplifier to eliminate the CLAMPABLE precondition, since this was added by the application of IS-CLAMPABLE. (This last specialization accomplishes the "backpropagation" or "regression" of constraints that has been a familiar aspect of earlier EBL work.) The resulting expression, shown next to Node 79 in Fig. 15, states that POLISH will eventually succeed when the preconditions of the sequence IS-CLAMPABLE, POLISH are satisfied.

Because the result from Node 79 also holds at Node 78, no further explanation is necessary at Node 78. LATHE's success at Node 1 can now be explained. The analysis is similar to that described above, in effect, the lower-level result from Node 78 is regressed across the LATHE operator. The final result states that LATHE is appropriate when the preconditions of the oeprator sequence LATHE, IS-CLAMPABLE, POLISH is applicable and the goal is to make an object cylindrical and then polish it. The control rule that is learned from this example is shown in Fig. 16. The rule is a preference rule, as are all rules learned from successes. (The analysis guarantees that the operator can solve the goals stated in the rule, not that it is the best operator under all circumstances.)

PRODIGY's method of learning from success is reminiscent of macro-operator formation.[10] In fact, variations of macro-operator learning have been employed by most other EBL problem solving systems to date. Unfortunately, we have found that the utility of this approach is fairly limited. Good performance depends on whether a small population of operator sequences can be identified that solve (or almost solve) most of the problems in the domain. Although PRODIGY's training example selection heuristics attempt to pick out only those training examples that illustrate particularly useful operator sequences (or subsequences), there may in fact be no small set of operator sequences that

---

```
IF (AND (CURRENT-NODE node)
        (CURRENT-GOAL node (SHAPE obj CYLINDRICAL))
        (CANDIDATE-OPERATOR node LATHE)
        (CANDIDATE-OPERATOR node other-op)
        (ADJUNCT-GOAL node (POLISHED obj))
        (KNOWN node
            (AND (LAST-SCHEDULED obj time-x)
                 (LATER time-y time-x)
                 (NOT (EXISTS obj-u SUCH-THAT
                          (SCHEDULED obj-u LATHE time-y)))
                 (HAS-CLAMP POLISHER)
                 (TEMPERATURE obj COOL)
                 (LATER time-z time-y)
                 (NOT (EXISTS obj-w SUCH-THAT
                          (SCHEDULED obj-w LATHE time-z))))))
THEN (PREFER OPERATOR LATHE OVER other-op)
```

---

Fig. 16. Preference rule learned by analyzing the success of LATHE.

[10] PRODIGY's method is not exactly macro-operator learning, since the learned rules only selected a single operator, not the entire operator sequence. In some cases macro-operators may be more efficient because the selection process happens once for the entire sequence. In other cases PRODIGY's control rules may be more efficient because they allow for more flexibility at each decision point, and because multiple control rules can be combined together by the simplifier. The various efficiency tradeoffs are discussed by Minton [52].

"covers" the domain. For this reason, we have included other methods of learning in PRODIGY, which distinguish it from most previous EBL systems. In the next section we show how learning from failure can be a valuable alternative to learning from success.

## 6.2. Learning from failure

In our machine-shop example, the problem solver constructed a plan to lathe and polish an object in order to make it cylindrical and polished. However, the problem solver did not immediately find this solution, but first explored the possibility of rolling the object and then polishing it. This possibility failed because the object could not be clamped to the polisher once it had been rolled due to its high temperature. In this section, we will describe how PRODIGY learns a control rule to avoid repeating this mistake in the future.

An illustrative subset of the axioms for explaining failures are shown in Fig. 17. (The axioms have been simplified for clarity.) They state that the failure of a node is implied by the failure of a goal at that node, which is in turn implied by failure of the available operators under all relevant bindings. The definition is recursive because bindings for an operator may fail if subgoaling generates a node that fails, or if applying the operator generates a node that fails. Other failure-related axioms (not shown in the figure) indicate that failure can occur if a loop is detected or a control rule rejects a candidate node, goal, operator or bindings. The full set of axioms for describing failures take up several pages, and are given in [52].

Figure 18 illustrates the portion of the failed search tree analyzed by PRODIGY as it explains the failure of ROLL at Node 1. The figure also shows for each of the nodes below Node 1 the intermediate results that describe why these nodes failed. As we have seen, PRODIGY begins the learning process by starting at the bottom left-most portion of the search tree and working upwards. The lower-level results serve as lemmas in explaining the higher-level failures.

As shown in Fig. 18, PRODIGY finds that Node 4 failed because there is no way to achieve the goal of cooling an object. (Objects can be heated as a side-effect of the ROLL operator.) This failure is propagated up the tree to Node 3, at which point PRODIGY can state that CLAMPING an object will fail if the object is not cool. Continuing the postorder traversal of the failed subtree, PRODIGY concludes that Node 5 failed because it is impossible to make an object rectangular. Thus Node 2 failed because polishing an object is impossible if the object is not rectangular and not cool (i.e., it is not stable and cannot be clamped). Finally, the top-level failure of ROLL is attributed to the fact the object had to be subsequently polished; as evidenced by the example, after applying ROLL, polishing is impossible. (Appendix C elaborates on PRODIGY's analysis of this example.)

Axiom-F1: A node fails if one of the goals at that node fails.
(NODE-FAILS *node*)
if (AND (ATOMIC-FORMULA *goal*)
      (IS-GOAL *node goal*)
      (GOAL-FAILS *goal node*))

Axiom-F2: A goal fails if all relevant operators fail to achieve it.
(GOAL-FAILS *goal node*)
if (FORALL *op* SUCH-THAT (IS-OPERATOR *op*)
    (OPERATOR-FAILS *op goal node*))

Axiom-F3: An operator fails if it is irrelevant to the goal.
(OPERATOR-FAILS *op goal node*)
if (FORALL *effect* SUCH-THAT (IS-EFFECT *effect op params*)
    (DOES-NOT-MATCH *effect goal* NIL))

Axiom-F4: An operator fails if it is relevant, but all bindings fail.
(OPERATOR-FAILS *op goal node*)
if (FORALL *bindings* SUCH-THAT
    (IS-RELEVANT-BINDINGS *bindings op goal*)
    (BINDINGS-FAIL *bindings op goal*))

Axiom-F5: A set of bindings fail if the operator cannot be applied with those bindings, and subgoaling fails.
(BINDINGS-FAIL *bindings op goal node*)
if (AND (NOT-APPLICABLE *bindings op node*)
      (IS-CHILD-NODE-AFTER-SUBGOALING *child-node bindings op node*)
      (NODE-FAILS *child-node*))

Axiom-F6: A set of bindings fail if applying the instantiated operator leads to failure.
(BINDINGS-FAIL *bindings op goal node*)
if (AND (IS-APPLICABLE *bindings op node*)
      (IS-CHILD-NODE-AFTER-APPLYING-OP *child-node bindings op node*)
      (NODE-FAILS *child-node*))

Fig. 17. Illustrative architecture-level axioms for FAILS.

The top-level result, which describes why applying ROLL at Node 1 failed, is converted directly into an operator rejection rule via the rule construction template for OPERATOR-FAILS. The resulting control rule was shown earlier in Fig. 8. (In addition, all of the node failure descriptions in Fig. 18 are converted into node rejection control rules, although our top-level result is by far the

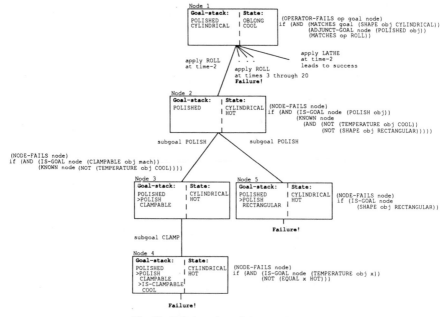

Fig. 18. Failed section of the search tree.

most useful.) This rule has high utility because its match cost is low, it is frequently applicable, and there is a large payoff when the rule is applicable. Specifically, by eliminating the need to consider the ROLL operator, the rule produces a savings on the order of $N \times T$, where $N$ is the size of the schedule, and $T$ is the cost of considering ROLL for a particular time period (the cost of searching Nodes 2 through 5 in Fig. 18).

In general, failure-driven learning is most beneficial when the reasons for the failure can be expressed by a concise, easily evaluated description. Notice that the rule learned from this example provides a much more general and efficient means for choosing between ROLL and LATHE than was gained from analyzing LATHE's success.

Our example also demonstrates that when a failure occurs, it may not be necessary to analyze the entire failed subtree to learn from the failure. To learn why applying ROLL at Node 1 failed, it was only necessary to analyze the subtree rooted at Node 2. Once this was accomplished PRODIGY immediately found that the other applications of ROLL (at TIME-2 through TIME-20) failed for the same reason. Thus, it was not necessary to construct separate explanations for each of these failures. In fact, had learning been interleaved with problem solving PRODIGY could have avoided these subsequent attempts to apply ROLL, thanks to the control rule learned from the failure of Node 2.

Thus, when learning and problem solving are interleaved, PRODIGY effectively carries out a general form of dependency-directed backtracking [24].

## 6.3. Learning from goal interference

Goal interactions are ubiquitous in planning. Goals may either interact constructively, or they may interfere with each other. This latter case can create serious difficulties for a domain-independent planner. For this reason, many previous planning systems have included built-in heuristics for avoiding and/or recovering from interferences [9, 70, 85]; PRODIGY improves on this by reasoning about interferences in order to learn domain-specific control rules. This type of learning method was pioneered by Sussman's HACKER program [79].

In order to illustrate how goals can interfere, we will modify our scheduling example. Let us assume that PRODIGY attempted to solve the goal (POLISHED OBJECT-A) before the goal (SHAPE OBJECT-A CYLINDRICAL), as shown in Fig. 19. (This figure explicitly shows these top-level goals as a conjunction, which is intended to illustrate that they are initially unordered and then PRODIGY selects a goal to solve first. Our previous figures did not show the top-level conjunction.) Thus, after successfully polishing the object, the system will attempt to reshape it. However, both lathing the object and rolling the object will have the unfortunate side-effect of deleting (POLISH OBJECT-A). This is referred to as a *goal protection violation*. Of course, PRODIGY can re-polish the object, in which case the resulting plan will involve polishing the object twice. However, because the EBL module notices the protection violation that occurs

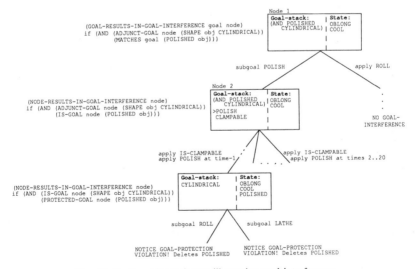

Fig. 19. Section of search tree illustrating goal interference.

when (POLISHED OBJECT-A) is deleted, PRODIGY can learn to order the goals correctly.

In the general case, we say that a plan exhibits goal interference if there is a goal in the plan that has been negated by a previous step in the plan. There are two complementary forms in which goal interference may manifest itself during the planning process. As we have seen, a *protection violation* occurs when an action undoes a previously achieved goal, requiring the goal to be re-achieved. A *prerequisite violation*, on the other hand, occurs when an action negates a goal that arises later in the planning process. Goal interferences may result in suboptimal plans or the outright failure to find a plan. In this section we will only consider the first case, since learning from failure is covered by the axioms described the previous section.

Since goal interferences can be unavoidable in some problems (and may even occur in optimal plans) PRODIGY learns rules that express preferences, thereby enabling solutions to be found even when interferences are unavoidable. When goal interferences can be avoided search time is typically reduced, and in addition, better solutions tend to be found. Learning to avoid goal interference is an optimization technique specifically designed for planning domains; in other types of domains (e.g., theorem proving) this technique may be irrelevant because interferences may not occur.

Returning to our example, to explain why the initial goal ordering resulted in goal interference, PRODIGY must show that all paths in the search tree subsequent to that goal selection decision resulted in either a failure or a goal interaction.[11] To formulate its explanation, PRODIGY will use the target concept GOAL-RESULTS-IN-GOAL-INTERFERENCE, which describes why selecting a goal at a node results in goal interference. The tree shown in Fig. 19 is annotated with some of the intermediate results derived during the EBS process. The high-level axioms for explaining goal interferences are shown in Appendix D. The axioms that are used to explain goal interferences are similar to (and overlap with) the axioms for failure, with the addition of several low-level axioms describing how protection and prerequisite violations occur.

As shown by Fig. 19, PRODIGY first notices that both ROLL and LATHE clobber the POLISHED property, causing a goal protection violation. In other words, all operators for making an object cylindrical result in a goal interfer-

---

[11] In normal problem solving mode, the PRODIGY problem solver will be quite content with a suboptimal solution that exhibits a goal interference, and will not continue searching for an optimal solution. Therefore, during the learning phase, if the solution exhibits a goal interference, the EBL module will call upon the problem solver to resume its search until all paths below the suspect decision point exhibit a protection violation, prerequisite violation or failure (i.e., until the example of goal interference has been verified). This is accomplished by the *training example recognition function* for goal interference. (Each target concept is associated with such a function, which is the code that actually picks out the training examples for that concept at a node.) The process of recognizing goal interferences and selecting appropriate training examples is discussed in more depth by Minton [52].

ence once the POLISHED property of the object has been achieved. Thus, at Node 2, the interaction is attributed to the fact that (SHAPE *obj* CYLINDRICAL) was an adjunct goal, and therefore slated to be achieved subsequently to (POLISHED *obj*). (The alternative paths emanating from Node 2 are not analyzed by the learning component because the system immediately determines that the reasons for the observed interaction are valid for each of them as well.) Finally at Node 1, PRODIGY determines that selecting a goal matching (POLISHED *obj*) will result in an interaction if (SHAPE *obj* CYLINDRICAL) must subsequently be achieved. The control rule resulting from the example is shown below, and states that PRODIGY should prefer the goal (SHAPE *obj* CYLINDRICAL) to the goal (POLISHED *obj*) when it is considering which goal to work on first.

```
       IF (AND (CURRENT-NODE node)
               (CANDIDATE-GOAL node (SHAPE obj CYLINDRICAL))
               (CANDIDATE-GOAL node (POLISHED obj)))
    THEN (PREFER GOAL (SHAPE obj CYLINDRICAL) OVER
               (POLISHED obj))
```

### 7. Comparison with Related Work

While the PRODIGY system illustrates one method of integrating EBL and problem solving, it is useful to analyze some other learning systems to compare how they exploit EBL. We will consider four prominent approaches, and compare how they address each of the issues outlined in Section 3: target concept coverage, scope of the theory, method of constructing explanations from examples, and the operationality criterion.

Perhaps the most widely known work on EBL is the EBG method by Mitchell et al. [56]. The main thrust of their effort was to clarify and unify much of the earlier research on explanation-based learning. As such, EBG is mainly a framework that is not closely tied to a particular performance system. However, there have been several implementations of EBG that do address the issues relevant to combining problem solving and learning. An alternate proposal for EBL, presented by DeJong and Mooney [20], discusses some deficiencies of and alternatives to Mitchell et al.'s EBG method. Their approach is primarily oriented towards schema-based problem solving. Among other points, they emphasize the necessity for a realistic operationality criterion appropriate to their problem solving architecture. They also describe techniques for improving explanations that are originally produced by observing the solution to a problem.

A third approach is illustrated by the SOAR system, developed by Laird, Newell, and Rosenbloom [42]. SOAR was not developed explicitly as an EBL system; instead, it is intended to be a general cognitive architecture utilizing an independently developed learning mechanism called chunking. Chunking operates by summarizing the information examined while processing each subgoal. The mechanism bears a strong resemblance to EBL, and Rosenbloom and Laird [69] have described how EBL can be implemented via chunking in SOAR. Finally, a discussion of EBL problem solving systems could not be complete without mentioning STRIPS [29]. Even though STRIPS far preceded the recent surge of work on EBL, the MACROP learning technique is now recognized as a simple form of EBL. In comparing these EBL approaches, we will only investigate how they have been integrated with a problem solver in order to optimize problem solving performance. However, we note that all of these systems address additional issues not considered here.

## 7.1. Target concepts

First, let us consider each system's target concepts to evaluate the diversity of the optimization strategies that have been pursued. Recall that a system's target concepts reflect the range of situations that can be optimized. Most of the implemented systems have demonstrated only a single strategy, namely learning from success. This includes STRIPS, LEX2 [54, 56] (an early implementation of EBG), and the systems discussed by DeJong and Mooney (e.g., GENESIS). These systems equate their target concepts with problem solving goals. They therefore learn descriptions of the states for which a specified operator (or sequence thereof) leads to success. Only recently have other optimization strategies begun to be considered. For example, Mostow and Bhatnagar [62] use EBG to learn from problem solving failures in their FAILSAFE system. In a related vein, DeJong and Mooney have also proposed using EBL to refine over-general concepts (as opposed to merely operationalizing them), which goes beyond the standard notion of learning from success. This proposal has been recently extended and implemented by Chien [14]. Even so, each of these systems employ a single optimization strategy, as opposed to PRODIGY, which employs multiple optimization strategies. PRODIGY currently learns from successes, failures, and goal interactions. Also, the set of target concepts are declaratively specified and thus easily extensible.

The one system, in addition to PRODIGY, that may be regarded as using multiple optimization strategies is SOAR. On one level, SOAR uses a single optimization technique, chunking. Chunking operates on the production level; whenever a result is returned for a goal, SOAR records the conditions matched by the productions that produced the result. Thus chunking is essentially a form of caching. However, if one looks at SOAR at a higher level of abstraction, chunking can be regarded as implementing alternate optimization strategies. For example, the system is able to learn from certain types of failures as it considers how to solve a goal. In particular, SOAR can learn to avoid an operator that leads to failure so long as there is a specific reason for the failure (returned as the result). Thus, explicit failure in the base domain can give rise to a preference that the choice is undesirable, and a chunk may be learned summarizing that conclusion. SOAR cannot learn if the failure is caused by exhausting all available alternatives [78]. Also, Rosenbloom, Laird and Newell have not addressed the use of explicit optimization goals, which would require the system to have a theory (i.e., problem space) describing itself.

## 7.2. Theory

The theory used by an EBL problem solving system provides a means for proving that an optimization applies in a given problem solving episode. There is a spectrum of approaches to providing a theory to drive the EBL process. One end of the spectrum is best exemplified by STRIPS, whose theory is completely represented by its domain operators. The system's "proofs" are not proofs in the usual sense, but sequences of domain operators.[12] The limited scope of the theory reflects the fact that STRIPS' target concepts are limited to the goals of the problem solver. At the other end, PRODIGY uses an explicit theory describing the relevant aspects of the problem solver in addition to a theory of the domain. This is necessary because PRODIGY's target concepts are meta-level problem solving phenomena (i.e., problem solving failures, goal interactions, etc.), rather than simply base-level problem solving goals. Since PRODIGY's theory is declarative and external to the problem solver, it can be extended easily to accommodate new target concepts. By contrast, STRIPS' domain operators and learning component are intimately intertwined with the problem solving system.

The other EBL systems can also be classified within this spectrum. The EBG approach clearly involves a separate, fully declarative theory describing the performance system, as illustrated by the LEX2 and FAILSAFE implementations. By contrast, the core of SOAR (i.e., the matcher, decision procedure, etc.) is not encoded as a declarative theory or problem space, it is only expressed in terms of the set of productions that implement the system. Thus, a theory of the problem solver is not used in the EBL process, and so there are some aspects of itself that SOAR cannot improve. This may be attributed to the view of chunking as a pervasive and automatic compilation mechanism that should not reflect on the workings of the agent. Laird, Rosenbloom and Newell [42] thus characterize SOAR as a "simple experience learner" rather than a "deliberate learner."[13] Finally, in DeJong and Mooney's scheme, as in STRIPS, explanations are constructed by observing operator sequences, and consequently the theory is limited to the task domain. To a certain extent, DeJong and Mooney expand on the STRIPS approach, because explanations may also

---

[12] As DeJong and Mooney [20] point out, however, operator sequences and proofs are isomorphic.

[13] It might be reasonable in SOAR to provide problems spaces for reasoning about itself. This would allow chunking to implement a wider variety of optimization strategies.

include inference rules and related information describing relevant features of the task domain. However, as with STRIPS, this approach operates by analyzing why a plan achieved a goal; thus the theory does not describe the problem solver itself, or allow learning based on other target concepts.

### 7.3. Mapping from an example to an explanation

One of the significant practical requirements for any EBL system is that it be able to efficiently construct explanations from examples. PRODIGY uses the search tree generated by the problem solver to control the construction of the explanation. This mapping is done efficiently by the EBS method's discriminator functions. In contrast, the EBG method does not specify any particular mechanism for identifying or constructing explanations. Recent implementations of EBG [36, 62] have relied on a theorem prover to construct explanations. However, if the theorem prover ignores the experience gained during problem solving, it must re-explore the search space traversed by the problem solver. In fact, as mentioned by Mostow and Bhatnagar [62], when learning from failure the explanation facility could discover a reason for an example's failure that is different from the one encountered by the problem solver.

For STRIPS and SOAR, the cost of mapping an example to an explanation is small. This is because the explanation is built directly from the sequence of operators or productions formed by the problem solver in a problem solving episode. That is, the explanation-based learner simply uses the results of the search already done by the problem solver. Similarly, in DeJong and Mooney's EBL scheme (as described in [20]), the explanation process starts with an observed operator sequence. However, the operator sequence is optional; if it is not available, an explanation will be built from scratch, as in EBG. Furthermore, the initial explanation can be improved so that a more operational and/or general schema is learned. (Recent extensions to their method for improving explanations are also described by Shavlik [74] and Mooney [60].) DeJong and Mooney do not discuss the costs involved in the explanation construction process in detail. However, their strategy of relying on observation whenever possible reduces the expense of the explanation construction process.

### 7.4. Operationality

A system's operationality criterion must reflect the computational costs and benefits of the control knowledge that is learned. However, the issue has been largely ignored in explanation-based learning. It is often assumed that the knowledge learned by an EBL problem solving system will improve the system's performance, but this may be an optimistic oversimplification. In general, the optimization techniques that have been implemented by EBL are *heuristic strategies*, not guaranteed to produce improvement in all circumstances. For example, the STRIPS MACROPS learning technique can actually decrease efficiency; if the cumulative time cost of testing the macro-operators preconditions outweighs the benefits in reduced search, then overall performance can decrease [49].

Mitchell et al.'s EBG proposal attempts to deal with this problem by including an explicit operationality criterion for testing an explanation's utility. However, as pointed out by DeJong and Mooney, the type of operationality criterion used by Mitchell et al. assures only that the new knowledge can be directly evaluated, it does not guarantee that it is actually useful. In the EBG examples, the operationality criterion simply specified that the explanation must refer only to directly computable or observable features. Later work on META-LEX extends the operationality criterion by considering the context of the learning [39]. In DeJong and Mooney's scheme, the cost of testing a "feature" may vary depending on the system's knowledge. Thus, their operationality criterion is dynamic, rather than static. PRODIGY refines the notion of operationality even further, specifying that the learned information must improve the efficiency of the problem solver. PRODIGY uses an explicit utility metric, described in Section 5.4, that depends on the time cost of evaluating, or matching, control knowledge compared to the time savings produced by that knowledge.

A very different approach to the operationality issue has been taken by the designers of SOAR, who, for the most part, intentionally ignore the utility issue. In part, this is because chunking is presumed to be an automatic process, and in part, because performance in SOAR is measured by the number of decisions necessary to perform a task. Since chunking will reduce the number of decisions that are made (so long as there is any overlap between tasks), it does very well according to its performance metric. However, making a decision may involve complex processing in its own right. For example, the cost of matching chunks is ignored in this simplistic metric; therefore, adding arbitrarily many and arbitrarily complex chunks can never hurt performance according to this metric. For this reason, the number of decisions may not correlate with actual CPU time, at least on conventional machines. The relationship between CPU time and decisions is a complex issue that depends in part upon the assumptions about the type of chunks typically formed. This issue has recently been investigated by Tambe and Newell [81], who have shown that in certain task domains SOAR will indeed learn expensive chunks that prolong the time per decision. Based on this work, Tambe and Rosenbloom [82] have considered restricting the language in which chunks are expressed to alleviate this problem.

## 8. Concluding Remarks

Having presented an in-depth investigation of explanation-based learning and its application to improving problem solving performance, let us return to a broader perspective. In essence, EBL enables the learning mechanism to take advantage of domain knowledge that specifies *why* some example is an instance of a target concept. This knowledge may not be available in all applications, but when it is available, it can serve as a strong means of guiding the generalization process. If we look at inductive learning, an alternative paradigm for learning from examples, the role of domain knowledge is much less direct. Inductive learning programs compare examples of a target concept in order to find a description that is consistent with all the examples, regardless of whether the common structure is coincidental or causally mandated. Thus, in inductive learning, the role of domain knowledge is merely to delimit the descriptions that the program considers, or at best to provide a heuristic bias for preferring certain descriptions over others among several consistent with the training data. For this reason, EBL is generally a preferable method if there is a strong source of domain knowledge available to guide the learning process.

One reason that EBL is an appropriate method for improving problem solving performance is that the necessary knowledge can be made available to the learner. In operator-based problem solving architectures, such as PRODIGY, the knowledge is provided by axiomatizing the domain operators and crucial aspects of the problem solving architecture itself. As we have shown in the paper, PRODIGY can use this theory to synthesize effective search control rules with the aid of problem solving traces. Since the descriptions of the task operators can be converted automatically into logic, the main requirement for incorporating EBL into a problem solver is to decide on appropriate target concepts, and then axiomatize the relevant aspects of the problem solving architecture, as we have done with PRODIGY.

We envision many extensions to our present EBL results, including scaling up to much larger task domains and learning from a partial domain theory (e.g., one where not all consequences or preconditions of an operator are known with certainty). Of particular interest is the integration of EBL with related parallel efforts that share the same PRODIGY problem solver: learning by derivational analogy [11] and learning to formulate effective abstractions for multi-level planning [41]. Both EBL and analogy strive to exploit past experience in order to reduce future search; therefore it is unclear whether a combination of the two will prove more effective than either in isolation. Plan abstraction, on the other hand, exploits orthogonal knowledge sources and therefore may yield complementary savings in search time, if EBL is applied to learn control rules at each level of abstraction. In all these extensions, however, we expect the underlying explanation-based learning mechanism to remain the same, allowing knowledge to play a strong role in the learning process.

### Appendix A. The PRODIGY Architecture

PRODIGY is a general problem solver combined with several learning modules. The PRODIGY architecture, in fact, was designed both as a unified testbed for different learning methods—including the EBL module discussed in this paper—and as a general architecture to solve interesting problems in complex task domains. Let us now focus on the architecture itself, as diagrammed in Fig. 20.

The operator-based problem solver produces a complete search tree, encapsulating all decisions—right ones and wrong ones—as well as the final solution. This information is used by each learning component in different ways, including the EBL component, which learns search control rules. In addition to the central problem solver,[14] PRODIGY has the following learning components:

– A user interface that can participate in an apprentice-like dialogue, enabling the user to evaluate and guide the system's problem solving and learning. The interface is graphic-based and tied directly to the problem solver, so that it can accept advice as it is solving a problem (i.e., coaching) or replay and analyze earlier solution attempts, all-the-while refining the factual or control knowledge.

– An explanation-based learning facility [52] for acquiring control rules from a problem solving trace, as indicated in Fig. 20. Explanations are constructed from an axiomatized theory describing both the domain and relevant aspects of the problem solver's architecture. Then the resulting descriptions are expressed

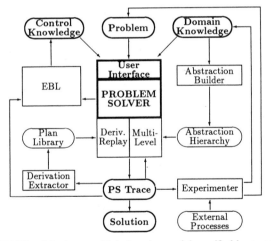

Fig. 20. The PRODIGY architecture: multiple learning modules unified by a common representation language and a shared general problem solver.

[14] The problem solver is an advanced operator-based planner that includes a simple reason-maintenance system and allows operators to have conditional effects. The problem solver's search (means-ends analysis) is guided by explicit domain-independent and domain-specific control rules. All of PRODIGY's learning modules share the same general problem solver and the same knowledge representation language, PDL.

in control rule form, and control rules whose utility in search reduction outweighs their application overhead are retained. The EBL method is discussed at length in this article.

– A derivational analogy engine [11, 23] that is able to replay entire solutions to similar past problems, calling the problem solver recursively to reduce any new subgoals brought about by known differences between the old and new problems. As indicated in Fig. 20, analogy and EBL are independent mechanisms to acquire domain-specific control knowledge. They coexist in PRODIGY and should be more tightly coupled than in the present architecture.

– A multi-level abstraction planning capability [41]. First, the axiomatized domain knowledge is divided into multiple abstraction levels based on an in-depth analysis of the domain. Then, during problem solving, PRODIGY proceeds to build abstract solutions and refine them by adding back details from the domain, solving new subgoals as they arise. This method is orthogonal to analogy and EBL, in that both can apply at each level of abstraction.

– A learning-by-experimentation module for refining domain knowledge that is incompletely or incorrectly specified [12]. Experimentation is triggered when plan execution monitoring detects a divergence between internal expectations and external expectations. As indicated in the figure, the main focus of experimentation is to refine the factual domain knowledge, rather than the control knowledge.

The problem solver and EBL component of PRODIGY have been fully implemented, and tested on several task domains including the blocks world domain, a machine-shop scheduling domain, and a 3-D robotics construction domain. The other components, while successfully prototyped, are at various stages of development and implementation.

### Appendix B. Partial Specification of the Machine-Shop Scheduling Domain

This appendix contains the definitions of the operators and inference rules that were used in the examples in this paper. A complete specification of all the operators and inferences rules for this domain can be found in [52].

**Example operators**

```
    ;Lathing makes an object cylindrical.

    (LATHE (obj time)
      (PRECONDITIONS
        (AND
          (LAST-SCHEDULED obj prev-time)
          (LATER time prev-time)
          (NOT (EXISTS other-obj SUCH-THAT
              (SCHEDULED other-obj LATHE time)))))
```

```
(EFFECTS
  (DELETE (SHAPE obj old-shape))
  (DELETE (LAST-SCHEDULED obj prev-time))
  (IF (POLISHED obj)
      (DELETE (POLISHED obj)))
  (ADD (LAST-SCHEDULED obj time))
  (ADD (SHAPE obj CYLINDRICAL))
  (ADD (SCHEDULED obj LATHE time))))
```

;**Rolling** makes an object cylindrical, and heats it

```
(ROLL (obj time)
  (PRECONDITIONS
    (AND
      (LAST-SCHEDULED obj prev-time)
      (LATER time prev-time)
      (NOT (EXISTS other-obj SUCH-THAT
            (SCHEDULED other-obj ROLLER time)))))
  (EFFECTS
    (DELETE (TEMPERATURE obj old-temp))
    (DELETE (SHAPE obj old-shape))
    (DELETE (LAST-SCHEDULED obj prev-time))
    (IF (POLISHED obj)
        (DELETE (POLISHED obj)))
    (ADD (TEMPERATURE obj HOT))
    (ADD (LAST-SCHEDULED obj time))
    (ADD (SHAPE obj CYLINDRICAL))
    (ADD (SCHEDULED obj ROLLER time))))
```

;Before **polishing**, nonrectangular objects must be clamped to the polisher.

```
(POLISH (obj time)
  (PRECONDITIONS
    (AND
      (OR (SHAPE obj RECTANGULAR)
          (CLAMPABLE obj POLISHER))
      (LAST-SCHEDULED obj prev-time)
      (LATER time prev-time)
      (NOT (EXISTS other-obj SUCH-THAT
            (SCHEDULED other-obj POLISHER time)))))
  (EFFECTS
    (DELETE (LAST-SCHEDULED obj prev-time))
    (ADD (LAST-SCHEDULED obj time))
    (ADD (POLISHED obj))
    (ADD (SCHEDULED obj POLISHER time))))
```

**An example inference rule**

> ;An object can be **clamped** to a machine only if the object is cool and the machine has a clamp.

> (IS-CLAMPABLE (*obj machine*)
>   (PRECONDITIONS
>     (AND (TEMPERATURE *obj* COOL)
>          (HAS-CLAMP *machine*)))
>   (EFFECTS
>     (ADD (CLAMPABLE *obj machine*)))))

## Appendix C. Explaining Failures: An In-Depth Example

In this appendix our intention is to provide the reader with a detailed illustration of PRODIGY's explanation process on an interesting example. For this purpose, we describe in more depth how PRODIGY explains the failure of Node 4 in our second example, originally presented in Section 6.2. As we have stated, Node 4 failed because the goal was (TEMPERATURE OBJECT-A COOL), and no operator is available for cooling objects. In fact, the only operator that changes an object's temperature is ROLL, which heats the object. Figure 21 lists the relevant lower-level architectural axioms needed to explain why the operators' postconditions did not match the goal. Normally, as we will see, much of this detail simplifies out during the specialization process.

The EBS process begins with the following target concept and example:

> Target concept: (NODE-FAILS *node*)

> Example: (NODE-FAILS Node 4)

NODE-FAILS is specialized by architectural-level Axiom-F1 and Axiom-F2 (described earlier in Fig. 17), to arrive at the following:

> (NODE-FAILS *node*)
> if (AND (ATOMIC-FORMULA *goal*)
>         (IS-GOAL *node goal*)
>         (FORALL *op* SUCH-THAT (IS-OPERATOR *op*)
>           (OPERATOR-FAILS *op goal node*)))

After specializing ATOMIC-FORMULA and simplifying IS-OPERATOR, we have the expression shown below. The description of the goal (TEMPERATURE *obj temp*), comes from the specialization of ATOMIC-FORMULA. Each of the references to OPERATOR-FAILS come from the simplifier's expansion of IS-OPERATOR.

The following axioms are used to explain why a match failed. The arguments to the matcher are a pattern (an atomic formula with variables), such as (TEMPERATURE *y x*), a list that is a ground formula, such as (TEMPERATURE OBJECT-A COOL), and an initial set of bindings for the variables in the pattern. A match fails if the list cannot be unified with the pattern.

Axiom MATCH-FAIL-1: A match fails if the head element of the pattern is a constant that is not equal to the head element of the list.
(DOES-NOT-MATCH *pattern list bindings*)
if (AND (HEAD-ELEMENT *list-head list*)
         (HEAD-ELEMENT *pat-head pattern*)
         (IS-CONSTANT *pat-head*)
         (NOT (EQUAL *list-head pat-head*)))

Axiom MATCH-FAIL-2: A match fails if the head element of the pattern is a variable, and its binding is not equal to the head element of the list.
(DOES-NOT-MATCH *pattern list bindings*)*C*
if AND (HEAD-ELEMENT *list-head list*)
       (HEAD-ELEMENT *pat-head pattern*)
       (IS-VARIABLE *pat-head*)
       (IS-BINDING *value pat-head bindings*)
       (NOT (EQUAL *value list-head*)))

Axiom MATCH-FAIL-3: A match fails if the head element of the pattern matches the head element of the list, but the remainder of the list does not match the remainder of the pattern.
(DOES-NOT-MATCH *pattern list bindings*)
if (AND (HEAD-ELEMENT *list-head list*)
         (HEAD-ELEMENT *pat-head pattern*)
         (TAIL *rest-of-list list*)
         (TAIL *rest-of-pattern pattern*)
         (UPDATE-BINDINGS *new-bindings list-head pat-head bindings*)
         (DOES-NOT-MATCH *rest-of-pattern rest-of-list new bindings*))

Fig. 21. Architecture-level axioms for DOES-NOT-MATCH.

(NODE-FAILS *node*)
if (AND (IS-GOAL *node* (TEMPERATURE *obj temp*))
         (OPERATOR-FAILS LATHE (TEMPERATURE *obj temp*) *node*)
         (OPERATOR-FAILS POLISH (TEMPERATURE *obj temp*) *node*)
         (OPERATOR-FAILS IS-CLAMPABLE (TEMPERATURE *obj temp*) *node*)
         (OPERATOR-FAILS ROLL (TEMPERATURE *obj temp*) *node*))

Except for ROLL, no operator or inference rule has a postcondition that can match (TEMPERATURE *obj temp*). Therefore after specialization, each of these operator failures (other than that of ROLL) simplify to TRUE, and we are left with the intermediate result shown below. (We omit a detailed discussion of this process in order to focus on the remainder of the example.)

```
(NODE-FAILS node)
if (AND (IS-GOAL node (TEMPERATURE obj temp))
        (OPERATOR-FAILS ROLL (TEMPERATURE obj temp) node))
```

OPERATOR-FAILS is then specialized by Axiom-F3 (see Fig. 17), which states that an operator fails if its postconditions (i.e., effects) do not match the goal:

```
(NODE-FAILS node)
if (AND (IS-GOAL node (TEMPERATURE obj temp))
        (FORALL effect SUCH-THAT (IS-EFFECT effect op params)
                (DOES-NOT-MATCH effect goal NIL)))
```

Then the simplifier expands IS-EFFECT, giving the following:

```
(NODE-FAILS node)
if (AND (IS-GOAL node (TEMPERATURE obj temp))
        (DOES-NOT-MATCH (TEMPERATURE obj HOT)
                        (TEMPERATURE obj temp) NIL)
        (DOES-NOT-MATCH (LAST-SCHEDULED obj time)
                        (TEMPERATURE obj temp) NIL)
        (DOES-NOT-MATCH (SHAPE obj CYLINDRICAL)
                        (TEMPERATURE obj temp) NIL)
        (DOES-NOT-MATCH (SCHEDULED obj ROLLER time)
                        (TEMPERATURE obj temp) NIL))
```

The first of the DOES-NOT-MATCH terms is successively specialized by Axiom MATCH-FAIL-3 (two applications) and MATCH-FAIL-2, because this match failed because COOL was not equal to HOT. The remaining DOES-NOT-MATCH terms are specialized by MATCH-FAIL-1, because the predicates are not equal. After simplifying we have the following final result:

```
(NODE-FAILS node)
if (AND (IS-GOAL node (TEMPERATURE obj temp))
        (NOT (EQUAL HOT temp)))
```

### Appendix D. Representative Axioms for Explaining Goal Interference

The following axioms illustrate the recursive nature of the GOAL-INTERFER-ENCE analysis.

Axiom-I1: A node results in goal interference if there exists a set of goals at that node that mutually interfere.
(NODE-RESULTS-IN-GOAL-INTERFERENCE *node*)
if (AND (SET-OF-GOALS *goals node*)
        (FORALL *goal* SUCH-THAT (MEMBER *goal goals*)
           (AND (GOAL-RESULTS-IN-GOAL-INTERFERENCE *goal node*)
              (INTERFERENCE-DEPENDS-ON-GOAL-SET *goal node*
                  *goals*))))

Axiom-I2: A goal results in goal interference if all operators result in goal interference once that goal is selected.
(GOAL-RESULTS-IN-GOAL-INTERFERENCE *goal node*)
if (FORALL *op* SUCH-THAT (IS-OPERATOR *op*)
    (OPERATOR-RESULTS-IN-GOAL-INTERFERENCE *op goal node*))

Axiom-I3: An operator results in goal interference if all bindings for that operator result in goal interference.
(OPERATOR-RESULTS-IN-GOAL-INTERFERENCE *op goal node*)
if (FORALL *bindings* SUCH-THAT
    (IS-RELEVANT-BINDINGS *bindings op goal*)
    (BINDINGS-RESULT-IN-GOAL-INTERFERENCE *bindings op goal*
      *node*))

Axiom-I4: A set of bindings for an operator results in goal interference if the operator cannot be applied with those bindings, and subgoaling results in goal interference.
(BINDINGS-RESULT-IN-GOAL-INTERFERENCE *bindings op goal node*)
if (AND (NOT-APPLICABLE *bindings op node*)
        (IS-CHILD-NODE-AFTER-SUBGOALING *child-node bindings op*
           *node*)
        (NODE-RESULTS-IN-GOAL-INTERFERENCE *child- node*))

Axiom-I5: A set of bindings for an operator results in goal interference if applying the instantiated operator results in goal interference.
(BINDINGS-RESULT-IN-GOAL-INTERFERENCE *bindings op goal node*)
if (AND (IS-APPLICABLE *bindings op node*)
        (IS-CHILD-NODE-AFTER-APPLYING-OP *child-node bindings op*
           *node*)
        (NODE-RESULTS-IN-GOAL-INTERFERENCE *child- node*))

As described in Section 6.3, to prove that goal interference occurs, PRODIGY must show that all paths result in failure or interference. The next four axioms illustrate how the definition of goal interference refers to the axioms for failure.

Axiom-I6: A node results in goal interference if the node fails.
(NODE-RESULTS-IN-GOAL-INTERFERENCE *node*)
if (NODE-FAILS *node*)

Axiom-I7: A goal results in goal interference if the goal fails.
(GOAL-RESULTS-IN-GOAL-INTERFERENCE *goal node*)
if (GOAL-FAILS *goal node*)

Axiom-I8: An operator results in goal interference if the operator fails.
(OPERATOR-RESULTS-IN-GOAL-INTERFERENCE *op goal node*)
if (OPERATOR-FAILS *op goal node*)

Axiom-I9: A set of bindings results in goal interference if the bindings fail.
(BINDINGS-RESULTS-IN-GOAL-INTERFERENCE *bindings op goal node*)
if (BINDINGS-FAIL *bindings op goal node*)

## ACKNOWLEDGMENT

The authors gratefully acknowledge the help of Michael Miller, Henrik Nordin, and Ellen Riloff in implementing the PRODIGY system and the contributions of the other members of the project, Robert Joseph, Alicia Perez, Santiago Rementeria, and Manuela Veloso. Comments and suggestions by Ranan Banerji, Murray Campbell, Jerry DeJong, Smadar Kedar-Cabelli, Rich Keller, Sridhar Mahadevan, Tom Mitchell, Jack Mostow, Allen Newell, David Steier, and Prasad Tadepalli have aided the development of the PRODIGY system, and the writing of this paper. Finally, we would like to thank the anonymous reviewers for their detailed comments on the paper.

This research was sponsored in part by the Defense Advanced Research Projects Agency (DOD), ARPA Order No. 4976, Amendment 20, under contract number F33615-87-C-1499, monitored by the Air Force Avionics Laboratory, in part by the Office of Naval Research under contracts N00014-84-K-0345 (N91) and N00014-84-K-0678-N123, in part by NASA under contract NCC 2-463, in part by the Army Research Institute under contract MDA903-85-C-0324, under subcontract 487650-25537 through the University of California, Irvine, and in part by small contributions from private institutions. The views and conclusions contained in this document are those of the authors and should not be interpreted as representing the official policies, either expressed or implied, of DARPA, ONR, NASA, ARI, or the US Government. The first and fifth authors were supported by AT&T Bell Labs Ph.D. Scholarships.

## REFERENCES

1. Aho, A.V., Sethi, R. and Ullman, J.D., *Compilers: Principles, Techniques and Tools* (Addison-Wesley, Reading, MA, 1986).
2. Anderson, J.R., Knowledge compilation: The general learning mechanism, in: *Proceedings International Machine Learning Workshop*, Montecello, IL (1983) 203–212.
3. Banerji, R.B., *Artificial Intelligence: A Theoretical Approach* (Elsevier North-Holland, New York, 1980).
4. Bennett, S.W., Approximation in mathematical domains, in: *Proceedings IJCAI-87*, Milan, Italy (1987) 239–241.
5. Bergadano, F. and Giordana, A., A knowledge intensive approach to concept induction, in: *Proceedings Fifth International Conference on Machine Learning*, Ann Arbor, MI (1988) 305–317.
6. Bhatnagar, N., A correctness proof of explanation-based generalization as resolution theorem proving, in: *Proceedings AAAI Spring Symposium on Explanation-Based Learning* (1988) 220–225.
7. Braverman, M.S. and Russell, S.J., IMEX: Overcoming intractability in explanation-based learning, in: *Proceedings AAAI-88*, St. Paul, MI (1988) 575–579.

8. Brownston, L., Farrell, R., Kant, E. and Marty, N., *Programming Expert Systems in OPS5*: *An Introduction to Rule-Based Programming* (Addison-Wesley, Reading, MA, 1985).

9. Carbonell, J.G., *Subjective Understanding*: *Computer Models of Belief Systems* (UMI Research Press, Ann Arbor, MI, 1981).

10. Carbonell, J.G., Derivational analogy and its role in problem solving, in: *Proceedings AAAI-83*, Washington, DC (1983) 64–69.

11. Carbonell, J.G., Derivational analogy: A theory of reconstructive problem solving and expertise acquisition, in: R.S. Michalski, J.G. Carbonell and T.M. Mitchell (Eds.), *Machine Learning*: *An Artificial Intelligence Approach* 2 (Morgan Kaufmann, Los Altos, CA, 1986).

12. Carbonell, J.G. and Gil, Y., Learning by experimentation, in: *Proceedings Fourth International Workshop on Machine Learning*, Irvine, CA (1987) 256–266.

13. Cheng, P.W. and Carbonell, J.G., Inducing iterative rules from experience: The FERMI experiment, in: *Proceedings AAAI-86*, Philadelphia, PA (1986) 490–495.

14. Chien, S.A., Extending explanation-based learning: Failure-driven schema refinement, in: *Proceedings Third IEEE Conference on Artificial Intelligence Applications*, Orlando, FL (1987) 106–111.

15. Cohen, P.R. and Feigenbaum, E.A. (Eds.), *The Handbook of Artificial Intelligence* 3 (Kaufmann, Los Altos, CA, 1982)

16. Cohen, W.W., Generalizing number and learning from multiple examples in explanation-based learning, in: *Proceedings Fifth International Conference on Machine Learning*, Ann Arbor, MI (1988) 256–269.

17. Danyluk, A.P., The user of explanations for similarity-based learning, in: *Proceedings IJCAI-87*, Milan, Italy (1987) 274–276.

18. Dean, T. and Boddy, M., An analysis of time dependent planning, in: *Proceedings AAAI-88*, St. Paul, MI (1988) 49–54.

19. DeJong, G.F., Acquiring schemata through understanding and generalizing plans, in: *Proceedings IJCAI-83*, Karlsruhe, F.R.G. (1983) 462–464.

20. DeJong, G.F. and Mooney, R., Explanation-based learning: An alternative view, *Mach. Learning* 1 (1986) 145–176.

21. DeJong, G.F., An approach to learning from observation, in: R.S. Michalski, J.G. Carbonell and T.M. Mitchell (Eds.), *Machine Learning*: *An Artificial Intelligence Approach* 2 (Morgan Kaufmann, Los Altos, CA, 1986) 571–590.

22. DeJong, G.F., Some thoughts on the present and future of explanation-based learning, in: *Proceedings ECAI-88*, Munich, F.R.G. (1988).

23. Carbonell, J.G. and Veloso, M.M., Integrating derivational analogy into a general problem-solving architecture, Case-Based Reasoning Workshop, Clearwater Beach, FL (1988) 104–124.

24. Doyle, J., A truth maintenance system, *Artificial Intelligence* 12 (1979) 231–272.

25. Doyle, R.J., Constructing and refining causal explanations from an inconsistent domain theory, in: *Proceedings AAAI-86*, Philadelphia, PA (1986) 538–544.

26. Ellman, T., Generalizing logic circuit designs by analyzing proofs of correctness, in: *Proceedings IJCAI-85*, Los Angeles, CA (1985) 643–646.

27. Ellman, T., Approximate theory formation: An explanation-based approach, in: *Proceedings AAAI-88*, St. Paul, MI (1988) 570–574.

28. Etzioni, O., Hypothesis filtering: A practical approach to reliable learning, in: *Proceedings Fifth International Conference on Machine Learning*, Ann Arbor, MI (1988) 416–429.

29. Fikes, R., Hart, P. and Nilsson, N., Learning and executing generalized robot plans, *Artificial Intelligence* 3 (1972) 251–288.

30. Flann, N.S. and Dietterich, T.G., Selecting appropriate representations for learning from examples, in: *Proceedings AAAI-86*, Philadelphia, PA (1986) 460–466.

31. Gupta, A., Explanation-based failure recovery, in *Proceedings AAAI-87*, Seattle, WA (1987) 606–610.

32. Hall, R.J., Learning by failing to explain: Using partial explanations to learn in incomplete or intractable domains, *Mach. Learning* 3 (1988) 45–77.

33. Hammond, K.J., Learning to anticipate and avoid planning problems through the explanation of failures, in: *Proceedings AAAI-86*, Philadelphia, PA (1986) 556–560.
34. Hirsh, H., Explanation-based generalization in a logic-programming environment, in: *Proceedings IJCAI-87*, Milan, Italy (1987) 221–227.
35. Hirsh, H., Reasoning about operationality for explanation-based learning, in: *Proceedings Fifth International Conference on Machine Learning*, Ann Arbor, MI (1988) 214–220.
36. Kedar-Cabelli, S.T. and McCarty, L.T., Explanation-based generalization as resolution theorem proving, in: *Proceedings Fourth International Workshop on Machine Learning*, Irvine, CA (1987) 383–389.
37. Kedar-Cabelli, S.T., Formulating concepts according to purpose, in: *Proceedings AAAI-87*, Seattle, WA (1987) 477–481.
38. Keller, R.M., Learning by re-expressing concepts for efficient recognition, in: *Proceedings AAAI-83*, Washington, DC (1983) 182–186.
39. Keller, R.M., The role of explicit knowledge in learning concepts to improve performance, Ph.D. Thesis, Department of Computer Science, Rutgers University, New Brunswick, NJ (1986).
40. Keller, R.M., Defining operationality for explanation-based learning, in: *Proceedings AAAI-87*, Seattle, WA (1987) 482–487.
41. Knoblock, C.A., Automatically generating abstractions for planning, in: *Proceedings First International Workshop in Change of Representation and Inductive Bias*, Briarcliff, NY (1988) 53–65.
42. Laird J.E., Rosenbloom, P.S. and Newell, A., Chunking in Soar: The anatomy of a general learning mechanism, *Mach. Learning* 1 (1986) 11–46.
43. Langley, P. and Carbonell, J.G., Approaches to machine learning, *J. Am. Soc. Inf. Sci.* 35 (1984) 306–316.
44. Lebowitz, M., Not the path to perdition: The utility of similarity-based learning, in: *Proceedings AAAI-86*, Philadelphia, PA (1986) 533–537.
45. Lebowitz, M., Integrated learning: Controlling explanation, *Cognitive Sci.* 10 (1986) 219–240.
46. Mahadevan, S., Verification-based learning: A generalization strategy for inferring problem-reduction methods, in: *Proceedings IJCAI-85*, Los Angeles, CA (1985) 616–623.
47. Mahadevan, S., Natarajan, B. and Tadepalli, P., A framework for learning as improving problem-solving performance in: *Proceedings AAAI Spring Symposium on Explanation-Based Learning* (1988) 215–219.
48. Minton, S., Constraint-based generalization, in: *Proceedings AAAI-84*, Austin, TX (1984) 251–254.
49. Minton S., Selectively generalizing plans for problem solving, in: *Proceedings IJCAI-85*, Los Angeles, CA (1985) 596–602.
50. Minton S., Carbonell, J.G., Knoblock, C.A., Kuokka, D. and Nordin, H., Improving the effectiveness of explanation-based learning, in: *Proceedings Workshop on Knowledge Compilation*, Inn at Otter Crest, OR (1986) 77–87.
51. Minton, S., Carbonell, J.G., Etzioni, O., Knoblock, C.A. and Kuokka, D.R., Acquiring effective search control rules: Explanation-based learning in the PRODIGY system, in: *Proceedings Fourth International Workshop on Machine Learning*, Irvine, CA (1987) 122–133.
52. Minton S., *Learning Search Control Knowledge: An Explanation-Based Approach* (Kluwer Academic Publishers, Boston, MA, 1988); also: Carnegie-Mellon CS Tech. Rept. CMU-CS-88-133.
53. Minton, S., EBL and weakest preconditions, in: *Proceedings AAAI Spring Symposium on Explanation-Based Learning* (1988) 210–214.
54. Mitchell, T., Utgoff, P. and Banerji, R., Learning by experimentation: Acquiring and refining problem-solving heuristics, in: R.S. Michalski, J.G. Carbonell and T.M. Mitchell (Eds.), *Machine Learning: An Artificial Intelligence Approach* (Tioga, Palo Alto, CA, 1983) 163–190.

55. Mitchell, T.M., The need for biases in learning generalizations, Tech. Rept. CBM-TR-117, Rutgers University, New Brunswick, NJ (1980).
56. Mitchell, T., Keller, R. and Kedar-Cabelli, S., Explanation-based generalization: A unifying view, *Mach. Learning* **1** (1986) 47–80.
57. Mooney, R. and DeJong, G., Learning schemata for natural language processing, in: *Proceedings IJCAI-85*, Los Angeles, CA (1985).
58. Mooney, R.J. and Bennett, S.W., A domain independent explanation-based generalizer, in: *Proceedings AAAI-86*, Philadelphia, PA (1986) 551–555.
59. Mooney, R.J., A general explanation-based learning mechanism and its application to narrative understanding, Ph.D. Thesis, University of Illinois at Urbana-Champaign (1987).
60. Mooney, R.J., Generalizing the order of operators in macro-operators, in: *Proceedings Fifth International Conference on Machine Learning*, Ann Arbor, MI (1988) 270–283.
61. Mostow, D.J., Machine transformation of advice into a heuristic search procedure, in: R.S. Michalski, J.G. Carbonell and T.M. Mitchell (Eds.), *Machine Learning: An Artificial Intelligence Approach* (Tioga, Palo Alto, CA, 1983) 367–403.
62. Mostow, J. and Bhatnagar, N., Failsafe: A floor planner that uses EBG to learn from its failures, *Proceedings IJCAI-87*, Milan, Italy (1987) 249–255.
63. O'Rorke, P., Generalization for explanation-based schema acquisition, in: *Proceedings AAAI-84*, Austin, TX (1984) 260–263.
64. Pazzani, M., Dyer, M. and Flowers, M., The role of prior causal theories in generalization, in: *Proceedings AAAI-86*, Philadelphia, PA (1986) 545–550.
65. Pazzani, M.J., Integrated learning with incorrect and incomplete theories, in: *Proceedings Fifth International Conference on Machine Learning*, Ann Arbor, MI (1988) 291–297.
66. Prieditis, A.E., Discovery of algorithms from weak methods, in: *Proceedings International Meeting on Advances in Learning*, Les Arcs, Switzerland (1986) 37–52.
67. Prieditis, A.E., Environment-guided program transformation, in: *Proceedings AAAI Spring Symposium on Explanation-Based Learning* (1988) 201–209.
68. Rajamoney, S.A., and DeJong, G.F., The classification, detection and handling of imperfect theory problems, in: *Proceedings IJCAI-87*, Milan, Italy (1987) 205–207.
69. Rosenbloom, P.S. and Laird, J.E., Mapping explanation-based generalization onto Soar, in: *Proceedings AAAI-86*, Philadelphia, PA (1986) 561–567.
70. Sacerdoti, E.D., *A Structure for Plans and Behavior* (Elsevier North-Holland, New York, 1977).
71. Schank, R.C., *Dynamic Memory* (Cambridge University Press, Cambridge, 1982).
72. Segre, A.M., Explanation-based learning of generalized robot assembly plans, Ph.D. Thesis, University of Illinois at Urbana-Champaign (1987).
73. Segre, A.M., On the operationality/generality trade-off in explanation-based learning, in: *Proceedings IJCAI-87*, Milan, Italy (1987) 242–248.
74. Shavlik, J.W. and DeJong, G.F., An explanation-based approach to generalizing number, in: *Proceedings IJCAI-87*, Milan, Italy (1987) 236–238.
75. Silver, B., Learning equation solving methods from worked examples, in: *Proceedings International Machine Learning Workshop*, Montecello, IL (1983).
76. Silver, B., Precondition analysis: Learning control information, in: R.S. Michalski, J.G. Carbonell and T.M. Mitchell (Eds.), *Machine Learning: An Artificial Intelligence Approach* **2** (Morgan Kaufmann, Los Altos, CA, 1986) 647–670.
77. Simon, H.A., Why should machines learn? in: R.S. Michalski, J.G. Carbonell and T.M. Mitchell (Eds.), *Machine Learning: An Artificial Intelligence Approach* (Tioga, Palo Alto, CA, 1983) 25–37.
78. Steier, D.M., Laird, J.E., Newell, A., Rosenbloom, P.S., Flynn, R.A., Golding, A., Polk, T.A., Shivers, O.G., Unruh, A. and Yost, G.R., Varieties of learning in Soar: 1987, in: *Proceedings Fourth International Workshop on Machine Learning*, Irvine, CA (1987) 300–311.

79. Sussman, G.J., *A Computer Model of Skill Acquisition* (American Elsevier, New York, 1975).
80. Tadepalli, P., Towards learning chess combinations, Tech. Rept. ML-TR-5, Department of Computer Science, Rutgers University, New Brunswick, NJ (1986).
81. Tambe, M. and Newell, A., Some chunks are expensive, in: *Proceedings Fifth International Conference on Machine Learning*, Ann Arbor, MI (1988) 451–458.
82. Tambe, M. and Rosenbloom, P., Eliminating expensive chunks, Tech. Rept. CMU-CS-88-189, Computer Science Department, Carnegie Mellon University, Pittsburgh, PA (1988).
83. Utgoff, P.E., Shift of bias for inductive concept learning, in: R.S. Michalski, J.G. Carbonell and T.M. Mitchell (Eds.), *Machine Learning: An Artificial Intelligence Approach* 2 (Morgan Kaufmann, Los Altos, CA, 1986) 107–148.
84. van Harmelen, F. and Bundy, A., Explanation-based generalization = Partial evaluation, *Artificial Intelligence* 36 (1988) 401–412.
85. Vere, S.A., Splicing plans to achieve misordered goals, in: *Proceedings IJCAI-86*, Los Angeles, CA (1985) 1016–1021.
86. Waterman, D., Generalization learning techniques for automating the learning of heuristics, *Artificial Intelligence* 1 (1970) 121–170.
87. Winston, P., Learning new principles from precedents and examples, *Artificial Intelligence* 19 (1982) 321–350.

# Design by Derivational Analogy: Issues in the Automated Replay of Design Plans

## Jack Mostow

*Computer Science Department, Rutgers University, Hill Center, Busch Campus, New Brunswick, NJ 08903, U.S.A.*

ABSTRACT

*Derivational analogy solves a problem by replaying the plan used to solve a previous problem, modifying it where necessary. We analyze how four published systems use this approach to help design (or redesign) complex artifacts like programs and circuits. We compare how they represent, acquire, and retrieve design plans; how they determine which parts of the old and new designs correspond; how they decide which steps of a design plan are appropriate to replay and adapt them to the new problem; and how they reuse partial plans. We show how each system's approach to these seven issues affects the SCOPE of problems it can solve, its EVOLVABILITY to solve new problems, the QUALITY of its solutions, the EFFICIENCY of its computation, and its AUTONOMY from the user.*

## 1. Introduction

Design is an important domain in which to study learning. To search an immense space of possible designs efficiently, it appears necessary to learn along the way (Mostow [62]). Moreover, such a space is sufficiently regular to make learning feasible: a design can be analyzed to guide subsequent iterations on the same problem (Mostow and Bhatnagar [67]), or modified to solve a related problem.

Design bears a deep resemblance to learning. In particular, design iteration seeks to improve an artifact description relative to various design goals, while incremental learning seeks to improve a system relative to various performance criteria. By viewing design as learning, we discern the role of credit/blame assignment in deciding which design decisions to revise. By viewing learning as redesigning a system to perform better, we discern how to evaluate the learned knowledge in context (Keller [41–43]). Conversely, we can view redesign as solving a new design problem by analogy with an old one.

The idea of solving a design (or planning) problem by modifying a previous solution is probably as old as design itself. In fact, redesign probably accounts for the majority of design activity today. Not only are many designs created by adapting previous successful designs, but even in innovative design there is a significant amount of design iteration, which consists of modifying a candidate design to satisfy design goals it failed to meet.

Modifying the *result* of the design process is like patching compiled code, and suffers from the same difficulties: a single change in the problem may require a multitude of patches and mess up the structure ot the design. If the effects of a single specification change or design decision are distributed throughout the implementation, it is easier to change one part of the derivation than to make patches all over the implementation. This distribution effect explains why patched code is hard to understand and maintain (Mostow [63]).

Those who forget history may be condemned to repeat it, but those who record history are allowed to replay it. Recent research in AI and design has emphasized the notion of reusing the *process* rather than the *product* of design: solving a problem by replaying the stored plan for solving a similar problem, modifying the plan wherever necessary to fit the new problem (Carbonell [13, 14, 16], Steinberg and Mitchell [86], Wile [93], Balzer et al. [5], Mostow [62, 63, 65], Kedar-Cabelli [38], Acosta et al. [1], Huhns and Acosta [36], Mostow and Barley [66]). Changing the problem definition and replaying the plan is like editing a high-level program and recompiling it, and should offer the same advantages. There are some important differences, though. First, compilation and recompilation are fully automatic. In contrast a plan may be constructed by recording design steps performed by hand, and the replay process may involve some user interaction. Second, the plan itself may be modified to represent a change in strategy; this is like modifying the compiler. Third, a compiler is supposed to handle all programs in its source language, and give error messages for those that violate rules of syntax or semantics. In contrast, a (design) plan is specific to a relatively narrow class of problems, and may fail ungracefully when applied to problems outside the class.

An effective mechanism for designing new circuits, programs, or widgets by analogy with old ones could greatly enhance design productivity. To date this approach has achieved only limited success, and it is worthwhile to analyze why. Previously we identified some of the issues that make this kind of analogy easier said than done (Mostow [65]). There are now (as of 1987) four implemented, published systems that replay design plans for complex artifacts: POPART (Wile [93]), REDESIGN (Steinberg and Mitchell [86]), BOGART (Mostow and Barley [66]), and ARGO (Huhns and Acosta [36]). We compare these systems by identifying an expanded list of issues and discussing how they are addressed in each system. The purpose of the analysis is to identify the various approaches to these issues, evaluate their effectiveness, explicate the assumptions on which they depend, and highlight the problems for which satisfactory solutions remain to be found.

Replaying a design plan is not the only way to automate redesign. One approach is to directly patch the description of the original artifact (Simoudis [78]). Another approach is to learn from the history of a design some general control knowledge that applies to other design problems as well (Tong [89]). Although these approaches are worth mentioning, they lie outside the scope of this article.

The rest of the article is organized as follows. Section 2 reviews relevant previous work. Section 3 characterizes design and redesign problems. Section 4 introduces several issues involved in replaying design plans. Sections 5–8 describe the four systems and how they address each of these issues. Section 9 summarizes the state of the art, exposes some important tradeoffs, identifies techniques for addressing them, and suggests directions for further work.

## 2. Related Work

Replay is related to previously developed methods for learning, replanning, dependency-directed backtracking, and analogical reasoning.

### 2.1. Rote learning

Simple mechanisms that capture and replay linear "plans" are not new. For example, by the early 1970s at least one text editor could transcribe a sequence of user-invoked commands and replay it on request (Weiner et al. [92]).[1] Such mechanisms do not represent information about the goal structure or applicability conditions of the command sequence. Neither do similar facilities in the INTERLISP programmer's assistant (Teitelman [88]), or operating systems that record the recent history of top-level user commands and "redo" a specified portion of it on request.

Of course any program is a replayable plan in the trivial sense that it can be re-executed. However, here we are interested in plans that are captured automatically, not just constructed by hand, and that produce complex designs when they are executed.

### 2.2. Macro-operators

The mechanism in STRIPS (Fikes and Nilsson [23]) for recording useful operator sequences and generalizing them into macro-rules can be viewed as a sort of replay facility. STRIPS improved on literal replay mechanisms by computing the preconditions of such macro-rules and variabilizing irrelevant constants. Checking a macro-rule's preconditions before applying it reduces the risk of misapplying it, while generalizing it expands the range of situations in which it can be applied.

---

[1] This was my first technical report; I never expected to cite it in an AI publication!

## 2.3. Dependency-directed backtracking

Dependency-directed backtracking (Stallman and Sussman [82]) or "truth maintenance" can be viewed as an alternative to replaying a computation in a new context. The results of the original computation are cached, along with their dependencies on various aspects of the original context. When the context changes, only the results invalidated by the change are discarded and recomputed (Mostow and Cohen [68]); the others can be reused without replaying the process of computing them.

When the changes consist of decisions made in the course of designing something, dependency-directed backtracking helps in redesign. Finer-grained dependency-directed backtracking is used in the DONTE circuit design system (Tong [90, 91]) to selectively retract individual consequences of a design decision.

The constraint propagation scheme used in the PRIDE system for designing paper paths in Xerox copiers (Mittal and Araya [58]) illustrates an interesting refinement to dependency-directed backtracking: whenever a constraint violation is detected, annotations attached to the constraint suggest ways to repair the constraint. These annotations come from hand-coded, domain-specific advice in the rule base, and reflect a knowledge-intensive expert systems approach.

Viewed as an alternative to replay, dependency-directed backtracking imposes the rather restrictive requirement that the new problem be encoded by modifying the same data structure that represented the old problem. That is, it helps in revising the same design, but not in solving a new problem by analogy with an old one. Moreover, other mechanisms must identify the dependencies and perform the repairs; dependency-directed backtracking itself merely propagates the changes via the encoded dependencies.

## 2.4. Replanning

Hayes-Roth et al. [34] described an interactive "planner's workbench" to assist replanning by consulting a "plan rationale." The rationale was represented as a network of uninterpreted English assertions linked by logical relations. The paper identified some of the key questions involved in replaying a plan: "Does the [new context] violate any of the assumptions underlying the plan, conflict with any of its goals, or usurp any of its resources? What alternatives are available if the planned actions are no longer effective? What considerations should determine the selection among alternative actions?" The replanning process was assumed to be interactive, and the project included some interesting explanation facilities for selecting and presenting elements of the original plan needed by the human replanner.

## 2.5. Analogy in theorem proving

Proofs are closely related to plans and programs; one can view a proof as a plan for getting from premises to conclusion via rules of inference, and constructive proofs can be interpreted as programs (Green [29], Bates and Constable [8]). Analogical proof techniques that adapted the proof of one theorem to solve another might turn out to be useful for redesign and replanning as well. Then again, they might not: while the parts of a proof are perfectly independent, in the sense that they can be proved independently, design problems are characterized by interactions among the parts. Analogical techniques that rely on the independence of subproblems might not apply to design.

Kling [45] reported a system named ZORBA that used the proof of one theorem to help find a proof for another. Rather than replaying the proof, ZORBA used it to identify which clauses might help prove the new theorem. By using only these clauses, ZORBA was able to speed up the search for a proof.

Constable et al. [17] describe the PRL proof-generating environment, which represents and manipulates hierarchical proof plans; the actual proof is constructed by executing the plan. PRL has a catalog of proof "tactics" for refining and transforming incomplete plans, and "tacticals" for building composite tactics. In particular, one tactic copies a proof from one plan to another. As the authors say [17, p. 318], "The result of the copy is almost a verbatim copy of the original proof. However, one could imagine writing more general tactics to construct proofs *by analogy* to existing proofs."

Bledsoe [9] and Brock et al. [10] focus on this analogy process. They describe theorem provers that are given a proof of one theorem and use it to find a proof for a similar theorem faster than proving it from scratch. The papers present heuristics for constructing and repairing analogies between theorems, but do not address the problem of selecting a good proof to use as a guide.

## 2.6. Analogical problem solving

Solving a new problem by analogy with a previously solved problem is an important type of analogical reasoning. Other types of analogical reasoning, both within one domain and across different domains, include generating explanations for students, learning facts (Greiner [30, 31]) and concepts (Burstein [11, 12], Kedar-Cabelli [39]), arguing legal cases (McCarty and Sridharan [52], Kedar-Cabelli [38], Nagel [70]), understanding metaphors (Gentner [26], Gentner and Gentner [28], Winston [94]), and taking intelligence tests (Evans [19]). For surveys of work on analogical reasoning, see Kedar-Cabelli [40], Hall [32], Prieditis [75], Holland et al. [35], Gentner [27].

Much of the recent work on analogical problem solving, including the work by Bledsoe et al. on analogical theorem proving, is based on Carbonell's work on transformational and derivational analogy. Carbonell began with a protocol study of human problem solving. His undergraduate subjects were initially unable to prove that the product of two even numbers is even. However, once they were shown the proof, most of them were able to solve the harder problem of proving that the product of two odd numbers is odd.

The "transformational analogy" mechanism inspired by this study was implemented in a production system model of the subjects' behavior (Carbonell [13, 14]). The program used various mutation operators to transform old plans to solve new problems. It generated proofs in geometry and simple number theory from proofs of related theorems. For instance, it proved Odd * Odd = Odd by patching and replaying the proof of Even * Even = Even. While the model simulated the behavior of human subjects, its linear representation of the proof plan failed to capture the underlying goal structure, and required somewhat unwieldy transforms to patch the plan.

The "derivational analogy" method was proposed to remedy the representational deficiencies of transformational analogy (Carbonell [15, 16]). It represents a problem solving plan as a hierarchical goal structure, showing how and why each goal was decomposed into subgoals. It solves a new problem by replaying this plan top-down. When the subplan for a subgoal fails, the plan is patched by solving that subgoal from scratch.

An implementation of the method solved a series of small route-planning problems. Carbonell observed that "one should be able to program a quicksort algorithm in LISP quite easily if one has recently implemented quicksort in Pascal" [16]. Interestingly, the next chapter of the same collection (Dershowitz [18]) presented a proposal for programming by analogy based on applying transformations guided by program annotations that describe the purpose and effect of different sections of code. However, problems as complex as programming remained too hard to automate.

Other research on analogical problem solving has gone under the name of "case-based reasoning" (Kolodner et al. [47]). Case-based reasoning has been investigated for several tasks, including dispute mediation (Simpson [79], Sycara [87]), recipe creation (Hammond [33]), meal planning (Kolodner [46]), diagnosis of hearing disorders (Bareiss et al. [6]), and landscape design (Navinchandra [71], Navinchandra et al. [72]). This body of work has focused on the indexing and retrieval of relevant precedents, largely ignored in other work on analogical problem solving, and also on the adaptation of old plans to solve new problems. Typically the solution "plan" is a parameterized script or schema whose structure is more or less fixed, rather than an arbitrary sequence of problem solving operators as in Carbonell's work. The task domain is sufficiently circumscribed that goals can be assumed to belong to a few predefined types, such as "resolve a physical dispute" or "plan a main course." Plans for solving instances of these goal types are indexed in a discrimination network by various distinguishing features. New problems are assumed to be expressed in terms of these goals, which can then be used as indices to retrieve relevant plans.

Additional work in analogical reasoning has examined which information to map from one case to another, and how to perform the mapping. In general, analogies abstract away superficial details and capture underlying commonalities at the level of higher-order causal relations (Falkenhainer et al. [20]). Related work on prototype-based reasoning (McCarty and Sridharan [52], Nagel [70]) has focused on complex analogies such as those involved in legal reasoning. Here the problem is to understand when and how two cases can be viewed as analogous. A mapping between a prototypical case (such as a legal precedent) and a new case is constructed by finding a series of successive deformations from one case to the other.

## 2.7. Evaluation of replay mechanisms

Replay mechanisms can be evaluated in terms of the following dimensions (Mitchell and Mostow [56]):

- SCOPE: What class of tasks can be solved by replaying a plan?
- EVOLVABILITY: How easily can the mechanism be extended to other tasks?
- QUALITY: How good are the solutions?
- EFFICIENCY: What computational resources does replay require?
- AUTONOMY: How little human intervention is required in the replay process?

The collection of replay mechanisms surveyed above illustrates the classic AI tradeoff between generality and power. Here generality is characterized by the SCOPE of tasks handled by replay, and the EVOLVABILITY of the mechanism to handle additional tasks, while power is measured by the QUALITY of the result, the computational EFFICIENCY of the process, and the AUTONOMY of the system. The completely automatic replay mechanisms are weak and/or brittle. The more sophisticated mechanisms are limited to a restricted class of tasks, or rely on the user to handle certain parts of a task. In both cases, the mechanisms' power is limited not only by their inferential capabilities but by missing knowledge, especially about the goal structure of the plan being replayed.

## 3. Design and Redesign Problems

This article focuses on replay in the context of design. Design can be defined as finding an artifact description that satisfies various kinds of constraints (Mostow [62], Tong [89]). We will illustrate these constraints in terms of a sample problem in circuit design.

The obvious aspects of a design problem are the constraints on the artifact:

(1) *Functional specification*: the operation to be performed by the circuit, e.g., add two 4-bit numbers.

(2) *Artifact costs*: time delay, surface area, and power consumption.

(3) *Target medium*: the materials and structures used in the artifact, such as the layers of silicon and metal used in VLSI NMOS fabrication technology.

(4) *Environmental criteria*: additional requirements imposed by the processes expected to operate on the artifact. For example, the fabrication process

imposes certain manufacturability constraints, while the testing process may require the ability to control and observe the state of circuit components.

A problem may impose additional restrictions on the artifact description:

(5) *Description requirements*: constraints on how the artifact is represented. For example, the circuit design may have to be expressed in a particular hardware description language.

(6) *Description costs*: as opposed to the costs of the artifact. For example, the circuit design requires space to store and time to draw.

Finally a design problem may impose meta-level restrictions on the process whereby this description is found:

(7) *Design resources*: the resources available for design may include knowledge bases like a standard cell library, and design tools like an editor, design rule checker, or simulator.

(8) *Design methodology*: additional restrictions on the order and kinds of design decisions, such as those imposed by Mead-Conway design rules or top-down decomposition.

(9) *Design costs*: design time, budget, expertise, etc.

Only the most general system would explicitly input complete descriptions of all these problem aspects. In real design systems, some aspects are fixed and/or implicit. For example, circuit design systems are often specific to a fixed target technology. Other aspects, such as the resources used in design, may vary, but as dependent parameters determined by the design process, rather than as controllable inputs that guide it. Finally, the various aspects needn't be specified independently, and some can be defined in terms of others. For example, instead of imposing a fixed deadline for creating the design, the decision about when to stop improving it might be based on some tradeoff between the quality of the design and the cost of delaying its completion.

Redesign consists of solving a design problem by modifying one or more previous designs. The new problem may differ from the old one(s) in one or more of the aspects listed above. We illustrate some of the difficulties caused by altering various aspects of our circuit design problem.

(1) *Functional specification*: What if the new design must add two 8-bit numbers? It is necessary to revise whichever design decisions implicitly or explicitly assumed a data width of 4.

(2) *Artifact costs*: What if chip area is no longer as important as chip speed? It may become preferable to implement certain operations in parallel, even though their serial implementations are still functionally correct.

(3) *Target medium*: What if the fabrication technology changes to CMOS? Not only will low-level decisions about implementation of transistors change, but some high-level design decisions that made sense for NMOS may be inappropriate for CMOS.

(4) *Environmental criteria*: What if the new design must produce a higher yield when fabricated? It may be necessary to widen the wires to compensate for misalignment between layers of the chip.

(5) *Description requirements*: What if the new design must be expressed in a different language? It might be possible to translate the previous design directly, or it might be necessary to rederive it using a different set of design tools. More interestingly, what if the new design must work for any data width? It might be possible to generalize the old design without modifying the circuit, by parameterizing the design description to work for any data width; or it might require changing the circuit itself, for example by using a bit slice style of design.

(6) *Description costs*: What if the description of the new design must fit on a single floppy disk? It might be necessary to replace custom-designed modules with pointers to standard cells in a library, even if they're not as good.

(7) *Design resources*: What if a better standard cell library becomes available? It may become feasible to reduce the size of the circuit by reimplementing some of its components.

(8) *Design methodology*: What if the new design must be proven correct? A more conservative design style might be needed to make the proof work.

(9) *Redesign costs*: What if very little time is available for redesign? It will be advisable to stick close to the original design rather than explore exotic alternatives.

(10) *Previous design plan(s)*: What information is available about how the 4-bit adder was designed? The system might be given just the circuit schematic for a 4-bit adder, without a description of the criteria the original solution was designed to satisfy. It might be given a single previous design to adapt, or it might be given a whole database of designs, in which case it must pick the relevant one(s) to retrieve.

As the examples suggest, changes in various aspects of a problem can subtly and pervasively affect the applicability of its solution. A redesign system might not be given explicit descriptions of all these aspects.

## 4. Issues in Replay

The derivational analogy approach to a redesign problem depends on replaying a *design plan*—an executable record of decisions made in the course of solving the original design problem. Replaying such a plan raises several issues:

(1) *Representation*: What information about the original design decisions is needed in order to replay them, and how should it be expressed?

(2) *Acquisition*: How can this information be captured?

(3) *Retrieval*: Given a problem, how can relevant previous designs be found?

(4) *Correspondence*: Which objects, goals, constraints, etc. in the new design correspond to which ones in the old design?

(5) *Appropriateness*: When should a given plan or plan step be replayed?

(6) *Adaptation*: How can a previous plan be altered to fit a new problem?

(7) *Partial reuse*: Which parts of a plan can be replayed by themselves?

The rest of this section discusses each of these issues. Sections 5–8 show how they are treated in POPART, REDESIGN, BOGART, and ARGO.

### 4.1. Representation of design plans

The capabilities of a replay mechanism are fundamentally constrained by the plan representation on which it operates. Its effectiveness depends on the extent to which it "understands" the design, which depends in turn on the knowledge represented in the design plan.

In an intelligent replay mechanism, a design plan should describe not only the final artifact, but the decision leading to that design, and the rationales for each decision (Mostow [62]). For example, consider a decision to decompose a 4-bit adder into four 1-bit adders. Its rationale might include such information as:

– *Goals*: The circuit should be fast and functionally correct.

– *Precondition*: The method for computing an $N$-bit function assumes it can be implemented using $N$ one-bit versions.

–*Justification for believing that the decision will achieve its goal*: The plan assumes that the 1-bit adders are properly implemented and connected.

– *Alternatives*: The sum of two 4-bit numbers can be computed in other ways, such as retrieving it from a 256-entry lookup table, building a large combinational circuit, or using a single 1-bit adder to compute the sum bit-serially.

– *Selection criteria*: Why is a particular option chosen instead of the alternatives? The particular implementation choice in the example might reflect a careful tradeoff between circuit speed and area. Or it might simply have been the first option considered, in which case it reflects a tradeoff between design EFFICIENCY and QUALITY.

A representation can be characterized not only by the knowledge it contains but also by how that knowledge is expressed. The more abstractly or generally a plan or plan step is represented, the larger the class of situations where it can be used; we call this property the *robustness* of the representation.

There can be a tradeoff between the robustness of a plan and the costs of acquiring, representing, and replaying it. A plan may be much easier to express, and possibly more efficient to replay, at a lower level of detail. For instance, it is much easier for a user to indicate a circuit module by pointing at it or naming it than to describe it in terms of the series of design decisions that led to its existence, yet the latter description may be far more robust. Similarly, it is much easier to analyze a partial design (e.g. its complexity, space usage, etc.) by examining it directly than by looking only at the design decisions that produced it. The conflicting demands of the various operations on a design plan suggest that they use different representations of it, with some provision for translating among them.

The representation of plans in a design system reflects its underlying model of the design process. As we shall see, the transformational model underlying POPART is more general—and therefore less constraining—than the top-down decomposition model underlying REDESIGN and BOGART. ARGO's model appears to lie somewhere in between.

## 4.2. Plan acquisition

The design plan to be replayed must first have been constructed, whether directly by the user, or by automatically recording the design process. The means by which it was constructed influences the difficulty of replaying it. The more problem solving knowledge captured during the plan acquisition process, the easier the plan may be to replay.

For instance, suppose the design process is recorded by "looking over the user's shoulder"—recording a series of edit commands in a circuit editor (Mitchell et al. [55]). The system can only guess at the goals motivating the commands.

On the other hand, if the system synthesizes the design plan itself, it has access to the underlying goal structure and can easily save that knowledge for use during replay. Of course, if the system is capable of generating the plan on its own, it should be able to solve the new problem too. Nonetheless, replay may still be useful to avoid the inefficiency of redesigning from scratch. Also, in domains where knowledge is imperfect, replaying a plan whose success has been validated by experience may be more reliable than creating a radically new plan.

The class of problems where we expect replay to be most useful are too hard to solve entirely automatically; much of design falls in this class. An interactive design system could ask its user to explain the reasons for each decision, but a complete rationale for a complex design would be burdensome for the user to provide and (if expressed in English) difficult for the system to interpret. One approach to reducing this burden is a division of labor in which the system performs the routine decisions but the user provides high-level guidance (Mostow [61]). A complementary approach is to have the system infer the rationale for the user's actions, given a domain theory strong enough to explain them (Mitchell et al. [55], Norton and Kelly [73]).

## 4.3. Plan retrieval

Given a design problem to solve by replay, one must retrieve a suitable stored design plan to replay. Plan retrieval is difficult for several reasons.

First, how can the relevance of a design plan to a problem be determined without incurring the computational expense of actually trying to replay it? Viewing plans as theories about how to solve problems sheds some light on this issue (Mostow [65]). If the plan is a design history constructed by recording the steps that solved the original problem, it constitutes a *descriptive* theory of how the original problem was solved. Replaying it means interpreting it as a *prescriptive* theory that specifies how to solve a new problem. But deciding whether it might help solve a new problem requires interpreting the plan as a *predictive* theory. These three uses impose different demands on the plan, and it is not surprising that a plan representation suitable for one purpose may fail for another.

Assessing the relevance of a plan is complicated by two additional factors. Theoretically one might compute the weakest precondition of the plan and test it to predict whether the entire plan applies to a given problem. However, a plan may be useful even if only part of it applies to the new problem. It's not clear how to predict what portion of a plan will apply without actually trying to replay it. Moreover, the question is not just whether a plan is sufficiently relevant to try, but which of several alternative plans to select.

Even if there were an efficient way to predict the relevance of a given plan to a given problem, it would be expensive to test every plan in a library of previous designs; scaling up to larger libraries would ultimately require some sort of indexing scheme to avoid computational costs proportional to the number of stored plans. However, the need to allow partial matches between problems and plans makes such indexing difficult.

Of the four systems reported here, only ARGO automates the retrieval of design plans. However, the retrieval problem goes away for redesign problems where the original design plan is a given. In particular, when replay is used to support design iteration, the design plan is the same for each iteration, except for whatever modifications the user chooses to introduce. In machine learning terminology, this use of replay in the course of solving a single design problem is a kind of within-task transfer, in contrast to the between-task transfer involved in solving a new design problem by analogy with an old one.

For solving new design problems by analogy with old ones, retrieval becomes problematic, and the effectiveness of replay is ultimately limited by the amount of work (whether manual or automatic) required to retrieve the design plan(s) relevant to a given problem. In short, although this article reports some attempts at automated retrieval of design plans, and some of the work on case-based reasoning described in Section 2.6 might eventually be extended to address it, it remains a hard open problem.

## 4.4. Object correspondence

A design plan serves as a prescription for how to solve some class of problems. If a plan step consists of applying a parameterized operator, then replaying it in the context of a new problem requires figuring out how to instantiate its parameters, that is, identifying which objects to apply the operator to. We say that these objects *correspond* to the ones to which the operator was applied in the original context where the plan was created.

The correspondence problem in replay consists of finding which objects in the new design correspond to which ones referred to in a previous design plan. There are various ways for a step in the plan to refer to the objects it involves. For example, the decision to decompose a 4-bit adder into four 1-bit adders might refer to it by description ("the 4-bit adder"), by name ("Module-0123"), by location on the screen ("$\langle 150, 300 \rangle$"), or by a direct pointer to the data structure representing the adder.

Replaying the plan requires re-interpreting such references in the context of the new problem so as to find the corresponding objects. However, references that made sense in the old problem might be anomalous in the new one:

– An *ambiguous* reference has multiple referents in the new context. "The 4-bit adder" is ambiguous if there is more than one of them to design in the new problem.

– A *meaningless* reference has no referent. If there is no module named Module-0123 in the new design, references to "Module-0123" are meaningless.

– A *misleading* reference has a unique but unintended referent. If there is a module named Module-0123 in the new design, but it's not an adder or something that makes sense to decompose like one, then the reference to "Module-0123" is misleading in the new context.

Overly specific references to objects in the old design are liable to be anomalous in the new one.

Several approaches to the problem of anomalous references are possible:

– Avoid them in the first place by representing the plan so it refers to objects in a robust fashion. For example, a detailed specification of the adder to be designed is a more robust reference than "Module-0123."

– Infer a more robust description based on the purpose of the step, later references to the same object, etc. For example, infer that "Module-0123" corresponds to a module to which the Decompose rule can be applied.

– Find an object in the new context that resembles the original object closely enough to be considered analogous. For example, an 8-bit adder could be considered analogous to the original 4-bit adder. A good similarity criterion would efficiently predict whether the new object can play the same role in the plan as the old one.

## 4.5. Appropriateness of replay

A design plan is a form of control knowledge: it prescribes a sequence of steps to solve a design problem. Without such a plan, finding an appropriate sequence of steps could take considerable search (by the system) or intervention (by the user). But when is a design plan, or a step in such a plan, appropriate to replay? The answer depends on the definition of "appropriate" and on what has changed since the plan was created.

The appropriateness issue has to do with deciding when a given plan step is appropriate to replay, and with what happens if it is replayed inappropriately. Each step of a plan depends on various aspects of the original problem, though it is unrealistic to expect the stored plan to represent all these dependencies explicitly. Plan steps will inevitably presume certain preconditions which were true in the original context. If they are false in the new context, the plan may fail.

Our discussion of the correspondence problem has already introduced a special case of such preconditions—the presumptions implicit in references. For example, a reference to "the 4-bit adder" presumes that there is exactly one 4-bit adder in the given context, and a reference to "Module-0123" presumes the existence of a module with that name. A reference is anomalous in contexts that violate such presumptions. It is useful to treat the correspondence problem as a separate case because it is amenable to specialized solutions.

Similarly, it is useful to distinguish several kinds of preconditions corresponding to different definitions of "appropriate," and to consider the effect of violating them. In a given context, a step may be:

(1) *Executable*: The plan step is syntactically applicable. If not, the step cannot be replayed. For instance, the step "Decompose Module-0123" presumes that the code for the Decompose operator can be applied to Module-0123.

(2) *Correct*: The plan step preserves the correctness of the design description (specification) to which it is applied. If not, replaying the step may produce an incorrect design. For instance, the Decompose operator might manage to decompose a 4-bit multiplier into four 1-bit multipliers, but the resulting circuit wouldn't work.

(3) *Successful*: The plan step achieves its original purpose. If not, the plan may fail even though the step can be replayed. For example, the purpose of decomposing the 4-bit adder into 1-bit adders is to help implement it. This purpose will not be achieved unless the 1-bit adders can be implemented.

(4) *Desirable*: The plan step still satisfies the criteria used to select it from the available alternatives. For example, suppose the reason for decomposing the 4-bit adder into 1-bit adders is to maximize speed. Even though it still achieves its purpose (implementation), the decomposition step can become undesirable if:
   (a) *The set of alternatives changes*: A faster but hitherto unknown or infeasible implementation becomes available, such as table lookup.
   (b) *The relative desirability of the alternatives changes*: Suppose the data width of 4 is increased so much that a cascade of 1-bit adders would

occupy more than one chip and therefore require a slower clock speed. A bit-serial implementation that reuses a single 1-bit adder may now be faster.

(c) *The selection criteria change*: If minimizing area becomes more important than maximizing speed, a parallel implementation may no longer be desirable.

While the successfulness of a step is a local property that depends only on whether the step achieves its purpose, its desirability is a global property that depends on the alternatives available and the selection criteria in force.

These types of preconditions are listed in order of increasingly stringent requirements on the *appropriateness* of replaying the design step: executability is a weak form of appropriateness; correctness is stronger, and desirability is stronger yet. Replaying a step that is no longer correct in the new context, or no longer achieves its original purpose, can lead to a functionally incorrect design, or a dead-end design that cannot be completed without retracting some of the decisions it embodies. In contrast, replaying a step that is successful but no longer desirable may merely lead to a suboptimal design.

Thus there is a potential tradeoff between the effort spent in evaluating the appropriateness of a design plan in a new context, and the quality of the design obtained by replaying the plan. At one extreme, replaying the plan without regard to its appropriateness may lead to an incorrect design. At the other extreme, selecting the most desirable alternative at each step ensures optimality, but incurs the expense of identifying and evaluating the alternatives. If the resources available for redesign are limited, it might make more sense to stick to the original plan wherever possible, even though there might be a better alternative. This preference is actually incorporated in some definitions of redesign: "In AI terms, design can be thought of as the creative process of developing plans and specifying, selecting, and arranging components in order that the goals and objectives of the designer (and the employing organization) can best be achieved. Redesign is the process of satisfying additional constraints on an existing system *with the aim of keeping the system intact where possible*" (Fisher [24], emphasis added).

The QUALITY of a replay mechanism depends on its ability to determine which steps in a design plan are appropriate in a new context, while its EFFICIENCY depends on identifying inappropriate steps before it tries to replay them. A fine-tuneable tradeoff between QUALITY and EFFICIENCY would require the ability to predict the cost of ensuring a given degree of appropriateness.

To summarize, the appropriateness problem in replay consists of deciding which plan steps should be replayed. We have defined increasing degrees of appropriateness: executability, correctness, success, and desirability. We will characterize each replay system by the degree to which it is sensitive to the various aspects of design listed in Section 3.

## 4.6. Plan adaptation

So far we have focused on deciding whether and how to replay a step in a plan. Although relatively few problems can be solved by repeating the exact same sequence of steps, many more can be solved by inserting, deleting, or changing a few steps, and replaying the modified plan. For example, a plan for designing a 4-bit adder might be adapted to design a 4-bit comparator. While appropriateness involves deciding which steps of a design plan can be replayed, adaptation involves deciding how to modify the plan to solve a new problem. Adapting a plan to a new problem involves a series of processes:

*Step* 1. *Detect* when the plan relies on assumptions violated by the new problem. For example, the original plan assumes the operation to be implemented is addition.

*Step* 2. *Localize* the adaptation by deciding which step(s) to modify. The 1-bit units should no longer be adders.

*Step* 3. *Repair* the plan by changing the chosen steps to fit the new problem. Replace the units with 1-bit comparators.

*Step* 4. *Propagate* the change by identifying the additional assumptions it violates. For example, the plan assumes each unit has two outputs, but a comparator has only one.

Since the change may invalidate additional steps, this cycle must be repeated to arrive at a consistent revised plan. In machine learning terms, Step 1 detects an error, Step 2 assigns blame, Step 3 updates the knowledge, and Step 4 tests it out.

Section 3 illustrated some of the possible differences between the problem the plan was constructed to solve and the new problem to be solved by modifying and replaying the plan. The amount of adaptation required to fit a new problem depends not only on these differences, but on how appropriate (in the sense of Section 4.5) the adapted plan must be.

The difficulty of adapting a plan to solve a new problem depends heavily on how explictly the assumptions it violates are represented. Inferring implicit assumptions can require arbitrary domain knowledge and reasoning capabilities. For example, it would be very difficult to infer how the decision to decompose the adder into 1-bit units depends on, say, the target technology. Even if the assumptions made by each step are represented explicitly, testing them all *before starting to replay the plan* would entail regressing each assumption through the preceding steps of the plan.

## 4.7. Partial reuse

Since a detailed design plan can rarely be replayed in its entirety, its usefulness depends in part on being able to replay pieces of it. What portions of a design plan can a given mechanism replay without replaying the whole plan?

We can characterize the flexibility of reuse in terms of which parts of a given plan can be replayed by themselves. At one extreme, a perfectly inflexible mechanism can only use a plan on an all-or-none basis. At the other extreme, a perfectly flexible mechanism can treat a plan as a set of independent decisions and replay any subset of them.

Intermediate cases arise when the plan is treated as a tree or lattice whose arcs show which decisions must precede which others. If one of the plan's subgoals arises in a new context, the appropriate subtree can be replayed. For example, to design a 1-bit adder, one might replay the corresponding subtree of the design plan for a 4-bit adder. Conversely, a plan's high-level strategy can be reused, minus the details, by replaying only the higher levels of the tree. For example, one might redesign the 4-bit adder by following the part of the plan for decomposing it into 1-bit adders and then using new subplans to implement and connect them.

Sections 5–8 describe how four replay systems address the issues of plan representation, acquisition, retrieval, correspondence, appropriateness, adaptation, and partial reuse. We present an overall assessment of each system, both in terms of addressing these issues and in terms of the purpose it was intended to achieve. We try to attribute each system's successes and limitations to the aspects responsible for them.

## 5. POPART

POPART stands for "Producer Of Parsers And Related Tools" (Wile [93]). Given a BNF grammar for a language, POPART generates a suite of grammar-driven tools, including a parser, pretty-printer, structure editor, pattern matcher, and transformation system. These tools are intended to support the transformational development of specifications and programs expressed in the given base language. In particular, POPART has facilities for recording, editing, and replaying a sequence of program transformation steps. It is these facilities which are of concern here. It should be pointed out that the following description of POPART refers to the published version, which was designed circa 1980. Since then POPART has continued to evolve in response to the limitations discussed below.

### 5.1. Plan representation in POPART

POPART is based on a transformational model of software development. In this model (Mostow [62]), a program specification is converted into an executable implementation by a series of transformation steps. In POPART, the plan for transforming a specification into a program is called a "development," and is expressed in a language called PADDLE. A PADDLE development is an executable object which applies a series of transformations to a program specification. Besides developing implementation plans, POPART has been used to support the process of specification design (Feather [21, 22]), and to construct executable proofs in the AFFIRM verification system.

A PADDLE development is essentially a tree whose root is a program development goal and whose leaves are the steps that transform the specification so as to achieve the goal. Each step invokes a structure-editing command or a transformation rule defined in terms of such commands. Unlike the top-down decomposition paradigm we will see in systems where each step refines a single module, POPART's transformational paradigm lets any step modify any part of the specification; Section 5.4 tells how the development describes which part to modify.

As Fig. 1 shows, PADDLE distinguishes functional specifications from the goals to be achieved by transforming them. Development goals document the purpose of each part of the development, e.g., elimination of various nonexecutable constructs from the specification. These goals are expressed in unrestricted (and uninterpreted) English. However, the relationship between a goal and its subgoals is expressed by one of several PASCAL-like constructs for representing conjunctive, disjunctive, conditional, sequenced, and iterated goals. Thus PADDLE is a "semiformal" language.

The sample development shown in Fig. 2 deletes redundant assignment statements in LISP expressions. For a more realistic example, see Wile [93].

A development is a plan for transforming programs. The top-level goal of the development in Fig. 2 is simplify-program; this symbol documents the purpose of the development but means nothing to POPART. The goal is achieved by a two-part plan that repeatedly searches for a PROGN expression and applies delete-redundant-assignment to it, continuing until the command can no longer be applied. The first part searches through a given program for a PROGN expression (the LISP equivalent of a begin-end block). The symbol progn-form denotes a typed pattern variable that only matches expressions described by the grammar rule

progn-form := '( 'PROGN { program + } ')

The second part invokes the command delete-redundant-assignment and finds the next progn-form if there is one, in which case it repeats.

Fig. 1. Transformational model of design.

```
simplify-program
  by begin
        Find !progn-form;
        while delete-redundant-assignment
             do Refind end
     end;
```

Fig. 2. A simple PADDLE development.

The delete-redundant-assignment command is defined in Fig. 3. Its body is also represented in PADDLE, and has three steps. To illustrate, let us see how it applies to the expression

(LAMBDA (Y) (PROGN (SETQ X 0) (SETQ X Y)))

The Find step moves the cursor to the subexpression

(PROGN (SETQ X 0) (SETQ X Y))

The Match step binds the pattern variable program#useless to the redundant statement (SETQ X 0) and program#keep to (SETQ X Y). Here the suffixes #useless and #keep distinguish two pattern variables of type program. The Replace step replaces the PROGN expression with (SETQ X Y), thereby simplifying the original expression to

(LAMBDA (Y) (SETQ X Y))

Various other PADDLE constructs make it possible to:

– Repeat part of the development, such as a replacement, throughout a given expression.

– Restrict the scope of a command to a given expression. This helps prevent Find from finding unintended matches.

– Group a sequence of commands as an atomic transaction. If one of them fails, the sequence has no effect.

```
command delete-redundant-assignment =
  begin
    Find (PROGN (SETQ !variable !program#1) (SETQ !variable !program#2))
    Match (PROGN !program#useless !program#keep)
    Replace !program#keep
  end
```

Fig. 3. A simple PADDLE command definition.

– Choose between alternative development paths based on various tests. In particular, one test is whether the path can be executed to completion.

– Invoke arbitrary LISP functions, permitting access to complex analysis tools like a type checker or semantic analyzer. Thus commands can be conditioned on, say, flow analysis, free variable usage, and reference (or nonreference) to various constructs.

– Include manual editing as part of the development. Whenever POPART encounters an undefined step in the course of executing a development, it returns control to the user, who can perform the step by hand and then resume execution of the development.

### 5.2. Plan acquisition in POPART

A POPART user can create a program development by applying a sequence of structure-editing and transformation commands to an initial specification; POPART transcribes this sequence as a PADDLE development. However, a real program derivation is not created left to right (Scherlis and Scott [77])—it is itself a complex artifact hand-constructed by a careful design process. In the course of this process, the designer may modify the specification, change the oder of transformations, and otherwise alter the derivation. For instance, a designer can start with an abstract implementation plan like the one in Fig. 4. POPART freely lets the designer refine the English goals top-down into executable transformation steps, work bottom-up to construct and combine pieces of the development, elaborate it to handle successively more detailed versions of the specification, or follow other strategies to construct the desired development. Since PADDLE developments are formal objects in a language whose grammar is accepted by POPART, users can manipulate them directly using the same generic grammar-driven tools they use to edit, parse, pretty-print, pattern match, and transform programs in the base language. Thus although a PADDLE development *executes* its transformation steps left to right, it is not generally *acquired* in that order.

In practice, to a large extent the user creates a development by editing it directly. Typically the user first tries out a sequence of commands in the context of an example to get it right, and then splices the recorded sequence into the development and reorganizes it more coherently. Thus POPART

```
implement-specification
    by begin
            remove specification constructs
            optimize algorithm
            select data structures
        end;
```

Fig. 4. An abstract PADDLE development.

combines the advantages of immediate interactive feedback on the concrete results of each step with the ability to inspect and edit a more or less readable representation of the abstract design plan.

As POPART executes a development, it annotates each step to show the transformations by which it was performed. To replay the development, it performs these transformations directly, instead of the original steps. The distinction is important when the original step involves user intervention, for example to carry out a step described in English. In such cases, POPART stops executing the development and lets the user perform the step by editing the program. POPART records the user's edit commands so it can splice them into the development as the way to perform the step.

## 5.3. Plan retrieval in POPART

Typically POPART is used to create a development from scratch. An alternative would be to start with a "similar" development and adapt it, but this strategy would require a database sufficiently rich to contain such a development, and the development itself would have to be expressed with sufficient generality that adapting it to the new problem would be less work than creating a development from scratch. Neither of these conditions appears to be met at present, in part because the examples to which POPART has been applied have been very diverse. However, POPART users do write reusable commands.

A development can be stored in a file and retrieved manually by specifying the file name. Generally the reason for retrieving a plan is not to solve a new problem by analogy to an old one—the plans tend to be too specific for that—but simply to resume work on a development in progress. Creating a PADDLE development is an iterative design process, in which the user repeatedly edits the specification or the development, and uses POPART to retransform the specification accordingly. As Section 4.3 observed, this use of replay avoids the retrieval issue.

## 5.4. Correspondence in POPART

In POPART, the correspondence problem consists of specifying which expression(s) each command in a development applies to, and its arguments if any. The user is responsible for designing the development so as to specify these objects as robustly as possible, but PADDLE provides various cursor positioning, pattern matching, and search constructs for the purpose.

A PADDLE command implicitly applies to the "current expression," represented by the current cursor location in a parse tree. A transformation step is preceded by commands that move the cursor to the desired location. For example, the Replace step in delete-redundant-assignment (Fig. 3) is preceded by a command to Find a PROGN expression containing a redundant assignment statement.

Some commands require other arguments besides the expression to transform. In PADDLE, these arguments are given as expressions that may contain pattern variables bound by earlier pattern matching. For example, the Match step in the definition of delete-redundant-assignment binds the variable program#keep, which is then used as an argument in the command Replace program#keep.

PADDLE's various cursor positioning commands make it possible to refer to the same subexpression in many different ways. The user is responsible for expressing references so as to avoid the three kinds of anomalous references described in Section 4.4, all of which can occur when a plan step is replayed:

– An ambiguous reference is a pattern that is intended by the designer of a development to match a unique subexpression, but which turns out to match more than one. POPART reports whether a match is unique, but does not prevent this anomaly.

– A meaningless reference in PADDLE occurs when a cursor positioning command fails, e.g., a search command fails to find a match. Unless the failed command is embedded in certain constructs, POPART generally reacts by halting. (Section 5.6 describes exceptions where POPART rewrites the current expression to match the search pattern.)

– A misleading reference means any sequence of cursor positioning commands that arrives at an expression other than the desired one.

While POPART lets users encode references as robustly as they can express them in PADDLE, the POPART replay mechanism itself gives very little help in preventing or detecting anomalous references. At best it responds to them by halting when a command fails. Since ambiguous and misleading references do not automatically cause a halt, replay may continue until well after the anomaly. To detect such anomalies, the user can insert explicit tests to make sure the current expression has the expected form, and halt if it doesn't. In particular, if the referent is supposed to satisfy a particular pupose, it may be possible to check at some later point whether that purpose has indeed been met.

## 5.5. Appropriateness in POPART

POPART does not automatically test whether a step is appropriate. even executable, before trying to replay it; if the step fails, replay halts, unless the step is part of a series of alternatives to try, in which case POPART tries the next one.

A plan step typically incorporates implicit assumptions about the current cursor position. Checking these assumptions is entirely up to the user, who can try to express them as explicit tests and insert them before the step. For example, the first step of delete-redundant-assignment checks that the current expression is a PROGN statement with successive assignments to the same variable.

POPART does not guarantee correctness or desirability; if a step is incorrect, replay proceeds anyway. Designing a PADDLE development for robustness is therefore a difficult art. It can be especially tricky to make the cursor positioning steps valid over a broad range of contexts. For example, delete-redundant-assignment does not apply to

(PROGN (SETQ X 0) (PRINT "Hello") (SETQ X Y))

Worse, it *does* apply to

(PROGN (SETQ X 0) (SETQ X (F X)))

In general, testing appropriateness is the responsibility of POPART's users, who are free to insert whatever tests of appropriateness they can encode in PADDLE. In this example, making delete-redundant-assignment correct would involve checking that the subexpression bound to the variable program#useless is really safe to eliminate. However, this test cannot readily be expressed in POPART's pattern language, because the semantic, context-sensitive concept of a "redundant assignment statement" cannot be defined syntactically as a nonterminal in a context-free language. A fully robust version of delete-redundant-assignment would require some powerful code analysis, and might be defined more conveniently in terms of a data flow graph representation of the code.

While this example involves a reference that becomes anomalous in new contexts, not all robustness problems in PADDLE developments involve the correspondence problem. For instance, POPART does not automatically test if the purpose of a given step in the development is already satisfied in the new context, in which case replaying the step anyway is liable to cause problems. In this example, if the redundant assignment statement has already been deleted, the Find step will fail, and replay will halt unless the development has been written to take this possibility into account. The user can try to make the development more robust by explicitly testing whether a goal is already satisfied before trying to achieve it, but such tests are not always easy to express in PADDLE.

A POPART user might try to write only correctness preserving commands, but POPART lacks the deductive engine needed to prove correctness. Moreover, such an engine would require much more information about the language it would operate on than the BNF grammar POPART uses to generate the transformation system. POPART allows, but does not enforce, the invocation of external tools to perform such analysis.

In short, POPART's users are responsible for the robustness of the developments they design. When a development is replayed outside the range of situations where it works properly, at best it breaks; at worst, it does something incorrect.

### 5.6. Plan adaptation in POPART

Given a change in the development or the code it transforms, the user is responsible for identifying and repairing the affected portions of the development.

*Detection*: When the development is replayed in the new context, it breaks where commands fail, but this does not necessarily occur at the steps that need to be changed; it might occur later in the development, or not at all, in which case the user must recognize that the result produced by executing the development is inappropriate.

*Localization*: After detecting a violated assumption, the user must figure out which step(s) to change.

*Repair*: The user modifies the development by editing it directly, but can try out a series of commands before splicing it into the development.

*Propagation*: Identifying the assumptions violated by changes in the development is up to the user, although it often helps to replay the modified development to see where it breaks.

Although adapting a development to solve a new problem is up to the user, POPART does have a limited "conditioning" facility for rewriting the current expression to make a pattern match succeed. For example, suppose delete-redundant-assignment is applied to a PROGN expression containing an extra statement, as in

      (PROGN (PRINT "Hello") (SETQ X 1) (SETQ X 2))

To make the Find step succeed, POPART will automatically rewrite the expression as

      (PROGN (PRINT "Hello") (PROGN (SETQ X 1) (SETQ X 2)))

The rewrite is based on the associativity of the PROGN operator, specified by the Kleene-plus construct { program + } in the grammar rule

      progn-form := '( 'PROGN { program + } ')

Unfortunately, expression conditioning in POPART is restricted to this one associativity-based kind of rewrite. A more general facility contemplated at one point would have allowed the user to define a set of transformations to use for conditioning. However, the problem solver that would have chosen which transformations to apply was never implemented. This task can be far from trivial, judging from BAR (Mostow [59, 60]), a means-ends analysis problem solver that rewrites a given expression to match a given pattern using a given set of transformations. In fact even POPART's restricted form of conditioning does not come for free: it buys robustness at the cost of the extra work it takes POPART—or the user—to determine that a pattern can *not* be matched. The more extensive the conditioning, the greater this cost becomes.

The inverse of conditioning is simplification, which enhances robustness by transforming the current expression into a semicanonical form to which subsequent steps are more likely to apply. The user can define a set of simplification rules for POPART to apply whenever possible. Unlike conditioning, simplification does not require sophisticated problem solving, since the rules are applied exhaustively. However, the user must ensure that the rules are correct, that the order in which they are applied does not matter, and that simplification eventually terminates. For example, simplification would fail to terminate if it used the transposition rule

> Match (AND !predicate#1 !predicate#2)
> Replace (AND ! predicate#2 !predicate#1)

## 5.7. Partial reuse in POPART

Since a PADDLE development is represented as a parse tree, one can replay a subplan by starting at a node below the root. Subtrees are easier to reuse if they reposition the cursor from scratch so as to avoid depending on it having been left in the right place by the preceding steps. In the course of creating a development in POPART, the user may reorganize it by reordering subtrees; one might view moving a subtree around in a development as "reusing" it in a new context.

A subtree that makes too many assumptions cannot be replayed in isolation; it is necessary to replay the development starting from the beginning and continuing until a step breaks. However, the subtree can be debugged by saving the state reached just before it applies. This state can then be used as a checkpoint to replay the subtree without starting over from the beginning. This method allows subtrees to be worked on in a different order than they're replayed.

While some pieces of a development may be reusable in other contexts, the user is responsible for identifying them, parameterizing them, and encapsulating them as transformation commands. In fact commands appear to be the normal unit of reuse. Thus PADDLE is not just a representation for design plans, but a language for expressing transformation rules, with POPART its interpreter.

## 5.8. Assessment of POPART

POPART's replay mechanism is syntactic in nature: it blindly executes a sequence of commands without understanding the goals motivating them or the conditions under which they are correct. Rectifying these deficiencies would involve adding a theorem prover to check the correctness of plan steps, formalizing the representation of development goals, and extending the interpreter to understand them. While some of these capabilities might be built on top of POPART, POPART as it exists does not provide them. Consequently, its replay facility, although indispensible for creating developments, is of limited usefulness for design iteration and not sufficiently powerful for design by analogy.

It is important to evaluate POPART in terms of the purpose for which it was evidently designed: providing a representation in which it is possible to express transformational program developments. Viewed as a permissive language for writing transformations, rather than a correctness enforcing language for design plans, PADDLE is considerably more successful. Its built-in parsing, conditioning, and simplification capabilities relieve the user of the considerable effort it would take to program such operations directly in a general-purpose programming language. So do its specialized search, matching, cursor positioning, and edit commands, though they do not always provide the power needed to express transformations without escaping to LISP.

POPART users have constructed developments hundreds of lines long. They have found its interactive edit-apply cycle very useful in this process, together with the ability to directly manipulate the development as a first-class object using the same generic facilities for manipulating base-level programs and specifications. PADDLE's various control constructs, including sequencing, iteration, and conditionality, enhance its ability to capture the goal structure of developments.

However, POPART is severely constrained by several assumptions implicit in its design:

– *POPART must work for any program language, given only its BNF grammar.* While developments can invoke language-specific semantic analysis tools, POPART's tools for parsing, pretty-printing, pattern matching, and editing are generic, and consequently cannot make or exploit strong assumptions about the objects they mainpulate. On the one hand, such code sharing is economical and enhances POPART's SCOPE and EVOLVABILITY by making it easy to extend to other languages. On the other hand, the lowest common denominator approach sacrifices QUALITY and AUTONOMY by making the users responsible for the robustness and appropriateness of the developments they write.

– *Programs and developments are displayed as text.* The same generic grammar-driven pretty-printer is used to display both base-level programs and the meta-level PADDLE developments for transforming them. More specialized

display tools might exploit language-specific features. While it appears feasible
to attach such tools to POPART, they would not share the generic character of
its built-in tools.

 – *Developments operate on a syntactic representation of programs.* Text is a
least common denominator for representing programs; program transformations are much easier to express in terms of a language-specific representation
that makes explicit the program's semantically important properties, like data
flow paths and side-effects, and suppresses irrelevant syntactic details, like the
order of function definitions in a LISP program. Expressing concepts like
"redundant assignment statement" in PADDLE without escaping to LISP appears
unwieldy or impossible. It might be possible to express such a command much
more concisely in a representation like the one used in the MIT programmer's
apprentice (Rich [76]). In fact, POPART is now being integrated into a system
(Baltzer et al. [2–4]) that provides such richer representations.

 – *Design goals are expressed in arbitrary English.* Therefore, POPART cannot
generate plans for achieving them, and must rely on the user to do so.

 – *Users are allowed to edit program developments directly.* Such unrestricted
intervention compromises development integrity, since by editing a step the
user may introduce internal inconsistencies that violate the assumptions on
which other steps depend.

## 6. REDESIGN

The REDESIGN system was created as an experiment to investigate some of the
requirements for an intelligent redesign tool, specifically the kinds of knowledge and inference needed in redesigning a circuit to implement a specification
change (Steinberg and Mitchell [86]). REDESIGN was not itself a tool, and was
only used on a single example, though its techniques were general. Given the
circuit schematic, functional specifications, and design plan for the display
controller in a computer terminal, REDESIGN was given the task of redesigning
the circuit so as to display characters in an italic font. It replayed the design
plan to identify which part of the circuit to modify, and then proposed
modifications for implementing the change. In this article we are interested
mainly in REDESIGN's replay mechanism.

### 6.1. Plan representation in REDESIGN

The representation of a "design plan" in REDESIGN is intended to capture the
knowledge a tool would need about the original design in order to automate or
intelligently assist the redesign process. A design plan in REDESIGN is a rational
reconstruction of the history by which a circuit could have been designed. This
idealized history is based on a top-down decomposition model of design
(Mostow [62]). In this model, a high-level specification is iteratively refined

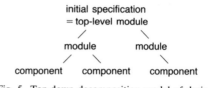

Fig. 5. Top-down decomposition model of design.

into a circuit by decomposing it into successively smaller modules, down to the level of primitive components.

REDESIGN's design plan for a circuit is a tree-like structure with a node for each module, as sketched in Fig. 5. Unlike PADDLE, REDESIGN's design plan representation identifies the goal structure with the decomposition structure. Thus a module represents both a part of the specification and the goal of implementing that part (Mostow [62]).

Figure 6 shows a simplified version of the design plan given in Steinberg and Mitchell [86] for a computer terminal display controller character generator module. The module must input an ASCII character code and output the corresponding pattern of pixels to display, encoded bit-serially. The root module represents the specification for the entire circuit, while the leaf modules are primitive components of the target technology. Each module has input and output ports and a specification describing their required properties, including their functional relationship, relative timing, data type, encoding, and so forth. Each nonprimitive module has one or more submodules, a description of the connections between them, and the name of the rule used to refine the module. The primitive components, plus the wires connecting them, constitute the circuit, and the modules represent the hierarchical goal structure of the design.

Refining modules independently can lead to inconsistencies at the interfaces between them. For example, the character decoder module in Fig. 6 outputs data in parallel, but the character generator is required to output data bit-serially. Such a problem is handled by inserting a "subgoal" module to resolve it, in this case a parallel-to-serial converter.

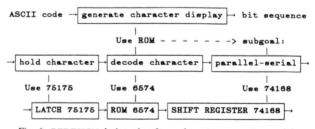

Fig. 6. REDESIGN design plan for a character generator module.

## 6.2. Plan acquisition in REDESIGN

Although a design plan in REDESIGN resembles an idealized design history, it is constructed by hand. In a realistic design tool, the plan would be constructed mechanically as part of the original design process, but REDESIGN was not intended to be a tool.

## 6.3. Plan retrieval in REDESIGN

REDESIGN finesses the retrieval problem in that its task is defined as redesigning a given circuit to satisfy a changed specification; the design plan for the original circuit is one of the givens.

## 6.4. Correspondence in REDESIGN

The top-down decomposition model assumed by REDESIGN greatly simplifies the correspondence problem, because it goes quite far toward inducing a correspondence between the old and new designs.

Given a circuit, its design plan, and a change in its specification, REDESIGN redesigns the circuit to incorporate the change. Consider a module that was originally decomposed into its submodules by some decomposition rule. Redesigning it involves one of three cases:

*Case 1. The module's specification is unchanged.* There is no need to change the module; it can be used as is.

*Case 2. The module's specification has changed, but the rule still applies.* REDESIGN must decide which submodules (and connections) created by the rule correspond to which original ones, so it can decide which submodule needs to be redesigned.

*Case 3. The module's specification has changed and no longer satisfies the rule.* REDESIGN assumes that the module must be redesigned by some means other than replaying its design plan.

Thus the correspondence problem arises only in Case 2 and consists of deciding which submodule specification to change, and how. REDESIGN assumes there is only one such submodule; if not, it complains.

To solve the correspondence problem, REDESIGN uses information about the variable bindings in the rule. To illustrate, consider the hypothetical rule RefineConjunction:

If a module's output specification has the form (AND ?a ?b), refine it into

where ?f outputs ?a, ?g outputs ?b, and ?and is an AND gate.

Consider a simple comparator module whose original specification was

(AND Testing (= In1 In2))

The module has three submodules, connected as follows:

F1 —[AND1]— G1

where F1 outputs Testing, and G1 outputs (= In1 In2).

When they were created, RefineConjunction bound the rule variables ?and, ?f, and ?g to the modules AND1, F1, and G1, respectively.
    Now suppose the original module's specification is changed to

(AND Testing (= StoredData Key)).

This specification still matches the left-hand side of RefineConjunction, so Case 2 holds, and REDESIGN applies RefineConjunction to the module, creating a new set of submodules and connections:

F2 —[AND2]— G2

where F2 outputs Testing, and G2 outputs (= StoredData Key).

REDESIGN's heuristic solution to the correspondence problem assumes that *the submodule bound to each rule variable corresponds to the same submodule as when the rule was originally applied*, even though its specification might be different. In this example, the new submodules F2 and G2 bound to ?f and ?g are assumed to correspond to F1 and G1, respectively. Since F2 outputs the same value as F1, Case 1 applies, and F1 can be used as is. Since G2 must compute (= StoredData Key) rather than (= In1 In2), it must be redesigned. This process applies recursively, continuing until Case 3 is reached.
    REDESIGN's treatment of the three correspondence anomalies described in Section 4.4 can be characterized as follows:

 – An ambiguous reference would mean a rule variable simultaneously bound to more than one module in the new context. REDESIGN's pattern matcher binds a rule variable to at most one module, so this anomaly does not arise.
 – A meaningless reference occurs when the rule used in the original plan step does not apply to the new context, so the bound-to-same-variable heuristic fails to identify modules corresponding to the ones originally bound to the rule variables. When this occurs, REDESIGN assumes the module must be redesigned from scratch.

– A misleading reference means a rule variable bound originally to one module and now to another module that doesn't truly correspond to it. The bound-to-same-variable heuristic permits such anomalies. On the other hand, REDESIGN's assumption that only one module needs to be changed makes such anomalies unlikely, since the other modules must have unchanged specifications. In Section 7.4 we will see what can happen when this assumption is dropped.

## 6.5. Appropriateness in REDESIGN

To analyze how REDESIGN addresses the appropriateness issue, we first identify the class of redesign problems it tackles. Consider the aspects of redesign problems listed in Section 3. How does REDESIGN address each one?

(1) *Functional specification*: REDESIGN is explicitly intended to assist in reimplementing a circuit to meet changes in its functional specification.

(2) *Artifact costs*: The only artifact cost modelled in REDESIGN is circuit delay, which is treated as a constraint. REDESIGN uses a constraint propagation mechanism to assure that timing constraints are satisfied.

(3) *Target medium*: REDESIGN implicitly assumes TTL technology as the target medium; this assumption is built into its circuit representation and repertoire of rules. To redesign a circuit in another technology, e.g. CMOS VLSI with asynchronous logic, it would be necessary to articulate implicit technology-specific assumptions, e.g., that the circuit has no bidirectional signals, and generalize the representation to remove them.

(4) *Environmental criteria*: Not considered in REDESIGN.

(5) *Description requirements*: REDESIGN has no explicit representation of the general design criteria motivating the circuit design and so cannot check if they are still satisfied by replaying the design plan, or if they have changed.

(6) *Description costs*: REDESIGN is not sensitive to the cost of representing or executing the design plan.

(7) *Design resources*: REDESIGN implicitly assumes the circuit must be redesigned using the same catalog of decomposition rules. It does not consider the effect on plan appropriateness of adding, changing, or deleting rules, except insofar as it tests rules to make sure they are still applicable, and it only does that for modules whose specifications have changed.

(8) *Design methodology*: REDESIGN assumes a model of design as top-down decomposition plus constraint propagation.

(9) *Redesign costs*: REDESIGN's built-in policy of adhering as closely as possible to the original design plan reflects an implicit bias toward minimizing redesign effort.

(10) *Previous design plan(s)*: REDESIGN is given a previous design plan to adapt.

In short, REDESIGN handles changes to a circuit's functional specification or timing requirements. Given such a change, to what extent does REDESIGN check that each step of the design plan is still appropriate?

(1) *Executability*: Replaying a design step means applying a decomposition rule to an abstract module; REDESIGN only replays a decomposition rule if it is applicable, which it checks by testing the rule conditions against the module description.

(2) *Correctness*: Unlike POPART's edit commands, REDESIGN's decomposition rules are expected to preserve correctness, except for inconsistencies detected by the CRITTER constraint propagator (Kelly [44]) described in Section 6.6.

(3) *Success*: Applying a decomposition rule is one step towards implementing a module, and enables subsequent steps to finish the job. Thus the step can be considered successful so long as the implementation can be completed by further decompositions. A step is unsuccessful if it creates an unimplementable submodule or overconstrains a module elsewhere in the circuit. When applying a rule, REDESIGN does not try to check a priori whether it might lead to such a dead end.

(4) *Desirability*: The design plan does not represent the original criteria for selecting one decomposition rule over another, and REDESIGN does not check whether these criteria are still in force and satisfied by the same rule. Instead, it implicitly uses a different desirability criterion: minimizing the change to the original design.

Since REDESIGN tests the correctness of every step it replays, and its criterion of desirability is to minimize redesign effort, every syntactically replayable step is appropriate to replay—unless it leads down a garden path. For example, suppose the specification of the comparator in Section 6.4 is changed to

(AND (= Data Key) Testing)

REDESIGN's correspondence heuristic would make it try to implement (= Data Key) as a wire like module F, and Testing as a comparator like module G. Both subplans would fail, causing REDESIGN to give up, since it assumes that only one module needs to be redesigned.

If REDESIGN could not replay a step properly, at worst it would give up or need extra help from the user; it would not design an incorrect circuit.

## 6.6. Plan adaptation in REDESIGN

The main focus of the REDESIGN project is on how to adapt a previous design to meet a change in its functional specification.

*Detetection*: REDESIGN is given a specification change as input.

*Localization*: Given a module with changed functional specifications or timing constraints, REDESIGN checks whether the rule originally used to refine the module still applies, that is, whether the modified specification satisfies the rule's precondition. If not, localization stops at the module, and REDESIGN then generates possible repairs. For example, suppose the specified output of a module changes from

> (AND Testing (= In1 In2))

to

> (AND Testing (= In1 In2) DataReady).

The RefineConjunction rule cannot be replayed, since it only applies to conjunctions of two arguments. When the original rule can be replayed, REDESIGN localizes the change to whichever submodule differs from the corresponding original submodule. The assumption that there is only one such submodule makes it easier to redesign, since it lets REDESIGN assume that the rest of the circuit remains unchanged.

*Repair*: Once REDESIGN has localized the specification change to a module it cannot re-implement by following the original design plan, it uses a form of means-ends analysis to systematically generate candidate patches to the original circuit. To illustrate, consider a module that inputs x and outputs $y = F(x)$:

Suppose the module must be redesigned to output y' instead of y.

REDESIGN uses three basic methods to repair a module whose output specification has changed:

(1) *Convert the module's output.* Insert a module to convert y to y':

(2) *Redesign the module from scratch.* Design a module F' that outputs y' rather than y:

(3) *Export the change.* Change the input x to some x' such that $F(x') = y'$, propagating the specification change upstream:

REDESIGN then recursively redesigns whatever module outputs x to output x′ instead.

In this fashion, REDESIGN generates a set of alternative patches to the design; the user is responsible for selecting and implementing the best one.

In our example, method (1) adds a postprocessor that converts the original output to the new output:

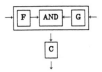

where C inputs (AND Testing (= In1 In2))
and outputs (AND Testing (= In1 In2) DataReady).

The postprocessor C can be implemented simply by gating its input with the DataReady signal, though REDESIGN would leave this decision to the user.

*Propagation*: REDESIGN uses the CRITTER inference engine (Kelly [44]) to check and propagate constraints. CRITTER computes the functional and timing behavior of a module from its submodules and their interconnections, compares it against the module specifications, and deduces consequences for modules elsewhere in the circuit. When the user patches the design, CRITTER propagates the consequences of the patch and detects any constraint violations in the form of conflicts between module behavior and specifications. For instance, suppose a module's output is specified to be serial, but is actually parallel. In principle, such conflicts could be repaired in the same manner as local specification changes. Like POPART's conditioning, the insertion of subgoal modules is a form of means-ends analysis.

### 6.7. Partial reuse in REDESIGN

REDESIGN replays an abstraction of a design plan when it recreates an abstract module without replaying its implementation. Since REDESIGN assumes that all the other modules can be reused without modification, it can only abstract one module in this manner. If this restriction were removed, partial reuse would be much more flexible, since many different subsets of modules could be modified.

### 6.8. Assessment of REDESIGN

REDESIGN was intended as an experimental vehicle, not as a redesign tool. For instance, its design plan was constructed by hand as a simulated history of a hypothetical original design process. A practical tool would capture this history automatically.

The top-down decomposition model of design underlying REDESIGN proved to be a mixed blessing. On the one hand, top-down decomposition is more restrictive than the general transformational paradigm embodied in POPART (Mostow [62]). On the other hand, it simplified or eliminated many of the difficulties that plagued POPART, such as the correspondence problem.

REDESIGN provided considerably more support for replay than POPART does, thanks to its correctness preserving rules, domain-specific knowledge, and CRITTER's inference capabilities. However, REDESIGN did not represent the motivations underlying the original design, worry about the desirability of the redesign, or try to handle changes in aspects of the original design problem other than functional specification and timing constraints. It variously ignored these aspects, left them to the user, or addressed them based on implicit and not altogether realistic assumptions, namely:

– *The implicit criterion of desirability is to minimize the amount of redesign.* This assumption trades QUALITY for EFFICIENCY and AUTONOMY.

– *The specification change can be implemented by redesigning a single module.* Thus constraints can be propagated based on the assumption that other modules remain unchanged.

Despite these and other deficiencies discussed above, REDESIGN succeeded in its objective of representing design plans well enough to help automate redesign. Although this representation was devised to encode the knowledge needed for redesign, since then it has proved useful for the initial design process as well, as we shall now see.

## 7. BOGART

BOGART (Mostow and Barley [66]) is a replay mechanism built on top of the VEXED (Mitchell et al. [57], Steinberg [84, 85]) circuit design system.[2]

### 7.0.1. *VEXED*

Like REDESIGN, VEXED is based on a model of design as top-down decomposition plus constraint propagation. The initial specification is represented as an abstract module to be implemented. At each point, the user selects which module to refine next; VEXED displays a menu of applicable decomposition rules; the user selects one; and VEXED applies the selected rule, decomposing the module into its submodules and interconnections. VEXED then uses CRITTER (the same constraint propagator used in REDESIGN) to propagate any

---

[2] The name BOGART refers to the famous line "Play it again, Sam" associated with the film *Casablanca*.

constraints added by the decomposition step, and the cycle continues until the design is complete.

Unlike REDESIGN, VEXED does not at present use subgoal modules; its decomposition rules are written so as to make each module conform fully to its specification. This strategy enhances design QUALITY and AUTONOMY at the cost of EFFICIENCY: it eliminates the need for patches, simplifies the representation of design plans, and reduces the amount of user intervention by eliminating inconsistent design choices before they can be chosen, but forces CRITTER to propagate many more constraints. When CRITTER does detect an inconsistency, which signals an overconstrained design, the user is expected to retract the decision that led to it. At any point the user can backtrack to an earlier state of the design to revise the specification or pursue an alternative implementation strategy.

### 7.0.2. LEAP

A user who doesn't like any of the decomposition rules applicable to a module can elect instead to refine it by hand, using VEXED's graphic circuit editor. The manual decomposition step is an opportunity for VEXED's learning apprentice, named LEAP (Mitchell et al. [55]), to learn a new decomposition rule. LEAP first invokes CRITTER to verify the manual step, and then generalizes the proof into a new, correctness preserving decomposition rule (Mahadevan [51], Mitchell et al. [54]).

### 7.0.3. Experience with BOGART

BOGART is arguably the first implementation of derivational analogy in a non-toy problem domain to be used productively other than by its developers. BOGART's functionality overlaps substantially with REDESIGN's; it can be considered a partial reimplementation of REDESIGN but is integrated into VEXED, which provides the interactive design-from-scratch capabilities lacking in REDESIGN. VEXED and BOGART have been used by students in a VLSI course to design small circuits. BOGART's purpose is to reduce the amount of user intervention required in VEXED, and it has demonstrably achieved this purpose in its trial by students. Uses for replay in BOGART include:

– *Structure copying*: replicating a module by replaying its design plan.
– *Design by analogy*: adapting a module by replaying part of its design plan.
– *Design iteration*: revising an early implementation decision and replaying subsequent decisions.
– *Design exploration*: comparing alternatives at a decision point by trying one; making additional decisions to drive the design down to where the consequences of the chosen alternative can be evaluated; backtracking to the decision point; trying another alternative; finding its consequences by replaying the same subsequent decisions; and finally choosing among the alternatives based on the results they lead to.

## 7.0.4. *MEET*

VEXED is factored into a domain-specific knowledge base and a generic shell, dubbed EVEXED for "empty VEXED" (analogous to EMYCIN). EVEXED, which includes BOGART, CRITTER, and LEAP, is based on the model of design as top-down decomposition plus constraint propagation; thus it is more specialized than POPART, which allows arbitrary transformations, and whose knowledge base (at least the part required by POPART) consists solely of a BNF grammar for the language being manipulated. VEXED's knowledge base consists of several dozen circuit decomposition rules and the circuit domain theory used in CRITTER and LEAP.

By replacing VEXED's circuit design knowledge base with a mechanical engineering knowledge base, a mechanical design system called MEET has been constructed (Langrana et al. [49], Mostow et al. [69]). MEET designs rotational power transmissions consisting of gears, belts, shafts, and pulleys. This task was selected precisely because of its similarity to circuit design. Other tasks, such as designing individual gears, are less amenable to top-down decomposition. In fact MEET invokes a separate program, named DPMED, to design the gears.

MEET inherits EVEXED's generic facilities, including BOGART. Although MEET is not yet sufficiently developed to conduct extensive experiments, BOGART has successfully replayed a sample MEET design plan, including the calls to DPMED.

## 7.1. Plan representation in BOGART

The VEXED design plans replayed by BOGART use essentially the same representation as REDESIGN, but have no subgoal modules. Figure 7, taken from Mostow and Barley [66], shows how BOGART displays the design plan for a simple comparator. Each node in black represents a decomposition step and is labeled with the name of the rule used in the step. The other nodes represent modules. The leaves represent the primitive components of the comparator circuit. The curved boundaries were added by hand to show how much of the plan BOGART was able to replay for two similar problems involving a content-addressable memory cell. In one case it replayed everything from the root down to the double boundary, while in the other case it got down to the triple boundary.

The display omits additional details encoded in the design plan. Most of this information is the same as in REDESIGN, such as the bindings of the rule parameters for each step. However, the design plan also includes the order in which the plan steps were originally performed. This information, partly lost in the tree structure, is needed to refine modules in the proper order. Refining a module constrains the possible implementations of modules connected to it, and VEXED propagates these constraints from one module to another. Some of

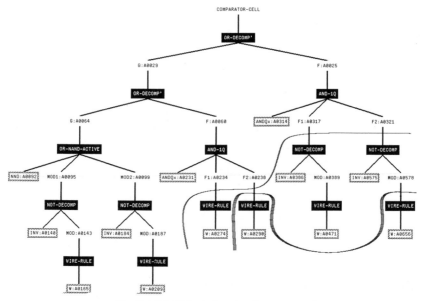

Fig. 7. BOGART's design plan for a comparator.

the rules are written in such a way that they do not become applicable until such constraint propagation has taken place. Thus recording the order of rule application, and replaying the steps in the same order, is a simple way to preserve the logical dependencies implicit in that order. A more sophisticated representation would represent such dependencies explicitly, as in DONTE (Tong [90, 91]).

VEXED design plans cannot represent alternative design paths; they are pure AND trees rather than AND/OR trees, let alone more complex control structures like PADDLE developments.

## 7.2. Plan acquisition in VEXED

The design plans replayed by BOGART are recorded automatically by VEXED. A design plan contains a node for each module. When the module is refined, the node is annotated with the name of the decomposition rule and the values of its parameters, and connected to a new child node for each submodule.

When the user backtracks to an earlier state of the design, any steps taken since then are retracted from the design and removed from the plan. Thus the plan *idealizes* the actual design history (Mostow [62]) by omitting dead ends. However, before backtracking, the user can save the current design plan to replay later.

When the user refines a module by hand, LEAP generalizes the decomposition step into a new rule. The manual step can then be recorded in the design

plan as if it had been performed by the rule.[3] This application of LEAP neatly
avoids the correspondence and appropriateness issues that arise when design
steps are represented at too low a level of detail to replay in a new context.

### 7.3. Plan retrieval in BOGART

Like POPART, BOGART makes the user retrieve the plan to replay, although
VEXED's circuit browsing facilities help somewhat in finding the relevant
subplan to replay (see Section 7.7). We expect that BOGART will mostly be
used for design iteration, at least until there is a library of design plans rich
enough to be useful and a population of users fluent enough to use them.

BOGART's capability for partial reuse of a design plan (see Section 7.7)
complicates the retrieval problem. Not only can BOGART stop replaying a plan
before reaching its leaves, it can also replay a subplan by starting at a node
below the root. One can imagine a retrieval scheme that rates the relevance of
each stored design plan based on how much of it can be replayed. However,
such a scheme appears almost as expensive as trying to replay every plan and
subplan, which would be prohibitive for a large catalog of plans.

### 7.4. Correspondence in BOGART

BOGART's correspondence finding method is similar to REDESIGN's in that it
identifies old and new modules if they are bound to the same rule variable.
However, REDESIGN only replays steps for modules whose specifications have
changed, while BOGART reimplements modules even if their specifications are
identical to the original. The reason for the difference is that the product of
REDESIGN is just a *plan* for redesigning the circuit, while BOGART must
produce the actual design. Also, while REDESIGN assumes that the difference
between the old and new specifications can be localized to a single module,
BOGART makes no such assumption.

For example, consider the hypothetical RefineConjunction step in the design
plan sketched in Fig. 8. The step refines a module whose output is specified to
be

(AND Testing (= Data Key))

The step uses the rule RefineConjunction, introduced in Section 6.4, to
decompose the module into

where F1 outputs Testing, and G1 outputs (= Data Key).

---

[3] At present this effect is achieved a bit awkwardly by retracting the manual step and applying
the learned rule.

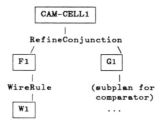

Fig. 8. Sketch of design plan for a content-addressable memory cell.

(Actual VEXED rules and modules are considerably more complicated; this example is deliberately simplified for clarity.)

VEXED rule conditions are written in a pattern language interpreted by a pattern matcher. To apply RefineConjunction to the example, VEXED matches the rule's left-hand pattern (AND ?a ?b) against the output specification, binding ?a to the input Test and ?b to the subexpression (= Data Key). The rule then refines the module into a submodule F1 that outputs Testing, a submodule G1 that computes (= Data Key), and an AND gate that conjoins the submodule outputs. RefineConjunction binds ?f to F1, ?g to G1, and ?and to the AND gate. Subsequent steps in the design plan refine F1 into a simple wire and G1 into a comparator.

Suppose this design step is replayed on a new module whose output specification is

(AND Testing (= Data[i] Key))

BOGART will bind ?a to Testing and ?b to (= Data[i] Key) and create the following structure, binding ?f to F2 and ?g to G2:

where F2 outputs Testing, and G2 outputs (= Data[i] Key).

Since the same rule variable ?f is bound to F1 in the original step and to F2 in the replayed step, BOGART assumes that F2 corresponds to F1, and it implements F2 as a wire using the same subplan used to implement F1. Similarly, it assumes that G2 corresponds to G1, and implements G2 as a comparator by replaying the subplan for G1.

As in REDESIGN, the robustness of a decomposition step in BOGART is determined by how its decomposition rule is written. For a manual step, robustness depends on how general a rule LEAP can learn from it. The robustness of a VEXED rule depends on the generality of its left-hand side and the appropriateness of its right-hand side for the cases where the left-hand side is satisfied.

Suppose the rule is the RefineConjunction rule described earlier. Let's see what happens if the module's output specification (AND Testing (= Data Key)) is changed by:

– *Adding an argument*: (AND Testing (= Data Key) InputReady). RefineConjunction no longer applies, since it only works for conjunctions of two arguments. A more robust rule would work for a conjunction of any number of arguments, but couldn't use the fixed names ?a and ?b for the arguments. The increased complexity of such a rule illustrates the tradeoff between concreteness and robustness. In fact, VEXED's actual rules for decomposing conjunctions handle this case because they work recursively, something like this:

A module to compute (AND ?a1 ... ?an) can be refined into

```
   ┌───┐   ┌─────┐   ┌───┐
 →─┤ A ├─┤ AND ├─┤ B ├─
   └───┘   └─────┘   └───┘
             ↓
```

where A outputs ?a1 and B outputs (AND ?a2 ... ?an)

– *Extracting a subexpression*: (= Data Key). The design step would no longer apply and replay would halt. A smarter replay facility would realize that it could skip the RefineConjunction step and replay the subplan for implementing the comparator submodule.

– *Embedding the expression*: (OR WildCard (AND Testing (= Data Key))). Again, the design step would no longer apply and replay would stop. A more robust replay mechanism could insert a design step to handle the conjunction, and replay the original plan to implement the embedded expression.

– *Changing the function*: (OR Testing (= Data Key)). RefineConjunction no longer applies here, since it only works for conjunctions. A more general-RefineCombination rule would allow other functions:

A module whose output has the form (?F ?a ?b)
can be decomposed into

```
   ┌───┐   ┌───┐   ┌───┐
 →─┤ A ├─┤ F ├─┤ B ├─
   └───┘   └───┘   └───┘
             ↓
```

where A outputs ?a, B outputs ?b and F computes ?F.

– *Transposing arguments*: (AND (= Data Key) Testing). RefineConjunction would still apply, but it would bind ?a to (= Data Key) and ?b to Testing and create the following structure, binding ?f to F3 and ?g to G3:

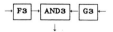

where F3 outputs (= Data Key), and G3 outputs Testing.

Replay would subsequently fail when, following the next steps in the design plan, BOGART tried to implement submodule F3 as a wire and submodule G3 as a comparator. Since the same rule variable ?f is bound to F1 in the original step and F3 in the replayed step, BOGART would assume that F3 corresponded to F1, and try to implement F3 as a wire using the same subplan used to implement F1. Similarly, it would assume that G3 corresponded to G1, and try to implement G3 as a comparator by replaying the subplan for G1. Both subplans fail in the new context. Obviously it should be the other way around: F3 should be implemented as a comparator, and G3 as a wire. The difficulty is caused by the simplistic assumption of correspondence between modules bound to the same rule variable, which ignores how the modules are implemented.

– *Relaxing the one-to-one correspondence between old and new plans*: (AND (= Data1 Key1) (= Data2 Key2)). RefineConjunction would still apply, binding ?a to (= Data1 Key1) and ?b to (= Data2 Key2). BOGART would try unsuccessfully to implement the first conjunct as a wire by replaying the plan for submodule F1, when in fact it would make more sense to implement both conjuncts as comparators by using the subplan for G1 twice and skipping the subplan for submodule F1 altogether. This example shows how correspondence is really a kind of plan retrieval: given a module to refine, find an appropriate subplan to replay.

The "bound-to-same-variable" correspondence heuristic is more likely to fail in BOGART, where any number of modules may differ from the ones in the original design plan, than in REDESIGN, where only one module can be modified. This heuristic could be strengthened by testing whether the specifications on a new module satisfy at least some preconditions of the design plan used to implement the old module it allegedly corresponds to Barley [7]. In the examples above, such a test would avoid trying to implement a comparator as a wire, or vice versa. In Section 8.4 we shall see how this idea is used in ARGO.

BOGART's treatment of the three correspondence anomalies described in Section 4.4 resembles REDESIGN's, with a few differences:

– An ambiguous reference would mean a rule variable simultaneously bound to more than one module in the new context. VEXED's pattern matcher binds a rule variable to at most one module, so this anomaly does not arise.

– A meaningless reference occurs when the rule used in the original plan step does not apply to the new context, so the bound-to-same-variable heuristic fails to identify modules corresponding to the ones originally bound to the rule variables.[4] When the heuristic fails in this way, BOGART simply refrains from replaying the step, though it continues replaying the other branches of the plan.

 – A misleading reference means a rule variable bound originally to one module and now to another module that doesn't truly correspond to it. BOGART's simple correspondence heuristic permits such anomalies.

### 7.5. Appropriateness in BOGART

The discussion in Section 6.5 about how REDESIGN treats the appropriateness problem applies to BOGART as well, with minor differences.

Like REDESIGN, BOGART tests the precondition of each step before replaying it. Thus BOGART guarantees that a replayed step is correct.[5] However, a replayed step is not necessarily successful, since it may lead to a dead end. Moreover, unlike REDESIGN, BOGART cannot assume that any step is desirable to replay provided it leads to a solution. A BOGART user may demand a good solution, not just a quick one. Lacking a representation of what constitutes a good solution, BOGART cannot guarantee that its behavior is desirable, only that it's correct.

Besides changes in functional specification and timing requirements, BOGART supports changes in implementation strategy. However, the changes and criteria motivating such changes are left implicit, and the user is responsible for identifying which steps to replay, though BOGART still tests their correctness first. Also, while REDESIGN assumes TTL technology as a target, VEXED's current rule base uses NMOS.

### 7.6. Plan adaptation in BOGART

Adaptation in BOGART consists of modifying a design plan that cannot be completely replayed to implement a module.

*Detection*: The user is responsible for detecting that a module needs to be redesigned, and for identifying decisions that rely on obsolete assumptions, though BOGART does detect design steps that are no longer correct.

*Localization*: By replaying as much of a design plan as possible, BOGART effectively localizes specification and timing changes to the modules that no longer satisfy the rules used to decompose the corresponding original modules. BOGART eliminates REDESIGN's assumption that there is only one such module.

---

[4] The same problem can occur if the rule does apply, but no longer binds the same variables; a VEXED rule doesn't necessarily bind the same set of variables every time it's applied.

[5] As correct as VEXED's rules and CRITTER, that is.

*Repair*: Unlike REDESIGN, BOGART does not use means-ends analysis to generate candidate patches to the design plan. When replay terminates, the user must complete whatever modules remain unimplemented, but can do so using any combination of manual decomposition, VEXED decomposition rules, and replaying other (sub)plans.

*Propagation*: VEXED uses a revised version of REDESIGN's constraint propagator CRITTER. After BOGART replays each step of a design plan, it pauses to let CRITTER perform constraint propagation, just as if the step had been chosen by the VEXED user. One approach to making BOGART more efficient would be to cache the results of the original constraint propagation, but this would require some dependency maintenance to handle cases where those results are invalidated by changes in the context or by revised decisions.

### 7.7. Partial reuse in BOGART

BOGART can replay any subtree of a design plan, including "abstract" subtrees that start at a nonroot and stop short of the leaves. The user specifies which subtree to replay by using the mouse to select its root and leaves from a graphic display like the one in Fig. 7; the default is the entire design plan. BOGART replays as much of the subtree as it can, but replays a step only if its precondition is still satisfied. If not, BOGART skips the branches beneath the step, but continues replaying other branches, and tries the step again later in case intervening steps have fulfilled its precondition.

Partial reuse is limited by representing design plans as trees. Design involves decisions about various properties of a module, such as its output value, timing, and data encoding. When these decisions are sufficiently independent to be made in more than one order, a strictly hierarchical design plan representation imposes an arbitrary order on them. If one decision is no longer applicable, replay stops without trying to replay subsequent decisions, even though they might still be suitable. Since BOGART can't "skip over" the first decision to replay others further down in the tree, the amount of the design plan it can replay is sensitive to the arbitrary order imposed by the hierarchical representation.

### 7.8. Assessment of BOGART

Thanks to the context in which it is used, BOGART finesses many of the problems listed in Section 4. BOGART relies on VEXED to help handle plan acquisition, on LEAP to generalize manual decomposition steps into replayable rules, on CRITTER to test preconditions and propagate constraints affected by design changes, and on the user to select the subplan(s) to replay and to complete the partial design that may result.

Although building on top of VEXED made it possible to implement BOGART quickly, VEXED also imposes some limitations on BOGART. In particular,

VEXED's failure to capture information about the rationales for design steps limits BOGART's robustness by preventing it from testing whether those steps are still desirable. Also, VEXED inherits several restrictions from REDESIGN:

– *Design is modeled as top-down decomposition plus constraint propagation.* This model is already proving inadequate. In particular, some VEXED rules cross module boundaries, but BOGART cannot replay them. For example, the GetSignal rule implements a computation by "stealing" its result from a module that computes it elsewhere in the circuit. Similarly, the Combine rule merges one module with another. Replaying such rules would require finding the corresponding module in a new circuit.

– *The design history is represented as a tree.* This model imposes an arbitrary ordering on logically independent design decisions about the same module.

– *Module decompositon is implemented by a few rules whose left-hand sides are variabilized patterns syntactically matched against a fixed list of features.* Comparison with POPART makes this restriction seem unrealistic for high-level software design, where the set of possible decompositions seems too rich to capture in a few rules, and an adequate list of features has not been identified. Perhaps the restriction will become more realistic for software design when we understand it better, or for specialized, well-studied types of software design, for example, divide-and-conquer algorithms (Kant [37], Smith [80], Smith et al. [81], Steier [83]).

Despite BOGART's limitations, experience with its use has confirmed our belief that even a simple replay mechanism can automate many of the repetitive aspects of design, freeing designers to concentrate on the design problem itself.

## 8. ARGO

The ARGO project is an attempt "to develop a robust and domain-independent system for applying analogical reasoning to the design process" (Huhns and Acosta [36]). In particular, it is exploring how analogical learning can increase EFFICIENCY in design problem solving.

ARGO builds on the ideas of REDESIGN and VEXED, but (unlike BOGART) uses none of the same code. Like VEXED, ARGO is based on a model of design that starts with a functional specification and performs successive top-down refinements. The initial implementation of ARGO (Acosta et al. [1]) synthesized digital circuits as complex as a 273-transistor barrel shifter, using refinement rules implemented directly in LISP. The rules were written so as to make it feasible to search for a design automatically, without requiring the user to choose the sequence of rules to apply. With some manual assistance, a design plan could be constructed and compiled into a macro-rule, which then reduced the amount of search needed to implement similar specifications.

The reimplemented version of ARGO discussed below resembles VEXED insofar as it is structured as a generic design system architecture that supports learning and analogy. ARGO uses the knowledge representation, inference mechanisms, and truth maintenance system provided by the PROTEUS expert system tool (Petrie et al. [74]). ARGO-V is an application of ARGO to VLSI design, and incorporates a knowledge base of rules, assertions, and frames. ARGO-V refines specifications into digital circuits. Huhns and Acosta [36] describe its synthesis of a content-addressable memory cell similar to the example in Mitchell et al. [57] and Mostow and Barley [66]. The discussion below is based on this description, but ARGO continues to evolve. In this article we are concerned with its mechanisms for analogical reasoning. We will use "ARGO" to refer to both the ARGO environment and the ARGO-V application.

ARGO's design cycle is much like VEXED's, but can operate either interactively or automatically, and does not separate the decision of which module to refine from the decision of how to refine it. At each step, ARGO computes the conflict set of all maximally specific refinement rule instances that apply anywhere in the current design state. ARGO further prunes the conflict set based on priorities assigned to the rules and on preferences of the form (PREFER ruleA ruleB) asserted by the user. The user selects which action(s) in the conflict set to fire; alternatively, ARGO can make an arbitrary choice based on the order in which the rules were defined. The user can intervene to assert new facts, rules, or preferences, causing ARGO to recompute the conflict set. The user can also contradict an undesired assertion, causing ARGO to invoke dependency-directed backtracking. As in BOGART, retracted steps are omitted from the plan, but ARGO's truth maintenance is more flexible than chronological backtracking. In any case, the conflict set is recomputed and the cycle repeats.

Once a design is completed and judged acceptable by the user, ARGO compiles its design plan into a reusable macro-rule and the preconditions for applying it. Like a chunk in SOAR (Laird et al. [48]), the macro-rule captures the net effect of applying all the rules in the plan. Since a macro-rule omits steps that add assertions retracted by later steps, it is somewhat faster than applying the rules individually. More importantly, it shortcuts the search needed to find the original sequence of rules.

## 8.1. Plan representation in ARGO

A design in ARGO is represented as a database of assertions stored as slots of frames in a truth maintenance system. A module is represented as a collection of assertions describing its specification, components, interconnections, and so forth, each with a belief status of IN or OUT supported by a set of justifications. Refinement steps are performed by rules. A rule's left-hand side (antecedent) is a set of parameterized assertions and is satisfied if it unifies with assertions in

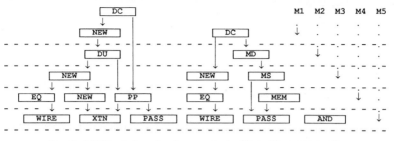

Fig. 9. ARGO's design plan for a content-addressable memory cell.

the database. A rule's right-hand side (consequent) adds new assertions and may retract old ones by moving them OUT in the truth maintenance system. Unlike BOGART, ARGO is not restricted to a hierarchical decomposition structure, since a rule may operate on more than one module.

As Fig. 9 shows, ARGO represents a design plan as an acyclic graph of dependencies among steps (instantiated rules). If one step adds an assertion that is used to satisfy the left-hand side of another, the second step depends on the first. (A finer-grained representation would distinguish the dependencies between individual assertions, as in DONTE (Tong [91]).) The dependency graph is not necessarily a tree, since one step can depend on several others. Nor is it necessarily connected, since the original design problem may contain independently solvable subproblems. In fact, the graph isn't even a separate data structure; it is implicitly represented by the justifications maintained by the truth maintenance system.

## 8.2. Plan acquisition in ARGO

ARGO uses explanation-based generalization (Mitchell et al. [54], Liuh and Huhns [50]) to compile dependency graphs into macro-rules in the same representation as its refinement rules, much as STRIPS did. A design plan is replayed by executing the corresponding macro-rule. For example, the design plan in Fig. 9 is compiled into rule M5.

The macro-rule learned from a complete design plan only applies when the plan can be replayed in its entirety, but a design plan may be useful even if it can be replayed only in part, as long as doing so leads toward an acceptable design. ARGO therefore also creates several increasingly abstract versions of an N-level design plan by dropping the leaves, then the next level, and so forth. A leaf is a set (rule instance) on which no other steps depend; typically it instantiates a library component. The more abstract a plan, the more often it can be replayed in its entirety, but the less it accomplishes. As Fig. 9 shows, rather than adopt a fixed tradeoff between these two considerations, ARGO creates macro-rules for each level of abstraction—but not for every possible abstraction of the plan, of which there are combinatorially many. This syntactic heuristic provides a domain-independent compromise between EFFICIENCY and SCOPE, as discussed in Section 4.7.

### 8.3. Plan retrieval in ARGO

At the start of each design cycle, ARGO finds all maximally specific rules and macro-rules applicable to the current design. A rule is applicable if its antecedent (left-hand side) matches (unifies with) assertions in the database. Rule 1 is considered an abstraction of (i.e., less specific than) rule 2 if its antecedent and consequent are weaker, that is, if rule 2's antecedent implies rule 1's antecedent and rule 2's consequent implies rule 1's consequent. For example, in Fig. 9, rule M1 is an abstraction of rule M2, and so forth.

Fortunately, ARGO does not have to test the preconditions of all the rules, since they are partially ordered by this static abstraction relation. By testing the most abstract rules first, ARGO can avoid testing some of the more specific ones. Thus if M1 is inapplicable, so is M2, and it doesn't have to be tested.

To select which rule to fire, ARGO uses several additional mechanisms, including rule priority classes, static rule ordering, and user-asserted preferences. Since none of these mechanisms distinguishes among multiple instantiations of the same rule, ARGO chooses one arbitrarily (in automatic mode) or makes the user choose (in interactive mode).

### 8.4. Correspondence in ARGO

For ARGO, the correspondence problem consists of binding the parameters of a macro-rule to objects in a new design problem. A macro-rule is retrieved if its preconditions match the specification of a new problem. ARGO's matching process finds all consistent sets of bindings for the parameters used in the macro-rule. For each set of bindings, ARGO constructs a separate rule instantiation to include in the conflict set.

ARGO's treatment of the three correspondence anomalies described in Section 4.4 can be characterized as follows:

– An ambiguous reference occurs when a macro-rule has more than one consistent set of bindings. Unlike BOGART, ARGO doesn't try to guess which object a parameter is intended to correspond to. In fact, applying the macro-rule to the same example from which it was learned is not guaranteed to recreate the same design. On the other hand, the object is guaranteed to satisfy all the constraints imposed by the design plan captured in the macro-rule. The more abstract the design plan from which the macro-rule was compiled, the fewer constraints it places on the bindings for a given parameter, the more ambiguous the reference becomes, and the likelier that ARGO will choose a different object than the one intended by the user.

– A meaningless reference would mean a rule parameter that violated one or more preconditions. Since the parameter bindings in a retrieved rule instance are guaranteed to satisfy the rule's preconditions, this problem does not arise.

– A misleading reference occurs when a parameter has only one binding, but it doesn't correspond to the object it was bound to originally. Since the original object satisfies all the constraints compiled into the macro-rule, this case should not arise unless the original rules left the relevant constraint(s) implicit.

As in the other systems, the robustness of replay in ARGO depends on how generally the rules are written. A reference may be misinterpreted if a constraint on a parameter is omitted from a rule. Also, while ARGO allows users to assert preferences among rules, they are not compiled into the macro-rules and anyway do not discriminate among multiple instantiations of the same rule.

## 8.5. Appropriateness in ARGO

To see how ARGO addresses the issue of appropriateness, we analyze its sensitivity to each aspect of redesign listed in Section 3.

(1) *Functional specification*: ARGO is intended to implement one functional specification by analogy to the implementation of another.

(2) *Artifact costs*: Like VEXED, ARGO-V treats timing goals as constraints included in the specification.

(3) *Target medium*: ARGO-V's current knowledge base assumes CMOS technology, but (unlike VEXED) represents this assumption explicitly by assert-ing CMOS as the value of an attribute named VHDL-PACKAGE. In principle, if each rule specific to CMOS were tagged as such, macro-rules that used them would automatically inherit the same tag, and would be moved OUT if the target technology changed.

(4) *Environmental criteria*: Like the other systems, ARGO does not consider environmental criteria not captured in the functional specification.

(5) *Description requirements*: ARGO assumes a fixed plan representation and is not sensitive to criteria concerning the form of the design plan itself.

(6) *Description costs*: ARGO ignores the costs of storing and using design plans, except insofar as its heuristic for which abstractions to store incorporates a fixed, domain-independent tradeoff between EFFICIENCY and flexibility of partial reuse (SCOPE).

(7) *Design resources*: If a rule is marked as invalid, ARGO's truth main-tenance mechanism automatically invalidates all macro-rules that depend on it.

(8) *Design methodology*: ARGO's model of top-down design is less restrictive than BOGART's, and largely implicit in its rules. A rule can operate on multiple modules.

(9) *Design costs*: ARGO incorporates an implicit bias toward reducing the

amount of search required to solve design problems similar to the ones solved previously.

(10) *Previous design plan(s)*: ARGO (or the user) must select from a library of macro-rules compiled from previous design plans and integrated with its catalog of rules.

Like REDESIGN and BOGART, then, ARGO is sensitive to differences in functional specification and timing constraints between the original and new design problems. However, it is somewhat better at checking the appropriateness of replaying a given step in light of such differences:

– *Executability*: Because the precondition of each step in the design plan is included in the macro-rule compiled from it, testing the preconditions of the macro-rule ensures that the step is executable.

– *Correctness*: As in BOGART, replay in ARGO is as correct as its rules. Unlike BOGART, which uses constraint propagation to prevent inconsistency, ARGO uses unification, which is a weaker form of inference.

– *Success*: Since ARGO tests the *entire* precondition of the macro-rule for a design plan, in effect it does not start to replay it unless it can replay every step in the plan. In contrast, BOGART may replay one step in a plan without being able to replay the next one. Thus ARGO provides somewhat better assurance that a replayed step won't lead to a dead end. However, neither system guarantees that the result of replay can be extended into a complete design.

– *Desirability*: As far as design goals other than functional specification and timing are concerned, the issue of appropriateness is somewhat murky. ARGO is only sensitive to such goals to the meager extent that they are captured in the user-defined rule preferences used to select among alternative actions in the conflict set, and these preferences are not compiled into the macro-rules. ARGO assumes that macro-rules are compiled from desirable solutions to design problems. It is therefore likely, but not guaranteed, that a macro-rule will lead toward a desirable solution for problems sufficiently similar to satisfy its preconditions. The likelihood diminishes for abstract macro-rules, which can apply to less similar problems.

### 8.6. Adaptation in ARGO

ARGO does not allow the modification of a macro-rule to fit a new problem. However, it achieves a similar effect by applying a macro-rule formed from an abstraction of the original design plan, and then searching for a sequence of rules to complete the design. This view yields the following analysis:

*Detection*: If a step in a design plan does not apply to a new problem, the preconditions of the macro-rule compiled from the plan will be violated. For example, if the XTN step in Fig. 9 does not apply, the precondition of macro-rule M5 will not be satisfied.

*Localization*: ARGO coarsely localizes the problematic step by retrieving the least abstract macro-rule that omits it. For example, retrieving M4 instead of M5 eliminates the XTN step, but also the five other steps at that level.

*Repair*: The parts of the original plan omitted from the abstract macro-rule are "repaired" by search. ARGO does not yet fully automate this search, but its predecessor did (Acosta et al. [1]). ARGO applies its rules, forward-chaining until quiescence. In this case it would need to find a substitute for XTN, and rediscover the other five steps. At this point the user is responsible for evaluating the appropriateness of the design and deciding which aspect(s) of the design to contradict.

*Propagation*: When a contradiction is detected by ARGO or asserted by the user, consistency is restored by retracting the assertion(s) responsible for the contradiction. ARGO lets the user choose which assertion(s) to retract; alternatively, it chooses the one(s) with the fewest other assertions depending on it. For instance, ARGO would rather retract an EQ step on which one other step depends, than a DU step on which more than one step depends. This domain-independent heuristic minimizes the change to the database.

## 8.7. Partial reuse in ARGO

Unlike BOGART, ARGO assumes that useful levels of abstraction can be determined a priori. ARGO performs plan abstraction in the context of the original design, without benefit of the additional information available at replay time. Thus ARGO sacrifices BOGART's flexibility of being able to replay any abstract subtree of a design plan.

ARGO retrieves a macro-rule only if all its preconditions are satisfied, and replays it only on an inflexible all-or-none basis. However, the formation of multiple macro-rules in effect allows a plan to be replayed down to any level of detail.

ARGO does not replay subplans of plans whose top-level steps are not applicable. For large designs, such subplans are likely to be reusable more often than the top-level plan: the top-level plan is generally only used once in a design, whereas the same subplan may be used to implement several similar modules. Presumably one could extend ARGO to create abstractions of the subplans at each level, but a plan may have many subplans, each of which has several possible levels of abstraction, and it is not clear how to avoid computing and storing a combinatorial number of macro-rules. One possibility is to identify connected subgraphs corresponding to independent subproblems.

ARGO's nonhierarchical plan representation would make ARGO more flexible than BOGART if the user were allowed to replay any "coherent" subgraph, that is, one that doesn't "skip over" functional dependencies in the original plan. However, ARGO uses the same macro-rule representation for both retrieval and replay. Partial reuse would need to operate on the original design plan representation, not just the compiled macro-rule.

## 8.8. Assessment of ARGO

ARGO appears to be the most complete system to date for design by derivational analogy. It uses dependency maintenance, a priori abstraction, explanation-based generalization, and search to provide at least a first-order solution to each of the problems discussed in this article. In particular, it uses abstract macro-rules to address the problems of plan acquisition, retrieval, correspondence, and appropriateness, based on the fact that a macro-rule whose preconditions are satisfied is guaranteed by EBG to behave like the (presumably correctness preserving) rules from which it was constructed. ARGO's predecessor (Acosta et al. [1]) demonstrated that such macro-rules can be used to speed up the search for a design.

ARGO's success is limited by several underlying assumptions, some of which characterize the other systems as well:

– *The original design plan is a good one.* Such an assumption is certainly not safe in BOGART, whose student users are far from expert. A design system that uses examples collected from its users should have some way to validate them. Moreover, ARGO treats the original example as prototypical of a class of design problems. If the problem or its solution are atypical, they may not be worth learning.

– *If a new problem resembles the original one enough to satisfy the preconditions of its design plan, the plan will lead toward a similarly good solution for the new problem.* The more abstract the plan, the more dubious this assumption. Even the entire original plan may produce a poor design if the new problem's design goals differ from those left implicit in the plan. In particular, the preconditions do not include the user-asserted preferences used to guide construction of the original design plan.

– *The criterion of desirability is to minimize redesign time.* For example, ARGO's bias in favor of maximally specific macro-rules reduces the amount of search required to complete the design. If a macro-rule applies, ARGO will not retrieve a more abstract version of it. Yet one can imagine cases where applying the more abstract rule and extending the design in a different direction would lead to a better design.

– *The replayable portions of a design plan can be precomputed.* Treating an abstracted design plan as an indivisible macro-rule depends on predicting a priori which portions of the plan might be useful to replay. This restriction might be eased by using the preconditions of the abstracted plan to decide whether to retrieve it, but still replaying as much as possible of the entire original plan. Such an extension would require giving ARGO a BOGART-like ability (see Section 7.7) to replay the applicable portion of the design plan, using the original plan representation rather than a macro-rule.

– *An (abstracted) design plan is reused without modification.* ARGO does not exploit previous designs as fully as possible. Searching for rules to complete a partial design adapts a design plan to solve more problems, but not as effectively as modifying the plan itself as in REDESIGN.

– *The design plans are small enough and few enough to compile into macro-rules.* Computing the conflict set of applicable rule instances is surprisingly fast at present, thanks to a small rule set, fast unification and inheritance mechanisms, and exploiting the abstraction relation to avoid testing some of the rules. The experimental results reported by Huhns and Acosta [36] indicate that each rule firing takes only about 5–20 seconds, including the time to compute the conflict set, select a rule instance, and apply it. However, this approach does not appear to scale up, since its time and space costs are linear in the number of known design plans, or even worse, the number of macro-rules formed from their abstractions. If the size of the conflict set is proportional to the number of refinable modules times the number of known rules, scaling up to larger designs and rule catalogs will require efficient techniques for incremental computation of the conflict set, such as the RETE matching algorithm described by Forgy [25] and used in various forward-chaining production system languages. However, such techniques would have to handle ARGO's use of LISP predicates and backchaining in rule antecedents. Even with such techniques, testing the preconditions of a large set of learned macro-rules may cost more than brute force search using the original operators:

> ... as more complex rules are learned the system slows down dramatically, despite the use of a fast pattern matcher (a version of the RETE algorithm (Forgy [25])). The problem is that the complexity of each new rule, in terms of the number of features in its left-hand side, grows rapidly as the depth of the analysis is extended. (Minton [53])

Various approaches might be used to speed up retrieval. A specialized database machine could test many design plan preconditions in parallel. Even if it took more total computation, macro-rule testing might be faster on a parallel machine than an inherently sequential search. An alternative to testing every plan (and subplan!) at retrieval time is to precompute a suitable index, something like an engineer's "data book." A database of previous design plans and subplans, indexed by functional category (e.g. micro-processor, memory, switching network, signal processor), resource constraints (e.g. fast, small, cheap, conservative), and various other properties, might help a design system or its user locate previous plans worth trying to replay. Compiling a good index requires considerable domain knowledge about what features to use and how to compute them. In contrast, ARGO's retrieval mechanism requires no domain

knowledge besides the rules used to compute the macro-rules. The practicality
of ARGO's approach will be limited if the user can look up relevant design plans
in an index faster than ARGO can test their preconditions.

In sum, ARGO's approach to analogy trades design QUALITY, computationally
feasible scaleup (EVOLVABILITY), and flexible exploitation of previous design
plans (SCOPE) for EFFICIENCY and AUTONOMY. Time will tell if ARGO can be
extended to remedy these shortcomings without abandoning the basic approach.

## 9. Conclusion

This article addresses the question, "What does it take to do (re)design by
replaying design plans?" It has identified some key issues in design by
derivational analogy, both as a framework for comparing the approaches
embodied in four published systems, and to expose unsolved problems.

Table 1 indicates the current state of the art by summarizing how each
system addresses each issue. Conspicuous deficiencies include insensitivity to

Table 1
How the four systems address several issues in replaying design plans

|  | POPART | REDESIGN | BOGART | ARGO |
|---|---|---|---|---|
| **Represent** | goal tree of global transformations | refinement tree with interface subgoals | refinement tree | acyclic graph of step dependencies |
| **Acquire** | record and edit command sequence | plan is given | record user choices of module and rule | record user's choices from conflict set, compile macro-rules |
| **Retrieve** | manually; invoke command by name | plan is given | manually | maximally specific applicable macro-rules |
| **Correspond** | by cursor positioning, pattern matching | if bound to same variable | if bound to same variable | if satisfy macro-rule preconditions |
| **- ambiguous** | non-unique match | doesn't happen | doesn't happen | multiple bindings |
| **- meaningless** | failed match | rule doesn't apply | unbound variable | doesn't happen |
| **- misleading** | wrong position | wrong submodule | wrong submodule | missing preconditions |
| **Check if appropriate** | if executable | if correct | if correct | if macro-rule successful |
| **- sensitive to** | changes in specification | changes in specification or timing | changes in specification or timing | changes in specification, timing, or rules |
| **- biassed to** | keep POPART generic | minimize redesign | reduce intervention | minimize search |
| **Adapt** | reformulate to match pattern | generate patches, propagate constraints | repair manually, propagate constraints | search to complete design |
| **Reuse subplan** | replay subtree until break | replay all but one module | replay abstract subtrees | replay to level i |

higher-level aspects of redesign problems, and the lack of a retrieval method that scales up efficiently to larger designs and design libraries.

Reasons for some of these deficiencies are suggested by Table 2, which summarizes how the four systems represent the various design problem aspects listed in Section 3. In particular, many of the higher-level aspects are left implicit or not represented at all.

Table 3 shows how the systems represent, or fail to represent, the various aspects of design plans listed in Section 4.1. As the table reveals, POPART contrasts with the other systems in some interesting ways. First, it is the only system that allows explicit representation of alternatives in a design plan.

Second, the PADDLE design plan representation distinguishes specifications from goals. The other systems allow only one or two types of goals, e.g., "implement a module" and "resolve an inconsistency," and have methods for achieving them (semi)automatically. In contrast, POPART "represents" arbitrary kinds of goals in English, but leaves the user entirely responsible for finding ways to achieve them.

Third, POPART uses the same uniform representation to encode design plans and to define the rules they invoke. The other systems use different representa-

Table 2
How the four systems represent design problems

| | POPART | REDESIGN | BOGART | ARGO |
|---|---|---|---|---|
| **Functional specification** | specified in base language | module I/O relation | module I/O relation | module I/O relation |
| **Artifact costs** | development goals in English | only timing represented | only timing represented | only timing represented |
| **Target medium** | base language | implicitly TTL | implicitly NMOS | implicitly CMOS |
| **Environmental criteria** | not represented | not represented | not represented | not represented |
| **Description requirements** | BNF grammar for base language | implicit module representation language | implicit module representation language | implicit module representation language |
| **Description costs** | not represented | not represented | not represented | not represented |
| **Design resources** | PADDLE commands | rules, constraint propagator, patcher | rules, constraint propagator | rules, unifier, TMS, search |
| **Design methodology** | implicitly transformational | implicitly top-down refinement + constraint propagation + means-ends analysis | implicitly top-down refinement + constraint propagation | implicitly top-down refinement + unification |
| **Redesign costs** | not represented | implicitly minimized | not represented | implicitly minimized |

Table 3
How the four systems represent design plans

| Goals | development goals in uninterpreted English | module to redesign, inconsistency to patch | module to refine | slot to fill, contradiction to resolve |
|---|---|---|---|---|
| **Goal-subgoal relations** | PADDLE control structures* | decomposition, subgoaling | decomposition | step dependencies |
| **Decisions** | apply command | apply rule | apply rule | apply rule |
| **Preconditions** | PADDLE tests* | match rule LHS | match rule LHS | satisfy rule antecedent |
| **Justifications** | not represented | rule + constraint propagation | rule + constraint propagation | rule + TMS |
| **Alternatives** | PADDLE developments* | not represented | not represented | not represented |
| **Selection criteria** | PADDLE tests* | not represented | not represented | rule preferences, implicit specificity ordering |
| **Rule definitions** | PADDLE developments* | frames, patterns, LISP | frames, patterns, LISP | frames, rewrite rules, LISP |

(\*) POPART represents design plans in the same PADDLE development language as the commands they invoke. PADDLE has constructs to express goal-subgoal subordination, sequencing, conditionals, iteration, patterns, and search, plus escape to arbitrary LISP code.

tions for these two purposes. Figure 10 illustrates the distinction in terms of an iceberg. The part of the iceberg above the waterline represents the goal structure of a design plan; the tip represents the top-level goal(s). The goals are achieved by decisions that invoke rules, shown at the waterline. Below the waterline are the rule definitions, expressed in a rule language that incorporates various representation constructs and is ultimately built on top of LISP. POPART uses the same language, PADDLE, both to express the goal structures above the waterline and to define the rules below. In contrast, the other

Fig. 10. The iceberg model of design plan representation.

systems distinguish between rules, which are expected to be correct, and the lower-level constructs used to implement them. Their design plan representations are much more constrained and hence more tractable. In particular, they guarantee that their design plans are correct, assuming the rules are; POPART makes no such guarantees.

In sum, PADDLE buys generality and expressiveness at the cost of tractability: POPART cannot rely on the correctness of the steps in a development or make strong assumptions about its structure, nor does it provide tools for analyzing correctness (though the user is free to invoke language-specific analysis tools). Moreover, the dual use of PADDLE above and below the rule level means that it should be compared not just with the other systems' design plan representations, but with their rule languages as well. In fact, the POPART project seems to be emphasizing the construction of a set of rules sufficiently general and correct to use as building blocks. Such rules seem easier to come by in circuit design than in the areas of software design where POPART has been used.

Why do the issues analyzed in this article matter? That is, how does a replay system's internal approach to those issues affect its externally measurable problem solving performance? Section 2.7 introduced some criteria for evaluating any system that solves design problems by replaying plans (or for that matter, any problem solving system):

- The SCOPE of problems solved.
- The EVOLVABILITY of the system to solve new problems.
- The QUALITY of its solution.
- The EFFICIENCY of its processing.
- The AUTONOMY of operation in terms of the amount of user intervention required.

Table 4 summarizes how each of these criteria is affected, positively or negatively, by the system's approach to the seven issues we have discussed.

The systems discussed in this article make various tradeoffs among these factors. We conclude by discussing some of the main tradeoffs, identifying the ideas used to address some of them, and evaluating the state of the art.

### 9.1. Tradeoffs that sacrifice SCOPE and QUALITY

To finesse various problems, each system discussed in this article relies on implicit assumptions about the purpose for which it will be used. These assumptions not only restrict SCOPE but often reduce design QUALITY as well.

For example, REDESIGN and ARGO incorporate similar assumptions about the cost of redesign. REDESIGN is biassed to find a minimal redesign, that is, one in which only one module is changed. ARGO is biassed to minimize the amount of search required to solve a new design problem. Both systems ignore the quality of the new design, so long as it's correct. Thus they sacrifice

Table 4
Overall positive (↑) and negative (↓) effects of approaches used in (a) POPART, (b) REDESIGN, (c) BOGART, and (d) ARGO

| | SCOPE | EVOLVABILITY | QUALITY | EFFICIENCY | AUTONOMY |
|---|---|---|---|---|---|
| **Represent** | ↑ many (d), robust (b,c,d) plans | ↓ strict refinement model (b,c), ↑ shell + knowledge (a,c,d) | ↑ correct rules (b,c,d) | ↓ space to store plans (c) and macro-rules (d) | ↓ write rules (a,b,c,d) |
| **Acquire** | ↑ generalize manual steps (c) | ↑ learn new rules (c) | ↑ learn correct rules (c) | ↓ time to learn rules (c,d) | ↑ record decisions (a,c,d), learn rules (c), ↓ edit plan (a) |
| **Retrieve** | ↑ retrieve all replayable plans (d) | ↓ failure to scale up (d) | ↑ most specific plan (d) | ↓ time to test preconditions (a,b,c,d) | ↓ manual (a,b,c) |
| **Correspond** | ↑ robust mapping (a,b,c,d) | ↓ ignore higher-level goals (a,b,c,d) | ↑ test plan preconditions (d), ↓ weak heuristics (b,c,d) | ↓ test plan preconditions (d) | ↓ user-specified (a) |
| **Check if appropriate** | ↓ domain-specific rules (a,b,c,d), propagator (b,c) | ↑ manual control (a,c,d) | ↑ user-specified tests (a), rule preconditions (b,c,d), constraint propagation (b,c), unification (d), preferences (d), ↓ weak heuristics (b,d) | ↓ constraint propagation (b,c) | ↓ user-specified (a), user-checked (d) |
| **Adapt** | ↑ means-ends analysis (a,b), editing (a), completion (b,c,d) | ↑ general heuristics (a,b,d) | ↑ search for good completion (d), ↓ weak heuristics (b,d) | ↓ conditioning (a), search (d), ↑ TMS (d) | ↓ manual editing (a), implementation (b), search (d,c) |
| **Reuse subplan** | ↑ replay subtree (a,c), abstract plan (c,d), partial ordering (d) | ↓ failure to scale up (d) | ↑ choose best replayable abstraction (d) | ↓ number of abstractions (d) | ↓ user chooses subplan (c) |

QUALITY for EFFICIENCY. BOGART has a similar bias—maximum AUTONOMY—but lets the user control the tradeoff by deciding which portion of the original design plan to replay and guiding the rest of the design by hand.

## 9.2. Pros and cons of user intervention

It is hardly surprising that user intervention makes some problems easier. For example, POPART, REDESIGN, and BOGART simply leave the problem of plan retrieval to the user. If the user is using the system to support repeated iteration on the same design, this strategy is quite reasonable. It becomes more burdensome for design by analogy.

REDESIGN and BOGART rely on the user to adapt an almost right plan; similarly, ARGO allows the user to add the rules needed to complete a design. Here, a bit of user intervention (reduced AUTONOMY) buys a lot of SCOPE, since the class of tasks a plan can solve completely is much smaller than the class of tasks it can almost solve.

On the other hand, user intervention makes certain problems harder when it requires the user and system to understand each other. For example, manual retrieval in BOGART, rule selection in VEXED, and manual selection from the conflict set in ARGO require the user to understand the alternatives well enough to decide which one to choose. Similarly, manual adaptation in POPART and BOGART requires the user to understand the plan well enough to decide which steps to select or modify.

Conversely, the system must understand the user's behavior well enough to replay it. While a manual decision may initially spare the system some work, re-interpreting it in a later context can be problematic. REDESIGN and BOGART suffer from this difficulty when they try to guess which object in the new context corresponds to the one the user originally chose to apply a rule to. POPART doesn't even try to guess; it makes the user responsible for spelling it out in the original plan, which can be very difficult to do robustly. The price ARGO pays for letting the user choose actions from the conflict set includes the design QUALITY sacrificed by omitting the reasons for the choice from the macro-rules compiled from the actions. *Every multiple choice decision input by the user is an opportunity to sneak in implicit, unreplayable knowledge.*

### 9.3. Techniques found useful

While tradeoffs among SCOPE, EVOLVABILITY, QUALITY, EFFICIENCY, and AU-TONOMY are inevitable, several attractive techniques have been identified that increase SCOPE, protect QUALITY, improve EFFICIENCY, or enhance AUTONOMY.

*Dependency-directed backtracking* can enhance both EFFICIENCY and AU-TONOMY. It can be viewed as a compiled form of replay. For example, to retract an early design decision in BOGART while keeping subsequent decisions, the user must backtrack the design to the decision point and then replay the subsequent decisions. In contrast, when a design decision is retracted in ARGO, only the assertions that actually depend on it are retracted.

To protect design QUALITY, it appears useful to represent design plans in terms of (*almost*) *correct rules*, complemented by global *deduction* mechanisms. A design plan composed of correct rules is guaranteed to produce a correct (though of course not necessarily desirable) implementation. POPART's failure to enforce this restriction is responsible for many of its limitations, and in fact its users are currently developing correct, reusable rules. However, while catalogs of correctness preserving transformations have been touted as a way to guarantee correctness, they are often hard to get right; it's simpler to verify a specific step than the general rule that produced it. To compensate, most of the systems complement their refinement rules with some sort of deduction mechanism. Thus REDESIGN and BOGART use CRITTER to propagate constraints imposed by a decision made in one part of the design to other parts they may affect. Similarly, ARGO uses its underlying unification and truth maintenance mechanisms to bind parameters consistently and detect contradictions. The absence of such a deductive mechanism appears to be one of the limiting factors in POPART, which lacks the nonsyntactic knowledge needed to reason about the expressions it transforms.

*Means-ends analysis* provides another way to exploit almost right rules, enhancing SCOPE and AUTONOMY, though sometimes at the cost of EFFICIENCY. One example is POPART's modest conditioning mechanism for rewriting an expression to permit a pattern match. The existence of this mechanism lets the user express development steps more simply and easily. When conditioning succeeds, it allows replay to continue, so it enhances robustness. However, conditioning adds to the cost of detecting a genuinely failed "near miss" pattern match. This wouldn't be so bad if mismatches always halted replay, since the delay would be minor compared to the subsequent user intervention. However, various PADDLE control constructs use matching to determine what step to replay next, so a repeated near miss in an inner loop of the development could degrade EFFICIENCY considerably.

Another example of means-ends analysis is REDESIGN's use of "subgoal modules" to repair constraint violations at interfaces. Omitting interface consistency tests from the preconditions of a refinement rule increases its coverage. As long as any inconsistencies are eventually detected and repaired, design correctness is protected. Thus means-ends analysis complements the SCOPE of refinement rules much as deduction complements their QUALITY. However, extensive use of subgoal modules can diminish design QUALITY compared to anticipating and preventing conflicts in advance: a circuit full of modules inserted to repair inconsistent interfaces is likely to be larger than necessary.

*Explanation-based learning* is finding some interesting applications in design system EVOLVABILITY. One of the first was the acquisition of decomposition rules in LEAP (Mahadevan [51], Mitchell et al. [55]). LEAP's contemplated use in BOGART for re-expressing manual decomposition steps as rules will protect their correctness (QUALITY) and increase their SCOPE. ARGO uses explanation-based generalization to compile (abstracted) design plans into macro-rules which are not only correct but guaranteed to be completely executable whenever their preconditions are satisfied. Automatic retrieval of the maximally specific macro-rule(s) enhances AUTONOMY.

## 9.4. Where do we go from here?

Crucial to the success of a derivational analogy system is its representation for plans. Further progress in SCOPE, EVOLVABILITY, QUALITY, EFFICIENCY, and AUTONOMY will require richer representations. In particular:

– Better design QUALITY and increased AUTONOMY will require explicit representations of design goals and decisions, as advocated by Mostow [62].

– Solving problems that involve reasoning about tradeoffs between QUALITY, EFFICIENCY, and AUTONOMY will require making explicit the higher-level considerations ignored or implicit in existing analogy systems: the criteria and costs associated with the design plan and the design process itself.

– EFFICIENCY in solving large problems will require the ability to form richer abstractions of the design plan, to simulate their effects, and to reorganize them so as to reformulate the search space (Tong [91]). The manipulation of large design plans will require special tools for operating on them, such as those proposed by Mostow [64, 65].

Design by derivational analogy has turned out to be easier said than done. Clearly much work remains to be done to remedy the deficiencies of current systems and make it a practical reality. The retrieval problem remains especially difficult. However, despite the difficult issues raised in this article, derivational analogy remains a promising approach to redesign and to problem solving in general. Even modest partial solutions offer a potentially enormous payoff. When designers "go back to the drawing board," they must repeat much of the tedious work that went into earlier designs. Eliminating a significant portion of this redundant effort could dramatically enhance design productivity.

ACKNOWLEDGMENT

This paper would not have been possible without the generous assistance and patient explanations provided by developers and users of the systems it describes: David Wile, Martin Feather, and Randy Kerber (POPART), Lou Steinberg (REDESIGN, VEXED, and BOGART), Mike Barley (VEXED and BOGART), and Ramon Acosta and Michael Huhns (ARGO). However, not all the views expressed in this paper necessarily agree with theirs. I am grateful to my colleagues Lou Steinberg and Chris Tong for many illuminating conversations on design, and to the entire Rutgers AI/Design group for the supportive and stimulating environment in which this research was performed. Finally, I would like to thank Jaime Carbonell, Ramon Acosta, Martin Feather, David Wile, Michael Huhns, Smadar Kedar-Cabelli, Lou Steinberg, and the anonymous reviewers for their numerous helpful comments on previous drafts.

The research reported here was supported in part by the Defense Advanced Research Projects Agency (DARPA) under Contract Number N00014-85-K-0116, in part by the National Science Foundation (NSF) under Grant Number DMC-8610507, and in part by the Center for Computer Aids to Industrial Productivity (CAIP), an Advanced Technology Center of the New Jersey Commission on Science and Technology, at Rutgers University, Piscataway, New Jersey. The opinions expressed in this paper are those of the author and do not reflect the policies, either expressed or implied, of any granting agency.

## REFERENCES

1. Acosta, R.D., Huhns, M.N. and Liuh, S.L., Analogical reasoning for digital system synthesis, in: *Proceedings 1986 International Conference on Computer-Aided Design* (1986).
2. Balzer, R., A 15 year perspective on automatic programming, *IEEE Trans. Softw. Eng.* **11** (1985) 1257–1268.
3. Balzer, R., Automated enhancement of knowledge representations, in: *Proceedings IJCAI-85*, Los Angeles, CA (1985) 203–207.
4. Balzer, R., Dyer, D., Morgenstern, M. and Neches, R., Specification-based computing environments, in: *Proceedings AAAI-83*, Washington, DC (1983) 12–16.
5. Balzer, R., Green, C. and Cheatham, T., Software technology in the 1990's using a new paradigm, *IEEE Computer* **16** (1983) 39–45.
6. Bareiss, E.R., Porter, B.W. and Wier, C.C., Protos: An exemplar-based learning apprentice, in: *Proceedings Fourth International Workshop on Machine Learning*, Irvine, CA (1987) 12–23.
7. Barley, M., Descendent support prediction: A first step in attacking the replay correspondence problem, Course project in CS671 Graduate Seminar on Artifical Intelligence Approaches to Design, Rutgers University, Computer Science Department, New Brunswick, NJ (1986).
8. Bates, J.L. and Constable, R.L., Proofs as programs, *ACM Trans. Program. Lang. Syst.* **7** (1) (1985) 113–136.
9. Bledsoe, W.W., The use of analogy in automatic proof discovery (preliminary report), Tech. Rept. AI-158-86, MCC, Microelectronics and Computer Technology Corporation, Austin, TX (1986).
10. Brock, B., Cooper, S. and Pierce, W., Some experiments with analogy in proof discovery (preliminary report), Tech. Rept. AI-347-86, MCC, Microelectronics and Computer Technology Corporation, Austin, TX (1986).
11. Burstein, M.H., A model of learning in analogical problem solving, in: *Proceedings AAAI-83*, Washington, DC (1983) 45–48.
12. Burstein, M.H., Concept formation by incremental analogical reasoning and debugging, in: R.S. Michalski, J.G. Carbonell and T.M. Mitchell (Eds.), *Machine Learning: An Artifical Intelligence Approach* **2** (Morgan Kaufman, Los Altos, CA, 1986) 351–369.
13. Carbonell, J.G., A computational model of analogical problem solving, in: *Proceedings IJCAI-81*, Vancouver, BC (1981) 147–152.
14. Carbonell, J.G., Learning by analogy: Formulating and generalizing plans from past experience, in: R.S. Michalski, J.G. Carbonell and T.M. Mitchell (Eds.), *Machine Learning: An Artificial Intelligence Approach* (Tioga, Palo Alto, CA, 1983) 137–161.
15. Carbonell, J.G., Derivational analogy and its role in problem solving, in: *Proceedings AAAI-83*, Washington, DC (1983) 64–69.
16. Carbonell, J.G., Derivational analogy: A theory of reconstructive problem solving and expertise acquisition, in: R.S. Michalski, J.G. Carbonell and T.M. Mitchell (Eds.), *Machine Learning: An Artificial Intelligence Approach* **2** (Morgan Kaufmann, Los Altos, CA, 1986) 371–392.
17. Constable, R.L., Knoblock, T.B. and Bates, J.L., Writing programs that construct proofs, *J. Autom. Reasoning* **1** (1985) 285–326.
18. Dershowitz, N., Programming by analogy, in: R.S. Michalski, J.G. Carbonell and T.M. Mitchell (Eds.), *Machine Learning: An Artificial Intelligence Approach* **2** (Morgan Kaufmann, Los Altos, CA, 1986) 395–432.
19. Evans, T.G., A program for the solution of a class of geometric-analogy intelligence test questions, in: M. Minsky (Ed.), *Semantic Information Processing* (MIT Press, Cambridge, MA, 1968) 271–353.
20. Falkenhainer, B., Forbus, K.D. and Gentner, D. The structure-mapping engine, in: *Proceedings AAAI-86*, Philadelphia, PA (1986) 272–277.

21. Feather, M.S., An incremental approach to constructing, explaining and maintaining specifications, in: M. Dowson (Ed.), *Proccedings 3rd International Software Process Workshop*, Breckenridge, CO (1986) 137–140.

22. Feather, M.S., Constructing specifications by combining parallel elaborations, *IEEE Trans. Softw. Eng.* **15** (1989) 198–208.

23. Fikes, R.E. and Nilsson, N.J., STRIPS: A new approach to the application of theorem proving to problem solving, *Artificial Intelligence* **2** (1971) 189–208.

24. Fisher, E.L., An AI-based methodology for factory design, *AI Mag.* **7** (4) (1986) 72–85.

25. Forgy, C., Rete: A fast algorithm for the many pattern/many object pattern matching problem, *Artificial Intelligence* **19** (1982) 17–37.

26. Gentner, D., Are scientific analogies metaphors? in: D. Miall (Ed.), *Metaphor: Problems and Perspectives* (Harvester Press, Brighton, England, 1982).

27. Gentner, D., The mechanisms of analogical learning, in: S. Vosniadou and A. Ortony (Eds.), *Similarity and Analogical Reasoning* (Cambridge University Press, Oxford, 1988).

28. Gentner, D. and Gentner, D.R., Flowing waters or teeming crowds: Mental models of electricity, in: D. Gentner and A.L. Stevens (Eds.), *Mental Models* (Erlbaum, Hillsdale, NJ, 1983).

29. Green, C.C., Theorem proving by resolution as a basis for question-answering systems, in: B. Meltzer and D. Michie (Eds.), *Machine Intelligence* **4** (Edinburgh University Press, Edinburgh, 1969) 183–205.

30. Greiner, R., Learning by understanding analogies, in: T.M. Mitchell, J.G. Carbonell and R.S. Michalski (Eds.), *Machine Learning: A Guide to Current Research* (Kluwer Academic Publishers, Boston, MA, 1986) 81–84.

31. Greiner, R., Learning by understanding analogies, in: A. Prieditis (Ed.), *Analogica '85: Proceedings of the First Workshop on Analogical Reasoning* (Pitman, London, 1987) 1–36.

32. Hall, R.P., Computational approaches to analogical reasoning: A comparative analysis, *Artificial Intelligence* **39** (1989) 29–120.

33. Hammond, K.J., Learning to anticipate and avoid planning problems through the explanation of failures, in: *Proceedings AAAI-86*, Philadelphia, PA (1986) 556–560.

34. Hayes-Roth, B., Hayes-Roth, F., Shapiro, N. and Wescourt, K., Planners' workbench: A computer aid to re-planning, Tech. Rept. P-6688, The Rand Corporation, Santa Monica, CA (1981).

35. Holland, J., Holyoak, K., Nisbett, R. and Thagard, P., *Induction: Processes of Inference, Learning, and Discovery* (MIT Press, Cambridge, MA, 1986).

36. Huhns, M.N. and Acosta, R.D., Argo: An analogical reasoning system for solving design problems, Tech. Rept. AI/CAD-092-87, MCC, Microelectronics and Computer Technology Corporation, Austin, TX (1987).

37. Kant, E., Understanding and automating algorithm design, *IEEE Trans. Softw. Eng.* **11** (1985) 1361–1374.

38. Kedar-Cabelli, S., Purpose-directed analogy, in: *Proceedings Seventh Annual Conference of the Cognitive Science Society*, Irvine, CA (1985).

39. Kedar-Cabelli, S.T., Toward a computational model of purpose-directed analogy, in: A. Prieditis (Ed.), *Analogica '85: Proceedings of the First Workshop on Analogical Reasoning* (Pitman, London, 1987) 89–107.

40. Kedar-Cabelli, S.T., Analogy: From a unified perspective, in: D.H. Helman (Ed.), *Analogical Reasoning* (Reidel, Dordrecht, Netherlands, 1988).

41. Keller, R.M., Defining operationality for explanation-based learning, *Artificial Intelligence* **35** (1988) 227–241.

42. Keller, R.M., Concept learning in context, in: *Proceedings Fourth International Machine Learning Workshop*, Irvine, CA (1987) 91–102.

43. Keller, R.M., The role of explicit contextual knowledge in learning concepts to improve performance, Ph.D. Thesis, Tech. Rept. ML-TR-7, Rutgers University, Computer Science Department, New Brunswick, NJ (1987).

44. Kelly, V., The CRITTER system: Automating critiquing of digital circuit designs, in: *Proceedings 21st IEEE Design Automation Conference* (1984) 419–425.
45. Kling, R.E., A paradigm for reasoning by analogy, *Artificial Intelligence* 2 (1971) 147–178.
46. Kolodner, J., Extending problem solver capabilities through case-based inference, in: *Proceedings Fourth International Workshop on Machine Learning*, Irvine, CA (1987) 167–178.
47. Kolodner, J.L., Simpson Jr., R.L., and Sycara-Cyranski, K., A process model of case-based reasoning in problem-solving, in: *Proceedings IJCAI-85*, Los Angeles, CA (1985) 284–290.
48. Laird, J.E., Rosenbloom, P.S. and Newell, A., Chunking in Soar: The anatomy of a general learning mechanism, *Mach. Learning* 1 (1) (1986) 11–46.
49. Langrana, N., Mitchell, T. and Ramachandran, N., Progress toward a knowledge-based aid for mechanical design, in: *Proceedings Symposium on Integrated and Intelligent Manufacturing*, Anaheim, CA (1986).
50. Liuh, S. and Huhns, M.N., Using a TMS for EBG, Tech. Rept. AI-445-86, MCC, Microelectronics and Computer Technology Corporation, Austin, TX (1986).
51. Mahadevan, S., Verification-based learning: A generalization strategy for inferring problem-reduction methods, in: *Proceedings IJCAI-85*, Los Angeles, CA (1985) 616–623.
52. McCarty, L.T. and Sridharan, N.S., The representation of an evolving system of legal concepts, II: Prototypes and deformations, in: *Proceedings IJCAI-81*, Vancouver, BC (1981) 246–253.
53. Minton, S., Constraint-based generalization: Learning game-playing plans from single examples, in: *Proceedings AAAI-84*, Austin, TX (1984) 251–254.
54. Mitchell, T.M., Keller, R.M. and Kedar-Cabelli, S.T., Explanation-based generalization: A unifying view, *Mach. Learning* 1 (1) (1986) 47–80.
55. Mitchell, T.M., Mahadevan, S. and Steinberg, L., LEAP: A learning apprentice for VLSI design, in: *Proceedings IJCAI-85*, Los Angeles, CA (1985) 573–580.
56. Mitchell, T.M. and Mostow, J., Artificial intelligence and design, Syllabus for 4-hour tutorial presented at AAAI-87, Seattle, WA (1987).
57. Mitchell, T.M., Steinberg, L.I., and Shulman, J., A knowledge-based approach to design, *IEEE Trans. Pattern Anal. Mach. Intell.* 7 (1985) 502–510.
58. Mittal, S. and Araya, A., A knowledge-based framework for design, in: *Proceedings AAAI-86*, Philadelphia, PA (1986) 856–865.
59. Mostow, J., Operationalizing advice: A problem-solving model, in: *Proceedings Second International Machine Learning Workshop*, Urbana, IL (1983) 110–116.
60. Mostow, J., A problem-solver for making advice operational, in: *Proceedings AAAI-83*, Washington, DC (1983) 279–283.
61. Mostow, J., A decision-based framework for comparing hardware compilers, *J. Syst. Softw.* 4 (1984) 39–50.
62. Mostow, J., Toward better models of the design process, *AI Mag.* 6 (1) (1985) 44–57.
63. Mostow, J., Response to Derek Partridge, *AI Mag.* 6 (3) (1985) 51–52.
64. Mostow, J., Some requirements for effective replay of derivations, in: *Proceedings Third International Machine Learning Workshop*, Skytop, PA (1985) 129–132.
65. Mostow, J., Why are design derivations hard to replay? in: T.M. Mitchell, J.G. Carbonell, and R.S. Michalski (Eds.), *Machine Learning: A Guide to Current Research* (Kluwer Academic Publishers, Hingham, MA, 1986) 213–218.
66. Mostow, J. and Barley, M., Automated reuse of design plans, in: W.E. Eder (Ed.), *Proceedings 1987 International Conference on Engineering Design* (ICED87), Boston, MA (1987) 632–647.
67. Mostow, J. and Bhatnagar, N., Failsafe: A floor planner that uses EBG to learn from its failures, in: *Proceedings IJCAI-87*, Milan, Italy (1987) 249–255.
68. Mostow, J. and Cohen, D., Automating program speedup by deciding what to cache, in: *Proceedings IJCAI-85*, Los Angeles, CA (1985) 165–172.

69. Mostow, J., Steinberg, L., Langrana, N. and Tong, C., Artificial intelligence aids for VLSI and a domain independent model of knowledge-based design: Research status report, Rutgers AI/Design Project Working Paper 79, Rutgers University, New Brunswick, NJ (1987).

70. Nagel, D.J., Learning concepts with a prototype-based model for concept representation, Ph.D. Thesis, Tech. Rept. DCS-TR-211, Rutgers University, Computer Science Department, New Brunswick, NJ (1987).

71. Navinchandra, D., Exploring innovative designs by relaxing criteria and reasoning from precedents, Ph.D. Thesis, MIT Department of Civil Engineering, Cambridge, MA (1987).

72. Navinchandra, D., Sriram, D. and Kedar-Cabelli, S.T., The role of analogy in engineering problem solving, in: *Proceedings Second International Conference on Applications of Artificial Intelligence in Engineering*, Boston, MA (1987).

73. Norton, S. and Kelly, K., Learning preference rules for a VLSI design problem-solver, in: *Proceedings Fourth IEEE Conference on AI Applications* (1988).

74. Petrie, C.J., Russinoff, D.M. and Steiner, D.D., PROTEUS: A default reasoning perspective, in: *Proceedings 5th Generation Computer Conference*, Washington, DC (1986).

75. Prieditis, A. (Ed.), *Analogica '85: Proceedings of the First Workshop on Analogical Reasoning* (Pitman, London, 1987).

76. Rich, C., The layered architecture of a system for reasoning about programs, in: *Proceedings IJCAI-85*, Los Angeles, CA (1985) 540–546.

77. Scherlis, W. and Scott, D., First steps towards inferential programming, in: *IFIP Congress 83* (North-Holland, Amsterdam, 1983).

78. Simoudis, E., A knowledge-based system for the analysis and redesign of digital circuit networks, *Int. J. Artif. Intell. Eng.* **2** (3) (1987) 167–172; Special Issue on AI in Engineering Design.

79. Simpson Jr., R.L., A computer model of case-based reasoning in problem solving: An investigation in the domain of dispute mediation, Ph.D. Thesis, Georgia Institute of Technology, Atlanta, GA (1985).

80. Smith, D.R., Top-down synthesis of divide-and-conquer algorithms, *Artificial Intelligence* **27** (1985) 43–96.

81. Smith, D., Kotik, G. and Westfold, S., Research on knowledge-based software environments at Kestrel Institute, *IEEE Trans. Softw. Eng.* **11** (1985) 1278–1295.

82. Stallman, R.M. and Sussman, G.J., Forward reasoning and dependency-directed backtracking in a system for computer-aided circuit analysis, *Artificial Intelligence* **9** (1977) 135–196.

83. Steier, D.M., Cypress-Soar: A case study in search and learning in algorithm design, in: *Proceedings IJCAI-87*, Milan, Italy (1987) 327–330.

84. Steinberg, L., Design as refinement plus constraint propagation: The VEXED experience, in: *Proceedings AAAI-87*, Seattle, WA (1987) 830–835.

85. Steinberg, L., Design = top down refinement plus constraint propagation plus what? in: *Proceedings 1987 IEEE International Conference on Systems, Man, and Cybernetics*, Alexandria, VA (1987) 498–502.

86. Steinberg, L.I. and Mitchell, T.M., The redesign system: A knowledge-based approach to VLSI CAD, *IEEE Design Test* **2** (1985) 45–54.

87. Sycara-Cyranski, K., Arguments of persuasion in labour mediation, in: *Proceedings IJCAI-85*, Los Angeles, CA (1985) 294–296.

88. Teitelman, W., Interlisp reference manual, Xerox Palo Alto Research Center, Palo Alto, CA (1978).

89. Tong, C., Learning justifiable design evaluation functions: A decomposable, multi-agent learning problem, Rutgers AI/VLSI Project Working Paper No. 48, Rutgers University, New Brunswick, NJ (1987).

90. Tong, C., Toward an engineering science of knowledge-based design, *Int. J. Artif. Intell. Eng.* **2** (3) (1987); Special Issue on AI in Engineering Design.

91. Tong, C., Knowledge-based circuit design, Ph.D. Thesis, Stanford University, Computer Science Department, Stanford, CA (1988).
92. Weiner, P., Singh, I., Mostow, D.J. and Irons, E.T., The Yale editor "E": A CRT-based text editing system, Tech. Rept., Yale University, Computer Science Department, New Haven, CT (1973).
93. Wile, D.S., Program developments: Formal explanations of implementations, *Commun. ACM* **26** (11) (1983) 902–911.
94. Winston, P., Learning and reasoning by analogy, *Commun. ACM* **23** (12) (1980) 689–703.

# Connectionist Learning Procedures

## Geoffrey E. Hinton

*Computer Science Department, University of Toronto,*
*10 King's College Road, Toronto, Ontario, Canada M5S 1A4*

ABSTRACT

*A major goal of research on networks of neuron-like processing units is to discover efficient learning procedures that allow these networks to construct complex internal representations of their environment. The learning procedures must be capable of modifying the connection strengths in such a way that internal units which are not part of the input or output come to represent important features of the task domain. Several interesting gradient-descent procedures have recently been discovered. Each connection computes the derivative, with respect to the connection strength, of a global measure of the error in the performance of the network. The strength is then adjusted in the direction that decreases the error. These relatively simple, gradient-descent learning procedures work well for small tasks and the new challenge is to find ways of improving their convergence rate and their generalization abilities so that they can be applied to larger, more realistic tasks.*

## 1. Introduction

Recent technological advances in VLSI and computer aided design mean that it is now much easier to build massively parallel machines. This has contributed to a new wave of interest in models of computation that are inspired by neural nets rather than the formal manipulation of symbolic expressions. To understand human abilities like perceptual interpretation, content-addressable memory, commonsense reasoning, and learning it may be necessary to understand how computation is organized in systems like the brain which consist of massive numbers of richly interconnected but rather slow processing elements.

This paper focuses on the question of how internal representations can be learned in "connectionist" networks. These are a recent subclass of neural net models that emphasize computational power rather than biological fidelity. They grew out of work on early visual processing and associative memories [28, 40, 79]. The paper starts by reviewing the main research issues for connectionist models and then describes some of the earlier work on learning procedures for associative memories and simple pattern recognition devices. These learning procedures cannot generate internal representations: They are limited to forming simple associations between representations that are specified externally. Recent research has led to a variety of more powerful connectionist learning procedures that can discover good internal representations and most of the paper is devoted to a survey of these procedures.

## 2. Connectionist Models

Connectionist models typically consist of many simple, neuron-like processing elements called "units" that interact using weighted connections. Each unit has a "state" or "activity level" that is determined by the input received from other units in the network. There are many possible variations within this general framework. One common, simplifying assumption is that the combined effects of the rest of the network on the $j$th unit are mediated by a single scalar quantity, $x_j$. The quantity, which is called the "total input" of unit $j$, is usually taken to be a *linear* function of the activity levels of the units that provide input to $j$:

$$x_j = -\theta_j + \sum_i y_i w_{ji} \, , \tag{1}$$

where $y_i$ is the state of the $i$th unit, $w_{ji}$ is the weight on the connection from the $i$th to the $j$th unit and $\theta_j$ is the threshold of the $j$th unit. The threshold term can be eliminated by giving every unit an extra input connection whose activity level is fixed at 1. The weight on this special connection is the negative of the threshold. It is called the "bias" and it can be learned in just the same way as the other weights. This method of implementing thresholds will generally be assumed in the rest of this paper. An external input vector can be supplied to the network by clamping the states of some units or by adding an input term, $I_j$, that contributes to the total input of some of the units. The state of a unit is typically defined to be a nonlinear function of its total input. For units with discrete states, this function typically has value 1 if the total input is positive and value 0 (or $-1$) otherwise. For units with continuous states one typical nonlinear input-output function is the logistic function (shown in Fig. 1):

$$y_j = \frac{1}{1 + e^{-x_j}} \, . \tag{2}$$

All the long-term knowledge in a connectionist network is encoded by where the connections are or by their weights, so learning consists of changing the weights or adding or removing connections. The short-term knowledge of the network is normally encoded by the states of the units, but some models also have fast-changing temporary weights or thresholds that can be used to encode temporary contexts or bindings [44, 96].

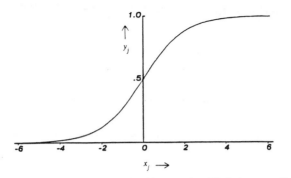

Fig. 1. The logistic input-output function defined by equation (2). It is a smoothed version of a step function.

There are two main reasons for investigating connectionist networks. First, these networks resemble the brain much more closely than conventional computers. Even though there are many detailed differences between connectionist units and real neurons, a deeper understanding of the computational properties of connectionist networks may reveal principles that apply to a whole class of devices of this kind, including the brain. Second, connectionist networks are massively parallel, so any computations that can be performed efficiently with these networks can make good use of parallel hardware.

## 3. Connectionist Research Issues

There are three main areas of research on connectionist networks: Search, representation, and learning. This paper focuses on learning, but a very brief introduction to search and representation is necessary in order to understand what learning is intended to produce.

### 3.1. Search

The task of interpreting the perceptual input, or constructing a plan, or accessing an item in memory from a partial description can be viewed as a constraint satisfaction search in which information about the current case (i.e. the perceptual input or the partial description) must be combined with knowledge of the domain to produce a solution that fits both these sources of constraint as well as possible [12]. If each unit represents a piece of a possible solution, the weights on the connections between units can encode the degree of consistency between various pieces. In interpreting an image, for example, a unit might stand for a piece of surface at a particular depth and surface orientation. Knowledge that surfaces usually vary smoothly in depth and orientation can be encoded by using positive weights between units that represent nearby pieces of surface at similar depths and similar surface orientations, and negative weights between nearby pieces of surface at very different depths or orientations. The network can perform a search for the most plausible interpretation of the input by iteratively updating the states of the units until they reach a stable state in which the pieces of the solution fit well with each other and with the input. Any one constraint can typically be overridden by combinations of other constraints and this makes the search procedure robust in the presence of noisy data, noisy hardware, or minor inconsistencies in the knowledge.

There are, of course, many complexities: Under what conditions will the network settle to a stable solution? Will this solution be the optimal one? How long will it take to settle? What is the precise relationship between weights and probabilities? These issues are examined in detail by Hummel and Zucker [52], Hinton and Sejnowski [45], Geman and Geman [31], Hopfield and Tank [51] and Marroquin [65].

### 3.2. Representation

For tasks like low-level vision, it is usually fairly simple to decide how to use the units to represent the important features of the task domain. Even so, there are some important choices about whether to represent a physical quantity (like the depth at a point in the image) by the state of a single continuous unit, or by the activities in a set of units each of which indicates its confidence that the depth lies within a certain interval [10].

The issues become much more complicated when we consider how a complex, articulated structure like a plan or the meaning of a sentence might be represented in a network of simple units. Some preliminary work has been done by Minsky [67] and Hinton [37] on the representation of inheritance hierarchies and the representation of frame-like structures in which a whole object is composed of a number of parts each of which plays a different role within the whole. A recurring issue is the distinction between local and distributed representations. In a local representation, each concept is represented by a single unit [13, 27]. In a distributed representation, the kinds of concepts that we have words for are represented by patterns of activity distributed over many units, and each unit takes part in many such patterns [42]. Distributed representations are usually more efficient than local ones in addition to being more damage-resistant. Also, if the distributed representation allows the weights to capture important underlying regularities in the task domain, it can lead to much better generalization than a local representation [78, 80]. However, distributed representations can make it difficult to represent several different things at the same time and so to use them effectively for representing structures that have many parts playing different roles it may be necessary to have a separate group of units for each role so that the assignment of a filler to a role is represented by a distributed pattern of activity over a group of "role-specific" units.

Much confusion has been caused by the failure to realize that the words "local" and "distributed" refer to the *relationship* between the terms of some descriptive language and a connectionist implementation. If an entity that is described by a single term in the language is represented by a pattern of activity over many units in the connectionist system, and if each of these units is involved in representing other entities, then the representation is distributed. But it is always possible to invent a new descriptive language such that, relative to this language, the very same connectionist system is using local representations.

## 3.3. Learning

In a network that uses local representations it may be feasible to set all the weights by hand because each weight typically corresponds to a meaningful relationship between entities in the domain. If, however, the network uses distributed representations it may be very hard to program by hand and so a learning procedure may be essential. Some learning procedures, like the perceptron convergence procedure [77], are only applicable if the desired states of all the units in the network are already specified. This makes the learning task relatively easy. Other, more recent, learning procedures operate in networks that contain "hidden" units [46] whose desired states are not specified (either directly or indirectly) by the input or the desired output of the network. This makes learning much harder because the learning procedure must (implicitly) decide what the hidden units should represent. The learning procedure is therefore constructing new representations and the results of learning can be viewed as a numerical solution to the problem of whether to use local or distributed representations.

Connectionist learning procedures can be divided into three broad classes: Supervised procedures which require a teacher to specify the desired output vector, reinforcement procedures which only require a single scalar evaluation of the output, and unsupervised procedures which construct internal models that capture regularities in their input vectors without receiving any additional information. As we shall see, there are often ways of converting one kind of learning procedure into another.

## 4. Associative Memories without Hidden Units

Several simple kinds of connectionist learning have been used extensively for storing knowledge in simple associative networks which consist of a set of input units that are directly connected to a set of output units. Since these networks do not contain any hidden units, the difficult problem of deciding what the hidden units should represent does not arise. The aim is simply to store a set of associations between input vectors and output vectors by modifying the weights on the connections. The representation of each association is typically distributed over many connections and each connection is involved in storing many associations. This makes the network robust against minor physical damage and it also means that weights tend to capture regularities in the set of input-output pairings, so the network tends to generalize these regularities to new input vectors that it has not been trained on [6].

## 4.1. Linear associators

In a linear associator, the state of an output unit is a linear function of the total input that it receives from the input units (see (1)). A simple, Hebbian procedure for storing a new association (or "case") is to increment each weight, $w_{ji}$, between the $i$th input unit and the $j$th output unit by the product of the states of the units

$$\Delta w_{ji} = y_i y_j , \qquad (3)$$

where $y_i$ and $y_j$ are the activities of an input and an output unit. After a set of associations have been stored, the weights encode the cross-correlation matrix between the input and output vectors. If the input vectors are orthogonal and have length 1, the associative memory will exhibit perfect recall. Even though each weight is involved in storing many different associations, each input vector will produce exactly the correct output vector [56].

If the input vectors are not orthogonal, the simple Hebbian storage procedure is not optimal. For a given network and a given set of associations, it may be impossible to store all the associations perfectly, but we would still like the storage procedure to produce a set of weights that minimizes some sensible measure of the differences between the desired output vectors and the vectors actually produced by the network. This "error measure" can be defined as

$$E = \tfrac{1}{2} \sum_{j,c} (y_{j,c} - d_{j,c})^2 ,$$

where $y_{j,c}$ is the actual state of output unit $j$ in input-output case $c$, and $d_{j,c}$ is its desired state. Kohonen [56] shows that the weight matrix that minimizes this error measure can be computed by an iterative storage procedure that repeatedly sweeps through the whole set of associations and modifies each weight by a small amount in the direction that reduces the error measure. This is a version of the least squares learning procedure described in Section 5. The cost of finding an optimal set of weights (in the least squares sense of optimal) is that storage ceases to be a simple "one-shot" process. To store one new association it is necessary to sweep through the whole set of associations many times.

## 4.2. Nonlinear associative nets

If we wish to store a small set of associations which have nonorthogonal input vectors, there is no simple, one-shot storage procedure for linear associative nets that guarantees perfect recall. In these circumstances, a nonlinear associative net can perform better. Willshaw [102] describes an associative net in which both the units and the weights have just two states: 1 and 0. The weights all start at 0, and associations are stored by setting a weight to 1 if ever its input and output units are both on in any association (see Fig. 2). To recall an association, each output unit must have its threshold dynamically set to be just less than $m$, the number of active input units. If the output unit should be on, the $m$ weights coming from the active input units will have been set to 1 during storage, so the output unit is guaranteed to come on. If the output unit should be off, the probability of erroneously coming on is given by the probability that all $m$ of the relevant weights will have been set to 1 when storing other associations. Willshaw showed that associative nets can make efficient use of the information capacity of the weights. If the number of active input units is the log of the total number of input units, the probability of incorrectly activating an output unit can be made very low even when the network is storing close to 0.69 of its information-theoretic capacity.

An associative net in which the input units are identical with the output units can be used to associate vectors with themselves. This allows the network to complete a partially specified input vector. If the input vector is a very degraded version of one of the stored vectors, it may be necessary to use an iterative retrieval process. The initial states of the units represent the partially specified vector, and the states of the units are then updated many times until they settle on one of the stored vectors. Theoretically, the network could oscillate, but Hinton [37] and Anderson and Mozer [7] showed that iterative retrieval normally works well. Hopfield [49] showed that if the weights are symmetrical and the units are updated one at a time the iterative retrieval process can be viewed as a form of gradient descent in an "energy function".

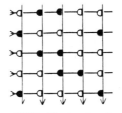

Fig. 2. An associative net (Willshaw [102]). The input vector comes in at the left and the output vector comes out at the bottom (after thresholding). The solid weights have value 1 and the open weights have value 0. The network is shown after it has stored the associations $01001 \rightarrow 10001$, $10100 \rightarrow 01100$, $00010 \rightarrow 00110$.

Hopfield nets store vectors whose components are all $+1$ or $-1$ using the simple storage procedure described in equation (3). To retrieve a stored vector from a partial description (which is a vector containing some 0 components), we start the network at the state specified by the partial description and then repeatedly update the states of units one at a time. The units can be chosen in random order or in any other order provided no unit is ever ignored for more than a finite time. Hopfield [49] observed that the behavior of the network is governed by the global energy function[1]

$$E = -\sum_{i<j} s_i s_j w_{ij} + \sum_j s_j \theta_j ,$$

(4)

where $s_i$ and $s_j$ are the states of two units. Each time a unit updates its state, it adopts the state that minimizes this energy function because the decision rule used to update a unit is simply the derivative of the energy function. The unit adopts the state $+1$ if its "energy gap" is positive and the state $-1$ otherwise, where the energy gap of the $j$th unit, $\Delta E_j$, is the increase in the global energy caused by changing the unit from state $+1$ to state $-1$.

$$\Delta E_j = E(s_j = -1) - E(s_j = +1) = -2\theta_j + 2\sum_i s_i w_{ij} .$$

(5)

So the energy must decrease until the network settles into a local minimum of the energy function. We can therefore view the retrieval process in the following way: The weights define an "energy landscape" over global states of the network and the stored vectors are local minima in this landscape. The retrieval process consists of moving downhill from a starting point to a nearby local minimum.

If too many vectors are stored, there may be spurious local minima caused by interactions between the stored vectors. Also, the basins of attraction around the correct minima may be long and narrow instead of round, so a downhill path from a random starting point may not lead to the nearest local minimum. These problems can be alleviated by using a process called "unlearning" [20, 50].

A Hopfield net with $N$ totally interconnected units can store about $0.15N$ random vectors.[2] This means that it is storing about 0.15 bits per weight, even though the weights are integers with $m + 1$ different values, where $m$ is the number of vectors stored. The capacity can be increased considerably by

---

[1] The energy function should not be confused with the error function described earlier. Gradient descent in the energy function is performed by changing the *states* of the units, not the *weights*.

[2] There is some confusion in the literature due to different ways of measuring storage capacity. If we insist on a fixed probability of getting *each* component of *each* vector correct, the number of vectors that can be stored is $O(N)$. If we insist on a fixed probability of getting *all* components of *all* vectors correct, the number of vectors that can be stored is $O(N/\log N)$.

abandoning the one-shot storage procedure and explicitly training the network on typical noisy retrieval tasks using the threshold least squares or perceptron convergence procedures described below.

## 4.3. The deficiencies of associators without hidden units

If the input vectors are orthogonal, or if they are made to be close to orthogonal by using high-dimensional random vectors (as is typically done in a Hopfield net), associators with no hidden units perform well using a simple Hebbian storage procedure. If the set of input vectors satisfy the much weaker condition of being linearly independent, associators with no hidden units can learn to give the correct outputs provided an iterative learning procedure is used. Unfortunately, linear independence does not hold for most tasks that can be characterized as mapping input vectors to output vectors because the number of relevant input vectors is typically much larger than the number of components in each input vector. The required mapping typically has a complicated structure that can only be expressed using multiple layers of hidden units.[3] Consider, for example, the task of identifying an object when the input vector is an intensity array and the output vector has a separate component for each possible name. If a given type of object can be either black or white, the intensity of an individual pixel (which is what an input unit encodes) cannot provide any direct evidence for the presence or absence of an object of that type. So the object cannot be identified by using weights on direct connections from input to output units. Obviously, it is necessary to explictly extract relationships among intensity values (such as edges) before trying to identify the object. Actually, extracting edges is just a small part of the problem. If recognition is to have the generative capacity to handle novel images of familiar objects the network must somehow encode the systematic effects of variations in lighting and viewpoint, partial occlusion by other objects, and deformations of the object itself. There is a tremendous gap between these complex regularities and the regularities that can be captured by an associative net that lacks hidden units.

## 5. Simple Supervised Learning Procedures

Consider a network that has input units which are directly connected to output units whose states (i.e. activity levels) are a continuous smooth function of their total input. Suppose that we want to train the network to produce particular "desired" states of the output units for each member of a set of input vectors. A measure of how poorly the network is performing with its current

---

[3] It is always possible to redefine the units and the connectivity so that multiple layers of simple units become a single layer of much more complicated units. But this redefinition does not make the problem go away.

set of weights is:

$$E = \tfrac{1}{2} \sum_{j,c} (y_{j,c} - d_{j,c})^2 , \qquad (6)$$

where $y_{j,c}$ is the actual state of output unit $j$ in input-output case $c$, and $d_{j,c}$ is its desired state.

We can minimize the error measure given in (6) by starting with any set of weights and repeatedly changing each weight by an amount proportional to $\partial E/\partial w$.

$$\Delta w_{ji} = -\varepsilon \frac{\partial E}{\partial w_{ji}} . \qquad (7)$$

In the limit, as $\varepsilon$ tends to 0 and the number of updates tends to infinity, this learning procedure is guaranteed to find the set of weights that gives the least squared error. The value of $\partial E/\partial w$ is obtained by differentiating (6) and (1).

$$\frac{\partial E}{\partial w_{ji}} = \sum_{\text{cases}} \frac{\partial E}{\partial y_j} \frac{dy_j}{dx_j} \frac{\partial x_j}{\partial w_{ji}} = \sum_{\text{cases}} (y_j - d_j) \frac{dy_j}{dx_j} y_i . \qquad (8)$$

If the output units are linear, the term $dy_j/dx_j$ is a constant.

The least squares learning procedure has a simple geometric interpretation. We construct a multi-dimensional "weight space" that has an axis for each weight and one extra axis (called "height") that corresponds to the error measure. For each combination of weights, the network will have a certain error which can be represented by the height of a point in weight space. These points form a surface called the "error surface". For networks with linear output units and no hidden units, the error surface always forms a bowl whose horizontal cross-sections are ellipses and whose vertical cross-sections are parabolas. Since the bowl only has one minimum,[4] gradient descent on the error surface is guaranteed to find it.

The error surface is actually the sum of a number of parabolic troughs, one for each training case. If the output units have a nonlinear but monotonic input-output function, each trough is deformed but no new minima are created in any one trough because the monotonic nonlinearity cannot reverse the sign of the gradient of the trough in any direction. When many troughs are added together, however, it is possible to create local minima because it is possible to change the sign of the total gradient without changing the signs of any of the conflicting case-wise gradients of which it is composed. But local minima cannot be created in this way if there is a set of weights that gives zero error for all training cases. If we consider moving away from this perfect point, the error must increase (or remain constant) for each individual case and so it must

[4] This minimum may be a whole subspace.

increase (or remain constant) for the sum of all these cases. So gradient descent is still guaranteed to work for monotonic nonlinear input-output functions provided a perfect solution exists. However, it will be very slow at points in weight space where the gradient of the input-output function approaches zero for the output units that are in error.

The "batch" version of the least squares procedure sweeps through all the cases accumulating $\partial E / \partial w$ before changing the weights, and so it is guaranteed to move in the direction of steepest descent. The "online" version, which requires less memory, updates the weights after each input-output case [99].[5] This may sometimes increase the total error, $E$, but by making the weight changes sufficiently small the total change in the weights after a complete sweep through all the cases can be made to approximate steepest descent arbitrarily closely.

### 5.1. A least squares procedure for binary threshold units

Binary threshold units use a step function, so the term $dy_j / dx_j$ is infinite at the threshold and zero elsewhere and the least squares procedure must be modified to be applicable to these units. In the following discussion we assume that the threshold is implemented by a "bias" weight on a permanently active input line, so the unit turns on if its total input exceeds zero. The basic idea is to define an error function that is large if the total input is far from zero and the unit is in the wrong state and is 0 when the unit is in the right state. The simplest version of this idea is to define the error of an output unit, $j$ for a given input case to be

$$E^*_{j,c} = \begin{cases} 0, & \text{if output unit has the right state}, \\ \frac{1}{2}x^2_{j,c}, & \text{if output unit has the wrong state}. \end{cases}$$

Unfortunately, this measure can be minimized by setting all weights and biases to zero so that units are always exactly at their threshold (Yann Le Cun, personal communication). To avoid this problem we can introduce a margin, $m$, and insist that for units which should be *on* the total input is at least $m$ and for units that should be *off* the total input is at most $-m$. The new error measure is then

$$E^*_{j,c} = \begin{cases} 0, & \text{if output unit has the right state by at least } m, \\ \frac{1}{2}(m - x_{j,c})^2, & \text{if output unit should be on but has } x_{j,c} < m, \\ \frac{1}{2}(m + x_{j,c})^2, & \text{if output unit should be off but has } x_{j,c} > -m. \end{cases}$$

[5] The online version is usually called the "least mean squares" or "LMS" procedure.

The derivative of this error measure with respect to $x_{j,c}$ is

$$\frac{\partial E^*_{j,c}}{\partial x_{j,c}} = \begin{cases} 0, & \text{if output unit has the right state by at least } m, \\ x_{j,c} - m, & \text{if output unit should be on but has } x_{j,c} < m, \\ x_{j,c} + m, & \text{if output unit should be off but has } x_{j,c} > -m. \end{cases}$$

So the "threshold least squares procedure" becomes:

$$\Delta w_{ji} = -\varepsilon \sum_c \frac{\partial E^*_{j,c}}{\partial x_{j,c}} y_{i,c}.$$

## 5.2. The perceptron convergence procedure

One version of the perceptron convergence procedure is related to the online version of the threshold least squares procedure in the following way: The magnitude of $\partial E^*_{j,c} / \partial x_{j,c}$ is ignored and only its sign is taken into consideration. So the weight changes are:

$$\Delta w_{ji,c} = \begin{cases} 0, & \text{if output unit behaves correctly by at least } m, \\ +\varepsilon y_{i,c}, & \text{if output unit should be on but has } x_{j,c} < m, \\ -\varepsilon y_{i,c}, & \text{if output unit should be off but has } x_{j,c} > -m. \end{cases}$$

Because it ignores the magnitude of the error, this procedure changes weights by at least $\varepsilon$ even when the error is very small. The finite size of the weight steps eliminates the need for a margin so the standard version of the perceptron convergence procedure does not use one.

Because it ignores the magnitude of the error this procedure does not even stochastically approximate steepest descent in $E$, the sum squared error. Even with very small $\varepsilon$, it is quite possible for $E$ to rise after a complete sweep through all the cases. However, each time the weights are updated, the perceptron convergence procedure is guaranteed to reduce the value of a different cost measure that is defined solely in terms of weights.

To picture the least squares procedure we introduced a space with one dimension for each weight and one extra dimension for the sum squared error in the output vectors. To picture the perceptron convergence procedure, we do not need the extra dimension for the error. For simplicity we shall consider a network with only one output unit. Each case corresponds to a constraint hyperplane in weight space. If the weights are on one side of this hyperplane, the output unit will behave correctly and if they are on the other side it will behave incorrectly (see Fig. 3). To behave correctly for all cases, the weights

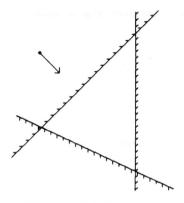

Fig. 3. Some hyperplanes in weight space. Each plane represents the constraint on the weights caused by a particular input-output case. If the weights lie on the correct (unshaded) side of the plane, the output unit will have the correct state for that case. Provided the weight changes are proportional to the activities of the input lines, the perceptron convergence procedure moves the weights perpendicularly towards a violated constraint plane.

must lie on the correct side of all the hyperplanes, so the combinations of weights that give perfect performance form a convex set. *Any* set of weights in this set will be called "ideal."

The perceptron convergence procedure considers the constraint planes one at a time, and whenever the current combination of weights is on the wrong side, it moves it perpendicularly towards the plane. This reduces the distance between the current combination of weights and *any* of the ideal combinations. So provided the weights move by less than twice the distance to the violated constraint plane, a weight update is guaranteed to reduce the measure

$$\sum_i \left( w_{i,\text{actual}} - w_{i,\text{ideal}} \right)^2 .$$

The perceptron convergence procedure has many nice properties, but it also has some serious problems. Unlike the threshold least squares procedure, it does not necessarily settle down to a reasonable compromise when there is no set of weights that will do the job perfectly. Also, there are obvious problems in trying to generalize to more complex, multi-layered nets in which the ideal combinations of weights do not form a single convex set, because the idea of moving towards *the* ideal region of weight space breaks down. It is therefore not surprising that the more sophisticated procedures required for multi-layer nets are generalizations of the least squares procedure rather than the perceptron convergence procedure: They learn by decreasing a squared performance error, not a distance in weight space.

## 5.3. The deficiencies of simple learning procedures

The major deficiency of both the least squares and perceptron convergence procedures is that most "interesting" mappings between input and output vectors cannot be captured by any combination of weights in such simple networks, so the guarantee that the learning procedure will find the best possible combination of weights is of little value. Consider, for example, a network composed of two input units and one output unit. There is no way of setting the two weights and one threshold to solve the very simple task of producing an output of 1 when the input vector is $(1, 1)$ or $(0, 0)$ and an output of 0 when the input vector is $(1, 0)$ or $(0, 1)$. Minsky and Papert [68] give a clear analysis of the limitations on what mappings can be computed by three-layered nets. They focus on the question of what preprocessing must be done by the units in the intermediate layer to allow a task to be solved. They generally assume that the preprocessing is fixed, and so they avoid the problem of how to make the units in the intermediate layer learn useful predicates. So, from the learning perspective, their intermediate units are not true hidden units.

Another deficiency of the least squares and perceptron learning procedures is that gradient descent may be very slow if the elliptical cross-section of the error surface is very elongated so that the surface forms a long ravine with steep sides and a very low gradient along the ravine. In this case, the gradient at most points in the space is almost perpendicular to the direction towards the minimum. If the coefficient $\varepsilon$ in (7) is large, there are divergent oscillations across the ravine, and if it is small the progress along the ravine is very slow. A standard method for speeding the convergence in such cases is recursive least squares [100]. Various other methods have also been suggested [5, 71, 75].

We now consider learning in more complex networks that contain hidden units. The next five sections describe a variety of supervised, unsupervised, and reinforcement learning procedures for these nets.

## 6. Backpropagation: A Multi-layer Least Squares Procedure

The "backpropagation" learning procedure [80, 81] is a generalization of the least squares procedure that works for networks which have layers of hidden units between the input and output units. These multi-layer networks can compute much more complicated functions than networks that lack hidden units, but the learning is generally much slower because it must explore the space of possible ways of using the hidden units. There are now many examples in which backpropagation constructs interesting internal representations in the hidden units, and these representations allow the network to generalize in sensible ways. Variants of the procedure were discovered independently by Werbos [98], Le Cun [59] and Parker [70].

In a multi-layer network it is possible, using (8), to compute $\partial E / \partial w_{ji}$ for *all* the weights in the network provided we can compute $\partial E / \partial y_j$ for all the units that have modifiable incoming weights. In a system that has no hidden units, this is easy because the only relevant units are the output units, and for them $\partial E / \partial y_j$ is found by differentiating the error function in (6). But for hidden units, $\partial E / \partial y_j$ is harder to compute. The central idea of backpropagation is that these derivatives can be computed efficiently by starting with the output layer and working backwards through the layers. For each input-output case, $c$, we first use a forward pass, starting at the input units, to compute the activity levels of all the units in the network. Then we use a backward pass, starting at the output units, to compute $\partial E / \partial y_j$ for all the hidden units. For a hidden unit, $j$, in layer $J$ the only way it can affect the error is via its effects on the units, $k$, in the next layer, $K$ (assuming units in one layer only send their outputs to units in the layer above). So we have

$$\frac{\partial E}{\partial y_j} = \sum_k \frac{\partial E}{\partial y_k} \frac{dy_k}{dx_k} \frac{dx_k}{dy_j} = \sum_k \frac{\partial E}{\partial y_k} \frac{dy_k}{dx_k} w_{kj} , \tag{9}$$

where the index $c$ has been suppressed for clarity. So if $\partial E / \partial y_k$ is already known for all units in layer $K$, it is easy to compute the same quantity for units in layer $J$. Notice that the computation performed during the backward pass is very similar in form to the computation performed during the forward pass (though it propagates error derivatives instead of activity levels, and it is entirely linear in the error derivatives).

### 6.1. The shape of the error surface

In networks without hidden units, the error surface only has one minimum (provided a perfect solution exists and the units use smooth monotonic input-output functions). With hidden units, the error surface may contain many local minima, so it is possible that steepest descent in weight space will get stuck at poor local minima. In practice, this does not seem to be a serious problem. Backpropagation has been tried for a wide variety of tasks and poor local minima are rarely encountered, provided the network contains a few more units and connections than are required for the task. One reason for this is that there are typically a very large number of qualitatively different perfect solutions, so we avoid the typical combinatorial optimization task in which one minimum is slightly better than a large number of other, widely separated minima.

In practice, the most serious problem is the speed of convergence, not the presence of nonglobal minima. This is discussed further in Section 12.

### 6.2. Backpropagation for discovering semantic features

To demonstrate the ability of backpropagation to discover important underlying features of a domain, Hinton [38] used a multi-layer network to learn the

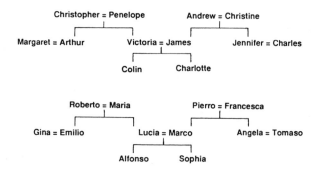

Fig. 4. Two isomorphic family trees.

family relationships between 24 different people (see Fig. 4). The information in a family tree can be represented as a set of triples of the form ($\langle$person1$\rangle$, $\langle$relationship$\rangle$, $\langle$person2$\rangle$), and a network can be said to "know" these triples if it can produce the third term of any triple when given the first two terms as input. Figure 5 shows the architecture of the network that was used to learn the triples. The input vector is divided into two parts, one of which specifies a person and the other a relationship (e.g. has-father). The network is trained to produce the related person as output. The input and output encoding use a different unit to represent each person and relationship, so all pairs of people are equally similar in the input and output encoding: The encodings do not give any clues about what the important features are. The architecture is designed so that all the information about an input person must be squeezed through a narrow bottleneck of 6 units in the first hidden layer. This forces the network

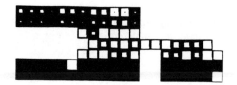

Fig. 5. The activity levels in a five-layer network after it has learned. The bottom layer has 24 input units on the left for representing person1 and 12 units on the right for representing the relationship. The white squares inside these two groups show the activity levels of the units. There is one active unit in the first group (representing Colin) and one in the second group (representing has-aunt). Each of the two groups of input units is totally connected to its own group of 6 units in the second layer. These two groups of 6 must learn to encode the input terms as distributed patterns of activity. The second layer is totally connected to the central layer of 12 units, and this layer is connected to the penultimate layer of 6 units. The activity in the penultimate layer must activate the correct output units, each of which stands for a particular person2. In this case, there are two correct answers (marked by black dots) because Colin has two aunts. Both the input and output units are laid out spatially with the English people in one row and the isomorphic Italians immediately below.

to represent people using distributed patterns of activity in this layer. The aim of the simulation is to see if the components of these distributed patterns correspond to the important underlying features of the domain.

After prolonged training on 100 of the 104 possible relationships, the network was tested on the remaining 4. It generalized correctly because during the training it learned to represent each of the people in terms of important features such as age, nationality, and the branch of the family tree that they belonged to (see Fig. 6), even though these "semantic" features were not at all explicit in the input or output vectors. Using these underlying features, much of the information about family relationships can be captured by a fairly small number of "micro-inferences" between features. For example, the father of a middle-aged person is an old person, and the father of an Italian person is an Italian person. So the features of the output person can be derived from the features of the input person and of the relationship. The learning procedure can only discover these features by searching for a set of features that make it easy to express the associations. Once these features have been discovered, the *internal* representation of each person (in the first hidden layer) is a distributed pattern of activity and similar people are represented by similar patterns. Thus the network constructs its own internal similarity metric. This is a significant advance over simulations in which good generalization is achieved because the experimenter chooses representations that already have an appropriate similarity metric.

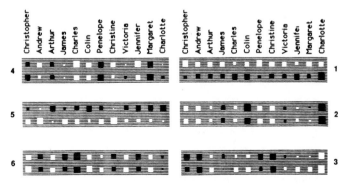

Fig. 6. The weights from the 24 input units that represent people to the 6 units in the second layer that learn distributed representations of people. White rectangles stand for excitatory weights, black for inhibitory weights, and the area of the rectangle encodes the magnitude of the weight. The weights from the 12 English people are in the top row of each unit. Beneath each of these weights is the weight from the isomorphic Italian. Unit 1 learns to encode nationality, unit 2 encodes generation (using three values), and unit 4 encodes the branch of the family tree to which a person belongs. During the learning, each weight was given a tendency to decay towards zero. This tendency is balanced by the error gradient, so the final magnitude of a weight indicates how useful it is in reducing the error.

## 6.3. Backpropagation for mapping text to speech

Backpropagation is an effective learning technique when the mapping from input vectors to output vectors contains both regularities and exceptions. For example, in mapping from a string of English letters to a string of English phonemes there are many regularities but there are also exceptions such as the word "women." Sejnowski and Rosenberg [84] have shown that a network with one hidden layer can be trained to pronounce letters surprisingly well. The input layer encodes the identity of the letter to be pronounced using a different unit for each possible letter. The input also encodes the local context which consists of the three previous letters and three following letters in the text (space and punctuation are treated as special kinds of letters). This seven-letter window is moved over the text, so the mapping from text to speech is performed sequentially, one letter at a time. The output layer encodes a phoneme using 21 articulatory features and 5 features for stress and syllable boundaries. There are 80 hidden units each of which receives connections from all the input units and sends connections to all the output units (see Fig. 7). After extensive training, the network generalizes well to new examples which demonstrates that it captures the regularities of the mapping. Its performance on new words is comparable to a conventional computer program which uses a large number of hand-crafted rules.

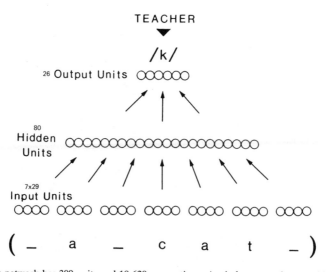

Fig. 7. The network has 309 units and 18,629 connections. A window seven letters wide is moved over the text, and the network pronounces the middle letter. It assumes a preprocessor to identify characters, and a postprocessor to turn phonemes into sounds.

## 6.4. Backpropagation for phoneme recognition

Speech recognition is a task that can be used to assess the usefulness of backpropagation for real-world signal-processing applications. The best existing techniques, such as hidden Markov models [9], are significantly worse than people, and an improvement in the quality of recognition would be of great practical significance.

A subtask which is well-suited to backpropagation is the bottom-up recognition of highly confusable consonants. One obvious approach is to convert the sound into a spectrogram which is then presented as the input vector to a multi-layer network whose output units represent different consonants. Unfortunately, this approach has two serious drawbacks. First, the spectrogram must have many "pixels" to give reasonable resolution in time and frequency, so each hidden unit has many incoming weights. This means that a very large number of training examples are needed to provide enough data to estimate the weights. Second, it is hard to achieve precise time alignment of the input data, so the spatial pattern that represents a given phoneme may occur at many different positions in the spectrogram. To learn that these shifts in position do not change the identity of the phoneme requires an immense amount of training data. We already know that the task has a certain symmetry—the same sounds occurring at different times mean the same phoneme. To speed learning and improve generalization we should build this a priori knowledge into the network and let it use the information in the training data to discover structure that we do not already understand.

An interesting way to build in the time symmetry is to use a multi-layer, feed-forward network that has connections with time delays [88]. The input units represent a single time frame from the spectrogram and the whole spectrogram is represented by stepping it through the input units. Each hidden unit is connected to each unit in the layer below by several different connections with different time delays and different weights. So it has a limited temporal window within which it can detect temporal patterns in the activities of the units in the layer below. Since a hidden unit applies the same set of weights at different times, it inevitably produces similar responses to similar patterns that are shifted in time (see Fig. 8).

Kevin Lang [58] has shown that a time delay net that is trained using a generalization of the backpropagation procedure compares favorably with hidden Markov models at the task of distinguishing the words "bee", "dee", "ee", and "vee" spoken by many different male speakers in a very noisy environment. Waibel et al. [97] have shown that the same network can achieve excellent speaker-dependent discrimination of the phonemes "b", "d", and "g" in varying phonetic contexts.

An interesting technical problem arises in computing the error derivatives for the output units of the time delay network. The adaptive part of the

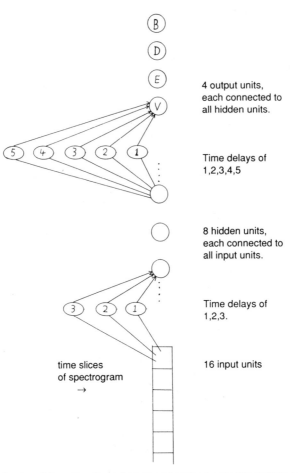

Fig. 8. Part of the time delay network used to recognize phonemes with variable onset times. A unit in one layer is connected to a unit in the layer below by several different connections which have different time delays and learn to have different weights.

network contains one output unit for each possible phoneme and these units respond to the input by producing a sequence of activations. If the training data is labeled with the exact time of occurrence of each phoneme, it is possible to specify the exact time at which an output unit should be active. But in the absence of precisely time-aligned training data, it is necessary to compute error derivatives for a sequence of activations without knowing when the phoneme occurred. This can be done by using a fixed postprocessing layer to integrate the activity of each output unit over time. We interpret the instantaneous activity of an output unit as a representation of the probability that the phoneme occurred at exactly that time. So, for the phoneme that really occurred, we know that the time integral of its activity should be 1 and for the other phonemes it should be 0. So at each time, the error derivative is simply the difference between the desired and the actual integral. After training, the network localizes phonemes in time, even though the training data contains no information about time alignment.

### 6.5. Postprocessing the output of a backpropagation net

Many people have suggested transforming the raw input vector with a module that uses unsupervised learning before presenting it to a module that uses supervised learning. It is less obvious that a supervised module can also benefit from a nonadaptive postprocessing module. A very simple example of this kind of postprocessing occurs in the time delay phoneme recognition network described in Section 6.4.

David Rumelhart has shown that the idea of a postprocessing module can be applied even in cases where the postprocessing function is initially unknown. In trying to imitate a sound, for example, a network might produce an output vector which specifies how to move the speech articulators. This output vector needs to be postprocessed to turn it into a sound, but the postprocessing is normally done by physics. Suppose that the network does not receive any direct information about what it should do with its articulators but it does "know" the desired sound and the actual sound, which is the transformed "image" of the output vector. If we had a postprocessing module which transformed the activations of the speech articulators into sounds, we could backpropagate through this module to compute error derivatives for the articulator activations.

Rumelhart uses an additional network (which he calls a mental model) that first learns to perform the postprocessing (i.e. it learns to map from output vectors to their transformed images). Once this mapping has been learned, backpropagation through the mental model can convert error derivatives for the "images" into error derivatives for the output vectors of the basic network.

### 6.6. A reinforcement version of backpropagation

Munro [69] has shown that the idea of using a mental model can be applied even when the image of an output vector is simply a single scalar value—the reinforcement. First, the mental model learns to predict expected reinforcement from the combination of the input vector and the output vector. Then the derivative of the expected reinforcement can be backpropagated through the mental model to get the reinforcement derivatives for each component of the output vector of the basic network.

## 6.7. Iterative backpropagation

Rumelhart, Hinton, and Williams [80] show how the backpropagation procedure can be applied to iterative networks in which there are no limitations on
the connectivity. A network in which the states of the units at time $t$ determine
the states of the units at time $t + 1$ is equivalent to a net which has one layer for
each time slice. Each weight in the iterative network is implemented by a
whole set of identical weights in the corresponding layered net, one for each
time slice (see Fig. 9). In the iterative net, the error is typically the difference
between the actual and desired final states of the network, and to compute the
error derivatives it is necessary to backpropagate through time, so the history
of states of each unit must be stored. Each weight will have many different
error derivatives, one for each time step, and the sum of all these derivatives is
used to determine the weight change.

Backpropagation in iterative nets can be used to train a network to generate
sequences or to recognize sequences or to complete sequences. Examples are
given by Rumelhart, Hinton and Williams [81]. Alternatively, it can be used to
store a set of patterns by constructing a point attractor for each pattern. Unlike
the simple storage procedure used in a Hopfield net, or the more sophisticated
storage procedure used in a Boltzmann machine (see Section 7), backpropagation takes into account the path used to reach a point attractor. So it will not
construct attractors that cannot be reached from the normal range of starting
points on which it is trained.[6]

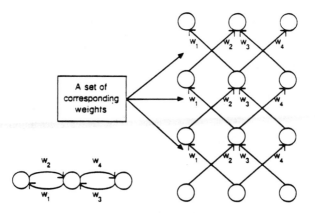

Fig. 9. On the left is a simple iterative network that is run synchronously for three iterations. On
the right is the equivalent layered network.

[6] A backpropagation net that uses asymmetric connections (and synchronous updating) is not
guaranteed to settle to a single stable state. To encourage it to construct a point attractor, rather
than a limit cycle, the point attractor can be made the desired state for the last few iterations.

## 6.8. Backpropagation as a maximum likelihood procedure

If we interpret each output vector as a specification of a conditional probability distribution over a set of output vectors given an input vector, we can interpret the backpropagation learning procedure as a method of finding weights that maximize the likelihood of generating the desired conditional probability distributions. Two examples of this kind of interpretation will be described.

Suppose we only attach meaning to binary output vectors and we treat a real-valued output vector as a way of specifying a probability distribution over binary vectors.[7] We imagine that a real-valued output vector is stochastically converted into a binary vector by treating the real values as the probabilities that individual components have value 1, and assuming independence between components. For simplicity, we can assume that the desired vectors used during training are binary vectors, though this is not necessary. Given a set of training cases, it can be shown that the likelihood of producing *exactly* the desired vectors is maximized when we minimize the cross-entropy, $C$, between the desired and actual conditional probability distributions:

$$C = -\sum_{j,c} d_{j,c} \log_2(y_{j,c}) + (1 - d_{j,c}) \log_2(1 - y_{j,c}),$$

where $d_{j,c}$ is the desired probability of output unit $j$ in case $c$ and $y_{j,c}$ is its actual probability.

So, under this interpretation of the output vectors, we should use the cross-entropy function rather than the squared difference as our cost measure. In practice, this helps to avoid a problem caused by output units which are firmly off when they should be on (or vice versa). These units have a very small value of $\partial y/\partial x$ so they need a large value of $\partial E/\partial y$ in order to change their incoming weights by a reasonable amount. When an output unit that should have an activity level of 1 changes from a level of 0.0001 to level of 0.001, the squared difference from 1 only changes slightly, but the cross-entropy decreases a lot. In fact, when the derivative of the cross-entropy is multiplied by the derivative of the logistic activation function, the product is simply the difference between the desired and the actual outputs, so $\partial C_{j,c}/\partial x_{j,c}$ is just the same as for a linear output unit (Steven Nowlan, personal communication).

This way of interpreting backpropagation raises the issue of whether, under some other interpretation of the output vectors, the squared error might not be the correct measure for performing maximum likelihood estimation. In fact, Richard Golden [32] has shown that minimizing the squared error is equivalent to maximum likelihood estimation if both the actual and the desired output vectors are treated as the centers of Gaussian probability density functions over the space of all real vectors. So the "correct" choice of cost function depends on the way the output vectors are most naturally interpreted.

---

[7] Both the examples of backpropagation described above fit this interpretation.

## 6.9. Self-supervised backpropagation

One drawback of the standard form of backpropagation is that it requires an external supervisor to specify the desired states of the output units (or a transformed "image" of the desired states). It can be converted into an unsupervised procedure by using the input itself to do the supervision, using a multi-layer "encoder" network [2] in which the desired output vector is identical with the input vector. The network must learn to compute an approximation to the identity mapping for all the input vectors in its training set, and if the middle layer of the network contains fewer units than the input layer, the learning procedure must construct a compact, invertible code for each input vector. This code can then be used as the input to later stages of processing.

The use of self-supervised backpropagation to construct compact codes resembles the use of principal components analysis to perform dimensionality reduction, but it has the advantage that it allows the code to be a nonlinear transform of the input vector. This form of backpropagation has been used successfully to compress images [19] and to compress speech waves [25]. A variation of it has been used to extract the underlying degrees of freedom of simple shapes [83].

It is also possible to use backpropagation to predict one part of the perceptual input from other parts. For example, in predicting one patch of an image from neighboring patches it is probably helpful to use hidden units that explicitly extract edges, so this might be an unsupervised way of discovering edge detectors. In domains with sequential structure, one portion of a sequence can be used as input and the next term in the sequence can be the desired output. This forces the network to extract features that are good predictors. If this is applied to the speech wave, the states of the hidden units will form a nonlinear predictive code. It is not yet known whether such codes are more helpful for speech recognition than linear predictive coefficients.

A different variation of self-supervised backpropagation is to insist that all or part of the code in the middle layer change as slowly as possible with time. This can be done by making the desired state of each of the middle units be the state it actually adopted for the previous input vector. This forces the network to use similar codes for input vectors that occur at neighboring times, which is a sensible principle if the input vectors are generated by a process whose underlying parameters change more slowly than the input vectors themselves.

## 6.10. The deficiencies of backpropagation

Despite its impressive performance on relatively small problems, and its promise as a widely applicable mechanism for extracting the underlying structure of a domain, backpropagation is inadequate, in its current form, for larger tasks because the learning time scales poorly. Empirically, the learning time on a serial machine is very approximately $O(N^3)$ where $N$ is the number of weights in the network. The time for one forward and one backward pass is $O(N)$. The number of training examples is typically $O(N)$, assuming the amount of information per output vector is held constant and enough training cases are used to strain the storage capacity of the network (which is about 2 bits per weight). The number of times the weights must be updated is also approximately $O(N)$. This is an empirical observation and depends on the nature of the task.[8] On a parallel machine that used a separate processor for each connection, the time would be reduced to approximately $O(N^2)$. Back-propagation can probably be improved by using the gradient information in more sophisticated ways, but much bigger improvements are likely to result from making better use of modularity (see Section 12.4).

As a biological model, backpropagation is implausible. There is no evidence that synapses can be used in the reverse direction, or that neurons can propagate error derivatives backwards (using a linear input-output function) as well as propagating activity levels forwards using a nonlinear input-output function. One approach is to try to backpropagate the derivatives using separate circuitry that *learns* to have the same weights as the forward circuitry [70]. A second approach, which seems to be feasible for self-supervised backpropagation, is to use a method called "recirculation" that approximates gradient descent and is more biologically plausible [41]. At present, backpropagation should be treated as a mechanism for demonstrating the kind of learning that can be done using gradient descent, without implying that the brain does gradient descent in the same way.

### 7. Boltzmann Machines

A Boltzmann machine [2, 46] is a generalization of a Hopfield net (see Section 4.2) in which the units update their states according to a *stochastic* decision rule. The units have states of 1 or 0,[9] and the probability that unit $j$ adopts the state 1 is given by

$$p_j = \frac{1}{1 + e^{-\Delta E_j / T}}, \tag{10}$$

where $\Delta E_j = x_j$ is the total input received by the $j$th unit and $T$ is the "temperature." It can be shown that if this rule is applied repeatedly to the units, the network will reach "thermal equilibrium." At thermal equilibrium the units still change state, but the *probability* of finding the network in any

---

[8] Tesauro [90] reports a case in which the number of weight updates is roughly proportional to the number of training cases (it is actually a 4/3 power law). Judd shows that in the worst case it is exponential [53].

[9] A network that uses states of 1 and 0 can always be converted into an equivalent network that uses states of +1 and −1 provided the thresholds are altered appropriately.

global state remains constant and obeys a Boltzmann distribution in which the probability ratio of any two global states depends solely on their energy difference:

$$\frac{P_A}{P_B} = e^{-(E_A - E_B)/T}$$

At high temperature, the network approaches equilibrium rapidly but low energy states are not much more probable than high energy states. At low temperature the network approaches equilibrium more slowly, but low energy states are much more probable than high energy states. The fastest way to approach low temperature equilibrium is generally to start at a high temperature and to gradually reduce the temperature. This is called "simulated annealing" [55]. Simulated annealing allows Boltzmann machines to find low energy states with high probability. If some units are clamped to represent an input vector, and if the weights in the network represent the constraints of the task domain, the network can settle on a very plausible output vector given the current weights and the current input vector.

For complex tasks there is generally no way of expressing the constraints by using weights on pairwise connections between the input and output units. It is necessary to use hidden units that represent higher-order features of the domain. This creates a problem: Given a limited number of hidden units, what higher-order features should they represent in order to approximate the required input-output mapping as closely as possible? The beauty of Boltzmann machines is that the simplicity of the Boltzmann distribution leads to a very simple learning procedure which adjusts the weights so as to use the hidden units in an optimal way.

The network is "shown" the mapping that it is required to perform by clamping an input vector on the input units and clamping the required output vector on the output units. If there are several possible output vectors for a given input vector, each of the possibilities is clamped on the output units with the appropriate frequency. The network is then annealed until it approaches thermal equilibrium at a temperature of 1. It then runs for a fixed time at equilibrium and each connection measures the fraction of the time during which both the units it connects are active. This is repeated for all the various input-output pairs so that each connection can measure $\langle s_i s_j \rangle^+$, the expected probability, averaged over all cases, that unit $i$ and unit $j$ are simultaneously active at thermal equilibrium when the input and output vectors are both clamped.

The network must also be run in just the same way but without clamping the output units. Again, it reaches thermal equilibrium with each input vector clamped and then runs for a fixed additional time to measure $\langle s_i s_j \rangle^-$, the expected probability that both units are active at thermal equilibrium when the output vector is determined by the network. Each weight is then updated by an amount proportional to the difference between these two quantities

$$\Delta w_{ij} = \varepsilon(\langle s_i s_j \rangle^+ - \langle s_i s_j \rangle^-).$$

It has been shown [2] that if $\varepsilon$ is sufficiently small this performs gradient descent in an information-theoretic measure, $G$, of the difference between the behavior of the output units when they are clamped and their behavior when they are not clamped.

$$G = \sum_{\alpha, \beta} P^+(I_\alpha, O_\beta) \log \frac{P^+(O_\beta | I_\alpha)}{P^-(O_\beta | I_\alpha)}, \tag{11}$$

where $I_\alpha$ is a state vector over the input units, $O_\beta$ is a state vector over the output units, $P^+$ is a probability measured when both the input and output units are clamped, and $P^-$ is a probability measured at thermal equilibrium when only the input units are clamped.

$G$ is called the "asymmetric divergence" or "Kullback information," and its gradient has the same form for connections between input and hidden units, connections between pairs of hidden units, connections between hidden and output units, and connections between pairs of output units. $G$ can be viewed as the difference of two terms. One term is the cross-entropy between the "desired" conditional probability distribution that is clamped on the output units and the "actual" conditional distribution exhibited by the output units when they are not clamped. The other term is the entropy of the "desired" conditional distribution. This entropy cannot be changed by altering the weights, so minimizing $G$ is equivalent to minimizing the cross-entropy term, which means that Boltzmann machines use the same cost function as one form of backpropagation (see Section 6.8).

A special case of the learning procedure is when there are no input units. It can then be viewed as an unsupervised learning procedure which learns to model a probability distribution that is specified by clamping vectors on the output units with the appropriate probabilities. The advantage of modeling a distribution in this way is that the network can then perform completion. When a partial vector is clamped over a subset of the output units, the network produces completions on the remaining output units. If the network has learned the training distribution perfectly, its probability of producing each completion is guaranteed to match the environmental conditional probability of this completion given the clamped partial vector.

The learning procedure can easily be generalized to networks where each term in the energy function is the product of a weight, $w_{i,j,k,...}$ and an arbitrary function, $f(i, j, k, \ldots)$, of the states of a subset of the units. The network must be run so that it achieves a Boltzmann distribution in the energy function, so each unit must be able to compute how the global energy would change if it were to change state. The generalized learning procedure is simply to change the weight by an amount proportional to the difference between $\langle f(i, j, k, \ldots) \rangle^+$ and $\langle f(i, j, k, \ldots) \rangle^-$.

The learning procedure using simple pairwise connections has been shown to produce appropriate representations in the hidden units [2] and it has also been used for speech recognition [76]. However, it is considerably slower than backpropagation because of the time required to reach equilibrium in large networks. Also, the process of estimating the gradient introduces several practical problems. If the network does not reach equilibrium the estimated gradient has a systematic error, and if too few samples are taken to estimate $\langle s_i s_j \rangle^+$ and $\langle s_i s_j \rangle^-$ accurately the estimated gradient will be extremely noisy because it is the difference of two noisy estimates. Even when the noise in the estimate of the difference has zero mean, its variance is a function of $\langle s_i s_j \rangle^+$ and $\langle s_i s_j \rangle^-$. When these quantities are near zero or one, their estimates will have much lower variance than when they are near 0.5. This nonuniformity in the variance gives the hidden units a surprisingly strong tendency to develop weights that cause them to be on all the time or off all the time. A familiar version of the same effect can be seen if sand is sprinkled on a vibrating sheet of tin. Nearly all the sand clusters at the points that vibrate the least, even though there is no bias in the direction of motion of an individual grain of sand.

One interesting feature of the Boltzmann machine is that it is relatively easy to put it directly onto a chip which has dedicated hardware for each connection and performs the annealing extremely rapidly using analog circuitry that computes the energy gap of a unit by simply allowing the incoming charge to add itself up, and makes stochastic decisions by using physical noise. Alspector and Allen [3] are fabricating a chip which will run about 1 million times as fast as a simulation on a VAX. Such chips may make it possible to apply connectionist learning procedures to practical problems, especially if they are used in conjunction with modular approaches that allow the learning time to scale better with the size of the task.

There is another promising method that reduces the time required to compute the equilibrium distribution and eliminates the noise caused by the sampling errors in $\langle s_i s_j \rangle^+$ and $\langle s_i s_j \rangle^-$. Instead of directly simulating the stochastic network it is possible to estimate its mean behavior using "mean field theory" which replaces each stochastic binary variable by a deterministic real value that represents the expected value of the stochastic variable. Simulated annealing can then be replaced by a deterministic relaxation procedure that operates on the real-valued parameters [51] and settles to a single state that gives a crude representation of the whole equilibrium distribution. The product of the "activity levels" of two units in this settled state can be used as an approximation of $\langle s_i s_j \rangle$ so a version of the Boltzmann machine learning procedure can be applied. Peterson and Anderson [74] have shown that this works quite well.

## 7.1. Maximizing reinforcement and entropy in a Boltzmann machine

The Boltzmann machine learning procedure is based on the simplicity of the expression for the derivative of the asymmetric divergence between the conditional probability distribution exhibited by the output units of a Boltzmann machine and a desired conditional probability distribution. The derivatives of certain other important measures are also very simple if the network is allowed to reach thermal equilibrium. For example, the entropy of the states of the machine is given by

$$H = -\sum_{\alpha} P_{\alpha} \log_e P_{\alpha} \,,$$

where $P_{\alpha}$ is the probability of a global configuration, and $H$ is measured in units of $\log_2 e$ bits. Its derivative is

$$\frac{\partial H}{\partial w_{ij}} = \frac{1}{T} \left( \langle Es_i s_j \rangle - \langle E \rangle \langle s_i s_j \rangle \right). \tag{12}$$

So if each weight has access to the global energy, $E$, it is easy to manipulate the entropy.

It is also easy to perform gradient ascent in expected reinforcement if the network is given a global reinforcement signal, $R$, that depends on its state. The derivative of the expected reinforcement with respect to each weight is

$$\frac{\partial R}{\partial w_{ij}} = \frac{1}{T} \left( \langle Rs_i s_j \rangle - \langle R \rangle \langle s_i s_j \rangle \right). \tag{13}$$

A recurrent issue in reinforcement learning procedures is how to trade off short-term optimization of expected reinforcement against the diversity required to discover actions that have a higher reinforcement than the network's current estimate. If we use entropy as a measure of diversity, and we assume that the system tries to optimize some linear combination of the expected reinforcement and the entropy of its actions, it can be shown that its optimal strategy is to pick actions according to a Boltzmann distribution, where the expected reinforcement of a state is the analog of negative energy and the parameter that determines the relative importance of expected reinforcement and diversity is the analog of temperature. This result follows from the fact that the Boltzmann distribution is the one which maximizes entropy (i.e. diversity) for a given expected energy (i.e. reinforcement).

This suggests a learning procedure in which the system represents the expected value of an action by its negative energy, and picks actions by allowing a Boltzmann machine to reach thermal equilibrium. If the weights are updated using equations (12) and (13) the negative energies of states will tend to become proportional to their expected reinforcements, since this is the way to make the derivative of $H$ balance the derivative of $R$. Once the system has learned to represent the reinforcements correctly, variations in the temperature can be used to make it more or less conservative in its choice of actions whilst always making the optimal tradeoff between diversity and expected reinforcement. Unfortunately, this learning procedure does not make use of the most important property of Boltzmann machines which is their ability to compute the quantity $\langle s_i s_j \rangle$ *given* some specified state of the output units. Also, it is much harder to compute the derivative of the entropy if we are only interested in the entropy of the state vectors over the output units.

### 8. Maximizing Mutual Information: A Semisupervised Learning Procedure

One "semisupervised" method of training a unit is to provide it with information about what category the input vector came from, but to refrain from specifying the state that the unit ought to adopt. Instead, its incoming weights are modified so as to maximize the information that the state of the unit provides about the category of the input vector. The derivative of the mutual information is relatively easy to compute and so it can be maximized by gradient ascent [73]. For difficult discriminations that cannot be performed in a single step this is a good way of producing encodings of the input vector that allow the discrimination to be made more easily. Figure 10 shows an example of a difficult two-way discrimination and illustrates the kinds of discriminant function that maximize the information provided by the state of the unit.

If each unit within a layer independently maximizes the mutual information between its state and the category of the input vector, many units are likely to discover similar, highly correlated features. One way to force the units to diversify is to make each unit receive its inputs from a different subset of the units in the layer below. A second method is to ignore cases in which the input vector is correctly classified by the final output units and to maximize the

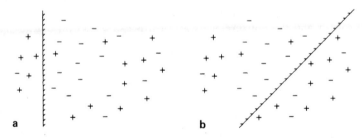

Fig. 10. (a) There is high mutual information between the state of a binary threshold unit that uses the hyperplane shown and the distribution (+ or −) that the input vector came from. (b) The probability, given that the unit is on, that the input came from the "+" distribution is not as high using the diagonal hyperplane. However, the unit is on more often. Other things being equal, a unit conveys most mutual information if it is on half the time.

mutual information between the state of each intermediate unit and the category of the input *given that the input is incorrectly classified.*[10]

If the two input distributions that must be discriminated consist of examples taken from some structured domain and examples generated at random (but with the same first-order statistics as the structured domain), this semisupervised procedure will discover higher-order features that characterize the structured domain and so it can be made to act like the type of unsupervised learning procedure described in Section 9.

## 9. Unsupervised Hebbian Learning

A unit can develop selectivity to certain kinds of features in its ensemble of input vectors by using a simple weight modification procedure that depends on the correlation between the activity of the unit and the activity on each of it input lines. This is called a "Hebbian" learning rule because the weight modification depends on both presynaptic and postsynaptic activity [36]. Typical examples of this kind of learning are described by Cooper, Liberman and Oja [18] and by Bienenstock, Cooper, and Munro [16]. A criticism of early versions of this approach, from a computational point of view, was that the researchers often postulated a simple synaptic modification rule and then explored its consequences rather than rigorously specifying the computational goal and then deriving the appropriate synaptic modification rule. However, an important recent development unifies these two approaches by showing that a relatively simple Hebbian rule can be viewed as the gradient of an interesting function. The function can therefore be viewed as a specification of what the learning is trying to achieve.

### 9.1. A recent development of unsupervised Hebbian learning

In a recent series of papers Linsker has shown that with proper normalization of the weight changes, an unsupervised Hebbian learning procedure in which the weight change depends on the correlation of presynaptic and postsynaptic activity can produce a surprising number of the known properties of the receptive fields of neurons in visual cortex, including center-surround fields [61], orientation-tuned fields [62] and orientation columns [63]. The procedure operates in a multi-layer network in which there is innate spatial structure so that the inputs to a unit in one layer tend to come from nearby locations in the layer below. Linsker demonstrates that the emergence of biologically suggestive receptive fields depends on the relative values of a few generic parameters. He also shows that for each unit, the learning procedure is performing gradient ascent in a measure whose main term is the ensemble average (across all the

---

[10] This method of weighting the statistics by some measure of the overall error or importance of a case can often be used to allow global measures of the performance of the whole network to influence local, unsupervised learning procedures.

various patterns of activity in the layer below) of

$$\sum_{i,j} w_i s_i w_j s_j \,,$$

where $w_i$ and $w_j$ are the weights on the $i$th and $j$th input lines of a unit and $s_i$ and $s_j$ are the activities on those input lines.

It is not initially obvious why maximizing the pairwise covariances of the weighted activities produces receptive fields that are useful for visual information processing. Linsker does not discuss this question in his original three papers. However, he has now shown [64] that the learning procedure maximizes the variance in the activity of the postsynaptic unit subject to a "resource" constraint on overall synaptic strength. This is almost equivalent to maximizing the ratio of the postsynaptic variance to the sum of the squares of the weights, which is guaranteed to extract the first principal component (provided the units are linear). This component is the one that would minimize the sum-squared reconstruction error if we tried to reconstruct the activity vector of the presynaptic units from the activity level of the postsynaptic unit. Thus we can view Linsker's learning procedure as a way of ensuring that the activity of a unit conveys as much information as possible about its presynaptic input vector. A similar analysis can be applied to competitive learning (see Section 10).

## 10. Competitive Learning

Competitive learning is an unsupervised procedure that divides a set of input vectors into a number of disjoint clusters in such a way that the input vectors within each cluster are all similar to one another. It is called competitive learning because there is a set of hidden units which compete with one another to become active. There are many variations of the same basic idea, and only the simplest version is described here. When an input vector is presented to the network, the hidden unit which receives the greatest total input wins the competition and turns on with an activity level of 1. All the other hidden units turn off. The winning unit then adds a small fraction of the current input vector to its weight vector. So, in future, it will receive even more total input from this input vector. To prevent the same hidden unit from being the most active in all cases, it is necessary to impose a constraint on each weight vector that keeps the sum of the weights (or the sum of their squares) constant. So when a hidden unit becomes more sensitive to one input vector it becomes less sensitive to other input vectors.

Rumelhart and Zipser [82] present a simple geometrical model of competitive learning. If each input vector has three components and is of unit length it can be represented by a point on the surface of the unit sphere. If the weight vectors of the hidden units are also constrained to be of unit length, they too can be represented by points on the unit sphere as shown in Fig. 11. The

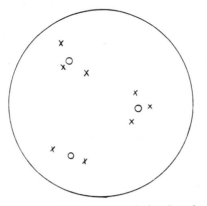

Fig. 11. The input vectors are represented by points marked "×" on the surface of a sphere. The weight vectors of the hidden units are represented by points marked "○." After competitive learning, each weight vector will be close to the center of gravity of a cluster of input vectors.

learning procedure is equivalent to finding the weight vector that is closest to the current input vector, and moving it closer still by an amount that is proportional to the distance. If the weight changes are sufficiently small, this process will stabilize when each weight vector is at the center of gravity of a cluster of input vectors.

We can think of the network as performing the following task: Represent the current input vector, $y_c$, as accurately as possible by using a single active hidden unit. The representation is simply the weight vector, $w_c$, of the hidden unit which is active in case $c$. If the weight changes are sufficiently small, this version of competitive learning performs steepest descent in a measure of the sum-squared inaccuracy of the representation. The solutions it finds are minima of the function

$$E = \tfrac{1}{2} \sum_c (w_c - y_c)^2 \ .$$

Although they use the geometrical analogy described above, Rumelhart and Zipser actually use a slightly different learning rule which cannot be interpreted as performing steepest descent in such a simple error function.

There are many variations of competitive learning in the literature [4, 29, 33, 95] and there is not space here to review them all. A model with similarities to competitive learning has been used by Willshaw and von der Malsburg [103] to explain the formation of topographic maps between the retina and the tectum. Recently, it has been shown that a variation of this model can be interpreted as performing steepest descent in an error function and can be applied to a range of optimization problems that involve topographic mappings between geometrical structures [23].

One major theme has been to show that competitive learning can produce topographic maps [57]. The hidden units are laid out in a spatial structure (usually two-dimensional) and instead of just updating the weight vector of the hidden unit that receives the greatest total input, the procedure also updates the weight vectors of adjacent hidden units. This encourages adjacent units to respond to similar input vectors, and it can be viewed as a way of performing gradient descent in a cost function that has two terms. The first term measures how inaccurately the weight vector of the most active hidden unit represents the input vector. The second term measures the dissimilarity between the input vectors that are represented by adjacent hidden units. Kohonen has shown that this version of competitive learning performs dimensionality reduction, so that surplus degrees of freedom are removed from the input vector and it is represented accurately by a point in a lower-dimensional space [57]. It is not clear how this compares in efficiency with self-supervised backpropagation (see Section 6.9) for dimensionality reduction.

Fukushima and Miyake [30] have demonstrated that a version of competitive learning can be used to allow a multi-layer network to recognize simple two-dimensional shapes in a number of different positions. After learning, the network can recognize a familiar shape in a novel position. The ability to generalize across position depends on using a network in which the layers of units that learn are interleaved with layers of nonlearning units which are prewired to generalize across position. Thus, the network does not truly learn translation invariance. By contrast, it is possible to design a backpropagation network that starts with no knowledge of the effects of translation and no knowledge of which input units are adjacent in the image. After sufficient experience, the network can correctly identify familiar, simple shapes in novel positions [39].

## 10.1. The relationship between competitive learning and backpropagation

Because it is performing gradient descent in a measure of how accurately the input vector could be reconstructed, competitive learning has a close relationship to self-supervised backpropagation. Consider a three-layer encoder network in which the desired states of the output units are the same as the actual states of the input units. Suppose that each weight from an input unit to a hidden unit is constrained to be identical to the weight from that hidden unit to the corresponding output unit. Suppose, also, that the output units are linear and the hidden units, instead of using the usual nonlinear input-output function, use the same "winner-take-all" nonlinearity as is used in competitive learning. So only one hidden unit will be active at a time, and the actual states of the output units will equal the weights of the active hidden unit. This makes it easy to compute the error derivatives of the weights from the hidden units to the output units. For weights from the active hidden unit the derivatives are simply proportional to the difference between the actual and desired outputs (which equals the difference between the weight and the corresponding component of the input vector). For weights from inactive hidden units the error derivatives are all zero. So gradient descent can be performed by making the weights of the active hidden unit regress towards the input vector, which is precisely what the competitive learning rule does.

Normally, backpropagation is needed in order to compute the error derivatives of the weights from the input units to the hidden units, but the winner-take-all nonlinearity makes backpropagation unnecessary in this network because all these derivatives are equal to zero. So long as the same hidden unit wins the competition, its activity level is not changed by changing its input weights. At the point where a small change in the weights would change the winner from one hidden unit to another, both hidden units fit the input vector equally well, so changing winners does not alter the total error in the output (even though it may change the output vector a lot). Because the error derivatives are so simple, we can still do the learning if we omit the output units altogether. This removes the output weights, and so we no longer need to constrain the input and output weights of a hidden unit to be identical. Thus the simplified version of competitive learning is a degenerate case of self-supervised backpropagation.

It would be interesting if a mechanism as simple as competitive learning could be used to implement gradient descent in networks that allow the $m$ most activated hidden units to become fully active (where $m > 1$). This would allow the network to create more complex, distributed representations of the input vectors. Unfortunately the implementation is not nearly as simple because it is no longer possible to omit the output layer. The output units are needed to combine the effects of all the active hidden units and compare the combined effect with the input vector in order to compute the error derivatives of the output weights. Also, at the point at which one hidden unit ceases to be active and another becomes active, there may be a large change in the total error, so at this point there are infinite error derivatives for the weights from the input to the hidden units. It thus appears that the simplicity of the mechanism required for competitive learning is crucially dependent on the fact that only one hidden unit within a group is active.

### 11. Reinforcement Learning Procedures

There is a large and complex literature on reinforcement learning procedures which is beyond the scope of this paper. The main aim of this section is to give an informal description of a few of the recent ideas in the field that reveals their relationship to other types of connectionist learning.

A central idea in many reinforcement learning procedures is that we can assign credit to a local decision by *measuring* how it correlates with the global reinforcement signal. Various different values are tried for each local variable (such as a weight or a state), and these variations are correlated with variations in the global reinforcement signal. Normally, the local variations are the result of independent stochastic processes, so if enough samples are taken each local variable can average away the noise caused by the variation in the other variables to reveal its own effect on the global reinforcement signal (given the current average behavior of the other variables). The network can then perform gradient ascent in the expected reinforcement by altering the probability distribution of the value of each local variable in the direction that increases the expected reinforcement. If the probability distributions are altered after each trial, the network performs a stochastic version of gradient ascent.

The main advantage of reinforcement learning is that it is easy to implement because, unlike backpropagation which *computes* the effect of changing a local variable, the "credit assignment" does not require any special apparatus for *computing* derivatives. So reinforcement learning can be used in complex systems in which it would be very hard to analytically compute reinforcement derivatives. The main disadvantage of reinforcement learning is that it is very inefficient when there are more than a few local variables. Even in the trivial case when all the local variables contribute independently to the global reinforcement signal, $O(NM)$ trials are required to allow the measured effects of each of the $M$ possible values of a variable to achieve a reasonable signal-to-noise ratio by averaging away the noise caused by the $N$ other variables. So reinforcement learning is very inefficient for large systems unless they are divided into smaller modules. It is as if each person in the United States tried to decide whether he or she had done a useful day's work by observing the gross national product on a day-by-day basis.

A second disadvantage is that gradient ascent may get stuck in local optima. As a network concentrates more and more of its trials on combinations of values that give the highest expected reinforcement, it gets less and less information about the reinforcements caused by other combinations of values.

## 11.1. Delayed reinforcement

In many real systems, there is a delay between an action and the resultant reinforcement, so in addition to the normal problem of deciding how to assign credit to decisions about hidden variables, there is a temporal credit assignment problem [86]. If, for example, a person wants to know how their behavior affects the gross national product, they need to know whether to correlate today's GNP with what they did yesterday or with what they did five years ago. In the iterative version of backpropagation (Section 6.7), temporal credit assignment is performed by explicitly computing the effect of each activity level on the eventual outcome. In reinforcement learning procedures, temporal credit assignment is typically performed by learning to associate "secondary" reinforcement values with the states that are intermediate in time between the action and the external reinforcement. One important idea is to make the reinforcement value of an intermediate state regress towards the weighted average of the reinforcement values of its successors, where the weightings reflect the conditional probabilities of the successors. In the limit, this causes the reinforcement value of each state to be equal to the expected reinforcement of its successor, and hence equal to the expected final reinforcement.[11] Sutton [87] explains why, in a stochastic system, it is typically more efficient to regress towards the reinforcement value of the next state rather than the reinforcement value of the final outcome. Barto, Sutton and Anderson [15] have demonstrated the usefulness of this type of procedure for learning with delayed reinforcement.

## 11.2. The $A_{R-P}$ procedure

One obvious way of mapping results from learning automata theory onto connectionist networks is to treat each unit as an automaton and to treat the states it adopts as its actions. Barto and Anandan [14] describe a learning procedure of this kind called "associative reward-penalty" or $A_{R-P}$ which uses stochastic units like those in a Boltzmann machine (see (10)). They prove that if the input vectors are linearly independent and the network only contains one unit, $A_{R-P}$ finds the optimal values of the weights. They also show empirically that if the same procedure is applied in a network of such units, the hidden units develop useful representations. Williams [101] has shown that a limiting case of the $A_{R-P}$ procedure performs stochastic gradient ascent in expected reinforcement.

## 11.3. Achieving global optimality by reinforcement learning

Thatachar and Sastry [91] use a different mapping between automata and connectionist networks. Each *connection* is treated as an automaton and the weight values that it takes on are its actions. On each trial, each connection chooses a weight (from a discrete set of alternatives) and then the network maps an input vector into an output vector and receives positive reinforcement if the output is correct. They present a learning procedure for updating the probabilities of choosing particular weight values. If the probabilities are changed slowly enough, the procedure is guaranteed to converge on the globally optimal combination of weights, even if the network has hidden layers. Unfortunately their procedure requires exponential space because it involves

---

[11] There may also be a "tax" imposed for failing to achieve the external reinforcement quickly. This can be implemented by reducing the reinforcement value each time it is regressed to an earlier state.

storing and updating a table of estimated expected reinforcements that contains one entry for every combination of weights.

## 11.4. The relative payoff procedure

If we are content to reach a local optimum, it is possible to use a very simple learning procedure that uses yet another way of mapping automata onto connectionist networks. Each connection is treated as a stochastic switch that has a certain probability of being closed at any moment [66]. If the switch is open, the "postsynaptic" unit receives an input of 0 along that connection, but if the switch is closed it transmits the state of the "presynaptic" unit. A real synapse can be modeled as a set of these stochastic switches arranged in parallel. Each unit computes some fixed function of the vector of inputs that it receives on its incoming connections. Learning involves altering the switch probabilities to maximize the expected reinforcement signal.

A learning procedure called $L_{R-I}$ can be applied in such networks. It is only guaranteed to find a local optimum of the expected reinforcement, but it is very simple to implement. A "trial" consists of four stages:

(1) Set the switch configuration. For each switch in the network, decide whether it is open or closed on this trial using the current switch probability. The decisions are made independently for all the switches.

(2) Run the network with this switch configuration. There are no constraints on the connectivity so cycles are allowed, and the units can also receive external inputs at any time. The constraint on the external inputs is that the probability distribution over patterns of external input must be stationary.

(3) Compute the reinforcement signal. This can be any nonnegative, stationary function of the behavior of the network and of the external input it received during the trial.

(4) Update the switch probabilities. For each switch that was closed during the trial, we increment its probability by $\varepsilon R(1-p)$, where $R$ is the reinforcement produced by the trial, $p$ is the switch probability and $\varepsilon$ is a small coefficient. For each switch that was open, we decrement its probability by $\varepsilon Rp$.

If $\varepsilon$ is sufficiently small this procedure stochastically approximates hill climbing in expected reinforcement. The "batch" version of the procedure involves observing the reinforcement signal over a large number of trials before updating the switch probabilities. If a sufficient number of trials are observed, the following "relative payoff" update procedure always increases expected reinforcement (or leaves it unchanged): Change the switch probability to be equal to the fraction of the total reinforcement received when the switch was closed. This can cause large changes in the probabilities, and I know of no proof that it hill-climbs in expected reinforcement, but in practice it always works. The direction of the jump in switch probability space caused by the batch version of the procedure is the same as the expected direction of the small change in switch probabilities caused by the "online" version.

A variation of the relative payoff procedure can be used if the goal is to make the "responses" of a network match some desired probability distribution rather than maximize expected reinforcement. We simply define the reinforcement signal to be the desired probability of a response divided by the network's current probability of producing that response. If a sufficient number of trials are made before updating the switch probabilities, it can be shown (Larry Gillick and Jim Baker, personal communication) that this procedure is guaranteed to decrease an information-theoretic measure of the difference between the desired probability distribution over responses and the actual probability distribution. The measure is actually the $G$ measure described in (11) and the proof is an adaptation of the proof of the EM procedure [22].

## 11.5. Genetic algorithms

Holland and his co-workers [21, 48] have investigated a class of learning procedures which they call "genetic algorithms" because they are explicitly inspired by an analogy with evolution. Genetic algorithms operate on a population of individuals to produce a better adapted population. In the simplest case, each individual member of the population is a binary vector, and the two possible values of each component are analogous to two alternative versions (alleles) of a gene. There is a fitness function which assigns a real-valued fitness to each individual and the aim of the "learning" is to raise the average fitness of the population. New individuals are produced by choosing two existing individuals as parents (with a bias towards individuals of higher than average fitness) and copying some component values from one parent and some from the other. Holland [48] has shown that for a large class of fitness functions, this is an effective way of discovering individuals that have high fitness.

## 11.6. Genetic learning and the relative payoff rule

If an entire generation of individuals is simultaneously replaced by a generation of their offspring, genetic learning has a close relationship to the batch form of the $L_{R-I}$ procedure described in Section 11.4. This is most easily understood by starting with a particularly simple version of genetic learning in which every individual in generation $t + 1$ has many different parents in generation $t$. Candidate individuals for generation $t + 1$ are generated from the existing individuals in generation $t$ in the following way: To decide the value of the $i$th component of a candidate, we randomly choose one of the individuals in generation $t$ and copy the value of its $i$th component. So the probability that the $i$th component of a candidate has a particular value is simply the relative frequency of that value in generation $t$. A selection process then operates on the candidates: Some are kept to form generation $t + 1$ and others are discarded. The fitness of a candidate is simply the probability that it is not discarded by the selection process. Candidates that are kept can be considered to have received a reinforcement of 1 and candidates that are discarded receive a reinforcement of 0. After selection, the probability that the $i$th component has a particular value is equal to the fraction of the successful candidates that have that value. This is exactly the relative payoff rule described in Section 11.4. The probabilities it operates on are the relative frequencies of alleles in the population instead of switch probabilities.

If the value of every component is determined by an independently chosen parent, information about the correlations between the values of different components is lost when generation $t + 1$ is produced from generation $t$. If, however, we use just two parents we maximize the tendency for the pairwise and higher-order correlations to be preserved. This tendency is further increased if components whose correlations are important are near one another and the values of nearby components are normally taken from the same parent. So a population of individuals can effectively represent the probabilities of small combinations of component values as well as the probabilities of individual values. Genetic learning works well when the fitness of an individual is determined by these small combinations, which Holland calls critical schemas.

## 11.7. Iterated genetic hill climbing

It is possible to combine genetic learning with gradient descent (or hill climbing) to get a hybrid learning procedure called "iterated genetic hill climbing" or "IGH" that works better than either learning procedure alone [1, 17]. IGH is as a form of multiple restart hill climbing in which the starting points, instead of being chosen at random, are chosen by "mating" previously discovered local optima. Alternatively, it can be viewed as genetic learning in which each new individual is allowed to perform hill climbing in the fitness function before being evaluated and added to the population. Ackley [1] shows that a stochastic variation of IGH can be implemented in a connectionist network that is trying to learn which output vector produces a high enough payoff to satisfy some external criterion.

## 12. Discussion

This review has focused on a small number of recent connectionist learning procedures. There are many other interesting procedures which have been omitted [24, 26, 34, 35, 47, 54, 94]. In particular, there has been no discussion of a large class of procedures which dynamically allocate new units instead of simply adjusting the weights in a fixed architecture. Rather than attempting to cover all of these I conclude by discussing two major problems that plague most of the procedures I have described.

## 12.1. Generalization

A major goal of connectionist learning is to produce networks that generalize correctly to new cases after training on a sufficiently large set of typical cases from some domain. In much of the research, there is no formal definition of what it means to generalize correctly. The network is trained on examples from a domain that the experimenter understands (like the family relationships domain described in Section 6) and it is judged to generalize correctly if its generalizations agree with those of the experimenter. This is sufficient as an informal demonstration that the network can indeed perform nontrivial generalization, but it gives little insight into the reasons why the generalizations of the network and the experimenter agree, and so it does not allow predictions to be made about when networks will generalize correctly and when they will fail.

What is needed is a formal theory of what it means to generalize correctly. One approach that has been used in studying the induction of grammars is to define a hypothesis space of possible grammars, and to show that with enough training cases the system will converge on the correct grammar with probability 1 [8]. Valiant [93] has recently introduced a rather more subtle criterion of success in order to distinguish classes of boolean function that can be induced from examples in polynomial time from classes that require exponential time. He assumes that the hypothesis space is known in advance and he allows the training cases to be selected according to *any* stationary distribution but insists that the same distribution be used to generate the test cases. The induced function is considered to be good enough if it differs from the true function on less than a small fraction, $1/h$, of the test cases. A class of boolean functions is considered to be learnable in polynomial time if, for any choice of $h$, there is a probability of at least $(1 - 1/h)$ that the induced function is good enough after a number of training examples that is polynomial in both $h$ and the number of arguments of the boolean function. Using this definition, Valiant has succeeded in showing that several interesting subclasses of boolean function are learnable in polynomial time. Our understanding of other connectionist learning procedures would be considerably improved if we could derive similar results that were as robust against variations in the distribution of the training examples.

The work on inducing grammars or boolean functions may not provide an appropriate framework for studying systems that learn inherently stochastic functions, but the general idea of starting with a hypothesis space of possible functions carries over. A widely used statistical approach involves maximizing the a posteriori likelihood of the model (i.e. the function) given the data. If the data really is generated by a function in the hypothesis space and if the amount of information in the training data greatly exceeds the amount of information required to specify a point in the hypothesis space, the maximum likelihood function is very probably the correct one, so the network will then generalize correctly. Some connectionist learning schemes (e.g. the Boltzmann machine learning procedure) can be made to fit this approach exactly. If a Boltzmann machine is trained with much more data than there are weights in the machine, and if it really does find the global minimum of $G$, and if the correct answer lies in the hypothesis space (which is defined by the architecture of the machine),[12] then there is every reason to suppose that it will generalize correctly, even if it has only been trained on a small fraction of the *possible* cases. Unfortunately, this kind of guarantee is of little use for practical problems where we usually know in advance that the "true" model does not lie in the hypothesis space of the network. What needs to be shown is that the best available point within the hypothesis space (even though it is not a perfect model) will also generalize well to test cases.

A simple thought experiment shows that the "correct" generalization from a set of training cases, however it is defined, must depend on how the input and output vectors are encoded. Consider a mapping, $M_I$, from entire input vectors onto entire input vectors and a mapping, $M_O$, from entire output vectors onto entire output vectors. If we introduce a precoding stage that uses $M_I$ and a postcoding stage that uses $M_O$ we can convert a network that generalizes in one way into a network that generalizes in any other way we choose simply by choosing $M_I$ and $M_O$ appropriately.

## 12.2. Practical methods of improving generalization

One very useful method of improving the generalization of many connectionist learning procedures is to introduce an extra term into the error function. This term penalizes large weights and it can be viewed as a way of building in an a priori bias is favor of simple models (i.e. models in which there are not too many strong interactions between the variables). If the extra term is the sum of the squares of the weights, its derivative corresponds to "weight decay"—each weight continually decays towards zero by an amount proportional to its magnitude. When the learning has equilibrated, the magnitude of a weight is equal to its error derivative because this error derivative balances the weight decay. This often makes it easier to interpret the weights. Weight decay tends to prevent a network from using table lookup and forces it to discover regularities in the training data. In a simple linear network without hidden units, weight decay can be used to find the weight matrix that minimizes the effect of adding zero-mean, uncorrelated noise to the input units [60].

Another useful method is to impose equality constraints between weights that encode symmetries in the task. In solving any practical problem, it is

---

[12] One popular idea is that evolution implicitly chooses an appropriate hypothesis space by constraining the architecture of the network and learning then identifies the most likely hypothesis within this space. How evolution arrives at sensible hypothesis spaces in reasonable time is usually unspecified. The evolutionary search for good architectures may actually be guided by learning [43].

wasteful to make the network learn information that is known in advance. If possible, this information should be encoded by the architecture or the initial weights so that the training data can be used to learn aspects of the task that we do not already know how to model.

## 12.3. The speed of learning

Most existing connectionist learning procedures are slow, particularly procedures that construct complicated internal representations. One way to speed them up is to use optimization methods such as recursive least squares that converge faster. If the second derivatives can be computed or estimated they can be used to pick a direction for the weight change vector that yields faster convergence than the direction of steepest descent [71]. It remains to be seen how well such methods work for the error surfaces generated by multi-layer networks learning complex tasks.

A second method of speeding up learning is to use dedicated hardware for each connection and to map the inner-loop operations into analog instead of digital hardware. As Alspector and Allen [3] have demonstrated, the speed of one particular learning procedure can be increased by a factor of about a million if we combine these techniques. This significantly increases our ability to explore the behavior of relatively small systems, but it is not a panacea. By using silicon in a different way we typically gain a large but constant factor (optical techniques may eventually yield a *huge* constant factor), and by dedicating a processor to each of the $N$ connections we gain at most a factor of $N$ in time at the cost of at least a factor of $N$ in space. For a learning procedure with a time complexity of, say, $O(N \log N)$ a speed up of $N$ makes a very big difference. For a procedure with a complexity of, say, $O(N^3)$ alternative technologies and parallelism will help significantly for small systems, but not for large ones.[13]

## 12.4. Hardware modularity

One of the best and commonest ways of fighting complexity is to introduce a modular, hierarchical structure in which different modules are only loosely coupled [85]. Pearl [72] has shown that if the interactions between a set of probabilistic variables are constrained to form a tree structure, there are efficient parallel methods for estimating the interactions between "hidden" variables. The leaves of the tree are the observables and the higher-level nodes are hidden. The probability distribution for each variable is constrained by the values of its immediate parents in the tree. Pearl shows that these conditional probabilities can be recovered in time $O(N \log N)$ from the pairwise correlations between the values of the leaves of the tree. Remarkably, it is also possible to recover the tree structure itself in the same time.

---

[13] Tsotsos [92] makes similar arguments in a discussion of the space complexity of vision.

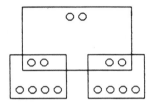

Fig. 12. The lower-level variables of a high-level module are the higher-level variables of several low-level modules.

Self-supervised backpropagation (see Section 6.9) was originally designed to allow efficient bottom-up learning in domains where there is hierarchical modular structure. Consider, for example, an ensemble of input vectors that are generated in the following modular way: Each module has a few high-level variables whose values help to constrain the values of a larger number of low-level variables. The low-level variables of each module are partitioned into several sets, and each set is identified with the high-level variables of a lower module as shown in Fig. 12.

Now suppose that we treat the values of all the low-level variables of the leaf modules as a single input vector. Given a sufficiently large ensemble of input vectors and an "innate" knowledge of the architecture of the generator, it should be possible to recover the underlying structure by using self-supervised backpropagation to learn compact codes for the low-level variables of each leaf module. It is possible to learn codes for all the lowest-level modules in parallel. Once this has been done, the network can learn codes at the next level up the hierarchy. The time taken to learn the whole hierarchical structure (given parallel hardware) is just proportional to the depth of the tree and hence it is $O(\log N)$ where $N$ is the size of the input vector. An improvement on this strictly bottom-up scheme is described by Ballard [11]. He shows why it is helpful to allow top-down influences from more abstract representations to less abstract ones, and presents a working simulation.

## 12.5. Other types of modularity

There are several other helpful types of modularity that do not necessarily map so directly onto modular hardware but are nevertheless important for fast learning and good generalization. Consider a system which solves hard problems by creating its own subgoals. Once a subgoal has been created, the system can learn how best to satisfy it and this learning can be useful (on other occasions) even if it was a mistake to create that subgoal on this particular occasion. So the assignment of credit to the decision to create a subgoal can be decoupled from the assignment of credit to the actions taken to achieve the subgoal. Since the ability to achieve the subgoals can be learned separately from the knowledge about when they are appropriate, a system can use achievable subgoals as building blocks for more complex procedures. This avoids the problem of learning the complex procedures from scratch. It may also constrain the way in which the complex procedures will be generalized to new cases, because the knowledge about how to achieve each subgoal may already include knowledge about how to cope with variations. By using subgoals we can increase modularity and improve generalization even in systems which use the very same hardware for solving the subgoal as was used for solving the higher-level goal. Using subgoals, it may even be possible to develop reasonably fast reinforcement learning procedures for large systems.

There is another type of relationship between easy and hard tasks that can facilitate learning. Sometimes a hard task can be decomposed into a set of easier constituents, but other times a hard task may just be a version of an easier task that requires finer discrimination. For example, throwing a ball in the general direction of another person is much easier than throwing it through a hoop, and a good way to train a system to throw it through a hoop is to start by training it to throw it in the right general direction. This relation between easy and hard tasks is used extensively in "shaping" the behavior of animals and should also be useful for connectionist networks (particularly those that use reinforcement learning). It resembles the use of multi-resolution techniques to speed up search in computer vision [89]. Having learned the coarse task, the weights should be close to a point in weight space where minor adjustments can tune them to perform the finer task.

One application where this technique should be helpful is in learning filters that discriminate between very similar sounds. The approximate shapes of the filters can be learned using spectrograms that have low resolution in time and frequency, and then the resolution can be increased to allow the filters to resolve fine details. By introducing a "regularization" term that penalizes filters which have very different weights for adjacent cells in the high resolution spectrogram, it may be possible to allow filters to "attend" to fine detail when necessary without incurring the cost of estimating all the weights from scratch. The regularization term encodes prior knowledge that good filters should generally be smooth and so it reduces the amount of information that must be extracted from the training data.

## 12.6. Conclusion

There are now many different connectionist learning procedures that can construct appropriate internal representations in small domains, and it is likely that many more variations will be discovered in the next few years. Major new advances can be expected on a number of fronts: Techniques for making the learning time scale better may be developed; attempts to apply connectionist procedures to difficult tasks like speech recognition may actually succeed; new technologies may make it possible to simulate much larger networks; and finally the computational insights gained from studying connectionist systems may prove useful in interpreting the behavior of real neural networks.

## ACKNOWLEDGMENT

This research was funded by grant IS8520359 from the National Science Foundation and by contract N00014-86-K-00167 from the Office of Naval Research. I thank Dana Ballard, Andrew Barto, David Rumelhart, Terry Sejnowski, and the members of the Carnegie-Mellon Boltzmann Group for many helpful discussions. Geoffrey Hinton is a fellow of the Canadian Institute for Advanced Research.

## REFERENCES

1. Ackley, D.H., Stochastic iterated genetic hill-climbing, Ph.D. Thesis, Carnegie-Mellon University, Pittsburgh, PA (1987).
2. Ackley, D.H., Hinton, G.E. and Sejnowski, T.J., A learning algorithm for Boltzmann machines, *Cognitive Sci.* **9** (1985) 147–169.
3. Alspector, J. and Allen, R.B., A neuromorphic VLSI learning system, in: P. Loseleben (Ed.), *Advanced Research in VLSI: Proceedings of the 1987 Stanford Conference* (MIT Press, Cambridge, MA, 1987).
4. Amari, S.-I., Field theory of self-organizing neural nets, *IEEE Trans. Syst. Man Cybern.* **13** (1983) 741–748.
5. Amari, S.-I., A theory of adaptive pattern classifiers, *IEEE Trans. Electron. Comput.* **16** (1967) 299–307.
6. Anderson, J.A. and Hinton, G.E., Models of information processing in the brain, in: G.E. Hinton and J.A. Anderson (Eds.), *Parallel Models of Associative Memory* (Erlbaum, Hillsdale, NJ, 1981).
7. Anderson, J.A. and Mozer, M.C., Categorization and selective neurons, in: G.E. Hinton and J.A. Anderson (Eds.), *Parallel Models of Associative Memory* (Erlbaum, Hillsdale, NJ, 1981).
8. Angluin, D. and Smith, C.H., Inductive inference: Theory and methods, *Comput. Surv.* **15** (1983) 237–269.
9. Bahl, L.R., Jelinek, F. and Mercer, R.L., A maximum likelihood approach to continuous speech recognition, *IEEE Trans. Pattern Anal. Mach. Intell.* **5** (1983) 179–190.
10. Ballard, D.H., Cortical connections and parallel processing: Structure and function, *Behav. Brain Sci.* **9** (1986) 67–120.
11. Ballard, D.H., Modular learning in neural networks, in: *Proceedings AAAI-87*, Seattle, WA (1987) 279–284.
12. Ballard, D.H., Hinton, G.E. and Sejnowski, T.J., Parallel visual computation, *Nature* **306** (1983) 21–26.
13. Barlow, H.B., Single units and sensation: A neuron doctrine for perceptual psychology? *Perception* **1** (1972) 371–394.
14. Barto, A.G. and Anandan, P., Pattern recognizing stochastic learning automata, *IEEE Trans. Syst. Man Cybern.* **15** (1985) 360–375.
15. Barto, A.G., Sutton, R.S. and Anderson, C.W., Neuronlike elements that solve difficult learning control problems, *IEEE Trans. Syst. Man Cybern.* **13** (1983).
16. Bienenstock, E.L., Cooper, L.N. and Munro, P.W., Theory for the development of neuron selectivity: Orientation specificity and binocular interaction in visual cortex, *J. Neurosci.* **2** (1982) 32–48.
17. Brady, R.M., Optimization strategies gleaned from biological evolution, *Nature* **317** (1985) 804–806.
18. Cooper, L.N., Liberman, F. and Oja, E., A theory for the acquisition and loss of neuron specificity in visual cortex, *Biol. Cybern.* **33** (1979) 9–28.

19. Cottrell, G.W., Munro, P. and Zipser, D., Learning internal representations from gray-scale images: An example of extensional programming, in: *Proceedings Ninth Annual Conference of the Cognitive Science Society* Seattle, WA (1987) 461–473.
20. Crick, F. and Mitchison, G., The function of dream sleep, *Nature* **304** (1983) 111–114.
21. Davis, L. (Ed.), *Genetic Algorithms and Simulated Annealing* (Pitman, London, 1987).
22. Dempster, A.P., Laird, N.M. and Rubin, D.B., Maximum likelihood from incomplete data via the EM algorithm, *Proc. Roy. Stat. Soc.* (1976) 1–38.
23. Durbin, R. and Willshaw, D., The elastic net method: An analogue approach to the travelling salesman problem, *Nature* **326** (1987) 689–691.
24. Edelman, G.M. and Reeke, G.N., Selective networks capable of representative transformations, limited generalizations, and associative memory, *Proc. Nat. Acad. Sci. USA* **79** (1982) 2091–2095.
25. Elman, J.L. and Zipser, D., Discovering the hidden structure of speech, Tech. Rept. No. 8701, Institute for Cognitive Science, University of California, San Diego, CA (1987).
26. Feldman, J.A., Dynamic connections in neural networks, *Biol. Cybern.* **46** (1982) 27–39.
27. Feldman, J.A., Neural representation of conceptual knowledge, Tech. Rept. TR189, Department of Computer Science, University of Rochester, Rochester, NY (1986).
28. Feldman, J.A. and Ballard, D.H., Connectionist models and their properties, *Cognitive Sci.* **6** (1982) 205–254.
29. Fukushima, K., Cognitron: A self-organizing multilayered neural network, *Biol. Cybern.* **20** (1975) 121–136.
30. Fukushima, K. and Miyake, S., Neocognitron: A new algorithm for pattern recognition tolerant of deformations and shifts in position, *Pattern Recogn.* **15** (1982) 455–469.
31. Geman, S. and Geman, D., Stochastic relaxation, Gibbs distributions, and the Bayesian restoration of images, *IEEE Trans. Pattern Anal. Mach. Intell.* **6** (1984) 721–741.
32. Golden, R.M., A unified framework for connectionist systems, Manuscript, Learning Research and Development Center, University of Pittsburgh, Pittsburgh, PA (1987).
33. Grossberg, S., Adaptive pattern classification and universal recoding, I: Parallel development and coding of neural feature detectors, *Biol. Cybern.* **23** (1976) 121–134.
34. Grossberg, S., How does the brain build a cognitive code? *Psychol. Rev.* **87** (1980) 1–51.
35. Hampson, S.E. and Volper, D.J., Disjunctive models of boolean category learning, *Biol. Cybern.* **55** (1987) 1–17.
36. Hebb, D.O., *The Organization of Behavior* (Wiley, New York, 1949).
37. Hinton, G.E., Implementing semantic networks in parallel hardware, in: G.E. Hinton and J.A. Anderson (Eds.), *Parallel Models of Associative Memory* (Erlbaum, Hillsdale, NJ, 1981).
38. Hinton, G.E., Learning distributed representations of concepts, in: *Proceedings Eighth Annual Conference of the Cognitive Science Society*, Amherst, MA (1986).
39. Hinton, G.E., Learning translation invariant recognition in a massively parallel network, in: *PARLE: Parallel Architectures and Languages Europe* **1** (Springer, Berlin, 1987) 1–14.
40. Hinton, G.E. and Anderson J.A., (Eds.), *Parallel Models of Associative Memory* (Erlbaum, Hillsdale, NJ, 1981).
41. Hinton, G.E. and McClelland, J.L., Learning representations by recirculation, in: D.Z. Anderson (Ed.), *Neural Information Processing Systems* (American Institute of Physics, New York, 1988).
42. Hinton, G.E., McClelland, J.L. and Rumelhart, D.E., Distributed representations, in: D.E. Rumelhart, J.L. McClelland and the PDP Research Group (Eds.), *Parallel Distributed Processing: Explorations in the Microstructure of Cognition*, I: *Foundations* (MIT Press, Cambridge, MA, 1986).
43. Hinton, G.E. and Nowlan, S.J., How learning can guide evolution, *Complex Syst.* **1** (1987) 495–502.
44. Hinton, G.E. and Plaut, D.C., Using fast weights to deblur old memories, in: *Proceedings Ninth Annual Conference of the Cognitive Science Society*, Seattle, WA (1987).

45. Hinton, G.E. and Sejnowski, T.J., Optimal perceptual inference, in: *Proceedings IEEE Conference on Computer Vision and Pattern Recognition*, Washington, DC (1983) 448–453.

46. Hinton, G.E. and Sejnowski, T.J., Learning and relearning in Boltzmann machines, in: D.E. Rumelhart, J.L. McClelland and the PDP Research Group (Eds.), *Parallel Distributed Processing: Explorations in the Microstructure of Cognition*, I: *Foundations* (MIT Press, Cambridge, MA, 1986).

47. Hogg, T. and Huberman, B.A., Understanding biological computation: Reliable learning and recognition, *Proc. Nat. Acad. Sci. USA* **81** (1984) 6871–6875.

48. Holland, J.H., *Adaptation in Natural and Artificial Systems* (University of Michigan Press, Ann Arbor, MI, 1975).

49. Hopfield, J.J., Neural networks and physical systems with emergent collective computational abilities, *Proc. Nat. Acad. Sci. USA* **79** (1982) 2554–2558.

50. Hopfield, J.J., Feinstein, D.I. and Palmer, R.G., "Unlearning" has a stabilizing effect in collective memories, *Nature* **304** (1983).

51. Hopfield, J.J. and Tank, D.W., "Neural" computation of decisions in optimization problems, *Biol. Cybern.* **52** (1985) 141–152.

52. Hummel, R.A. and Zucker, S.W., On the foundations of relaxation labeling processes, *IEEE Trans. Pattern Anal. Mach. Intell.* **5** (1983) 267–287.

53. Judd, J.S., Complexity of connectionist learning with various node functions, COINS Tech. Rept. 87-60, University of Amherst, Amherst, MA (1987).

54. Kerszberg, M. and Bergman, A., The evolution of data processing abilities in competing automata, in: *Proceedings Conference on Computer Simulation in Brain Science*, Copenhagen, Denmark (1986).

55. Kirkpatrick, S., Gelatt, C.D. and Vecchi, M.P., Optimization by simulated annealing, *Science* **220** (1983) 671–680.

56. Kohonen, T., *Associative Memory: A System-Theoretical Approach* (Springer, Berlin, 1977).

57. Kohonen, T., Clustering, taxonomy, and topological maps of patterns, in: *Proceedings Sixth International Conference on Pattern Recognition*, Munich, F.R.G. (1982).

58. Lang, K.J., Connectionist speech recognition, Thesis proposal, Carnegie-Mellon University, Pittsburgh, PA (1987).

59. Le Cun, Y., A learning scheme for asymmetric threshold networks, in: *Proceedings Cognitiva 85*, Paris, France (1985) 599–604.

60. Le Cun, Y., Modèles connexionnistes de l'apprentissage, Ph.D. Thesis, Université Pierre et Marie Curie, Paris, France (1987).

61. Linsker, R., From basic network principles to neural architecture: Emergence of spatial opponent cells, *Proc. Nat. Acad. Sci. USA* **83** (1986) 7508–7512.

62. Linsker, R., From basic network principles to neural architecture: Emergence of orientation-selective cells, *Proc. Nat. Acad. Sci. USA* **83** (1986) 8390–8394.

63. Linsker, R., From basic network principles to neural architecture: Emergence of orientation columns, *Proc. Nat. Acad. Sci. USA* **83** (1986) 8779–8783.

64. Linsker, R., Development of feature-analyzing cells and their columnar organization in a layered self-adaptive network, in: R. Cotterill (Ed.), *Computer Simulation in Brain Science* (Cambridge University Press, Cambridge, 1987).

65. Marroquin, J.L., Probabilistic solution of inverse problems, Ph.D. Thesis, MIT, Cambridge, MA (1985).

66. Minsky, M.L., Theory of neural-analog reinforcement systems and its application to the brain-model problem, Ph.D. Dissertation, Princeton University, Princeton, NJ (1954).

67. Minsky, M.L., Plain talk about neurodevelopmental epistemology, in: *Proceedings IJCAI-77*, Cambridge, MA (1977) 1083–1092.

68. Minsky, M.L. and Papert, S., *Perceptrons* (MIT Press, Cambridge, MA, 1969).

69. Munro, P.W., A dual back-propagation scheme for scalar reinforcement learning, in: *Proceedings Ninth Annual Conference of the Cognitive Science Society*, Seattle, WA (1987).

70. Parker, D.B., Learning-logic, Tech. Rept. TR-47, Sloan School of Management, MIT, Cambridge, MA (1985).
71. Parker, D.B., Second order back-propagation: An optimal adaptive algorithm for any adaptive network, Unpublished manuscript (1987).
72. Pearl, J., Fusion, propagation, and structuring in belief networks, *Artificial Intelligence* **29** (1986) 241–288.
73. Pearlmutter, B.A. and Hinton, G.E., G-maximization: An unsupervised learning procedure for discovering regularities, in: J.S. Denker (Ed.), *Neural Networks for Computing: American Institute of Physics Conference Proceedings* **151** (American Institute of Physics, New York, 1986) 333–338.
74. Peterson, C. and Anderson, J.R., A mean field theory learning algorithm for neural networks, MCC Tech. Rept. E1-259-87, Microelectronics and Computer Technology Corporation, Austin, TX (1987).
75. Plaut, D.C. and Hinton, G.E., Learning sets of filters using back-propagation, *Comput. Speech Lang.* **2** (1987) 36–61.
76. Prager, R., Harrison, T.D. and Fallside, F., Boltzmann machines for speech recognition, *Comput. Speech Lang*, **1** (1986) 1–20.
77. Rosenblatt, F., *Principles of Neurodynamics* (Spartan Books, New York, 1962).
78. Rumelhart, D.E. and McClelland, J.L., On the acquisition of the past tense in English, in: J.L. McClelland, D.E. Rumelhart and the PDP Research Group (Eds.), *Parallel Distributed Processing: Explorations in the Microstructure of Cognition*, II: *Applications* (MIT Press, Cambridge, MA, 1986).
79. Rumelhart, D.E., McClelland, J.L. and the PDP Research Group (Eds.), *Parallel Distributed Processing: Explorations in the Microstructure of Cognition*, I: *Foundations* (MIT Press, Cambridge, MA, 1986).
80. Rumelhart, D.E., Hinton, G.E. and Williams, R.J., Learning internal representations by back-propagating errors, *Nature* **323** (1986) 533–536.
81. Rumelhart, D.E., Hinton, G.E. and Williams, R.J., Learning internal representations by error propagation, in: D.E. Rumelhart, J.L. McClelland and the PDP Research Group (Eds.), *Parallel Distributed Processing: Explorations in the Microstructure of Cognition*, I: *Foundations* (MIT Press, Cambridge, MA, 1986).
82. Rumelhart, D.E. and Zipser, D., Competitive learning, *Cognitive Sci.* **9** (1985) 75–112.
83. Saund, E., Abstraction and representation of continuous variables in connectionist networks, in: *Proceedings AAAI-86*, Philadelphia, PA (1986) 638–644.
84. Sejnowski, T.J. and Rosenberg, C.R., Parallel networks that learn to pronounce English text, *Complex Syst.* **1** (1987) 145–168.
85. Simon, H.A., *The Sciences of the Artificial* (MIT Press, Cambridge, MA, 1969).
86. Sutton, R.S., Temporal credit assignment in reinforcement learning, Ph.D. Thesis, COINS Tech. Rept. 84-02, University of Massachusetts, Amherst, MA (1984).
87. Sutton, R.S., Learning to predict by the method of temporal differences, Tech. Rept. TR87-509.1, GTE Laboratories, Waltham, MA (1987).
88. Tank, D.W. and Hopfield, J.J., Neural computation by concentrating information in time, *Proc. Nat. Acad. Sci. USA* **84** (1987) 1896–1900.
89. Terzopoulos, D., Multiresolution computation of visible surface representations., Ph.D. Dissertation, Department of Electrical Engineering and Computer Science, MIT, Cambridge MA (1984).
90. Tesauro, G., Scaling relationships in back-propagation learning: Dependence on training set size, *Complex Syst.* **2** (1987) 367–372.
91. Thatachar, M.A.L. and Sastry, P.S., Learning optimal discriminant functions through a cooperative game of automata, Tech. Rept. EE/64/1985, Department of Electrical Engineering, Indian Institute of Science, Bangalore, India (1985).

92. Tsotsos, J.K., A "complexity level" analysis of vision, in: *Proceedings First International Conference on Computer Vision*, London (1987) 346–355.
93. Valiant, L.G., A theory of the learnable, *Commun. ACM* **27** (1984) 1134–1142.
94. Volper, D.J. and Hampson, S.E., Connectionist models of boolean category representation, *Biol. Cybern.* **54** (1986) 393–406.
95. von der Malsburg, C., Self-organization of orientation sensitive cells in striate cortex, *Kybernetik* **14** (1973) 85–100.
96. von der Malsburg, C., The correlation theory of brain function. Internal Rept. 81-2, Department of Neurobiology, Max-Plank Institute for Biophysical Chemistry, Göttingen, F.R.G. (1981).
97. Waibel, A., Hanazawa, T., Hinton, G., Shikano, K. and Lang, K., Phoneme recognition using time-delay neural networks, Tech. Rept. TR-1-0006, ATR Interpreting Telephony Research Laboratories, Japan (1987).
98. Werbos, P.J., Beyond regression: New tools for prediction and analysis in the behavioral sciences, Ph.D. Thesis, Harvard University, Cambridge, MA (1974).
99. Widrow, B. and Hoff, M.E., Adaptive switching circuits, in: *IRE WESCON Conv. Record* **4** (1960) 96–104.
100. Widrow, B. and Stearns, S.D., *Adaptive Signal Processing* (Prentice-Hall, Englewood Cliffs, NJ, 1985).
101. Williams, R.J., Reinforcement learning in connectionist networks: A mathematical analysis, Tech. Rept., Institute for Cognitive Science, University of California San Diego, La Jolla, CA (1986).
102. Willshaw, D., Holography, associative memory, and inductive generalization, in: G.E. Hinton and J.A. Anderson (Eds.), *Parallel Models of Associative Memory* (Erlbaum, Hillsdale, NJ, 1981).
103. Willshaw, D.J. and von der Malsburg, C., A marker induction mechanism for the establishment of ordered neural mapping: Its application to the retino-tectal connections, *Philos. Trans. Roy. Soc. Lond. B* **287** (1979) 203–243.

# Classifier Systems and Genetic Algorithms

**L.B. Booker, D.E. Goldberg and J.H. Holland**

*Computer Science and Engineering, 3116 EECS Building,*
*The University of Michigan, Ann Arbor, MI 48109, U.S.A.*

ABSTRACT

*Classifier systems are massively parallel, message-passing, rule-based systems that learn through credit assignment (the bucket brigade algorithm) and rule discovery (the genetic algorithm). They typically operate in environments that exhibit one or more of the following characteristics: (1) perpetually novel events accompanied by large amounts of noisy or irrelevant data; (2) continual, often real-time, requirements for action; (3) implicitly or inexactly defined goals; and (4) sparse payoff or reinforcement obtainable only through long action sequences. Classifier systems are designed to absorb new information continuously from such environments, devising sets of competing hypotheses (expressed as rules) without disturbing significantly capabilities already acquired. This paper reviews the definition, theory, and extant applications of classifier systems, comparing them with other machine learning techniques, and closing with a discussion of advantages, problems, and possible extensions of classifier systems.*

## 1. Introduction

Consider the simply defined world of checkers. We can analyze many of its complexities and with some real effort we can design a system that plays a pretty decent game. However, even in this simple world novelty abounds. A good player will quickly learn to confuse the system by giving play some novel twists. The real world about us is much more complex. A system confronting this environment faces perpetual novelty—the flow of visual information impinging upon a mammalian retina, for example, never twice generates the same firing pattern during the mammal's lifespan. How can a system act other than randomly in such environments?

It is small wonder, in the face of such complexity, that even the most carefully contrived systems err significantly and repeatedly. There are only two cures. An outside agency can intervene to provide a new design, or the system can revise its own design on the basis of its experience. For the systems of most interest here—cognitive systems or robotic systems in realistic environments, ecological systems, the immune system, economic systems, and so on—the first option is rarely feasible. Such systems are immersed in continually changing environments wherein timely outside intervention is difficult or impossible. The only option then is learning or, using the more inclusive word, adaptation.

In broadest terms, the object of a learning system, natural or artificial, is the expansion of its knowledge in the face of uncertainty. More directly, a learning system improves its performance by generalizing upon past experience. Clearly, in the face of perpetual novelty, experience can guide future action only if there are relevant regularities in the system's environment. Human experience indicates that the real world abounds in regularities, but this does not mean that it is easy to extract and exploit them.

In the study of artificial intelligence the problem of extracting regularities is the problem of discovering useful representations or categories. For a machine learning system, the problem is one of constructing relevant categories from the system's primitives (pixels, features, or whatever else is taken as given). Discovery of relevant categories is only half the job; the system must also discover what kinds of action are appropriate to each category. The overall process bears a close relation to the Newell–Simon [40] problem solving paradigm, though there are differences arising from problems created by perpetual novelty, imperfect information, implicit definition of the goals, and the typically long, coordinated action sequences required to attain goals.

There is another problem at least as difficult as the representation problem. In complex environments, the actual attainment of a goal conveys little information about the overall process required to attain the goal. As Samuel [42] observed in his classic paper, the information (about successive board configurations) generated during the play of a game greatly exceeds the few bits conveyed by the final win or a loss. In games, and in most realistic environments, these "intermediate" states have no associated payoff or direct information concerning their "worth." Yet they play a stage-setting role for goal attainment. It may be relatively easy to recognize a triple jump as a critical step toward a win; it is much less easy to recognize that something done many moves earlier set the stage for the triple jump. How is the learning system to recognize the implicit value of certain stage-setting actions?

Samuel points the way to a solution. Information conveyed by intermediate states can be used to construct a model of the environment, and this model can be used in turn to make predictions. The verification or falsification of a prediction by subsequent events can be used then to improve the model. The model, of course, also includes the states yielding payoff, so that predictions about the value of certain stage-setting actions can be checked, with revisions made where appropriate.

In sum, the learning systems of most interest here confront some subset of the following problems:

(1) a perpetually novel stream of data concerning the environment, often noisy or irrelevant (as in the case of mammalian vision),

(2) continual, often real-time, requirements for action (as in the case of an organism or robot, or a tournament game),

(3) implicitly or inexactly defined goals (such as acquiring food, money, or some other resource, in a complex environment),

(4) sparse payoff or reinforcement, requiring long sequences of action (as in an organism's search for food, or the play of a game such as chess or go).

In order to tackle these problems the learning system must:

(1) invent categories that uncover goal-relevant regularities in its environment,

(2) use the flow of information encountered along the way to the goal to steadily refine its model of the environment,

(3) assign appropriate actions to stage-setting categories encountered on the way to the goal.

It quickly becomes apparent that one cannot produce a learning system of this kind by grafting learning algorithms onto existing (nonlearning) AI systems. The system must continually absorb new information and devise ranges of competing hypotheses (conjectures, plausible new rules) without disturbing capabilities it already has. Requirements for consistency are replaced by competition between alternatives. Perpetual novelty and continual change provide little opportunity for optimization, so that the competition aims at satisficing rather than optimization. In addition, the high-level interpreters employed by most (nonlearning) AI systems can cause difficulties for learning. High-level interpreters, by design, impose a complex relation between primitives of the language and the sentences (rules) that specify actions. Typically this complex relation makes it difficult to find simple combinations of primitives that provide plausible generalizations of experience.

A final comment before proceeding: Adaptive processes, with rare exceptions, are far more complex than the most complex processes studied in the physical sciences. And there is as little hope of understanding them without the help of theory as there would be of understanding physics without the attendant theoretical framework. Theory provides the maps that turn an uncoordinated set of experiments or computer simulations into a cumulative exploration. It is far from clear at this time what form a unified theory of learning would take, but there are useful fragments in place. Some of these fragments have been provided by the connectionists, particularly those following the paths set by Sutton and Barto [98], Hinton [23], Hopfield [36] and others. Other fragments come from theoretical investigations of complex adaptive systems such as the investigations of the immune system pursued by Farmer, Packard and Perelson [14]. Still others come from research centering on genetic algorithms and classifier systems (see, for example, [28]). This paper focuses on contributions deriving from the latter studies, supplying some illustrations of the interaction between theory, computer modeling, and data in that context. A central theoretical concern is the process whereby structures (rule clusters and the like) emerge in response to the problem solving demands imposed by the system's environment.

## 2. Overview

The machine learning systems discussed in this paper are called *classifier systems*. It is useful to distinguish three levels of activity (see Fig. 1) when looking at learning from the point of view of classifier systems:

At the lowest level is the *performance system*. This is the part of the overall system that interacts directly with the environment. It is much like an expert system, though typically less domain-dependent. The performance systems we will be talking about are rule-based, as are most expert systems, but they are message-passing, highly standardized, and highly parallel. Rules of this kind are called classifiers. The performance system is discussed in detail in Section 3; Section 4 relates the terminology and procedures of classifier systems to their counterparts in more typical AI systems.

Because the system must determine which of its rules are effective, a second level of activity is required. Generally the rules in the performance system are of varying usefulness and some, or even most, of them may be incorrect. Somehow the system must evaluate the rules. This activity is often called *credit assignment* (or apportionment of credit); accordingly this level of the system will be called the *credit assignment system*. The particular algorithms used here for credit assignment are called *bucket brigade algorithms*; they are discussed in Section 5.

The third level of activity, the *rule discovery system*, is required because,

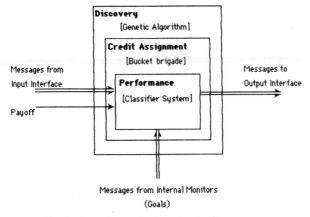

Fig. 1. General organization of a classifier system.

even after the system has effectively evaluated millions of rules, it has tested only a minuscule portion of the plausibly useful rules. Selection of the best of that minuscule portion can give little confidence that the system has exhausted its possibilities for improvement; it is even possible that none of the rules it has examined is very good. The system must be able to generate new rules to replace the least useful rules currently in place. The rules could be generated at random (say by "mutation" operators) or by running through a predetermined enumeration, but such "experience-independent" procedures produce improvements much too slowly to be useful in realistic settings. Somehow the rule discovery procedure must be biased by the system's accumulated experience. In the present context this becomes a matter of using experience to determine useful "building blocks" for rules; then new rules are generated by combining selected building blocks. Under this procedure the new rules are at least plausible in terms of system experience. (Note that a rule may be plausible without necessarily being useful of even correct.) The rule discovery system discussed here employs *genetic algorithms*. Section 6 discusses genetic algorithms. Section 7 relates the procedures implicit in genetic algorithms to some better-known machine learning procedures.

Section 8 reviews some of the major applications and tests of genetic algorithms and classifier systems, while the final section of the paper discusses some open questions, obstacles, and major directions for future research.

Historically, our first attempt at understanding adaptive processes (and learning) turned into a theoretical study of genetic algorithms. This study was summarized in a book titled *Adaptation in Natural and Artificial Systems* (Holland [28]). Chapter 8 of that book contained the germ of the next phase. This phase concerned representations that lent themselves to manipulation by genetic algorithms. It built upon the definition of the *broadcast language* presented in Chapter 8, simplifying it in several ways to obtain a standardized class of parallel, rule-based systems called *classifier systems*. The first descriptions of classifier systems appeared in Holland [29]. This led to concerns with apportioning credit in parallel systems. Early considerations, such as those of Holland and Reitman [34], gave rise to an algorithm called the *bucket brigade algorithm* (see [31]) that uses only local interactions between rules to distribute credit.

## 3. Classifier Systems

The starting point for this approach to machine learning is a set of rule-based systems suited to rule discovery algorithms. The rules must lend themselves to processes that extract and recombine "building blocks" from currently useful rules to form new rules, and the rules must interact simply and in a highly parallel fashion. Section 4 discusses the reasons for these requirements, but we define the rule-based systems first to provide a specific focus for that discussion.

## 3.1. Definition of the basic elements

Classifier systems are parallel, message-passing, rule-based systems wherein all rules have the same simple form. In the simplest version all messages are required to be of a fixed length over a specified alphabet, typically $k$-bit binary strings. The rules are in the usual *condition/action* form. The condition part specifies what kinds of messages satisfy (activate) the rule and the action part specifies what message is to be sent when the rule is satisfied.

A classifier system consists of four basic parts (see Fig. 2).

– The *input interface* translates the current state of the environment into standard messages. For example, the input interface may use property detectors to set the bit values (1: the current state has the property, 0: it does not) at given positions in an incoming message.

– The *classifiers*, the rules used by the system, define the system's procedures for processing messages.

– The *message list* contains all current messages (those generated by the input interface and those generated by satisfied rules).

– The *output interface* translates some messages into effector actions, actions that modify the state of the environment.

A classifier system's basic execution cycle consists of the following steps:

*Step* 1. Add all messages from the input interface to the message list.

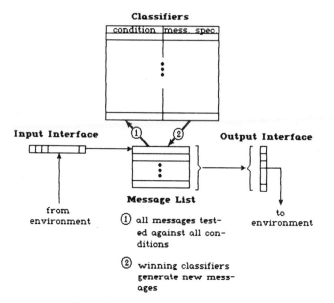

Fig. 2. Basic parts of a classifier system.

*Step* 2. Compare all messages on the message list to all conditions of all classifiers and record all matches (satisfied conditions).

*Step* 3. For each set of matches satisfying the condition part of some classifier, post the message specified by its action part to a list of new messages.

*Step* 4. Replace *all* messages on the message list by the list of new messages.

*Step* 5. Translate messages on the message list to requirements on the output interface, thereby producing the system's current output.

*Step* 6. Return to Step 1.

Individual classifiers must have a simple, compact definition if they are to serve as appropriate grist for the learning mill; a complex, interpreted definition makes it difficult for the learning algorithm to find and exploit building blocks from which to construct new rules (see Section 4).

The major technical hurdle in implementing this definition is that of providing a simple specification of the condition part of the rule. Each condition must specify exactly the set of messages that satisfies it. Though most large sets can be defined only by an explicit listing, there is one class of subsets in the message space that can be specified quite compactly, the hyperplanes in that space. Specifically, let $\{1, 0\}^k$ be the set of possible $k$-bit messages; if we use "#" as a "don't care" symbol, then the set of hyperplanes can be designated by the set of all ternary strings of length $k$ over the alphabet $\{1, 0, \#\}$. For example, the string $1\#\# \ldots \#$ designates the set of all messages that start with a 1, while the string $00 \ldots 0\#$ specifies the set $\{00 \ldots 01, 00 \ldots 00\}$ consisting of exactly two messages, and so on.

It is easy to check whether a given message satisfies a condition. The condition and the message are matched position by position, and if the entries at all non-# positions are identical, then the message satisfies the condition. The notation is extended by allowing any string $c$ over $\{1, 0, \#\}$ to be prefixed by a "$-$" with the intended interpretation that $-c$ is satisfied just in case *no* message satisfying $c$ is present on the message list.

### 3.2. Examples

At this point we can introduce a small classifier system that illustrates the "programming" of classifiers. The sets of rules that we'll look at can be thought of as fragments of a simple simulated organism or robot. The system has a vision field that provides it with information about its environment, and it is capable of motion through that environment. Its goal is to acquire certain kinds of objects in the environment ("targets") and avoid others ("dangers"). Thus, the environment presents the system with a variety of problems such as "What sequence of outputs will take the system from its present location to a visible target?" The system must use classifiers with conditions sensitive to messages from the input interface, as well as classifiers that integrate the messages from other classifiers, to send messages that control the output interface in appropriate ways.

In the examples that follow, the system's input interface produces a message
for each object in the vision field. A set of *detectors* produces these messages
by inserting in them the values for a variety of properties, such as whether or
not the object is moving, whether it is large or small, etc. The detectors and
the values they produce will be defined as needed in the examples.

The system has three kinds of *effectors* that determine its actions in the
environment. One effector controls the VISION VECTOR, a vector indicating the
orientation of the center of the vision field. The VISION VECTOR can be rotated
incrementally each time step (V-LEFT or V-RIGHT, say in 15-degree increments).
The system also has a MOTION VECTOR that indicates its direction of motion,
often independent of the direction of vision (as when the system is scanning
while it moves). The second effector controls rotation of the MOTION VECTOR
(M-LEFT or M-RIGHT) in much the same fashion as the first effector controls the
VISION VECTOR. The second effector may also align the MOTION VECTOR with
the VISION VECTOR, or set it in the opposite direction (ALIGN and OPPOSE,
respectively), to facilitate behaviors such as pursuit and flight. The third
effector sets the rate of motion in the indicated direction (FAST, CRUISE, SLOW,
STOP). The classifiers process the information produced by the detectors to
provide sequences of effector commands that enable the system to achieve
goals.

For the first examples let the system be supplied with the following property
detectors:

$$d_1 = \begin{cases} 1, & \text{if the object is moving}, \\ 0, & \text{otherwise}; \end{cases}$$

$$(d_2, d_3) = \begin{cases} (0,0), & \text{if the object is centered in the vision field}, \\ (1,0), & \text{if the object is left of center}, \\ (0,1), & \text{if the object is right of center}; \end{cases}$$

$$d_4 = \begin{cases} 1, & \text{if the system is adjacent to the object}, \\ 0, & \text{otherwise}; \end{cases}$$

$$d_5 = \begin{cases} 1, & \text{if the object is large}, \\ 0, & \text{otherwise}; \end{cases}$$

$$d_6 = \begin{cases} 1, & \text{if the object is striped}, \\ 0, & \text{otherwise}. \end{cases}$$

Let the detectors specify the rightmost six bits of messages from the input interface,
$d_1$ setting the rightmost bit, $d_2$ the next bit to the left, etc. (see Fig. 3).

**Example 3.1.** A simple *stimulus-response* classifier.

> IF there is "prey" (*small, moving, nonstriped object*), centered in
> the vision field (*centered*), and not adjacent (*nonadjacent*),
> THEN move toward the object (ALIGN) rapidly (FAST).

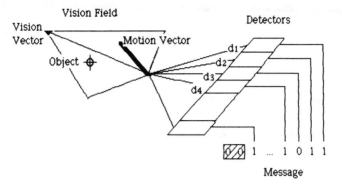

Fig. 3. Input interface for a simple classifier system.

Somewhat fancifully, we can think of the system as an "insect eater" that seeks out small, moving objects unless they are striped ("wasps"). To implement this rule as a classifier we need a condition that attends to the appropriate detector values. It is also important that the classifier recognize that the message is generated by the input interface (rather than internally). To accomplish this we assign messages a prefix or *tag* that identifies their origin—a two-bit tag that takes the value $(0, 0)$ for messages from the input interface will serve for present purposes (see Example 3.5 for a further discussion of tags). Following the conventions of the previous subsection the classifier has the condition

$$00\#\#\#\#\#\#\#\#000001 \, ,$$

where the leftmost two loci specify the required tag, the # specify the loci (detectors) not attended to, and the rightmost 6 loci specify the required detector values ($d_1 = 1 = moving$, being the rightmost locus, etc.). When this condition is satisfied, the classifier sends an outgoing message, say

$$0100000000000000 \, ,$$

where the prefix 01 indicates that the message is *not* from the input interface. (Though these examples use 16-bit messages, in realistic systems much longer messages would be advantageous.) We can think of this message as being used directly to set effector conditions in the output interface. For convenience these *effector settings*, ALIGN and FAST in the present case, will be indicated in capital letters at the right end of the classifier specification. The complete specification, then, is

$$00\#\#\#\#\#\#\#\#000001 \, / \, 0100000000000000, \text{ALIGN, FAST} \, .$$

**Example 3.2.** A set of classifiers detecting a compound object defined by the *relations* between its parts.

The following pair of rules emits an identifying message when there is a moving T-shaped object in the vision field.

> IF there is a centered object that is large, has a long axis, and is moving *along* the direction of that long axis ,
> THEN move the vision vector FORWARD (along the axis in the direction of motion) and record the presence of a moving object of type "I" .

> IF there was a centered object of type "I" observed on the previous time step, and IF there is currently a centered object in contact with "I" that is large, has a long axis, and is moving *crosswise* to the direction of that long axis ,
> THEN record the presence of a moving object of type "T" (blunt end forward) .

The first of these rules is "triggered" whenever the system "sees" an object moving in the same direction as its long axis. When this happens the system scans forward to see if the object is preceded by an attached cross-piece. The two rules acting in concert detect a compound object defined by the relation between its parts (cf. Winston's [53] "arch"). Note that the pair of rules *can* be fooled; the moving "cross-piece" might be accidentally or temporarily in contact with the moving "I". As such the rules constitute only a first approximation or default, to be improved by adding additional conditions or exception rules as experience accumulates. Note also the assumption of some sophistication in the input and output interfaces: an effector "subroutine" that moves the center of vision along the line of motion, a detector that detects the absence of a gap as the center of vision moves from one object to another, and beneath all a detector "subroutine" that picks out moving objects. Because these are intended as simple examples, we will not go into detail about the interfaces— suffice it to say that reasonable approximations to such "subroutines" exist (see, for example, [37]).

If we go back to our earlier fancy of the system as an insect eater, then moving T-shaped objects can be thought of as "hawks" (not too farfetched, because a "T" formed of two pieces of wood and moved over newly hatched chicks causes them to run for cover, see [43]).

To redo these rules as classifiers we need two new detectors:

$$d_7 = \begin{cases} 1, & \text{if the object is moving in the direction of its long axis ,} \\ 0, & \text{otherwise ;} \end{cases}$$

$$d_8 = \begin{cases} 1, & \text{if the object is moving in the direction of its short axis ,} \\ 0, & \text{otherwise .} \end{cases}$$

We also need a command for the effector subroutine that causes the vision vector to move up the long axis of an object in the direction of its motion, call it V-FORWARD. Finally, let the message 0100000000000001 signal the detection of the moving "I" and let the message 0100000000000010 signal the detection of the moving T-shaped object. The classifier implementing the first rule then has the form

$$00\#\#\#\#\#\#01\#1\#001 \; / \; 0100000000000001, \text{ V-FORWARD} \; .$$

The second rule must be contingent upon *both* the just previous detection of the moving "I", signalled by the message 0100000000000001, and the current presence of the cross-piece, signalled by a message from the environment starting with tag 00 and having the value 1 for detector $d_8$.

$$0100000000000001, \; 00\#\#\#\#\#\#10\#1\#001 \; / \; 0100000000000010 \; .$$

**Example 3.3.** Simple memory.

The following set of three rules keeps the system on alert status if there has been a moving object in the vision field recently. The duration of the alert is determined by a timer, called the ALERT TIMER, that is set by a message, say 0100000000000011, when the object appears.

> IF there is a moving object in the vision field ,
> THEN set the ALERT TIMER and send an alert message .
>
> IF the ALERT TIMER is not zero ,
> THEN send an alert message .
>
> IF there is *no* moving object in the vision field and the ALERT TIMER
>   is not zero ,
> THEN decrement the ALERT TIMER .

To translate these rules into classifiers we need an effector subroutine that sets the alert timer, call it SET ALERT, and another that decrements the alert timer, call it DECREMENT ALERT. We also need a detector that determines whether or not the alert timer is zero.

$$d_9 = \begin{cases} 1 \, , & \text{if the ALERT TIMER is } not \text{ zero ,} \\ 0 \, , & \text{otherwise .} \end{cases}$$

The classifiers implementing the three rules then have the form

$$00\#\#\#\#\#\#\#\#\#\#\#\#1 \; / \; 0100000000000011, \text{ SET ALERT}$$
$$00\#\#\#\#\#1\#\#\#\#\#\#\#\# \; / \; 0100000000000011$$
$$00\#\#\#\#\#1\#\#\#\#\#\#\#0 \; / \; \text{DECREMENT ALERT} \; .$$

Note that the first two rules send the same message, in effect providing an OR of the two conditions, because satisfying either the first condition *or* the second will cause the message to appear on the message list. Note also that these rules check on an *internal* condition via the detector $d_9$, thus providing a system that is no longer driven solely by external stimuli.

**Example 3.4.** Building blocks.

To illustrate the possibility of combining several active rules to handle complex situations we introduce the following three pairs of rules.

(A)   IF there is an alert and the moving object is near ,
      THEN move at FAST in the direction of the MOTION VECTOR .

      IF there is an alert and the moving object is far ,
      THEN move at CRUISE in the direction of the MOTION VECTOR .

(B)   IF there is an alert, and a small, nonstriped object in the vision
      field ,
      THEN ALIGN the motion vector with the vision vector .

      IF there is an alert, and a large T-shaped object in the vision field ,
      THEN OPPOSE the motion vector to the vision vector .

(C)   IF there is an alert, and a moving object in the vision field ,
      THEN send a message that causes the vision effectors to CENTER the
      object .

      IF there is an alert, and *no* moving object in the vision field,
      THEN send a message that causes the vision effectors to SCAN .

(Each of the rules in pair (C) sends a message that invokes additional rules. For example "centering" can be accomplished by rules of the form,

      IF there is an object in the left vision field ,
      THEN execute V-LEFT .

      IF there is an object in the right vision field ,
      THEN execute V-RIGHT .

realized by the pair of classifiers

      00###########10# / V-LEFT
      00###########01# / V-RIGHT.)

Any combination of rules obtained by activating one rule from each of the three subsets (A), (B), (C) yields a potentially useful behavior for the system. Accordingly the rules can be combined to yield behavior in eight distinct situations; moreover, the system need encounter only two situations (involving disjoint sets of three rules) to test all six rules. The example can be extended easily to much larger numbers of subsets. The number of potentially useful combinations increases as an *exponent* of the number of subsets; that is, $n$ subsets, of two alternatives apiece, yield $2^n$ distinct combinations of $n$ simultaneously active rules. Once again, only two situations (appropriately chosen) need be encountered to provide testing for *all* the rules.

The six rules are implemented as classifiers in the same way as in the earlier examples, noticing that the system is put on alert status by using a condition that is satisfied by the alert message 0100000000000011. Thus the first rule becomes

$$0100000000000011, \ 00\#\#\#\#0\#\#\#\#\#\#\#\#1 \ / \ \text{FAST} \ ,$$

where a new detector $d_{10}$, supplying values at the tenth position from the right in environmental messages, determines whether the object is far (value 1) or near (value 0).

It is clear that the building block approach provides tremendous combinatorial advantages to the system (along the lines described so well by Simon [45]).

**Example 3.5.** Networks and tagging.

Networks are built up in terms of *pointers* that couple the elements (nodes) of the network, so the basic problem is that of supplying classifier systems with the counterparts of pointers. In effect we want to be able to couple classifiers so that activation of a classifier $C$ in turn causes activation of the classifiers to which it points. The passing of activation between coupled classifiers then acts much like Fahlman's [13] marker-passing scheme, except that the classifier system is passing, and processing, messages. In general we will say a classifier $C_2$ is *coupled* to a classifier $C_1$ if some condition of $C_2$ is satisfied by the message(s) generated by the action part of $C_1$. Note that a classifier with very specific conditions (few #) will be coupled typically to only a few other classifiers, while a classifier with very general conditions (many #) will be coupled to many other classifiers. Looked at this way, classifiers with very specific conditions have few incoming "branches," while classifiers with very general conditions have many incoming "branches."

The simplest way to couple classifiers is by means of *tags*, bits incorporated in the condition part of a classifier that serve as a kind of identifier or address. For example, a condition of the form 1101## ... # will accept any message with the prefix 1101. Thus, to send a message to this classifier we need only prefix the message with the tag 1101. We have already seen an example of this use of tags in Example 3.1, where messages from the input interface are "addressed" only to classifiers that have conditions starting with the prefix 00. Because $b$ bits yield $2^b$ distinct tags, and tags can be placed anywhere in a condition (the component bits need not even be contiguous), large numbers of conditions can be "addressed" uniquely at the cost of relatively few bits.

By using appropriate tags one can define a classifier that attends to a specific *set* of classifiers. Consider, for example, a pair of classifiers $C_1$ and $C_2$ that send messages prefixed with 1101 and 1001, respectively. A classifier with the condition $1101\#\# \ldots \#$ will attend only to $C_1$, whereas a classifier with condition $1\#01\#\# \ldots \#$ will attend to both $C_1$ and $C_2$. This approach, in conjunction with recodings (where the prefix of the outgoing message differs from that of the satisfying messages), provides great flexibility in defining the sets of classifiers to which a given classifier attends. Two examples will illustrate the possibilities:

**Example 3.5.1.** Producing a message in response to an arbitrarily chosen subset of messages.

An arbitrary logical (boolean) combination of conditions can be realized through a combination of couplings and recodings. The primitives from which more complex expressions can be constructed are AND, OR, and NOT. An AND-condition is expressed by a single multi-condition classifier such as $M_1, M_2/M$, for $M$ is only added to the message list if *both* $M_1$ *and* $M_2$ are on the list. Similarly the *pair* of classifiers $M_1/M$ and $M_2/M$ express an OR-condition, for $M$ is added to the message list if *either* $M_1$ *or* $M_2$ is on the list. NOT, of course, is expressed by a classifier with the condition $-M$. As an illustration, consider the boolean expression

$$(M_1 \text{ AND } M_2) \text{ OR } ((\text{NOT } M_3) \text{ AND } M_4).$$

This is expressed by the following set of classifiers with the message $M$ appearing if and only if the boolean expression is satisfied.

$$M_1, M_2/M, \qquad -M_3, M_4/M.$$

The judicious use of # and recodings often substantially reduces the number of classifiers required when the boolean expressions are complex.

**Example 3.5.2.** Representing a network

The most direct way of representing a network is to use one classifier for each pointer (arrow) in the network (though it is often possible to find clean representations using one classifier for each node in the network).

As an illustration of this approach consider the following network fragment (Fig. 4). In marker-passing terms, the ALERT node acquires a marker when there is a MOVING object in the vision field. For the purposes of this example, we will assume that the conjunction of arrows at the TARGET node is a requirement that all three nodes (ALERT, SMALL, and NOT STRIPED) be marked

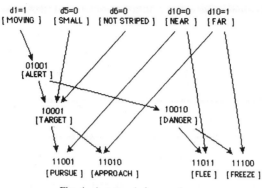

Fig. 4. A network fragment.

before TARGET is marked. Similarly, PURSUE will only be marked if both TARGET and NEAR are marked, etc.

To transform this network into a set of classifiers, begin by assigning an identifying tag to each node. (The tags used in the diagram are 5-bit prefixes). The required couplings between the classifiers are then simply achieved by coordinating the tags used in conditions with the tags on the messages ("markers") to be passed. Henceforth, we extend the notation to allow #'s in the action part of classifiers, where they designate *pass-throughs*: Wherever the message part contains a #, the bit value of the outgoing message is identical to the bit value of the message satisfying the classifier's first condition. That is, the bit value of the incoming (satisfying) message is "passed through" to the outgoing message.

On the basis, assuming that the MOVING node is marked by the detector $d_1$, the arrow between MOVING and ALERT would be implemented by the classifier

$$00\#\#\#\#\#\#\#\#\#\#\#\#\#1 \; / \; 01001\#\#\#\#\#\#\#\#\#\# ,$$

while the arrows leading from SMALL, NOT STRIPED, and ALERT to TARGET could be implemented by the single classifier

$$00\#\#\#\#\#\#\#\#\#00\#\#\#\# , \quad 01001\#\#\#\#\#\#\#\#\#\# \; /$$
$$10001\#\#\#\#\#\#\#\#\#\# .$$

In turn, the arrows from NEAR and TARGET to PURSUE could be implemented by

$$00\#\#\#\#0\#\#\#\#\#\#\#\#\# , \quad 10001\#\#\#\#\#\#\#\#\#\# \; /$$
$$11001\#\#\#\#\#\#\#\#\#\# .$$

The remainder of the network would be implemented similarly.

Some comments are in order. First, the techniques used in Example 3.5.1 to implement boolean connectives apply equally to arrows. For example, we could set conditions so that TARGET would be activated if *either* MOVING and SMALL *or* MOVING and NOT STRIPED were activated. Relations between categories can be introduced following the general lines of Example 3.2. Second, tags can be assigned in ways that provide direct information about the structure of the network. For example, in the network above the first two bits of the tag indicate the level of the corresponding category (the number of arrows intervening between the category and the input from the environment). Finally, effector-oriented categories such as PURSUE would presumably "call subroutines" (sets of classifiers) that carry out the desired actions. For instance, the message from PURSUE would involve such operations as centering the object (see the classifiers just after (C) in Example 3.4), followed by rapid movement toward the object (see the classifier in Example 3.1).

Forrest [15] has produced a general complier for producing coupled classifiers implementing any semantic net specified by KL-ONE expressions.

A final comment on the use of classifiers: Systems of classifiers, when used with learning algorithms, are *not* adjusted for consistency. Instead individual rules are treated as partially confirmed hypotheses, and conflicts are resolved by competition. The specifics of this competition are presented in Section 5.

### 4. The Relation of Classifier Systems to Other AI Problem Solving Systems

As noted previously, many of the problem solving and learning mechanisms in classifier systems have been motivated by broad considerations of adaptive processes in both natural and artificial systems. This point of view leads to a collection of computation procedures that differ markedly from the symbolic methods familiar to the AI community. It is therefore worthwhile to step back from the details of classifier systems and examine the core ideas that make classifier systems an important part of machine learning research.

When viewed solely as rule-based systems, classifier systems have two apparently serious weaknesses. First, the rules are written in a language that lacks descriptive power in comparison to what is available in other rule-based systems. The left-hand side of each rule is a simple conjunctive expression having a limited number of terms. It clearly cannot be used to express arbitrary, general relationships among attributes. Even though sets of such expressions are adequate in principle, most statements in the classifier language can be expressed more concisely or easily as statements in LISP or logic. Second, because several rules are allowed to fire simultaneously, control issues are raised that do not come up in conventional rule-based systems. Coherency can be difficult to achieve in a distributed computation. Explicit machinery is needed for insuring a consistent problem solving focus, and the requisite control knowledge may be hard to come by unless the problem is inherently parallel to begin with. These two properties suggest an unconventional approach if a classifier system is to be used to build a *conventional* expert system, though the computational completeness of classifier systems assures it could be done in the usual way.

The key to understanding the advantages of classifier systems is to understand the kind of problems they were designed to solve. A perpetually novel stream of data constitutes an extremely complex and uncertain problem solving environment. A well-known strategy for resolving uncertainty is exemplified by the blackboard architecture (see [12]). By coordinating multiple sources of hierarchically organized knowledge, hypotheses and constraints, problem solving can proceed in an opportunistic way, guided by the summation of converging evidence and building on weak or partial results to arrive at confident conclusions. However, managing novelty requires more than this kind of problem solving flexibility. A system must dynamically construct and modify the representation of the problem itself! Flexibility is required at the more basic level of concepts, relations, and the way they are organized. Classifier systems were designed to make this kind of flexibility possible.

Building blocks are the technical device used in classifier systems to achieve this flexibility. The message list is a global database much like a blackboard, but the possibilities for organizing hypotheses are not predetermined in advance. Messages and tags are building blocks that provide a flexible way of constructing arbitrary hierarchical or heterarchical associations among rules and concepts. Because the language is simple, modifying these associations can be done with local syntactic manipulations that avoid the need for complex interpreters or knowledge-intensive critics. In a similar way, rules themselves are building blocks for representing complex concepts, constraints and problem solving behaviors. Because rules are activated in parallel, new combinations of existing rules and rule clusters can be used to handle novel situations. This is tantamount to building knowledge sources as needed during problem solving.

The apparently unsophisticated language of classifier systems is therefore a deliberate tradeoff of descriptive power for adaptive efficiency. A simple syntax yields building blocks that are easy to identify, evaluate, and recombine in useful ways. Moreover, the sacrifice of descriptive power is not as severe as it might seem. A complex environment will contain concepts that cannot be specified easily or precisely even with a powerful logic. For example, a concept might be an equivalence class in which the members share no common features. Or it might be a relation with a strength that is measured by the distance from some prototype. Or it might be a network of relationships so variable that there are no clearly defined concept boundaries. Rather than construct a syntactically complex representation of such a concept that would be difficult to use or modify, a classifier system uses *groups* of rules as the representation. The structure of the concept is *modeled* by the organization, variability, and distribution of strength among the rules. Because the members of a group compete to become active (see Section 5), the appropriate aspects of the representation are selected only when they are relevant in a given problem solving context. The modularity of the concept thereby makes it easier to use as well as easier to modify.

This distributed approach to representing knowledge is similar to the way complex concepts are represented in connectionist systems (see [24]). Both frameworks use a collection of basic computing elements as epistemic building blocks. Classifier systems use condition/action rules that interact by passing messages. Connectionist systems use simple processing units that send excitatory and inhibitory signals to each other. Concepts are represented in both systems by the simultaneous activation of several computing elements. Every computing element is involved in representing several concepts, and the representations for similar concepts share elements. Retrieval of a concept is a constructive process that simultaneously activates constituent elements best fitting the current context. This technique has the important advantage that some relevant generalizations are achieved automatically. Modifications to elements of one representation automatically affect all similar representations that share those elements.

There are important differences between classifier systems and connectionist systems, however, that stem primarily from the properties of the building blocks they use. The interactions among computing elements in a connectionist system make "best-fit" searches a primitive operation. Activity in a partial pattern of elements is tantamount to an incomplete specification of a concept. Such patterns are automatically extended into a complete pattern of activity representing the concept most consistent with the given specification. Content-addressable memory can therefore be implemented effortlessly. The same capability is achieved in a classifier system using pointers and tags to link related rules. A directed spreading activation is then required to efficiently retrieve the appropriate concept.

Other differences relate to the way inductions are achieved. Modification of connection strengths is the only inductive mechanism available in most connectionist systems (see [36, 48]). Moreover, the rules for updating strength are part of the initial system design that cannot be changed except perhaps by tuning a few parameters. Classifier systems, on the other hand, permit a broad spectrum of inductive mechanisms ranging from strength adjustments to analogies. Many of these mechanisms can be controlled by, or can be easily expressed in terms of, inferential rules. These inferential rules can be evaluated, modified and used to build higher-level concepts in the same way that building blocks are used to construct lower-level concepts.

Classifier systems are like connectionist systems in emphasizing microstructure, multiple constraints and the emergence of complex computations from simple processes. However, classifier systems use rules as a basic epistemic unit, thereby avoiding the reduction of all knowledge to a set of connection strengths. Classifier systems thus occupy an important middle ground between the symbolic and connectionist paradigms.

We conclude this section by comparing classifier systems to SOAR (see [38]), another system architecture motivated by broad considerations of cognitive processes. SOAR is a general-purpose architecture for goal-oriented problem solving and learning. All behavior in SOAR is viewed as a search through a problem space for some state that satisfies the goal (problem solution) criteria. Searching a problem space involves selecting appropriate operators to transform the initial problem state, through a sequence of operations, into an acceptable goal state. Whenever there is an impasse in this process, such as a lack of sufficient criteria for selecting an operator, SOAR generates a subgoal to resolve the impasse. Achieving this subgoal is a new problem that SOAR solves recursively by searching through the problem space characterizing the subgoal. SOAR's knowledge about problem states, operators, and solution criteria is represented by a set of condition/action rules. When an impasse is resolved, SOAR seizes the opportunity to learn a new rule (or set of rules) that summarizes important aspects of the subgoal processing. The new rule, or chunk of knowledge, can then be used to avoid similar impasses in the future. The learning mechanism that generates these rules is called *chunking*.

There are some obvious points of comparison between classifier systems and the SOAR architecture. Both emphasize the flexibility that comes from using rules as a basic unit of representation, and both emphasize the importance of tightly coupling induction mechanisms with problem solving. However, classifier systems do not enforce any one particular problem solving regime the way SOAR does. At a broader level, these systems espouse very different points of view about the mechanisms necessary for intelligent behavior. SOAR emphasizes the sufficiency of a single problem solving methodology coupled with a single learning mechanism. The only way to break a problem solving impasse is by creating subgoals, and the only way to learn is to add rules to the knowledge base by chunking. Classifier systems, on the other hand, place an emphasis on flexibly modeling the problem solving environment. A good model allows for prediction-based evaluation of the knowledge base, and the assignment of credit to the model's building blocks. This, in turn, makes it possible to modify, replace, or add to existing rules via inductive mechanisms such as the recombination of highly rated building blocks. Moreover, a model can provide the constraints necessary to generate plausible reformulations of the representation of a problem. To resolve problem solving impasses, then, classifier systems hypothesize new rules (by recombining building blocks), instead of recompiling (chunking) existing rules.

We will make comparisons to other machine learning methods (Section 7), after we have defined and discussed the learning algorithms for classifier systems.

## 5. Bucket Brigade Algorithms

The first major learning task facing any rule-based system operating in a complex environment is the *credit assignment* task. Somehow the performance system must determine both the rules responsible for its successes and the representativeness of the conditions encountered in attaining the successes. (The reader will find an excellent discussion of credit assignment algorithms in Sutton's [47] report.) The task is difficult because overt rewards are rare in complex environments; the system's behavior is mostly "stage-setting" that makes possible later successes. The problem is even more difficult for parallel systems, where only some of the rules active at a given time may be instrumental in attaining later success. An environment exhibiting perpetual novelty adds still another order of complexity. Under such conditions the performance system can *never* have an absolute assurance that any of its rules is "correct." The perpetual novelty of the environment, combined with an always limited sampling of that environment, leaves a residue to uncertainty. Each rule in effect serves as a hypothesis that has been more or less confirmed.

The *bucket brigade* algorithm is designed to solve the credit assignment problem for classifier systems. To implement the algorithm, each classifier is assigned a quantity called its *strength*. The bucket brigade algorithm adjusts the strength to reflect the classifier's overall usefulness to the system. The strength is then used as the basis of a competition. Each time step, each satisfied classifier makes a *bid* based on its strength, and only the highest bidding classifiers get their messages on the message list for the next time step.

It is worth recalling that there are no consistency requirements on posted messages; the message list can hold any set of messages, and any such set can direct further competition. The only point at which consistency enters is at the output interface. Here, different sets of messages may specify conflicting responses. Such conflicts are again resolved by competition. For example, the strengths of the classifiers advocating each response can be summed so that one of the conflicting actions is chosen with a probability proportional to the sum of its advocates.

The bidding process is specified as follows. Let $s(C, t)$ be the strength of classifier $C$ at time $t$. Two factors clearly bear on the bidding process: (1) relevance to the current situation, and (2) past "usefulness." Relevance is mostly a matter of the specificity of the rule's condition part—a more specific condition satisfied by the current situation conveys more information about that situation. The rule's strength is supposed to reflect its usefulness. In the simplest versions of the competition the bid is a product of these two factors, being 0 if the rule is irrelevant (condition not satisfied) or useless (strength 0), and being high when the rule is highly specific to the situation (detailed conditions satisfied) and well confirmed as useful (high strength).

To implement this bidding procedure, we modify Step 3 of the basic execution cycle (see Section 3.1).

*Step 3.* For each set of matches satisfying the condition part of classifier $C$, *calculate a bid* according to the following formula,

$$B(C, t) = bR(C)s(C, t),$$

where $R(C)$ is the specificity, equal to the number of non-# in the condition part of $C$ divided by the length thereof, and $b$ is a constant considerably less than 1 (e.g., $\frac{1}{8}$ or $\frac{1}{16}$). The size of the bid determines the *probability* that the classifier posts its message (specified by the action part) to the new message list. (E.g., the probability that the classifier posts its message might decrease exponentially as the size of the bid decreases.)

The use of probability in the revised step assures that rules of lower strength sometimes get tested, thereby providing for the occasional testing of less-favored and newly generated (lower strength) classifiers ("hypotheses").

The operation of the bucket brigade algorithm can be explained informally via an economic analogy. The algorithm treats each rule as a kind of "middleman" in a complex economy. As a "middleman," a rule only deals with its "suppliers"—the rules sending messages satisfying its conditions—and its "consumers"—the rules with conditions satisfied by the messages the "middleman" sends. Whenever a rule wins a bidding competition, it initiates a transaction wherein it pays out part of its strength to its suppliers. (If the rule does not bid enough to win the competition, it pays nothing.) As one of the winners of the competition, the rule becomes active, serving as a supplier to its consumers, and receiving payments from them in turn. Under this arrangement, the rule's strength is a kind of capital that measures its ability to turn a "profit." If a rule receives more from its consumers than it paid out, it has made a profit; that is, its strength has increased.

More formally, when a winning classifier $C$ places its message on the message list it pays for the privilege by having its strength $s(C, t)$ reduced by the amount of the bid $B(C, t)$,

$$s(C, t + 1) = s(C, t) - B(C, t).$$

The classifiers $\{C'\}$ sending messages matched by this winner, the "suppliers," have their strengths increased by the amount of the bid—it is shared among them in the simplest version—

$$s(C', t + 1) = s(C', t) + aB(C, t),$$

where $a = 1/$(no. of members of $\{C'\}$).

A rule is likely to be profitable only if its consumers, in their local transactions, are also (on the average) profitable. The consumers, in turn, will be profitable only if *their* consumers are profitable. The resulting chains of consumers lead to the ultimate consumers, the rules that directly attain goals and receive payoff directly from the environment. (Payoff is added to the strengths of all rules determining responses at the time the payoff occurs.) A rule that regularly attains payoff when activated is of course profitable. The profitability of other rules depends upon their being coupled into sequences leading to these profitable ultimate consumers. The bucket brigade ensures that early acting, "stage-setting" rules eventually receive credit if they are coupled into (correlated with) sequences that (on average) lead to payoff.

If a rule sequence is faulty, the final rule in the sequence loses strength, and the sequence will begin to disintegrate, over time, from the final rule backwards through its chain of precursors. As soon as a rule's strength decreases to the point that it loses in the bidding process, some competing rule will get a chance to act as a replacement. If the competing rule is more useful than the one displaced, a revised rule sequence will begin to form using the new rule. The bucket brigade algorithm thus searches out and repairs "weak links" through its pervasive local application.

Whenever rules are coupled into larger hierarchical knowledge structures, the bucket brigade algorithm is still more powerful than the description so far would suggest. Consider an abstract rule $C^*$ of the general form, "if the goal is $G$, and if the procedure $P$ is executed, then $G$ will be achieved." $C^*$ will be active throughout the time interval in which the sequence of rules comprising $P$ is executed. If the goal is indeed achieved, this rule serves to activate the response that attains the goal, as well as the stage-setting responses preceding that response. Under the bucket brigade $C^*$ will be strengthened immediately by the goal attainment. On the very next trial involving $P$, the earliest rules in $P$ will have their strengths substantially increased under the bucket brigade. This happens because the early rules act as suppliers to the strengthened $C^*$ (via the condition "if the procedure $P$ is executed"). Normally, the process would have to be executed on the order of $n$ times to backchain strength through an $n$-step process $P$. $C^*$ circumvents this necessity.

## 6. Genetic Algorithms

The rule discovery process for classifier systems uses a *genetic algorithm* (GA). Basically, a genetic algorithm selects high strength classifiers as "parents," forming "offspring" by recombining components from the parent classifiers. The offspring displace weak classifiers in the system and enter into competition, being activated and tested when their conditions are satisfied. Thus, a genetic algorithm crudely, but at high speed, mimics the genetic processes underlying evolution. It is vital to the understanding of genetic algorithms to know that even the simplest versions act much more subtly than "random search with preservation of the best," contrary to a common misreading of genetics as a process primarily driven by mutation. (Genetic algorithms have been studied intensively by analysis, Holland [28] and Bethke [4], and simulation, DeJong [11], Smith [46], Booker [6], Goldberg [18], and others.)

Though genetic algorithms act subtly, the basic execution cycle, the "central loop," is quite simple:

*Step* 1. From the set of classifiers, select pairs according to strength—the stronger the classifier, the more likely its selection.

*Step* 2. Apply *genetic operators* to the pairs, creating "offspring" classifiers. Chief among the genetic operators is *cross-over*, which simply exchanges a randomly selected segment between the pairs (see Fig. 5).

*Step* 3. Replace the weakest classifiers with the offspring.

The key to understanding a genetic algorithm is an understanding of the way it manipulates a special class of building blocks called *schemas*. In brief, under a GA, a good building block is a building block that occurs in good rules. The GA biases future constructions toward the use of good building blocks. We will soon see that a GA rapidly explores the space of schemas, a very large space, implicitly rating and exploiting schemas according to the strengths of the rules employing them. (The term *schema* as used here is related to, but should not be confused with, the broader use of that term in psychology).

The first step in making this informal description precise is a careful definition of *schema*. To start, recall that a condition (or an action) for a classifier is defined by a string of letters $\alpha_1 \alpha_2 \ldots \alpha_j \ldots \alpha_k$ of length $k$ over the 3-letter alphabet $\{1, 0, \#\}$. It is reasonable to look upon these strings as built up from the component letters $\{1, 0, \#\}$. It is equally reasonable to look upon certain combinations of letters, say 11 or 0##1, as components. All such possibilities can be defined with the help of a new "don't care" symbol "∗." To define a given *schema*, we specify the letters at the positions of interest, filling out the rest of the string with "don't cares." (The procedure mimics that for defining conditions, but we are operating at a different level now.) Thus, ∗0##1∗∗ . . . ∗ focuses attention on the combination 0##1 at positions 2 through 5. Equivalently, ∗0##1∗∗ . . . ∗ specifies a *set* of conditions, the set of *all* conditions that can be defined by using the combination 0##1 at positions 2 through 5. Any condition that has 0##1 at the given positions is an *instance* of schema ∗0##1∗∗ . . . ∗. The set of all *schemas* is just the set $\{1, 0, \#, *\}^k$ of all strings of length $k$ over the alphabet $\{1, 0, \#, *\}$. (Note that a *schema* defines a subset of the set of all possible conditions, while each condition defines a subset of the set of all possible messages.)

A classifier system, at any given time $t$, typically has many classifiers that contain a given component or schema $\sigma$; that is, the system has many instances of $\sigma$. We can assign a value $s(\sigma, t)$ to $\sigma$ at time $t$ by averaging the strengths of its instances. For example, let the system contain classifier $C_1$, with condition $10\#\#110\ldots0$ and strength $s(C_1, t) = 4$, and classifier $C_2$, with condition $00\#\#1011\ldots1$ and strength $s(C_2, t) = 2$. If these are the only two instances of schema $\sigma = *0\#\#1**\ldots*$ at time $t$, then we assign to the schema the value

$$s(\sigma, t) = \tfrac{1}{2}[s(C_1, t) + s(C_2, t)] = 3 ,$$

the average of the strengths of the two instances. The general formula is

$$s(\sigma, t) = (1/[\text{no. of instances of } \sigma]) \sum_{C \text{ an instances of } \sigma} s(C, t) .$$

$s(\sigma, t)$ can be looked upon as an *estimate* of the mean value of $\sigma$, formed by taking the average value of the samples (instances) of $\sigma$ present in the classifier system at time $t$. It is a crude estimate and can mislead the system; nevertheless it serves well enough as a heuristic guide if the system has procedures that compensate for misleading estimates. This the algorithm does, as we will see, by evaluating additional samples of the schema; that is, it constructs new classifiers that are instances of the schema and submits them to the bucket brigade.

Consider now a system with $M$ classifiers that uses the observed averages $\{s(\sigma, t)\}$ to guide the construction of new classifiers from schemas. Two questions arise: (1) How many schemas are present (have instances) in the set of $M$ classifiers? (2) How is the system to calculate and use the $\{s(\sigma, t)\}$?

The answer to the first question has important implications for the use of schemas as building blocks. A single condition (or action) is an instance of $2^k$ schemas! (This is easily established by noting that a given condition is an instance of *every* schema obtained by substituting an "$*$" for one or more letters in the definition of the condition.) In a system of $M$ single-condition classifiers, there is enough information to calculate averages for somewhere between $2^k$ and $M2^k$ schemas. Even for very simple classifiers and a small system, $k = 32$ and $M = 1000$, this is an enormous number, $M2^k \sim 4$ trillion.

The natural way to use the averages would be to construct more instances of above-average schemas, while constructing fewer instances of below-average schemas. That is, the system would make more use of above-average building blocks, and less use of below-average building blocks. More explicitly: Let $s(t)$ be the average strength of the classifiers at time $t$. Then schema $\sigma$ is above average if $s(\sigma, t)/s(t) > 1$, and vice versa. Let $M(\sigma, t)$ be the number of instances of schema $\sigma$ in the system at time $t$, and let $M(\sigma, t + T)$ be the number of instances of $\sigma$ after $M$ new classifiers (samples) have been constructed. The simplest heuristic for using the information $s(\sigma, t)/s(t)$ would be to require that the number of instances (uses) of $\sigma$ increase (or decrease) at time $t + T$ according to that ratio,

$$M(\sigma, t + T) = c[s(\sigma, t)/s(t)]M(\sigma, t) ,$$

where $c$ is an arbitrary constant. It is even possible, *in principle*, to construct the new classifiers so that *every* schema $\sigma$ *with at least a few instances present at* $t$ receives the requisite number of samples. (This is rather surprising since there are so many schemas and only $M$ new classifiers are constructed; however a little thought and some calculation, exploiting the fact that a single classifier is an instance of $2^k$ distinct schemas, shows that it is possible.)

A generating procedure following this heuristic, setting aside problems of implementation for the moment, has many advantages. It samples each schema with above-average instances with increasing intensity, thereby further confirming (or disconfirming) its usefulness and exploiting it (if it remains above average). This also drives the overall average $s(t)$ upward, providing an ever-increasing criterion that a schema must meet to be above average. Moreover, the heuristic employs a distribution of instances, rather than working only from the "most recent best" instance. This yields both robustness and insurance against being caught on "false peaks" (local optima) that misdirect development. Overall, the power of this heuristic stems from its rapid accumulation of better-than-average building blocks. Because the strengths underlying the $s(\sigma, t)$ are determined (via the bucket brigade) by the regularities and interactions in the environment, the heuristic provides a sophisticated way of exploiting such regularities and interactions.

Though these possibilities exist in principle, there is no feasible *direct* way to calculate and use the large set of averages $\{s(\sigma, t)/s(t)\}$. However, genetic algorithms do *implicitly* what is impossible explicitly. To see this, we must specify exactly the steps by which a genetic algorithm generates new classifiers.

The algorithm acts on a set $B(t)$ of $M$ strings $\{C_1, C_2, \ldots, C_M\}$ over the alphabet $\{1, 0, \#\}$ with assigned strengths $s(C_j, t)$ via the following steps:

*Step* 1. Compute the average strength $s(t)$ of the strings in $B(t)$, and assign the normalized value $s(C_j, t)/s(t)$ to each string $C_j$ in $B(t)$.

*Step* 2. Assign each string in $B(t)$ a probability proportional to its normalized value. Then, using this probability distribution, select $n$ pairs of strings, $n \ll M$, from $B(t)$, and make copies of them.

*Step* 3. Apply *cross-over* (and, possibly, other *genetic operators*) to each copied pair, forming $2n$ new strings. *Cross-over* is applied to a pair of strings as follows: Select at random a position $i$, $1 \le i \le k$, and then exchange the segments to the left of position $i$ in the two strings (see Fig. 5).

*Step* 4. Replace the $2n$ lowest strength strings in $B(t)$ with the $2n$ strings newly generated in Step 3.

*Step* 5. Set $t$ to $t + 1$ in preparation for the next use of the algorithm and return to Step 1.

Figure 6 illustrates the operation of the algorithm. In more sophisticated versions of the algorithm, the selection of pairs for recombination may be biased toward classifiers active at the time some triggering condition is satisfied. Also Step 4 may be modified to prevent one kind of string from

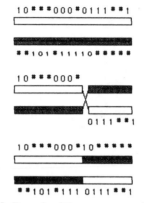

Fig. 5. Example of the cross-over operator.

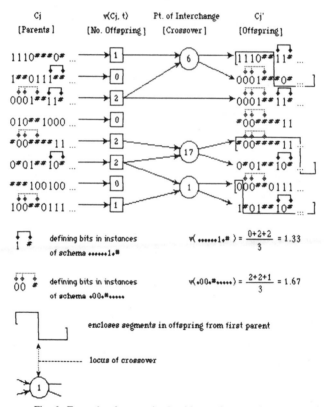

Fig. 6. Example of a genetic algorithm acting on schemas.

"overcrowding" $B(t)$ (see [4, 11] for details).

Contiguity of constituents, and the building blocks constructed from them, are significant under the cross-over operator. Close constituents tend to be exchanged together. Operators for rearranging the atomic constituents defining the rules, such as the genetic operator *inversion*, can bias the rule generation process toward the use of certain *kinds* of building blocks. For example, if "color" is nearer to "shape" than to "taste" in a condition, then a particular "color"-"shape" combination will be exchanged as a unit more often than a "color"-"taste" combination. *Inversion*, by rearranging the positions of "shape" and "taste," could reverse this bias. Other genetic operators, such as *mutation*, have lesser roles in this use of the algorithm, mainly providing "insurance" (see [28, Chapter 6, Sections 2–4] for details).

To see how the genetic algorithm implicitly carries out the schema search heuristic described earlier, it is helpful to divide the algorithm's action into two phases: phase 1 consists of Steps 1–2; phase 2 consists of Steps 3–4.

First consider what would happen if phase 1 were iterated, without the execution of phase 2, but with the replacement of strings in $B(t)$. In particular, let phase 1 be iterated $M/2n$ times (assuming for convenience that $M$ is a multiple of $2n$). Under $M/2n$ repetitions of phase 1, *each instance C* of a given schema $\sigma$ can be expected to produce $s(\sigma, t)/s(t)$ "offspring" copies. The total number of instances of schema $\sigma$ after the action of phase 1 is just the *sum* of the copies of the individual instances. Dividing this total by the original number of instances, $M(\sigma, t)$, gives the average rate of increase, and is just $s(\sigma, t)/s(t)$ as required by the heuristic. This is true of every schema with instances in $B(t)$, as required by the heuristic.

Given that phase 1 provides just the emphasis for each schema required by the heuristic, why is phase 2 necessary? Phase 2 is required because phase 1 introduces no *new* strings (samples) into $B(t)$, it merely introduces copies of strings already there. Phase 1 provides emphasis but no new trials. The genetic operators, applied in phase 2, obviously modify strings. It can be proved (see [28, Theorem 6.2.3]) that the genetic operators of Step 3 leave the emphasis provided by phase 1 largely undisturbed, while providing *new* instances of the various schemas in $B(t)$ in accord with that emphasis. Thus, phase 1 combined with phase 2 provides, implicitly, just the sampling scheme suggested by the heuristic.

The fundamental theorem for genetic algorithms [28, Theorem 6.2.3] can be rewritten as a procedure for progressively biasing a probability distribution over the space $\{1, 0, \#\}^k$:

**Theorem 6.1.** *Let* $P_{\text{cross}}$ *be the probability that a selected pair will be crossed, and let* $P_{\text{mut}}$ *be the probability that a mutation will occur at any given locus. If* $p(\sigma, t)$ *is the fraction of the population occupied by the instances of* $\sigma$ *at time* $t$, *then*

$$p(\sigma, t+1) \geq [1 - \lambda(\sigma, t)][1 - P_{\text{mut}}]^{d(\sigma)}[u(\sigma, t)/u(t)]p(\sigma, t)$$

*gives the expected fraction of the population occupied by instances of $\sigma$ at time $t+1$ under the genetic algorithm.*

The right-hand side of this equation can be interpreted as follows: $[u(\sigma, t)/u(t)]$, the ratio of the observed average value of the schema $s$ compared to the overall population average, determines the rate of change of $p(\sigma, t)$, subject to the "error" terms $[1 - \lambda(\sigma, t)][1 - P_{\text{mut}}]^{d(\sigma)}$. If $u(\sigma, t)$ is above average, then schema $\sigma$ tends to increase, and vice versa.

The "error" terms are the result of breakup of instances of $\sigma$ because of cross-over and mutation, respectively. In particular, $\lambda(\sigma, t) = P_{\text{cross}}(l(\sigma)/k)p(\sigma, t)$ is an upper bound on the loss of instances of $\sigma$ resulting from crosses that fall within the interval of length $l(\sigma)$ determined by the outermost defining loci of the schema, and $[1 - P_{\text{mut}}]^{d(\sigma)}$ gives the proportion of instances of $\sigma$ that escape a mutation at one of the $d(\sigma)$ defining loci of $\sigma$.

(The underlying algorithm is stochastic so the equation only provides a bound on expectations at each time step. Using the terminology of mathematical genetics, the equation supplies a *deterministic model* of the algorithm under the assumption that the expectations are the values actually achieved on each time step.)

In any population that is not too small—from a biological view, a population not so small as to be endangered from a lack of genetic variation—distinct schemas will almost always have distinct subsets of instances. For example, in a randomly generated population of size 2500 over the space $\{1, 0\}^k$, any schema defined on 8 loci can be expected to have about 10 instances. (For ease of calculation, we consider populations of binary strings in the rest of this section, but the same results hold for $n$-letter alphabets.) There are

$$\binom{2500}{10} \simeq 3 \times 10^{26}$$

ways of choosing this subset, so that it is extremely unlikely that the subsets of instances for two such schemas will be identical. (Looked at another way, the chance that two schemas have even *one* instance in common is less than $10 \times 2^{-8} \simeq \frac{1}{25}$ if they are defined on disjoint subsets of loci.) Because the sets of instances are overwhelmingly likely to be distinct, the observed averages $\hat{u}(\sigma, t)$, will have little cross-correlation. As a consequence, the rate of increase (or decrease) of a schema $\sigma$ under a genetic algorithm is largely uncontaminated by the rates associated other such schemas. Loosely, the rate is uninfluenced by "cross-talk" from the other schemas.

To gain some idea of how many schemas are so processed consider the following:

**Theorem 6.2.** *Select some bound e on the transcription error under reproduction and cross-over, and pick l such that $l/k \le \frac{1}{2}e$. Then in a population of size $M = c_1 2^{l/k}$, obtained as a uniform random sample from $\{1, 0\}^k$, the number of schemas propagated with an error less than e greatly exceeds $M^3$.*

**Proof.** (1) Consider a "window" of $2l$ contiguous loci in a string of length $k$ such that $2l/k = e$. Clearly any schema having all its defining loci within this window will be subject to a transcription error less than $e$ under cross-over.

(2) There are

$$\binom{2l}{l} \simeq 2^{2l}/[\pi l]^{-1/2}$$

ways of selecting $l$ defining positions in the window, and there are $2^l$ different schemas that can be defined using any given set of $l$ of defining loci. Therefore, there are approximately $2^{3l}/[\pi l]^{-1/2}$ distinct schemas with $l$ defining positions that can be defined in the window.

(3) A population of size $M = c_1 2^l$, for $c_1$ a small integer, obtained by a uniform random sampling of $\{1, 0\}^k$ can be expected to have $c_1$ instances of *every* schema defined on $l$ defining positions. Therefore, for the given window, there will be approximately $M^3/(c_1)^3[\pi l]^{-1/2}$ schemas having instances in the population and defined on some set of $l$ loci in the window.

(4) The same argument can be given for schemas of length $l - 1, l - 2, \ldots$, and for $l + 1, l + 2, \ldots$, with values of

$$\binom{2l}{l \pm j}$$

decreasing in accord with the binomial distribution. There are also $k - l - 1$ distinct positionings of the window on strings of length $k$. It follows that many more than $M^3$ schemas, with instances in the population of size $M$, increase or decrease at a rate given by their observed marginal averages with a transcription error less than $e$. $\square$

From the point of view of sampling theory, 20 or 30 instances of a schema $\sigma$ constitute a sample large enough to give some confidence to the corresponding estimate of $u(\sigma)$. Thus, for such schemas, the biases $p(\sigma, t)$ produced by a genetic algorithm over a succession of generations are neither much distorted by sampling error nor smothered by "cross-talk."

It is important to recognize that the genetic algorithm only manipulates $M$ strings while implicitly generating and testing the new instances of the very large number of schemas involved ($\gg M^3$, early on). Moreover, during this procedure, samples (instances) of schemas not previously tried are generated. This implicit manipulation of a great many schemas through operations on $2n$ strings per step is called *implicit parallelism* (it is called *intrinsic parallelism* by Holland [28]).

## 7. Comparison with Other Learning Methods

The rule discovery procedures in a classifier system—genetic algorithms—are just as unconventional as the problem solving procedures. Here again, it is important to look beyond the details and examine the core ideas. In terms of the weak methods familiar to the AI community, a genetic algorithm can be thought of as a complex hierarchical generate-and-test process. The generator produces building blocks which are combined into complete objects. At various points in the procedure, tests are made that help weed out poor building blocks and promote the use of good ones. The information requirements of the process are modest: a generator for building blocks and objects, and an evaluator that allows them to be tested and compared with alternatives. It is altogether appropriate to label the procedure a weak method, if one is referring to its lack of domain-dependent requirements.

On closer examination, though, it is apparent that there are important differences between genetic algorithms and the standard assortment of weak methods. The differences are centered on the formulation of the search for useful rules. The familiar weak methods focus on managing the *complexity* of the search space, emphasizing ways to avoid computationally prohibitive exhaustive searches. Such methods use small amounts of knowledge to focus the search and prune the space of alternatives. Genetic algorithms proceed by managing the *uncertainty* of the search space. Uncertainty enters in the sense that the desirability of an element of the search space as a solution or partial solution is unknown until it has been tested. Managing complexity reduces uncertainty as more of the search space is explored; on the other hand, it is also clear that reducing uncertainty makes the search more effective, with complexity becoming more manageable in the process.

This shift of viewpoint is subtle, but has important consequences for the way the search is carried out. Typical AI search procedures use heuristic evaluation functions to prune search paths, and it often suffices that they provide bounds on test outcomes. On the other hand, uncertainty management requires the use of test outcomes (samples) to estimate regularities in the search space. Acquiring and using this knowledge as the search proceeds requires that more attention be paid to the *distribution* of test outcomes over the search space. The focus is on subspaces and the kinds of elements they contain, rather than on paths and their ultimate destinations. That is, the emphasis is on sample-based induction [33].

This point of view is captured by a weak method we will call *sample-select-and-recombine*. Assume that the elements of the search space are structured, that is, that they are constructed of components or building blocks. To find an element in this space:

*Step* 1. Draw a sample from the space.

*Step* 2. Order the elements in the sample according to some preference criterion related to the goals of the search.

*Step* 3. Use this ranking to estimate the usefulness of the building blocks present in the sample's elements.

*Step* 4. Generate a new sample by selecting building blocks on the basis of this evaluation, recombining them to construct new elements.

*Step* 5. Repeat Steps 1–4 until the desired element is found.

This method has the obvious advantage that the memory requirements are small and it can be used when a conventional generator or heuristic evaluation function is hard to find. All that is needed is a set of building blocks and a capability to order a sample in terms of a goal-relevant preference. Just as generate-and-test procedures are made more effective by incorporating as much of the test as possible into the generation process, genetic algorithms derive their power by tightly coupling the sampling and selection process. It is important that there are theoretical results that show that genetic algorithms implement the sample-select-and-recombine method in a near-optimal way.

We can make a direct comparison of this approach with more familiar AI learning procedures. This is most easily accomplished in the realm of concept learning tasks where the problem is to find a concept description consistent with a given set of (positive and negative) examples of the concept. Wilson [52] gives a detailed account of the way in which genetic algorithms acting on classifier systems learn complex multiple disjunctive concepts. Here we will refer to the description of genetic algorithms given above, and will briefly examine two well-known learning algorithms: the interference matching algorithm (Hayes-Roth and McDermott [22]), and the candidate elimination algorithm (Mitchell [39]).

### 7.1. Interference matching

Interference matching is a general technique for inferring the common attributes of several positive examples. (Interference matching is closely related to techniques, such as those examined by Valiant [49], for inferring boolean functions from true and false instances, but interference matching makes less stringent requirements on the match between problem, algorithm and representation.) A schema describing the shared characteristics is constructed using the attribute value for attributes shared, and a place holder symbol (essentially a "don't care" symbol) for attributes that differ over the examples. For example, interference matching of the two descriptors [RED, ROUND, HEAVY] and [RED, SQUARE, HEAVY] yields the schema [RED, HEAVY]. This technique can be used to compute a set of schemas accounting for all positive examples of a concept—called a *maximal decomposition*—by using the following algorithm:

> Let $S$ be the list of schemas, initially empty .
> Let $\{E_1, \ldots, E_N\}$ be the set of $N$ examples .
> **For** $i = 1$ to $N$
>> **For** $j = 1$ to $|S|$
>>> Form a schema $s$ by interference matching $E_i$ with the $j$th element of $S$ .
>>> Form a new schema $s'$ by interference matching all examples that satisfy (are instances of) $s$ .
>>> Add $s'$ to the list $S$ if it is not already there .
>>> Repeat until no new schemas are created (for the given value of $i$) .
>> Add $E_i$ to $S$ unaltered .

A simple example is given in Fig. 7.

The list of schemas comprising a maximal decomposition is the minimal complete set of nonredundant schemas that occur in the examples. For instance, in Fig. 7, the schemas ***1 and **0* are redundant because they designate the same subset of examples; they are therefore summarized by the more restrictive schema **01. The algorithm is more complicated when there is more than one concept to be learned or, equivalently, negative examples are available. A separate maximal decomposition is computed for each concept, but, in addition, a performance value is computed for each schema. The performance value rates each schema according to its ability to discriminate instances of a concept from noninstances in the set of examples.

| Examples | Maximal Decomposition |
|:--------:|:---------------------:|
| 1001 | 1001 |
|  | ------- |
| 1110 | 1*** |
|  | 1110 |
|  | ------- |
| 0101 | **01 |
|  | **** |
|  | *1** |
|  | 0101 |
|  | ------- |
| 0010 | *0** |
|  | **10 |
|  | 0*** |
|  | 0010 |

Fig. 7. Example of a maximal decomposition.

Similar algorithms have been suggested for inferring the structure of boolean functions from presentations of true instances (see, for example, Valiant [49]).

Because a maximal decomposition is an exhaustive list of the structural characteristics of a concept, the size of the list becomes unmanageable as the number of examples grows. Hayes-Roth suggests discarding schemas with low performance values to keep the size of the list under control. This strategy can only work, though, if all the examples are available at once. If the examples occur incrementally, the performance value assigned to a schema at any given time is an estimate subject to error. The only obvious way to recover from a mistakenly discarded schema is to recompute the entire maximal decomposition.

Therein lies the major difference between interference matching and genetic algorithms. Genetic algorithms implicitly work with the building blocks for a decomposition. Iterative application of a genetic algorithm produces a population of concept descriptions in which the number of occurrences of each building block is proportional to the observed average performance of its carriers. In this sense, the population is a database that compactly and usefully summarizes the examples so far encountered. If a new example is introduced, it is assimilated by an automatic revision of the proportions of the relevant building blocks. This updating occurs without keeping explicit or exhaustive records about performance, thereby avoiding the large computational burdens associated with updating a maximal decomposition.

## 7.2. Candidate elimination

The candidate elimination algorithm is similar to genetic algorithms in that it cleverly implements a procedure that would be intractable if attempted by brute force. The basic idea is to enumerate the set of all possible concept descriptions and, for each example, remove from consideration any description that is inconsistent with that example. When there is only one description left the problem is solved. Mitchell [39] makes this idea tractable by ordering the set of possible descriptions according to *generality*. One description is more general than another if it includes as instances all the instances specified by the other description. Thus the schema $**0*$ is more general than the schema $**01$. This is a partial ordering because not all descriptions are comparable—there can be several maximally general or maximally specific descriptions in the space. The key to this approach is the observation that the set of most specific descriptions and the set of most general descriptions consistent with an example *bound* the set of all descriptions consistent with the example. An algorithm therefore need only keep track of these bounds to converge to the description consistent with all examples.

In more detail, the candidate elimination algorithm maintains two sets that bound the space of consistent descriptions: the set $S$ of most specific possible descriptions, and the set $G$ of most general possible descriptions. Given a new positive example, the elements of $S$ are generalized the smallest amount that allows inclusion of the new example as an instance. Any element of $G$ that is inconsistent with this example is removed. Similarly, given a new negative example, the elements of $G$ are specialized the smallest amount that precludes the example as an instance. Any element of $S$ that includes this example as an instance is removed. This process is repeated for each new example, the set $S$ becoming more general and the set $G$ becoming more specific, until $S$ and $G$ are identical. The concept description remaining is the one that is consistent with all the examples.

This algorithm obviously has no problems assimilating new examples and it converges to a solution quickly. The basic limitations are: (i) the $S$ and $G$ can be quite large, even for relatively simple concepts, (ii) only conjunctive concepts can be learned, and (iii) the algorithm usually fails if the data are noisy (some instances incorrect). Genetic algorithms avoid these limitations by characterizing the search space in a fundamentally different way: (i) the data set corresponding to the $S$ and $G$ sets is carried implicitly in the proportions of the building blocks, (ii) disjunctions are handled by the parallelism of the rule set, and (iii) noise is handled effortlessly because uncertainty reduction is at the heart of the procedure. The price paid by the genetic algorithm is that it robustly samples the space without concern for the difficulty of the problem; it cannot use an obvious path to a solution to curtail its search unless there are strong building blocks that can be combined to construct that path.

## 8. Applications

Research on genetic algorithms has paralleled work in mainstream artificial intelligence in the sense that simpler studies of search and optimization in straightforward problem domains have preceded the more complex investigations of machine learning. This is no surprise. Search and optimization applications, with their well-defined problems, objective functions, constraints and decision variables provide a tame environment where alternatives may be compared easily. By contrast, machine learning problems, with their ill-defined goal statements, subjective evaluation criteria and multitudinous decision options, constitute an unwieldy environment not easily given to comparison or analysis. The application of GAs in search and optimization has both tested and improved GAs, and it has encouraged their successful application to search problems that have not succumbed to more traditional procedures. Accordingly this review of applications starts by examining GA applications in search and optimization.

### 8.1. Genetic algorithms in search and optimization

(Because much of the inspiration for early studies of genetic algorithms came from genetics, much of the work described in this section was set forth using the terminology of genetics. We have not explained these terms in detail, but we have eliminated any terms that would not appear in a high-school biology text.)

The first *application* of a GA—in fact, the first published use of the words "genetic algorithm"—came in Bagley's [3] pioneering dissertation. At that time there was much interest in game playing computer programs, and in that spirit Bagley devised a controllable testbed of game tasks modeled after the game hexapawn. Bagley's GA operated successfully on "diploid chromosomes" (paired strings) which were decoded to construct parameter sets for a game board evaluation function. The GA contained the three basic operators—reproduction, cross-over, and mutation—along with dominance and inversion. At about the same time, Rosenberg [41] was completing his Ph.D. study of the simulated growth and genetic interaction of a population of single-celled organisms. His organisms were characterized by a simple rigorous biochemistry, a permeable membrane, and a classical, one-gene/one-enzyme structure. He introduced an interesting adaptive cross-over scheme that associated linkage factors with each gene, thereby permitting different linkages between adjacent genes. Rosenberg's work is sometimes overlooked by GA researchers because of its emphasis on biological simulation, but its nearness to root finding and function optimization make it an important contribution to the search domain.

In 1971 Cavicchio [7] investigated the application of GAs to a subroutine selection task and a pattern recognition task. He adopted the pixel weighting scheme of Bledsoe and Browning [5] and used a GA to search for good sets of detectors (subsets of pixels). His GA found good sets of detectors more quickly than a competing "hill-climbing" algorithm. Cavicchio was one of the first to implement a scheme for maintaining population diversity.

The first dissertation to apply GAs to well-posed problems in mathematical optimization was Hollstien's [35] which used a testbed of 14 functions of two variables. The work is notable in its use of allele dominance and schemes of mating preference adopted from traditional breeding practices. Hollstien's GA located optima for his functions much more rapidly than traditional algorithms, but it was difficult to draw general conclusions because he used very small populations ($n = 16$). Frantz [17] studied positional effects on function optimization. Specifically, he considered functions wherein the value assigned to an argument string could not be well approximated by assigning a least mean squares estimate to each component bit of the argument. (From the point of view of a geneticist, this amounts to saying there are strong epistatic interactions between the genes.) He tested the hypothesis that an inversion (string permutation) operator might improve the efficiency of a GA for such functions. Because the standard GA found near-optimal results quickly in all cases, the inversion operator had little effect. However, for substantially more difficult problems, such as the traveling salesman problem, job shop scheduling and bin packing, Frantz's hypothesis remains a fruitful avenue of research (see Davis [8, 9], Goldberg and Lingle [19], and Grefenstette, Gopal, Rosmaita and van Gucht [21]). More recently, Bethke [4] has added rigor to the study of functions that are hard for GAs through his investigation of schema averages using Walsh transforms (following a suggestion of Andrew Barto). Goldberg [19] has also contributed to the understanding of GA-hard functions with his definition and analysis of the *minimal deceptive problem*.

De Jong's [11] dissertation was particularly important to subsequent applications of genetic algorithms. He recognized the importance of carefully controlled experimentation in an uncluttered function optimization setting. Varying population size, mutation and cross-over probabilities, and other operator parameters, he examined GA performance in a problem domain consisting of five test functions ranging from a smooth, unimodal function of two variables to functions characterized by high dimensionality (30 variables), great multimodality, discontinuity and noise. To quantify GA performance he defined online and offline performance measures, emphasizing interim performance and convergence, respectively. He also defined a measure of robustness of performance over a range of environments and demonstrated by experiment the robustness of GAs over the test set.

In Appendix A we display a representative group of GA search and optimization applications ranging from an archeological model of the transition from hunting and gathering to agriculture, through VLSI layout problems and medical image registration, to structural optimization. (A complete bibliography covering the entries in Appendices A and B is available from any one of the authors.) The broad successes in these domains have encouraged experiments with GAs in machine learning problems.

## 8.2. Machine learning using genetic algorithms

The goals for GAs in the context of machine learning have always been clear:

> The study of adaptation involves the study of both the adaptive system and its environment. In general terms, it is a study of how systems can generate procedures enabling them to adjust efficiently to their environments. If adaptability is not to be arbitrarily restricted at the outset, the adapting system must be able to generate any method or procedure capable of an effective definition. (Holland [25])

The original intent, and the original outline of the attendant theory, encompassed a class of adaptive systems much broader than those concerned with search and optimization. The theoretical foundation was used as a basis for defining a series of increasingly sophisticated *schemata processors* (Holland

[26]). Although the 1968 conference at which this paper was presented predates the first application of a classifier system by a full decade [34], schemata processors resemble modern day classifier systems in both outline and detail. The 1978 implementation of Holland and Reitman [34], called CS-1 (Cognitive System Level One), was trained to learn two maze-running tasks. It used (i) a performance system with a message list and simple classifiers, (ii) a credit assignment algorithm that retained information about all classifiers active between successive payoffs and adjusted their strengths at the time of payoff, and (iii) a GA with reproduction, cross-over, mutation and crowding that generated new classifiers. The main result demonstrated that the system could transfer its experience in a simpler maze to improve its rate of learning in a more complex maze.

Smith's [46] study of a classifier system used a purely GA approach, sidestepping the need for a credit assignment algorithm. He represented a rule *set* by a single string, obtained by stringing the rules end to end. He then devised a micro-level cross-over operator, for exchanging segments of individual rules, and a macro-level cross-over operator, for exchanging segments of rule strings (equivalent to exchanging subsets of rules). Smith successfully applied this system, LS-1 (Learning System One) to the Holland and Reitman maze-running task and to a draw poker betting task. In the draw poker task, Smith's system learned to beat Waterman's [50] adaptive poker playing program consistently, a substantial achievement given the amount of domain-specific knowledge in Waterman's program.

The next major application of classifier systems was Booker's [6] study. Booker concentrated on the formal connections between cognitive science and classifier systems. His computer simulations investigated the adaptive behavior of an artificial creature, moving about in a two-dimensional environment containing "food" and "poison," controlled by a classifier system "brain." Booker's classifier system contained a number of innovations including the use of sharing to promote "niche" exploitation, and the use of mating restrictions to reduce the production of ineffective offspring (lethals).

In 1983, Goldberg [18] applied a classifier system to the control of two engineering systems: the pole-balancing problem and a natural gas pipeline-compressor system. The simulations were in the SR (stimulus-response) format, with payoff being presented at each computational time step by a critic. In both cases Goldberg observed the formation of stable subpopulations of rules serving as *default hierarchies*. In a default hierarchy, fairly general rules cover the most frequent cases and more specific rules (that typically contradict the default rules) cover exceptions.

Wilson [51, 52], working along different lines, studied a number of applications of classifier systems. While at Polaroid, he was able to construct and test a classifier system that learned to focus and center a moveable videocamera on an object placed in its field of vision. These experiments, though successful, caused him to turn to a simpler environment and a simpler version of the classifier system to better understand its behavior. In the later experiments, performed at the Rowland Institute for Science, a classifier system called ANIMAT operated in a two-dimensional environment, searching for food hidden behind obstacles. ANIMAT did not use a message list and hence could not employ a standard bucket brigade algorithm. Instead all classifiers contributing to a chosen action, the *action set*, received strength increments derived either from subsequent environmental payoff or from the bids of the next action set. This bucket brigade-like algorithm successfully propagated credit to early stage-setting rules under conditions of intermittent and noisy payoff.

A number of GA-based machine learning applications and extensions have followed the early works. A representative list, ranging from the evolution of cooperation (Axelrod [2]) and prediction of international events (Schrodt [44]) to VLSI compaction (Fourman [16]), is presented in Appendix B. There are now standard software tools for exploring these systems, including Forrest's [15] KL-ONE-to-classifier-system translator and Riolo's general-purpose, classifier system C-package.[1]

Recent work on classifier systems and genetic algorithms may be found in the books *Genetic Algorithms and Simulated Annealing* (Davis [10]) and *Genetic Algorithms and Their Applications* (Grefenstette [20]), the latter book containing papers presented at a conference held at MIT in the summer of 1987.

## 9. The Future: Advantages, Problems, Techniques, and Prospects

Up to this point we have reviewed and commented upon established aspects of classifier systems and their learning algorithms. Now we want to look to the future. Section 9.1, as a prologue, reviews some properties of classifier systems that afford future opportunities, while Section 9.2 points up some of the problems that currently impede progress. Section 9.3 outlines some untried techniques that broaden the possibilities for classifier systems, and Section 9.4 offers a look at some of the directions we think will be productive for future research.

### 9.1. Advantages

When it comes to describing advantages, pride of place goes to the genetic algorithm. The genetic algorithm operating on classifiers discovers potentially useful building blocks, tests them, and recombines them to form plausible new classifiers. It does this at the large "speedup" implied by Theorem 6.2 on

---

[1]Available on request from R. Riolo, Division of Computer Science and Engineering, 3116 EECS Building, The University of Michigan, Ann Arbor, MI 48109, U.S.A.

*implicit parallelism*, searching through and testing large numbers of building blocks while manipulating relatively few classifiers.

Competition based on rule strength, in conjunction with the parallelism of classifier systems provides several additional advantages. New rules can be added without imposing the severe computational burden of checking their consistency with all the extant rules. Indeed the system can retain large numbers of mutually contradictory, partially confirmed rules, an important advantage because these rules serve as alternative hypotheses to be invoked when currently favored rules prove inadequate. Moreover, this approach in conjunction with the genetic algorithm provides the overall system with a robust incremental means of handling noisy data. The system has no need of an archival memory of all past examples; its memory resides in the sets of competing alternatives.

## 9.2. Problems

To this point in time our problems are largely those attending a new approach wherein the experimental landmarks only sparsely cover the landscape of possibilities.

The most serious problem we have encountered concerns the stability of emergent default hierarchies. The hierarchies *do* emerge (see, for example, Goldberg [18], a first as far as we know), but in long runs there may be a catastrophic collapse in which whole subsets of good rules are lost. The rules, or rules similar in effect, are then reacquired, but this instability is highly undesirable.

Forrest [15] has demonstrated that semantic nets can be implemented simply and directly with coupled classifiers, but the question of how such structures can emerge in response to experience has been barely touched. This is, of course, more a research objective than a fault.

We also have only the faintest guidelines as to the functioning of the bucket brigade when the rule sequences are long and intertwined. Again, we have uncovered no faults, we simply have very little knowledge.

## 9.3. Techniques

There are several new techniques that should substantially increase the power and robustness of classifier systems. Chief among these is the *triggering* of genetic operators. For example, when an input message receives only weak bids from very general classifiers, it is a sign that the system has little specific information for dealing with the current environmental situation. A cross between the input message and the condition parts of some of the active general rules will yield plausible new rules with more specific conditions. This amounts to a bottom-up procedure for producing candidate rules that will automatically be tested for usefulness when similar situations recur. As another example, when a rule makes a large profit under the bucket brigade, this can be used as a signal to cross it with rules active on the immediately preceding time step. An appropriate cross between the message part of the precursor and the condition part of the profit making successor can produce a new pair of *coupled* rules. (The trigger is only activated if the precursor is *not* coupled to the active profit maker.) The coupled pair models the state transition mediated by the original pair of (uncoupled) rules. Such coupled rules can serve as the building blocks for models of the environment. Because the couplings serve as "bridges" for the bucket brigade, these building blocks will be assigned credit in accord with the efficacy of the models constructed from them. Interestingly enough there seems to be a rather small number of robust triggering conditions (see Holland et al. [33]), but each of them would appear to add substantially to the responsiveness of the classifier system.

*Support* is another technique that adds considerably to the system's flexibility. Basically, support is a technique that enables the classifier system to integrate many pieces of partial information (such as several views of a partially obscured object) to arrive at strong conclusions. Support is a quantity that travels *with* messages, rather than being a counterflow as in the case of bids. When a classifier is satisfied by several messages from the message list, each such message adds its support into that classifier's *support counter*. Unlike a classifier's strength, the support accrued by a classifier lasts for only the time step in which it is accumulated. That is, the support counter is reset at the end of each time step (other techniques are possible, such as a long or short half-life). Support is used to modify the size of the classifier's bid on that time step; large support increases the bid, small support decreases it. If the classifier wins the bidding competition, the message it posts carries a support proportional to the size of its bid. The propagation of support over sets of coupled classifiers acts somewhat like spreading activation (see [1]), but it is much more directed. Like spreading activation, support can serve to bring associations (coupled rules) into play; but, as mentioned at the outset, it is meant to act primarily as a means of integrating partial information (as when several weakly bidding, general rules bearing on the same topic are activated simultaneously).

### 9.4. Prospects

The number of feasible directions for exploring the possibilities and applications of classifier systems is almost daunting. Here we will mention only some of the broader paths.

Perhaps the most important thing that can be done at this point is an expansion of the theory. Classifier systems serve as a "testbed" for concepts applicable to a wide range of complex adaptive systems. In developing a mathematics to deal with the interaction of the genetic algorithm and classifier systems we perforce develop a mathematics for dealing with a much wider range of adaptive systems.

The process is reciprocal. For instance, in mathematical economics there are pieces of mathematics that deal with (1) hierarchical organization, (2) retained earnings (fitness) as a measure of past performance, (3) competition based on retained earnings, (4) distribution of earnings on the basis of local interactions of consumers and suppliers, (5) taxation as a control on efficiency, and (6) division of effort between production and research (exploitation versus exploration). Many of these fragments, mutatis mutandis, can be used to study the counterparts of these processes in classifier systems.

Similarly, in mathematical ecology there are pieces of mathematics dealing with (1) niche exploitation (models exploiting environmental regularities), (2) phylogenetic hierarchies, polymorphism and enforced diversity (competing subsystems), (3) functional convergence (similarities of subsystem organization enforced by environmental requirements on payoff attainment), (4) symbiosis, parasitism, and mimicry (couplings and interactions in a default hierarchy, such as an increased efficiency for extant generalists simply because related specialists exclude them from some regions in which they are inefficient), (5) food chains, predator-prey relations, and other energy transfers (apportionment of energy or payoff amongst component subsystems), (6) recombination of multifunctional coadapted sets of genes (recombination of building blocks), (7) assortative mating (biased recombination), (8) phenotypic markers affecting interspecies and intraspecies interactions (coupling), (9) "founder" effects (generalists giving rise to specialists), and (10) other detailed commonalities such as tracking versus averaging over environmental changes (compensation for environmental variability), allelochemicals (cross-inhibition), linkage (association and encoding of features), and still others. Once again, though mathematical ecology is a younger science than mathematical economics, there is much in the mathematics already developed that is relevant to the study of classifier systems and other nonlinear systems far from equilibrium.

In addition to attempting to adapt and extend these fragments, there are at least two broader mathematical tasks that can be undertaken. One is an attempt to produce a general characterization of systems that exhibit *implicit parallelism*. Up to now all such attempts have led to sets of algorithms which are easily recast as genetic algorithms—in effect, we still only know of one example of an algorithm that exhibits implicit parallelism. The second task involves developing a mathematical formulation of the process whereby a system can develop a useful internal model of an environment exhibiting perpetual novelty. In our (preliminary) experiments to date these models typically exhibit a (tangled) hierarchical structure with associative couplings. Such structures have been characterized mathematically as quasi-homomorphisms (see [33]). The perpetual novelty of the environment can be characterized by a Markov process in which each state has a recurrence time that is large relative to any feasible observation time. Considerable progress has been made along these lines (see [32]), but much remains to be done. In particular, we need to construct an interlocking set of theorems based on:

(1) a stronger set of fixed point theorems that relates the strengths of classifiers under the bucket brigade to observed payoff statistics,

(2) a set of theorems that relates building blocks exploited by the "slow" dynamics of the genetic algorithm to the sampling rates for rules at different levels of the emerging default hierarchy (more general rules are tried more often), and

(3) a set of theorems (based on the previous two sets) that detail the way in which various kinds of environmental regularities are exploited by the genetic algorithm acting in terms of the strengths assigned by the bucket brigade.

In the realm of experiment, aside from interesting new applications, the design of experiments centered on the *emergence* of tags under triggered coupling offers intriguing possibilities. Tags serve as the glue of larger systems, providing both associative and temporal (model building) pointers (see Example 3.5). Under certain kinds of triggered coupling (see the previous section) the message sent by the precursor in the coupled pair can have a "hash-coded" section (say a prefix or suffix). The purpose of this hash-coded tag is to prevent accidental eavesdropping by other classifiers—a sufficient number of randomly generated bits in the tag will prevent accidental matches with other conditions (unless the conditions have a lot of # in the tag region). If the coupled pair proves useful to the system then it will have further offspring under the genetic algorithm, and these offspring often will be coupled to other rules in the system. Typically, the tag will be passed on to the offspring, serving as a common element in all the couplings; the tag will only persist if the resulting cluster of rules proves to be a useful "subroutine." In this case, the "subroutine" can be "called" by messages that incorporate the tag, because the conditions of the rules in the cluster are satisfied by such messages. In short, the tag that was initially determined at random now "names" the developing subroutine. It even has a *meaning* in terms of the actions it calls forth. Moreover, the tag is subject to the same kinds of recombination as other parts of the rules (it is, after all, a schema). As such it can serve as a building block for other tags. It is as if the system were inventing symbols for its internal use. Clearly, any simulation that provides for a test of these ideas will be an order of magnitude more sophisticated than anything we have tried to date. Runs involving hundreds of thousands of time steps will probably be required.

Another set of possibilities, far beyond anything we yet understand either theoretically or empirically, is fully directed rule generation. In the *broadcast language* that was the precursor of classifier systems, provision was made for the generation of rules by other rules. With minor changes to the definition of classifier systems, this possibility can be reintroduced. (Both messages and rules are strings. By enlarging the message alphabet, lengthening the message string, and introducing a special symbol that indicates whether a string is to be interpreted as a rule or a message, the task can be accomplished.) With this provision the system can invent its own candidate operators and rules of inference. Survival of these meta- (operator-like) rules should then be made to depend on the net usefulness of the rules they generate (much as a schema takes its value from the average value of its carriers). It is probably a matter of a decade or two before we can do anything useful in this area.

Another interesting possibility rests on the fact that classifier systems are general-purpose systems. They can be programmed initially to implement whatever expert knowledge is available to the designer; learning then allows the system to expand, correct errors, and transfer information from one domain to another. It is important to provide ways of instructing such systems so that they can generate rules—tentative hypotheses—on the basis of advice. Little has been done in this direction. It is also particularly important that we understand how lookahead and virtual explorations can be incorporated without disturbing other activities of the system.

Our broadest hopes turn on reincarnating in machine learning the cycle of theory and experiment so fruitful in physics. The close control of initial conditions, parameters, and environment made possible by simulation should enable the design of critical tests of the unfolding theory. And the simulations should suggest new directions for the theory. We hope to gain an understanding, not just of classifier systems, but of the consequences of competition in a changing population wherein subsystems are defined by combinations of building blocks that interact in a nonlinear fashion. In this context, classifier systems serve as a well-defined, precisely controllable testbed for a general theory.

## Appendix A. Genetic Algorithm Applications in Search and Logic

| Cat. | Year | Investigators | Description |
|------|------|---------------|-------------|
| *Biology* | | | |
| B | 1967 | Rosenberg | Simulation of the evolution of single-celled organism populations. |
| B | 1970 | Weinberg | Outline of cell population simulation including meta-level GA. |
| B | 1984 | Perry | Investigation of niche theory and specification with GAs. |
| B | 1985 | Grosso | Simulation of diploid GA with explicit subpopulations and migration. |
| *Computer science* | | | |
| CS | 1967 | Bagley | GA-directed parameter search for evaluation function in hexapawn-like game. |
| CS | 1983 | Gerardy | Probabilistic automaton identification attempt via GA. |
| CS | 1983 | Gordon | Adaptive document description using GA. |
| CS | 1984 | Rendell | GA search for game evaluation function. |

| Cat. | Year | Investigators | Description |
|------|------|---------------|-------------|
| *Engineering* | | | |
| E | 1981 | Goldberg | Mass-spring-dashpot system identification with simple GA. |
| E | 1982 | Etter, Hicks, Cho | Recursive adaptive filter design using a simple GA. |
| E | 1983 | Goldberg | Steady state and transient optimization of gas pipeline using GA. |
| E | 1985 | Davis | Outline of job shop scheduling procedure using GA. |
| E | 1985 | Davis, Smith | VLSI circuit layout via GA. |
| E | 1985 | Fourman | VLSI layout compaction via GA. |
| E | 1985 | Goldberg, Kuo | On-off, steady state optimization of oil pump-pipeline system via GA. |
| E | 1986 | Goldberg, Samtani | Structural optimization (plane truss) via GA. |
| E | 1986 | Minga | Aircraft landing strut weight optimization via GA. |
| E | 1987 | Davis, Coombs | Communications network link size optimization using GA plus advanced operators. |
| E | 1987 | Davis, Ritter | Classroom scheduling via simulated annealing with meta-level GA. |
| *Function optimization* | | | |
| FO | 1985 | Ackley | Connectionist algorithm with GA-like properties. |
| FO | 1985 | Brady | Traveling salesman problem via genetic-like operators. |
| FO | 1985 | Davis | Bin-packing and graph-coloring problems via GA. |
| FO | 1985 | Grefenstette, Gopal, Rosmaita, van Gucht | Traveling salesman problem via knowledge-augmented genetic operators. |
| FO | 1986 | Goldberg, Smith | Blind knapsack problem via simple GA. |
| *Genetic algorithm parameters* | | | |
| GA | 1971 | Hollstien | 2-D function optimization with mating and selection rules. |
| GA | 1972 | Bosworth, Foo, Zeigler | GA-like operators on simulated genes with sophisticated mutation. |
| GA | 1972 | Frantz | Investigation of positional nonlinearity and inversion. |
| GA | 1973 | Martin | Theoretical study of GA-like probabilistic algorithms. |
| GA | 1975 | DeJong | Base-line parametric study of simple GA in 5-function testbed. |
| GA | 1976 | Bethke | Brief theoretical investigation of possible parallel GA implementation. |
| GA | 1977 | Mercer | GA controlled by meta-level GA. |
| GA | 1981 | Bethke | Application of Walsh functions to schema average analysis. |
| GA | 1981 | Brindle | Investigation of selection and dominance in GAs. |
| GA | 1981 | Grefenstette | Brief theoretical investigation of possible parallel GA implementation. |
| GA | 1983 | Pettit, Swigger | Cursory investigation of GAs in nonstationary search problems. |
| GA | 1983 | Wetzel | Traveling salesman problem via GA. |
| GA | 1984 | Mauldin | Study of several heuristics to maintain diversity in simple GA. |

| Cat. | Year | Investigators | Description |
|------|------|---------------|-------------|
| GA | 1985 | Baker | Trial of ranking selection procedure on DeJong testbed. |
| GA | 1985 | Booker | Suggestion for partial match scores, sharing, and mating restrictions. |
| GA | 1985 | Goldberg, Lingle | Traveling salesman problem using partially matched cross-over and schema analysis. |
| GA | 1985 | Schaffer | Multi-objective optimization using GAs with sub-populations. |
| GA | 1986 | Goldberg | Maximization of marginal schema content by optimization of estimated population size. |
| GA | 1986 | Grefenstette | GA controlled by meta-level GA. |
| GA | 1986 | Grefenstette, Fitzpatrick | Test of simple genetic algorithm with noisy functions. |
| GA | 1987 | Goldberg | Analysis of minimal deceptive problem for simple GAs. |

*Image processing*

| | | | |
|------|------|---------------|-------------|
| IP | 1970 | Cavicchio | Selection of detectors for pixel-based pattern recognition. |
| IP | 1984 | Fitzpatrick, Grefenstette, van Gucht | Image registration via GA to highlight selected properties. |
| IP | 1985 | Englander | Selection of detectors for known image classification. |
| IP | 1985 | Gillies | GA search for diagnostic image feature subroutines in Cytocomputer. |

*Physical sciences*

| | | | |
|------|------|---------------|-------------|
| PS | 1985 | Shaefer | Nonlinear equation solving with GA for fitting molecular potential surfaces. |

*Social sciences*

| | | | |
|------|------|---------------|-------------|
| SS | 1979 | Reynolds | GA-guided adaptation in hunter gatherer/agricultural transition model. |
| SS | 1981 | Smith, DeJong | Calibration of population migration model using GA search. |
| SS | 1985 | Axelrod | Iterated prisoner's dilemma problem solution using GA. |
| SS | 1985 | Axelrod | Simulation of the evolution of behavioral norms with GA. |

## Appendix B. Genetic Algorithm Applications in Machine Learning

| Cat. | Year | Investigators | Description |
|------|------|---------------|-------------|
| *Business* | | | |
| BU | 1986 | Frey | Architectural classification using CS. |
| BU | 1986 | Thompson, Thompson | GA search for rule sets to predict company profitability. |

| Cat. | Year | Investigators | Description |
|------|------|---------------|-------------|
| *Computer science* | | | |
| CS | 1980 | Smith | Draw poker bet decisions learned by pure GA (LS-1). |
| CS | 1985 | Cramer | GA learning of multiplication task using assembler-like instruction set. |
| CS | 1985 | Forrest | Interpreter to convert KL-ONE networks to CSs. |
| CS | 1986 | Riolo | General-purpose C-package for classifier system study. |
| CS | 1986 | Riolo | Letter sequence prediction task via CS. |
| CS | 1986 | Robertson | LISP version of letter sequence prediction task implemented on Connection Machine |
| CS | 1986 | Zeigler | GA searches for rule sets in symbolic rule-based system. |
| CS | 1986 | Zhou | GA builds finite automata from I/O examples. |
| *Engineering* | | | |
| E | 1983 | Goldberg | Pole-balancing task and gas pipeline control tasks learned by CS. |
| E | 1984 | Schaffer | LS-2 (see Smith) learns parity and signal problems. |
| E | 1985 | Kuchinski | GA search for battle management system rules. |
| E | 1986 | Liepins, Hilliard | Simple scheduling problem learned via CS. |
| E | 1986 | Wilson | Boolean multiplexer task learned via CS. |
| *Psychology and social sciences* | | | |
| SS | 1978 | Holland, Reitman | CS-1 learns to transfer information between maze-running tasks. |
| SS | 1982 | Booker | Animal-like automaton with CS "brain" learns in simple 2-D environment. |
| SS | 1983 | Wilson | Video eye learns to focus when driven by CS. |
| SS | 1985 | Axelrod | GA searches for rule-based strategies in iterated prisoner's dilemma. |
| SS | 1985 | Wilson | ANIMAT automaton with CS "brain" learns to acquire obstacle-hidden objects in 2-D environment. |
| SS | 1986 | Schrodt | Prediction of international events using CS. |
| SS | 1986 | Haslev (Skanland) | Past tense for Norwegian verb forms learned by CS. |

## REFERENCES

1. Anderson, J.R., *The Architecture of Cognition* (Harvard University Press, Cambridge, MA, 1983).
2. Axelrod, R., The evolution of strategies in the iterated prisoner's dilemma, in: L. Davis (Ed.), *Genetic Algorithms and Simulated Annealing* (Pitman, London, 1987).
3. Bagley, J.D., The behavior of adaptive systems which employ genetic and correlation algorithms, Ph.D. Dissertation, University Microfilms No. 68-7556, University of Michigan, Ann Arbor, MI (1967).
4. Bethke, A.D., Genetic algorithms as function optimizers, Ph.D. Dissertation, University Microfilms No. 8106101, University of Michigan, Ann Arbor, MI (1981).
5. Bledsoe, W.W. and Browning, I., Pattern recognition and reading by machine, in: *Proceedings Eastern Joint Computer Conference* (1959) 225–232.
6. Booker, L.B., Intelligent behavior as an adaptation to the task environment, Ph.D. Dissertation, University Microfilms No. 8214966, University of Michigan, Ann Arbor, MI (1982).

7. Cavicchio, D.J., Adaptive search using simulated evolution, Ph.D. Dissertation, University of Michigan, Ann Arbor, MI (1970).
8. Davis, L.D., Applying adaptive algorithms to epistatic domains, in: *Proceedings IJCAI-85*, Los Angeles, CA (1985) 162–164.
9. Davis, L.D., Job shop scheduling with genetic algorithms, in: J.J. Grefenstette (Ed.), *Proceedings of an International Conference on Genetic Algorithms and Their Applications* (Carnegie-Mellon University Press, Pittsburgh, PA, 1985) 136–140.
10. Davis, L.D., *Genetic Algorithms and Simulated Annealing* (Morgan Kaufmann, Los Altos, CA, 1987).
11. DeJong, K.A., An analysis of the behavior of a class of genetic adaptive systems, Ph.D. Dissertation, University Microfilms No. 76-9381, University of Michigan, Ann Arbor, MI (1975).
12. Erman, L.D., Hayes-Roth, F., Lesser, V.R. and Reddy, D.R., The Hearsay-II speech-understanding system: Integrating knowledge to resolve uncertainty, *Comput. Surv.* **12** (1980) 213–253.
13. Fahlman, S., *NETL: A System for Representing and Using Real World Knowledge* (MIT Press, Cambridge, MA, 1979).
14. Farmer, J.D., Packard, N.H. and Perelson, A.S., The immune system and artificial intelligence, in: J.J. Grefenstette (Ed.), *Proceedings of an International Conference on Genetic Algorithms and Their Applications* (Carnegie-Mellon University Press, Pittsburgh, PA, 1985) supplement; revised: *Phys. D* **22** (1986) 187–204.
15. Forrest, S., A study of parallelism in the classifier system and its application to classification in KL-ONE semantic networks, Ph.D. Dissertation, University of Michigan, Ann Arbor, MI (1985).
16. Fourman, M.P., Compaction of symbolic layout using genetic algorithms, in: J.J. Grefenstette (Ed.), *Proceedings of an International Conference on Genetic Algorithms and Their Applications* (Carnegie-Mellon University Press, Pittsburgh, PA, 1985) 141–153.
17. Frantz, D.R., Non-linearities in genetic adaptive search, Ph.D. Dissertation, University Microfilms No. 73-11116, University of Michigan, Ann Arbor, MI (1973).
18. Goldberg, D.E., Computer-aided gas pipeline operation using genetic algorithms and rule learning, Ph.D. Dissertation, University Microfilms No. 8402282, University of Michigan, Ann Arbor, MI (1983).
19. Goldberg, D.E. and Lingle, R., Alleles, loci, and the travelling salesman problem, in: J.J. Grefenstette (Ed.), *Proceedings of an International Conference on Genetic Algorithms and Their Applications* (Carnegie-Mellon University Press, Pittsburgh, PA, 1985) 154–159.
20. Grefenstette, J.J., *Genetic Algorithms and Their Applications* (Erlbaum, Hillsdale, NJ, 1987).
21. Grefenstette, J.J., Gopal, R., Rosmaita, B.J. and van Gucht, D., Genetic algorithms for the traveling salesman problem, in: J.J. Grefenstette (Ed.), *Proceedings of an International Conference on Genetic Algorithms and Their Applications* (Carnegie-Mellon University Press, Pittsburgh, PA, 1985) 160–168.
22. Hayes-Roth, F. and McDermott, J., An interference matching technique for inducing abstractions, *Commun. ACM* **21** (1978) 401–410.
23. Hinton, G.E. and Anderson, J.A., *Parallel Models of Associative Memory* (Erlbaum, Hillsdale, NJ, 1981).
24. Hinton, G.E., McClelland, J.L. and Rumelhart, D.E., Distributed representations, in: D.E. Rumelhart and J.L. McClelland (Eds.), *Parallel Distributed Processing*, I: *Foundations* (MIT Press, Cambridge, MA, 1986).
25. Holland, J.H., Outline for a logical theory of adaptive systems, *J. ACM* **3** (1962) 297–314.
26. Holland, J.H., Processing and processors for schemata, in: E.L. Jacks (Ed.), *Associative Information Processing* (American Elsevier, New York, 1971) 127–146.
27. Holland, J.H., Genetic algorithms and the optimal allocation of trials, *SIAM J. Comput.* **2** (1973) 88–105.
28. Holland, J.H., *Adaptation in Natural and Artificial Systems* (University of Michigan Press, Ann Arbor, MI, 1975).

29. Holland, J.H., Adaptation, in: R. Rosen and F.M. Snell (Eds.), *Progress in Theoretical Biology* IV (Academic Press, New York, 1976) 263–293.

30. Holland, J.H., Adaptive algorithms for discovering and using general patterns in growing knowledge-bases, *Int. J. Policy Anal. Inf. Syst.* **4** (1980) 245–268.

31. Holland, J.H., Escaping brittleness: The possibilities of general purpose learning algorithms applied to parallel rule-based systems, in: R.S. Michalski, J.G. Carbonell and T.M. Mitchell (Eds.), *Machine Learning: An Artificial Intelligence Approach* **2** (Morgan Kaufmann, Los Altos, CA, 1986) 593–623.

32. Holland, J.H., A mathematical framework for studying learning in classifier systems, *Phys. D* **22** (1986) 307–317.

33. Holland, J.H., Holyoak, K.J., Nisbett, R.E. and Thagard, P.R., *Induction: Processes of Inference, Learning, and Discovery* (MIT Press, Cambridge, MA 1986).

34. Holland, J.H. and Reitman, J.S., Cognitive systems based on adaptive algorithms, in: D.A. Waterman and F. Hayes-Roth (Eds.), *Pattern-Directed Inference Systems* (Academic Press, New York, 1978) 313–329.

35. Hollstien, R.B., Artificial genetic adaptation in computer control systems, Ph.D. Dissertation, University Microfilms No. 71-23773, University of Michigan, Ann Arbor, MI (1971).

36. Hopfield, J.J., Neural networks and physical systems with emergent collective computational abilities, *Proc. Nat. Acad. Sci. USA* **79** (1982) 2554–2558.

37. Jain, R., Dynamic scene analysis using pixel-based processes, *IEEE Computer* **14** (1981) 12–18.

38. Laird, J.E., Newell, A. and Rosenbloom, P.S., SOAR: An architecture for general intelligence, *Artificial Intelligence* **33** (1987) 1–64.

39. Mitchell, T.M., Version spaces: A candidate elimination approach to rule learning, in: *Proceedings IJCAI-77*, Cambridge, MA (1977).

40. Newell, A. and Simon, H.A., *Human Problem Solving* (Prentice-Hall, Englewood Cliffs, NJ, 1972).

41. Rosenberg, R.S., Simulation of genetic populations with biochemical properties. Ph.D. Dissertation, University Microfilms No. 67-17836, University of Michigan, Ann Arbor, MI (1967).

42. Samuel, A.L., Some studies in machine learning using the game of checkers, *IBM J. Res. Dev.* **3** (1959) 210–229.

43. Schleidt, W.M., Die historische Entwicklung der Begriffe "Angeborenes Auslosendes Schema" und "Angeborener Auslosmechanismus", *Z. Tierpsychol.* **21** (1962) 235–256.

44. Schrodt, P.A., Predicting international events, *Byte* **11** (12) (1986) 177–192.

45. Simon, H.A., *The Sciences of the Artificial* (MIT Press, Cambridge, MA, 1969).

46. Smith, S.F., A learning system based on genetic adaptive algorithms, Ph.D. Dissertation, University of Pittsburg, Pittsburgh, PA (1980).

47. Sutton, R.S., Learning to predict by the methods of temporal difference, Tech. Rept. TR87-509.1, GTE, Waltham, MA (1987).

48. Sutton, R.S. and Barto, A.G., Toward a modern theory of adaptive networks: Expectation and prediction, *Psychol. Rev.* **88** (1981) 135–170.

49. Valiant, L.G., A theory of the learnable, *Commun. ACM* **27** (1984) 1134–1142.

50. Waterman, D.A., Generalization learning techniques for automating the learning of heuristics, *Artificial Intelligence* **1** (1970) 121–170.

51. Wilson, S.W., On the retinal-cortical mapping, *Int. J. Man-Mach. Stud.* **18** (1983) 361–389.

52. Wilson, S.W., Knowledge growth in an artificial animal, in: J.J. Grefenstette (Ed.), *Proceedings of an International Conference on Genetic Algorithms and Their Applications* (Carnegie-Mellon University Press, Pittsburgh, PA, 1985) 16–23.

53. Winston, P.H., Learning structural descriptions from examples, in: P.H. Winston (Ed.), *The Psychology of Computer Vision* (McGraw-Hill, New York, 1975).

# Data-Driven Approaches
# to Empirical Discovery

## Pat Langley

*Department of Information and Comptuer Science,*
*University of California, Irvine, CA 92717, U.S.A.*

## Jan M. Zytkow*

*Computer Science Department, Wichita State University,*
*Wichita, KS 67208, U.S.A.*

ABSTRACT

*In this paper we track the development of research in empirical discovery. We focus on four machine discovery systems that share a number of features: the use of data-driven heuristics to constrain the search for numeric laws; a reliance on theoretical terms; and the recursive application of a few general discovery methods. We examine each system in light of the innovations it introduced over its predecessors, providing some insight into the conceptual progress that has occurred in machine discovery. Finally, we reexamine this research from the perspectives of the history and philosophy of science.*

## 1. Introduction

In the last decade, a few AI researchers have turned their attention to a domain often considered the realm of genius—scientific discovery. The vast majority of this work has focused on empirical discovery, and much of the effort has been concerned with the induction of numeric laws. In this paper we trace one evolutionary chain of research on discovery, in particular the development of data-driven methods relating to numeric law induction. We examine four systems—Gerwin's function induction system, Langley, Bradshaw, and Simon's BACON, Zytkow's FAHRENHEIT, and Nordhausen and Langley's IDS—and describe how each program introduces abilities lacking in earlier systems. The conceptual advances involve three different but interrelated aspects of discovery: the form of laws and theoretical terms discovered; the ability to determine the scope and context of laws; and the ability to design

* On leave of absence at Department of Computer Science, George Mason University, Fairfax, VA 22030, U.S.A.

experiments. We evaluate each of the systems, but we focus on their theoretical contributions rather than on reporting their behavior in specific domains. We close the paper by reviewing the work on machine discovery from the views of the history and philosophy of science.

## 1.1. Machine learning and discovery

One of the central insights of AI is that intelligence relies on large amounts of domain-specific knowledge. The field of machine learning is concerned with methods for acquiring such knowledge, and one approach to this problem involves machine discovery (Langley and Michalski [19]). This approach can be distinguished from other work in machine learning by the degree of supervision provided to the learner. Some learning research focuses on direct instruction, in which a teacher gives explicit advice or declarative knowledge (e.g., Mostow [27]). In work on learning from examples, the learner must acquire its own concepts or rules from experience, but the teacher preclassifies instances into useful classes (e.g., Dietterich and Michalski [3]). Both of these approaches are supervised in that a teacher provides information that constrains the learning task. In contrast, discovery occurs in domains where no such teacher is available, forcing the learner to operate without supervision.

Within this view of discovery as unsupervised learning, one can further identify three different aspects of discovery which borrow from distinctions that occur within the philosophy of science. Some discoveries involve the organization of objects or events into categories and taxonomies; within machine learning, work on this problem generally goes by the name of *conceptual clustering* (e.g., Michalski and Stepp [25]). Other discoveries involve the induction of descriptive regularities, some qualitative and others quantitative in nature. Finally, some discovery involves the formulation of explanatory theories. The dichotomy between description and explanation is actually a continuum, but one can identify extreme cases at both ends of the spectrum. For example, the ideal gas law has a clear descriptive flavor, relating the temperature, volume, and pressure of gas in a container. In contrast, the kinetic theory of gases, with its analogy to colliding balls, has a clear explanatory flavor.

Much of the research in machine discovery has focused on the induction of descriptive laws,[1] and in this paper we will limit our attention to that aspect of the scientific process. We can define the task of empirical discovery as:

– *Given*. A set of observations or data.
– *Find*. One or more general laws that summarize those data.

---

[1] There has also been considerable work on conceptual clustering (Michalski and Stepp [25], Fisher [6]), and there have been recent efforts to use analogy in constructing explanatory theories (Falkenhainer [5], Langley and Jones [18]).

In the domains we will examine, an observation consists of a conjunction of attribute-value pairs, either numeric or symbolic in nature.[2] For instance, one might observe a particular combination of values for the temperature ($T$), volume ($V$), and pressure ($P$) for a contained gas. Laws take the form of relations (usually arithmetic) between these terms (such as $PV/T = k$ in the case of gases) and the conditions under which these relations hold. Empirical discovery in the task of finding such laws that account for a given set of data.

We have chosen to focus on empirical discovery in this paper for two main reasons. First, most research in machine discovery has dealt with this task, including our own work. Second, empirical discovery often occurs in the early stages of a field's evolution, before scientists have acquired much knowledge of the domain. As a result, it seems likely that general, domain-independent heuristics play a more central role in this task than in the process of theory formation and revision. Nonetheless, empirical discoveries are rare even among trained scientists, making them eminently worthy of attention. This combination makes them a good starting point for the mechanistic study of discovery.

## 1.2. A framework for empirical discovery

There are many paths to empirical discovery, but all of the systems we will describe in this paper share a common approach to this problem. Before describing the systems themselves, we should attempt to characterize this commonality. Taken together, the features that we will examine let one construct relatively simple and general discovery systems that still have considerable power.

First, all of the systems define *theoretical terms* that let them state laws in simple forms and that aid in the discovery process. The concept of momentum, defined as the product of mass and velocity, is one example of such a theoretical term. Using this product, one can state the law of conserved momentum as a simple linear relation. We will see that other types of theoretical terms are also possible. This can be viewed as a simple form of representation change, but we will not emphasize this aspect.

Second, the systems all employ *data-driven* heuristics to direct their searches through the space of theoretical terms and numeric laws. These heuristics match against different possible regularities in the data and take different actions depending on which regularity they detect. Some heuristics propose laws or hypotheses, others define a new theoretical term, and yet others alter the proposed scope of a law. Different data lead to the application of alternative sequences of heuristics, and thus to different sets of empirical laws.

---

[2] Some researchers (Lenat [23], Jones [10], Langley, Simon, Bradshaw and Zytkow [21]) have studied empirical discovery in domains involving more complex relational data, but we will discuss these only in passing.

Finally, all the systems can apply their methods *recursively* to the results of previously applications, and they achieve much of their power in this fashion. Thus, knowledge resulting from the application of one heuristic can later be examined and extended by other heuristics. For instance, once a theoretical term has been defined, it can be used as the basis for defining still other terms. In general, this recursive structure leads to synergistic behaviors that would not otherwise occur.

### 1.3. Alternative frameworks for empirical discovery

For the sake of completeness, we should briefly consider some other frameworks for empirical discovery. Clearly, one might construct a discovery system that formulates laws without the aid of theoretical terms. For example, given one dependent term and a set of independent terms, one might use a regression algorithm to fit a curve to observed data. Such a law would directly predict the data with no intervening theoretical constructs. Few machine discovery systems operate in this manner; the construction of higher-level terms plays some role in nearly all AI work on empirical discovery. Moreover, all use some form of heuristic search in place of the algorithmic curve-fitting methods commonly used in statistics, and the notion of recursive application also plays a central role in most systems.

The mention of statistical methods raises an important issue. Statisticians have developed a variety of algorithms for summarizing data, most of which are firmly based in mathematics. Given the existence of these methods, why attempt to develop alternatives? One reason is that, historically, human scientists have not relied on such methods in making their discoveries. Even when AI does not attempt to model the details of human cognition, it generally borrows its inspiration from this area. Another reason is that AI methods, with their emphasis on heuristic methods, generally apply to broader range of tasks than algorithmic approaches. Thus, heuristic approaches to numeric discovery may handle a wider class of numeric laws than existing statistical techniques, and may even suggest methods for discovering qualitative laws.

Let us briefly review some other AI discovery work that has employed a heuristic search approach, but that differs from the methods we will describe in later sections. One example in Lenat's AM [23], which incorporates a variety of heuristics to direct its search in the domain of number theory. Starting with about 100 basic concepts such as sets, lists, equality, and so forth, AM uses operators like specialization, generalization, and composition to generate new concepts. It then applies these operators to the resulting theoretical terms, eventually generating concepts such as multiplication, natural numbers, and prime numbers. The system also finds qualitative laws that relate these concepts, such as the unique factorization theorem. Although AM clearly creates new terms and applies its heuristics recursively, these heuristics are used primarily to *evaluate* new concepts rather than to create them. Thus, it should be viewed as a *model-driven* system rather than as a data-driven one.

Kokar's [12] work on COPER shows that one can also apply the model-driven approach to numerical discovery. This system has considerable knowledge embedded into its generator, employing information about attributes' dimensions to generate a restricted class of theoretical terms. COPER then tests the resulting set of terms for consistency with the observed data. Its knowledge of physical dimensions lets it determine whether this set is complete and, if not, to search for additional (unobserved) terms. Once it has found a consistent set of higher-level terms, it searches a space of polynomial functions to find a numeric law that summarizes the observations. COPER has discovered the law of falling bodies and Bernoulli's law of fluid flow in this fashion.

Falkenhainer and Michalski's [4] ABACUS takes a middle ground, basing its generation of new terms on some knowledge of dimensions but also on a simple measure of correlation between variables. The latter heuristic has a data-driven flavor, making ABACUS more similar to the programs we will discuss later than either AM or COPER. The system also incorporates a component that clusters subsets of the data according to the laws they obey and uses these clusters to formulate conditions under which these laws hold. This component employs the AQ algorithm (Michalski and Larson [24]) to search through the space of possible conditions; this process also has a mixed flavor, using some data to generate hypotheses and other data to evaluate them.

In the following pages, we describe four other discovery systems in greater detail. Given the variety of efforts on empirical discovery, our focus on a subset of this work deserves some justification. Our main reason is historical continuity. The four systems represent an evolutionary chain through the space of approaches to empirical discovery, with each system introducing innovations on its predecessors. We believe the evolutionary view reveals aspects of the discovery process that would remain hidden in a more traditional review. We also believe that the incremental development of AI systems, in which each program adds capabilities to previous ones, is an important methodological paradigm that deserves more widespread use. However, readers should not interpret our emphasis on these systems as downplaying the importance of other research in discovery.

## 2. Gerwin's Model of Function Induction

Gerwin [8] described one of the earliest machine discovery systems. He was concerned with inducing complex functions of one variable in the presence of noisy data. To this end, he collected and analyzed verbal protocols of humans solving a set of function induction tasks, as well as constructing a system that operated on the same class of problems. We will not review his experimental results here, except to note that he observed subjects using heuristic methods in their search for laws. The task itself and the system are more interesting for our purposes.

Gerwin's research on function induction introduced some important ideas that were to influence later work in empirical discovery. For instance, it served to clearly define the task of numeric discovery. At the same time, it also presented evidence that humans invoked heuristic search methods to solve such problems; the use of such methods (rather than algorithmic methods borrowed from statistics) made numeric discovery an interesting task for artificial intelligence.

Although Gerwin focused on functions of only one variable, some of his functions were quite complex. All were defined in terms of one or more primitive functions, taken from the set $e^{x/2}$, $x^2$, $x$, $x^{1/2}$, $\ln x$, $\sin x$, and $\cos x$, and combined using the connectives $+$, $-$, $/$, and $\times$. For instance, one such function is $y = x^2 \sin x - \ln x$; another is $y = x/\cos x$. However, a random component was included in each of the 15 test functions used, so the functions did not describe the data perfectly. In each case, Gerwin presented his subjects (and his program) with 10 $x$ values and their associated $y$ values. From these data, the subjects and program were to infer the function best fitting the observations.

## 2.1. Detecting patterns and computing residuals

Gerwin's system included a number of condition-action rules for detecting regularities in the data. For instance, it looked for patterns having periodic trends with increasing (or decreasing) amplitudes; it also noted monotonic increasing (or decreasing) trends when they occurred. Each such pattern suggested an associated class of functions (or combination of functions) that could lead to its production. Thus, when the program noted a trend, it hypothesized that some member of the associated class was an additive component of the overall function.

Having identified a set of likely components, the system selected one of those functions and used it to generate predicted $y$ values for each $x$ value. It then subtracted the predicted data from the actual values, checking to see whether these *residuals* had less variance than the original observations. If not, the system tried some other function from the same class and repeated the process. If none of these were successful, it looked for some other pattern in the data.

Upon finding a useful component function, Gerwin's system applied the same induction method to the residual data. It looked for patterns in these data, proposed component functions, tested their effect, and either rejected them or included them as another component in the developing overall function. This process continued until the system could no longer detect any patterns in the residual data. Since no regularity remained, the program would halt at this point, assuming it had found the best description of the original data. Using this approach, Gerwin's program was able to discover many of the functions used in his experiment, some of them quite complex.

## 2.2. Evaluating Gerwin's system

The particular system that Gerwin implemented relied on three important notions that we have already discussed. The first was the use of data-driven heuristics—his pattern-detecting condition-action rules—to direct the discovery process. The second was the notion of adding component functions, which can be viewed as a nascent form of theoretical term, and calculating residuals, which can be viewed as computing the values of those new terms. The final idea involved the recursive application of the original heuristics to these residuals, leading to new residuals and new data until a satisfactory function had been obtained. Taken together, these three features led to a simple yet powerful method for empirical discovery.

Despite its innovations, Gerwin's system was simplistic along a number of dimensions. It could discover only functions in one variable; it could define only one form of theoretical term; and its data-driven heuristics were specific to particular classes of functions. Moreover, the system was tested only on a set of artificially generated functions, so its implications for real-world discovery tasks was not clear. Later work in machine discovery would address all of these issues.

## 3. The BACON System

Although Gerwin's early work had many limitations, it provided an initial definition of the numeric discovery task and it suggested that this problem was amenable to the same heuristic search methods that had been used to explain other forms of intelligent behavior. These insights led directly to the BACON project (Langley [14, 15], Bradshaw, Langley and Simon [2], Langley, Bradshaw and Simon [6]), an attempt to construct a more general and more comprehensive model of empirical discovery.

## 3.1. Representing data and laws

BACON is actually a sequence of discovery systems that were developed over a number of years. In this paper, we will focus on BACON.4, since that program incorporates the main ideas and tells the most coherent story. As input, the system accepts a set of independent terms and request the corresponding values of the dependent terms. As an example, BACON might be given three independent terms—the pressure $P$ on a gas, the temperature $T$ of the gas, and the quantity $N$ of the gas—and the single dependent term $V$, the resulting volume of the gas. Independent terms may take on either numeric or nominal (symbolic) values, whereas dependent terms are always numeric.

As output, BACON.4 generates three interrelated structures that constitute its empirical discoveries:

(1) a set of numeric laws stated as simple constancies or linear relations, such as $X = 8.32$ and $U = 1.57V + 4.6$, along with some simple conditions under which each law holds;

(2) a set of definitions that relate theoretical terms to directly observable variables, such as $X = Y/T$ and $Y = PV$; it is these definitions that let BACON state its laws in such a simple form;

(3) a set of intrinsic properties, such as *mass* and *specific heat*, that take on numeric values; these values are associated with the symbolic values of nominal terms; thus, the *mass* of *object A* may be 1.43 while the *mass* of *object B* is 2.61.

Although each structure has a very simple form, taken together they provide BACON with considerable representational power. Using these three knowledge types, the system has rediscovered a wide range of laws from the history of physics and chemistry, including forms of the ideal gas law, Coulomb's law, Snell's law of refraction, Black's law of specific heat, Gay–Lussac's law of combining volumes, and Canizzaro's determination of relative atomic weights. Now let us examine the process by which BACON accomplishes these discoveries.

### 3.2. Discovering simple laws

BACON's most basic operation involves discovering a functional relation between two numeric terms. This is the direct analog to Gerwin's function induction task. For example, Galileo's law of falling bodies relates the distance $D$ from which an object is dropped to the time $T$ it takes to reach the ground. This law can be stated as $D/T^2 = k$, where $k$ is a constant. To discover laws relating two numeric variables, BACON employs three simple heuristics:

INCREASING
IF the values of $X$ increase as the values of $Y$ increase,
THEN define the ratio $X/Y$ and examine its values.

DECREASING
IF the values of $X$ increase as the values of $Y$ decrease,
THEN define the product $XY$ and examine its values.

CONSTANT
IF the values of $X$ are nearly constant for a number of values,
THEN hypothesize that $X$ always has this value.

Table 1
Data obeying the law of uniform acceleration

| Time ($T$) | Distance ($D$) | $D/T$ | $D/T^2$ |
| --- | --- | --- | --- |
| 0.1 | 0.098 | 0.98 | 9.80 |
| 0.2 | 0.390 | 1.95 | 9.75 |
| 0.3 | 0.880 | 2.93 | 9.78 |
| 0.4 | 1.572 | 3.93 | 9.83 |
| 0.5 | 2.450 | 4.90 | 9.80 |
| 0.6 | 3.534 | 5.89 | 9.82 |

Table 1 presents some idealized data that obey the law of falling bodies. Given the cooccurring values of $D$ and $T$ shown in the table, BACON notices that one term increases as the other increases. This leads the INCREASING rule to apply, defining the ratio $D/T$ and computing its values. Since the resulting values increase as those of $D$ decrease, they lead the system to apply the DECREASING heuristic, which defines the product $D^2/T$. When it computes the values for this new term, BACON notes that all the values are very near the mean of 9.795. This causes the rule CONSTANT to apply, hypothesizing that $D^2/T$ always has this value; the system has rediscovered a form of Galileo's law. From this example, one can see that BACON makes no distinction between directly observable terms and those it has defined itself. The system can also discover other complex relations in this way, such as Kepler's third law of planetary motion: $d^3/p^2 = k$, where $d$ is the planet's distance from the Sun, $p$ its period, and $k$ is a constant.

### 3.3. Discovering complex laws

In order to see how BACON discovers more complex laws involving a number of independent terms, let us consider a simple form a Black's heat law. This relates the initial temperatures of two substances ($T_1$ and $T_2$) with their temperature after they have been combined ($T_f$). The law can be stated as: $(c_1 M_1 + c_2 M_2) T_f = c_1 M_1 T_1 + c_1 M_2 T_2$, where $M_1$ and $M_2$ are the two initial masses and $c_1$ and $c_2$ are constants associated with the particular substances used in the experiment. For now we will assume the same substance is used in both cases; this makes $c_1 = c_2$ and lets us cancel them out from the equation. This gives the simpler law $T_f = (M_1/(M_1 + M_2)) T_1 + (M_2/(M_1 + M_2)) T_2$.

Given a set of independent terms such as $M_1$, $M_2$, $T_1$, and $T_2$, BACON constructs a simple factorial design experiment involving all combinations of independent values, and proceeds to collect data. In this case, the system begins by holding $M_1$, $M_2$, and $T_1$ constant and varying the values of $T_2$, examining the effect on the final temperature $T_f$ in each situation. In this way, the program collects the cooccurring independent and dependent values it requires to discover a simple law. In this case it finds the linear relation $T_f = aT_2 + b$, where $a$ is the slope of the line and $b$ its intercept. However, the system follows a conservative strategy upon discovering such a law, stating only that it holds when the other independent terms ($M_1$, $M_2$, and $T_1$) take on their observed values.

Nevertheless, BACON's ultimate goal is to discover a more general relation that incorporates all the independent variables. Thus, the system runs the same experiment again, but this time with different values for $T_1$, the temperature of the other substance. The result is a number of specific laws that hold for different values of $T_1$, but which all have the form $T_f = aT_2 + b$. At this point, the program shifts perspectives and begins to treat $a$ and $b$ as higher-level dependent terms, the values of which it has determined from the earlier experiments.

BACON then uses its methods for finding simple laws to uncover a relation between the values of $T_1$ and these two terms. In this example, the system finds that the slope $a$ is unaffected by $T_1$, which it states as the second-level law $a = c$. It also discovers a linear relation between the temperature and the intercept that can be stated as $b = dT_1$; since the intercept of this line is zero, it is omitted.

Having established two second-level laws, BACON now proceeds to vary $M_2$, the mass of the second substance, and to observe its effects on the parameters in these laws. This involves running additional experiments by varying $T_1$ and $T_2$, but once this has been done the system has a set of values for the parameters $c$ and $d$, each pair associated with a different value of $M_2$. Upon examining these values, BACON does not find any simple law but it notes that $c$ and $M_2$ increase together; as a result, it defines the ratio term $M_2/c$. This new term is linearly related to $M_2$, giving the third-level law $M_2 = e(M_2/c) + f$. Similar regularities lead the program to define the product $dM_2$ and to find the linear relation $dM_2 = gd + h$.

Now that it has incorporated the independent terms $T_2$, $T_1$, and $M_2$ into its laws, BACON turns to the final variable, $M_1$. Varying this leads to a set of additional experiments in which the other terms are varied, and from these the system estimates values for the parameters $e$, $f$, $g$, and $h$ for each value of $M_1$. The slope term $e$ has the constant value 1.0 in all cases, but the remaining terms vary. Closer inspection reveals that $f$, $g$, and $h$ are all linearly related to $M_1$ and that each line has a zero intercept, with slopes respectively $j$, $k$, and $l$.

At this point, BACON has rediscovered the simplified version of Black's law presented above, though not in the form we specified. Table 2 traces the steps followed by the system, listing the laws formulated at each level of the discovery process; at this point of the discussion we are at level 4. We should note that, as it finds laws at each level, the program places conditions on these laws corresponding to the values of the terms that it has not yet varied. As it incorporates these terms into higher-level laws, the conditions are generalized.

Table 2
Relations discovered at different levels for Black's law

| Level | Term varied | Laws found | Laws implied |
|---|---|---|---|
| 1 | $T_2$ | $T_f = aT_2 + b$ | $T_f = aT_2 + b$ |
| 2 | $T_1$ | $a = c$ <br> $b = dT_1$ | $T_f = cT_2 + dT_1$ |
| 3 | $M_2$ | $M_2 = e(M_2/c) + f$ <br> $dM_2 = gd + h$ | $T_f = eM_2T_2/(M_2 - f)$ <br> $+ hT_1/(M_2 - g)$ |
| 4 | $M_1$ | $f = jM_1, \quad g = kM_1$ <br> $h = lM_1, \quad e = 1.0$ | $T_f = M_2T_2/(M_2 - jM_1)$ <br> $+ lM_1T_1/(M_2 - kM_1)$ |
| 5 | Substance$_2$ | $j = pc_2, \quad k = qc_2$ <br> $l = rc_2$ | $T_f = M_2T_2/(M_2 - pc_2M_1)$ <br> $+ rc_2M_1T_1/(M_2 - gc_2M_1)$ |
| 6 | Substance$_1$ | $pc_1 = -1.0$ <br> $qc_1 = -1.0,$ <br> $rc_1 = 1.0$ | $T_f = M_2T_2/(M_2 + (c_2/c_1)M_1)$ <br> $+ (c_2/c_1)M_1T_1/(M_2 + (c_2/c_1)M_1)$ |

Thus, BACON gradually expands the scope of its laws as it moves to higher levels of description. We will return to the issue of scope later in the paper.

### 3.4. Postulating intrinsic properties

The above methods suffice to discover laws that relate numeric terms, such as occur in the ideal gas law. However, there are many historical cases in which scientists were also confronted with nominal or symbolic attributes. For instance, the two substances in Black's law are best described in this manner; one can combine water with water, water with mercury, and so forth. Upon varying the substances in this manner, one finds that the values of parameters in the various law also change. However, one cannot incorporate such symbolic terms directly into its numeric laws; some other step is required.

BACON's response in such cases is to *postulate* numeric terms that are associated with the observable nominal ones; we call these *intrinsic properties*. In the Black's law example, one can introduce such a property (called *specific heat*), the values of which are associated with different substances. Thus, if we let the specific heat $c$ for *water* be 1.0, then the specific heat for *mercury* is 0.0332 and the specific heat for *ethyl alcohol* is 0.456. Once BACON has established these values, it can relate the values of $c$ to parameters from its various laws, giving a higher-level law that effectively incorporates the two substances.

Let us continue with the Black's law example where we left off. BACON had incorporated the numeric terms $M_1$, $M_2$, $T_1$, and $T_2$ into a coherent set of laws, all ultimately related to the final temperature $T_f$. The system had also arrived at values for four parameters at the fourth level of description. One of these (call it $i$) involved a simple constancy; the others, $j$, $k$, and $l$, were the slopes of linear relations. The values for these parameters were conditional on the particular pair of substances used in the experiment, in this case two containers of water.

BACON's next step is to vary the second substance, using different materials such as mercury and ethyl alcohol with the first substance (still held constant as water). Upon doing this, the system notes that the values of $j$, $k$, and $l$ all vary, though the value of $i$ remains unchanged. In order to incorporate these terms into a higher-level law, the program requires some numeric independent variable associated with the second substance; we will call this $c_2$. BACON must assign values for this term, one for each nominal value of the substance, and it bases these values on those for the parameter $j$ (though $k$ or $l$ would have served equally well). The term $c_2$ is an intrinsic property, and the numeric values assigned to it are intrinsic values. These are initially stored with the condition that the first substance be water.

At this point BACON notes a linear relation between $c_2$ and $j$, but this is tautological, since it had defined the intrinsic property using the values of the latter term. However, the system also discovers linear relations between $c_2$ and $k$ and between $c_2$ and $l$; these are not guaranteed to hold and so have empirical content. The program has moved beyond tautologies and into laws capable of making predictions. Even more interesting events occur when the program varies the first substance in the experiment.

Upon placing mercury in contact with water, with mercury, and with ethyl alcohol, BACON finds that the values of the slope $j$ differ from when the first substance was water. But more important, they are linearly related to the earlier values of $j$. This tells BACON that the values of its intrinsic property should be useful regardless of the first substance; the condition that the first substance be water is dropped and the intrinsic values are stored with only the values of the second substance as a condition for retrieval. Thus, one value of $c_2$ is associated with water, another with mercury, and a third with ethyl alcohol. This lets the system retrieve the values of $c_2$ that it identified earlier and to note a linear relation between $c_2$ and the parameter $j$. Moreover, this law is nontautological; the values of $c_2$ were based on earlier values of $j$, not the current ones.

This generalization of the conditions on the intrinsic values also proves useful at the next (and highest) level of description. Different linear relations occur when different substances are placed in the first container, and the slopes of these lines provide the dependent terms for BACON to relate to the first substance. Since this is a nominal term, one could define a new intrinsic property, but there is no need; the conditions on the property $c$ have been sufficiently generalized to let its values be used in this case as well. Thus, BACON infers the values of $c_1$ and relates these to the various slope terms. The final set of relations correspond to Black's heat law, and the terms $c_1$ and $c_2$ correspond to the specific heats of the first and second substance, respectively. Table 2 summarizes the forms of the final laws.

### 3.5. Evaluating BACON

Now that we have examined BACON's representation and heuristics, we can evaluate its behavior in terms of some general issues relating to empirical discovery. Basically, we will conclude that on two dimensions—the forms of laws it can handle and the types of new terms it can define—the system performs quite well. However, the program's ability to determine the scope of laws and its ability to design experiments leave much to be desired.

Recall that BACON states all laws as either simple constancies or linear relations between two variables. However, when combined with the ability to define new ratio/product terms and to introduce intrinsic properties, this is sufficient to state a wide range of laws. For instance, the system can formulate laws involving exponents; one example is Kepler's law $(d^3/p^2 = k)$ and another is Coulomb's law $(FD^2/q_1q_2 = k)$. Another is Ohm's law for electric circuits, which in its most general form can be stated as $TD^2/(LI - rI) = b$. BACON can also discover a general version of the ideal gas law that does not rely on the absolute temperature scale: $PV = aNT + bN$. These suggest that the system can discover a respectable variety of empirical laws.

BACON also fares well in its ability to define new terms, and as we have stated, much of its overall power resides in this capability. The method of defining products and ratios may seem very weak at first glance, but recall that once a new term has been defined, the system does not distinguish it from observable terms. Thus, the program can define products of ratios, ratios of products of products, and so forth. Also, upon discovering a linear relation at one level of description, the system treats the slope and intercept as new dependent terms at the next level. This means that slopes and intercepts can themselves be incorporated in complex relations, as we saw in the general version of the ideal gas law above. The ability to introduce intrinsic properties provides power of an entirely different type, letting BACON effectively transform nominal variables into numeric ones, which can then be incorporated into numeric laws.

However, the system is less robust in representing and discovering the scope of laws. We have seen that BACON places conditions—in the form of the values of unvaried terms—on both its laws and its intrinsic values, and that it cautiously drops these conditions if the data merit such action. But one can imagine other alternatives that BACON ignores. For instance, Black's law holds across a broad range of temperatures, but not across the phase boundaries at which substances change from liquid to solid. Similarly, the ideal gas law is an excellent approximation for normal temperatures, but it breaks down at high levels. Ideally, an empirical discovery system should be able to detect and represent such constraints on the laws it formulates.

BACON's ability to generate experiments is also quite limited. The system is presented with independent terms and their suggested values, and from this it algorithmically produces a combinatorial design. There is no sense in which the system gathers data adaptively in response to the observations it makes. Such intelligent experiment generation is an important component of scientific discovery, and a robust empirical discovery system should have this capacity. In the following section, we examine another system that responds to the issues of scope and experiment generation.

## 4. The FAHRENHEIT System

We have seen that BACON constituted a significant step beyond Gerwin's early discovery work, but that it still had a number of limitations. The most pressing of these revolved around identifying the scope of the discovered laws and generating experiments in an intelligent manner. In this section, we describe FAHRENHEIT (Zytkow [34], Koehn and Zytkow [11]), a successor to BACON that responds to these issues.

### 4.1. Representing laws and their scope

The FAHRENHEIT system borrows heavily from the earlier work by Langley, Simon, and Bradshaw, including a BACON-like routine as one of its basic components. This component is similar enough to BACON.4 that we will ignore the differences and focus instead on its interaction with the remainder of the system. In other words, Zytkow's work does not question the basic validity of the earlier system; rather, it argues that BACON told only part of the story. The form of FAHRENHEIT's input is identical to that given to BACON: a set of independent and dependent attributes that take on numeric or symbolic values. Zytkow's program interacts with a separate simulated environment that eases the running of experiments, but this difference is not theoretically significant.

The system's output is also very similar: a set of numeric laws that summarize the data, stated through a set of theoretical terms defined using observables. The existing version does not incorporate intrinsic properties, but these could be easily added. The main difference from BACON lies in the form of the numeric laws. Rather than stating the scope of a law as a simplistic set of independent values, FAHRENHEIT specifies these limits as another set of numeric laws.[3] It accomplishes this feat through a familiar ploy—defining new theoretical terms.

Let us consider a simple form of Black's specific heat law, in which one combines the substances water and mercury and in which one holds their masses constant at 0.1 kg and 5.0 kg, respectively. The simplified law can be stated as: $T_f = jT_M + kT_W$, where $T_M$ and $T_W$ are the initial temperatures for

---

[3] Falkenhainer and Michalski [4] also address the issue of limiting the scope of laws in their ABACUS system. However, they represent boundaries either as symbolic conditions or as simple maxima and minima on the values of numeric terms.

mercury and water, and $T_f$ is the final temperature of both. The terms $j$ and $k$ are constants that hold for this particular pair of substances and the given masses. In fact, this relationship holds only for limited values of the temperature $T_M$ and $T_W$, and it is with representing this limitation that we are concerned.

Like its laws, FAHRENHEIT represents limits on laws at varying levels of description. For instance, suppose the system has formulated the first-level law $T_f = aT_M + b$, where $a$ and $b$ are constants for a given temperature $T_W$. Along with these parameters, FAHRENHEIT also defines two *limit* terms, one representing the maximum value of $T_M$ for which the law holds and another for the minimum value. We will call these terms $T_{M\,max}$ and $T_{M\,min}$, respectively.

These limit terms may have different values for different settings of $T_W$, and these values are carried to the second level of description along with $a$ and $b$. At this level, the limit terms themselves may enter into relations with the independent variable. In this case, simple laws exist for both boundary terms: $T_{M\,max} = -0.6T_W + 160$ and $T_{M\,min} = -0.6T_W$. Of course, the system also states laws involving the slope and intercept parameters from the first level; in this case, $a$ is constant and $b = dT_M$.

In addition, FAHRENHEIT also specifies limits on all four of these higher-level laws, defining versions of $T_{W\,max}$ and $T_{W\,min}$, the maximum and minimum temperatures for which each law is valid. This means that the system not only has the ability to place limits on its basic laws; it can also state the boundary conditions under which its boundary laws hold. This is another instance of the recursive theme underlying the class of discovery systems we have been considering. Figure 1 summarizes the boundary conditions found in the Black's law example we have just considered.

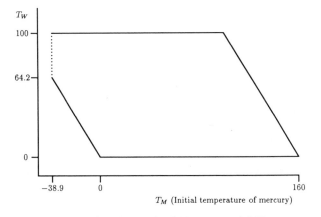

Fig. 1. The scope of Black's law for 0.1 kg water and 5.0 kg mercury.

## 4.2. Determining the scope of laws

Now that we have examined FAHRENHEIT's representation of empirical laws, let us turn to the method by which it discovers them. The system's basic organization is very similar to that used in BACON, and it begins in exactly the same manner—by varying the values of one independent term and examining the effect on the dependent variables. Returning to the Black's law example, suppose FAHRENHEIT varies $T_M$ and observes the resulting values of $T_f$. Using the same heuristics as BACON.4, the program notes a linear relationship between the two terms and formulates the law $T_f = aT_M + b$, where the slope $a = 0.624$ and the intercept $b = 11.28$.

At this point, BACON would assume that the only conditions on the new law are the values of the independent terms that have not yet been varied; i.e., that the substances are mercury and water, that $T_W = 30°$, that $M_M = 5$ kg, and that $M_W = 0.1$ kg. It would proceed to vary these terms in order to determine their effect on the parameters $a$ and $b$. FAHRENHEIT does not make this assumption, realizing that the law relating $T_M$ and $T_f$ may hold for only *some* values of $T_W$. To check this possibility, the system selectively gathers additional data, varying the value of $T_M$ in an attempt to determine upper and lower boundaries on the law.

FAHRENHEIT first increments the independent term by the same user-specified amount used in its earlier data-gathering steps. If the law still holds, it increments by double this amount and checks again. This doubling continues until the system arrives at some value of the variable for which the law is violated, or until it reaches values beyond the range of the measuring instrument. In the latter case, the program assumes the law has no upper limit; in the former case, it attempts to find the exact point at which the law ceases to hold. For this the system uses a successive approximation method, halving the distance between the highest known value that obeys the law and the lowest known value that violates the law. This process continues until it has determined the upper limit within the desired (user-specified) degree of precision. FAHRENHEIT employs the same method to determine the lower limit on the law.[4]

Returning to our example, after discovering the law $T_f = aT_M + b$ when $T_W = 30°$, the system would determine the upper and lower bounds on this law. For this situation, the law holds only between $T_M = 142°$ and $T_M = -18°$; for values outside this range, the linear relation cannot be used to predict the

---

[4] FAHRENHEIT considers only independent terms in its search for boundary conditions. One can imagine cases in which dependent variables would also be useful, though the resulting laws could not be used for making predictions. One can also envision domains in which the boundaries are not clear-cut; phase boundaries are a good example. To the extent these can be handled as "noisy boundaries," the system can discover approximate constraints. Extending FAHRENHEIT in both directions is a task for future research.

dependent term. Other limits hold for other values of $T_W$, and this leads to the next stage in FAHRENHEIT's discovery process.

### 4.3. Discovering complex laws and limits

Recall that once BACON has induced a law relating one independent term to a dependent term (say $T_f$ and $T_M$), it recurses to a higher level. The program varies another independent term (say $T_W$) and, for each value of that term, repeats the experimentation that led to the original law. In each case, the system finds the same form of the law, but the parameters (say $a$ and $b$) in that law may take on different values. These become dependent values at the next higher level of description and are associated with the independent values under which they occurred. Once it has collected enough higher-level data, BACON applies its heuristics to induce a higher-level law (say $a = c$ and $b = dT_W$).

BACON's successor follows the same basic strategy, but as we have seen, it defines two additional theoretical terms for each law discovered at the lower level. The system treats these terms as dependent variables at the next higher level and attempts to relate their values to those of the varied independent term.[5] In our Black's law example, the limit terms are $T_{M\,max}$ and $T_{M\,min}$, whereas the second independent term (to which they must be related) is $T_W$. In this case, FAHRENHEIT discovers the two linear relations described above, one between $T_{M\,max}$ and $T_W$ ($T_{M\,max} = -0.6T_W + 160$) and the other between $T_{M\,min}$ and $T_W$ ($T_{M\,min} = -0.6T_W$). They state that, as the temperature of mercury increases, there is a decrease in both the maximum and minimum temperatures of water for which the law holds. These relations are shown as slanted lines in Fig. 1. Although both have slopes of $-0.6$, the two lines are independent of each other and have different intercepts.

FAHRENHEIT's next step follows from its inherently recursive nature—it attempts to establish limits on these limit laws. It uses the same scheme it employed at the lower level, exploring values of the independent term (this time $T_W$) until it finds the upper and lower limits one each law. In Fig. 1, the upper limit on the maximum law is 100, the upper limit on the minimum law is 64.2, and the lower limit on both laws is zero. The limits for the two laws need not be the same, though the two lower limits are equal (this results from the phase change of water into ice).

However, recall that FAHRENHEIT has also discovered another law at the current level; this is $b = dT_W$, which relates the intercept of the lower-level law to the temperature of water. Naturally, the program also searches for the limits on this law in terms of $T_W$. The lower limit for this law (zero) corresponds to the lower limit for both the maximum and minimum laws, and the upper limit

---

[5] This means that the number of dependent terms increases by a factor of three, at minimum, for each level ascended. Thus, higher levels of abstraction require that ever more discoveries be made.

(100) corresponds to the upper limit for the maximum law. However, the latter differs from the upper limit (64.2) for the minimum law, indicating a range of the basic law ($a = cT_w$) for which the lower limit is unknown. We have marked this range with a dotted line in the figure. The current version of FAHRENHEIT leaves this range unspecified, but future versions should attempt to determine its functional form as well.

In summary, the new system employs the same recursive structure as BACON, which lets it discover the same higher-level laws (relating multiple variables) as did the earlier system. However, FAHRENHEIT's inclusion of theoretical terms for the scope of a law also lets it discover:

(1) upper and lower limits on the higher-level laws;
(2) laws that express upper and lower limits as functions of other terms; and
(3) limits on these limit-based laws themselves.

The example we have considered is relatively simple in that it involved only two independent terms and thus generated only two levels of description. But FAHRENHEIT's discovery strategy applies equally well to more complex situations involving many variables and levels, and the system will recursively apply its heuristics until it can discover no further regularities.

In the introduction, we reviewed Falkenhainer and Michalski's [4] ABACUS, a system that determines the scope of laws using a different method. One can view their system as searching for the regions that are composed of hyperectangles in an $N$-dimensional space, using the AQ algorithm. In contrast, FAHRENHEIT searches for regions bounded by the class of laws that BACON can discover. As a result, the latter system would seem more appropriate for domains with complex boundaries that involve relations between two or more variables.

## 4.4. Additional capabilities of FAHRENHEIT

In addition to determining the scope of laws, FAHRENHEIT also includes a number of other abilities beyond those found in BACON. One of these involves irrelevant independent variables. In experiments involving such terms, Langley, Simon, and Bradshaw's system would note a constancy for all dependent variables and state simple laws to this effect. In this sense, BACON could handle irrelevant terms. However, upon coming to a new experimental context involving the same terms, the program would go through the same process of varying the independent term, observing dependent values, noting their constancies, and stating trivial laws. FAHRENHEIT avoids this extra effort and unneeded data gathering by marking such independent attributes as irrelevant and bypassing them in later experiments. This can lead to substantial savings, especially if the irrelevant terms are ones that would have been varied earlier in the discovery process and thus would have been included at lower levels of description.[6]

Another of BACON's limitations involved the order in which independent terms were varied. Although in many cases the system was insensitive to the order, this did not hold for some of the more complex laws. Let us return to Black's law for an example. In its full form, this law relates the final temperature $T_f$ not only to the initial temperatures $T_1$ and $T_2$ of the combined substances, but also to the masses $M_1$ and $M_2$ of those substances. In the reported runs on Black's law (Langley, Bradshaw and Simon [16], Langley, Simon, Bradshaw and Zytkow [21]), the temperatures were always varied first, but let us examine the result when the mases are used instead.

Suppose we place two containers of water into contact, with $T_1 = 20°$, $T_2 = 40°$, and $M_1 = 1$. Upon varying the mass of the second container $M_2$ and observing the resulting values of $T_f$, we obtain data that obey the law $T_f = 20(1 + 2M_2)/(1 + M_2)$. However, BACON's heuristics are not powerful enough to discover this law. When we tell the system to vary the independent terms in this order, it will fail to recognize any regularity in the resulting data. One response would be to replace BACON's law-finding rules with more powerful curve-fitting methods, but this is sidestepping the real issue. Any law-finding method will have some limits, and these limits will eventually emerge when encountering the right order of variation.

FAHRENHEIT responds to this possibility by considering different orders of varying the independent terms. The system operates in normal Baconian mode until it encounters some term that appears relevant, but for which it cannot find any regular law. In such cases, the program sidesteps the variable and places it at the end of the queue to ensure that it will be reconsidered later. It then varies the next independent term in the queue and attempts to incorporate this variable into some law. If this also fails, FAHRENHEIT considers the next term, and so forth. If it cannot find laws for any of the remaining independent terms, the system halts with only a partial law.

Although this strategy is more robust than BACON's method and can handle the Black's law example given above, it does not consider all possible orders and thus is not guaranteed to find the maximal laws. FAHRENHEIT's authors have experimented with a variant on the above algorithm that, upon failing to find laws for any of the remaining terms, backtracks to consider different orders of variables that have already been successfully related. This scheme is more complete, but it is also more expensive. In the worst case, the simpler method has a computational complexity of $\frac{1}{2}N(N + 1)$, where $N$ is the number

---

[6] Langley [15] describes an earlier version of BACON that identified irrelevant terms in a similar manner and modified its experiments in response. These abilities were dropped in later versions to devote attention to other issues.

of independent terms. In contrast, the backtracking method has a worst-case complexity of $N!$, though we doubt this would occur very often.

## 4.5. Evaluating FAHRENHEIT

We have seen that FAHRENHEIT introduced a number of improvements over BACON. The system's ability to consider alternative orders of varying indepen- dent variables lets it discover laws under conditions in which BACON would have failed. The program also handles irrelevant terms in a more sensible way than its precursor, leading to savings in both time and in the amount of data required.

Most important, FAHRENHEIT represents the scope of laws in a more robust manner than did BACON, and it incorporates heuristics to discover such limits in scope. This requires a more intelligent data-gathering strategy than was present in the earlier program, involving the selective generation of experi- ments that depend on the results of earlier experiments. Moreover, FAHRENHEIT does not halt upon finding the upper and lower limits on a law; it defines theoretical terms for these limits and carries them to the next level of description, along with the parameters for its basic laws. Using its recursive structure, the system then searches for laws relating these limit terms to new independent variables, and searches for limits on these laws in turn.

The resulting limits and limit-related laws establish a clear context in which FAHRENHEIT believes its basic laws to hold. But this context is still based largely on "number games," and it tells one little about the qualitative structure of situations in which the laws are valid. In the following section, we will see another approach to representing and discovering the context on empirical laws that responds to this issue.

## 5. The IDS System

Langley and Nordhausen [20] have described IDS, an integrated discovery system that formulates both qualitative laws and discovers numeric relation- ships. Although this program is superficially responding to the same task as the other systems we have examined, it differs significantly in both its representa- tion of laws and in its discovery process. This research effort is still in its early stages, but in this section we report the progress to date. As before, we will begin by considering representational issues.

## 5.1. The need for qualitative descriptions

Like FAHRENHEIT, the IDS system interacts with a simulated world in which it can gather data. But this environment differs from Zytkow's simulation in two important ways: (1) all attribute-value pairs are associated with specific objects; and (2) the values of these attributes change over time. Thus, IDS has available to it a more realistic environment than earlier systems, and this is reflected in its representation of laws.

This representation is best explained through an example, and since we have used Black's law earlier in the paper, let us consider it again. The previous versions of this law, as represented by BACON and FAHRENHEIT, related the masses ($M_1$ and $M_2$), specific heats ($c_1$ and $c_2$), and initial temperatures ($T_1$ and $T_2$) of two substances to their final temperature ($T_f$) after they had been in contact for some time. However, Black's law actually involves much more than this single equation. Let us walk through what actually transpires in such an experiment.

We begin with two substances, having known masses and stable temperatures, which are then placed in contact. If we measure the temperatures over time, we will observe that the higher one gradually decreases and the lower one gradually increases. This process continues until the two temperatures become equal, at which point both remain constant. Note that much of the interesting detail in the example is lost in the BACON/FAHRENHEIT representation. Some might be regained by including separate final temperatures for each object, but there would still be no sense of two quantities gradually moving towards equilibrium.

## 5.2. Representing change with qualitative schemas

IDS is able to represent such knowledge by using *qualitative schemas* that summarize changes over time in the values of one or more objects. A schema consists of a finite state diagram in which successive states represent succeeding intervals of time. For instance, the schema for Black's law contains three such states: the first describes temperatures before contact; the second describes temperatures after contact but before equilibrium is reached; and the last describes temperatures after the physical system achieves equilibrium. Figure 2 presents a graphical description of this three-state schema.

Each state in the schema has an associated description of the observed attributes. These descriptions state whether a given attribute's values are increasing, decreasing, or constant during that state. In fact, these "qualitative derivatives" define the boundaries of each state. In matching the schema against a new instance of Black's law, IDS knows when the physical system has moved into the next state by noting when the signs of the various derivatives change. For instance, the second state in the figure applies only to those time steps in which the first object's temperature is increasing (the qualitative derivative is positive) and the second object's temperature is decreasing (the derivative is negative).

This knowledge representation is very similar to that suggested by Forbus [7] in his qualitative process (QP) theory, and we have been strongly influenced by this work. Given a set of physical processes and some initial description of the environment, QP theory describes how one can generate an *envisionment* of the states the physical system will enter as those processes operate. The qualitative schemas of IDS are nearly identical to Forbus' envisionments. We have used a different term because IDS induces its schemas directly from observations, whereas in qualitative process theory, envisionments are deduced from process descriptions. We do not have the space to describe the generality of this approach to representing physical systems, but it can be used to provide qualitative descriptions for a substantial range of phenomena from both physics and chemistry. For this reason, we believe it provides an excellent basis for machine discovery.

## 5.3. Inducing qualitative schemas

In its initial knowledge state, IDS contains a simple set of qualitative schemas. For instance, the initial schema for heating includes two states: one in which a heater near an object is turned off (and in which the object's temperature is constant); and another in which the heater is turned on (and in which the object's temperature is increasing). The initial schema for placing objects in contact is even simpler; IDS expects that the only effect of placing one object adjacent to another is to change its location.

However, experiments with objects having different temperatures lead to violated expectations, and these in turn cause IDS to modify the qualitative structure of this second schema. We do not have the space to detail the processes used in acquiring qualitative schemas, but we can list the three basic methods:

– If IDS encounters entirely new behavior, it creates a new state and adds this to the current schema.

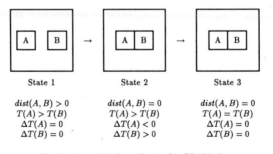

| State 1 | State 2 | State 3 |
|---|---|---|
| $dist(A, B) > 0$ | $dist(A, B) = 0$ | $dist(A, B) = 0$ |
| $T(A) > T(B)$ | $T(A) > T(B)$ | $T(A) = T(B)$ |
| $\Delta T(A) = 0$ | $\Delta T(A) < 0$ | $\Delta T(A) = 0$ |
| $\Delta T(B) = 0$ | $\Delta T(B) > 0$ | $\Delta T(B) = 0$ |

Fig. 2. A qualitative schema for Black's law.

– If the system recognizes itself in a known state that was not predicted, it adds a connection between this state and the previous one.

– Upon finding evidence that a state's description is overly general, IDS makes that description more specific.

Taken together, these methods let the program incrementally improve its qualitative schemas as it gains more experience with its environment. They lead from the initial "place-in-contact" schema to the schema shown in Fig. 2. This latter schema accurately describes the qualitative structure underlying Black's law.

## 5.4. Embedding numeric laws in qualitative schemas

We have focused on representating qualitative knowledge in IDS, but the system can also state numeric laws. The form of these laws is intimately related to the structure of the schemas, which are both object-oriented and time-oriented. As a result, numeric terms are specified using two subscripts, one for the object involved and another for the state. In the Black's law schema, the temperature of the first object ($A$) in the second state would be $T_{A,2}$, whereas the temperature of the second object ($B$) in the third (final) state would be $T_{B,3}$. Thus, IDS would state the numeric aspects of Black's law as

$$T_{A,3} = \frac{c_A M_A T_{A,2} + c_B M_B T_{B,2}}{c_A M_A + c_B M_B} \quad \text{and} \quad T_{B,3} = T_{A,3}.$$

Qualitative schemas serve two main purposes with respect to numeric laws. First, they provide a context within which the law has meaning. Clearly, if one places two objects into contact and they do not obey the qualitative structure of the schema in Fig. 2, then one would not expect their quantitative relations to obey Black's law. For example, some substances might be so well insulated that their temperature loss is negligible. This approach also lets one qualitatively handle phase shifts, which FAHRENHEIT modeled in a purely quantitative fashion.

Second, qualitative schemas constrain the search for numeric laws. Different instances of the Black's law schema provide IDS with data that differ in terms of the masses, temperatures, and substances involved. However, these data are much more structured than those available to BACON or FAHRENHEIT, simplifying the law discovery process.

IDS applies data-driven heuristics to these numeric data in hopes of finding constant terms and simple linear relations. In the Black's law example, it follows a path much like that taken by BACON, though the terms involved are slightly different. One important difference is that *all* terms that are constant throughout the schema can be viewed as intrinsic properties of the objects used in the experiment. Moreover, when IDS encounters the same qualitative situation involving different objects, different substances, or different classes of substances, it may discover the same values for these terms. In such cases, it raises the retrieval conditions for the intrinsic value to the appropriate level of generality. In this framework, intrinsic values are associated directly with objects or classes of objects, not with nominal values themselves.

In addition, new types of intrinsic properties arise within the IDS scheme that do not appear within earlier approaches. The system may note that the schema shifts from one state to its successor whenever the value of a particular term reaches a certain value. The introduction of such *limit conditions* lets one represent and discover concepts like melting points and boiling points, which signal changes of qualitative state. IDS may also note that the *duration* of a state is constant or that it is related to some other term. This leads to concepts such as heat of fusion and heat of vaporization. All of these concepts are types of intrinsic property, with different values associated with different substances. Thus, the use of qualitative schemas provides representational support for intrinsic terms that could not be handled in earlier frameworks.

## 5.5. Evaluating IDS

Our research on IDS is still in its early stages, though we have a running system that we have tested on a variety of heat-related laws. The representational power of the system seems considerably greater than that of BACON, and it provides more context for its numeric laws than does FAHRENHEIT, that does not mean that one system is superior to the other. The current version of IDS does not include the methods for determining scope that Zytkow's system introduced, and these should definitely be considered for future versions. Nor does the system consider different orders of independent variables, though the use of qualitative schemas significantly simplifies the search for numeric relations.

We would argue that IDS's greatest significance lies in its attempt to integrate the discovery of qualitative and quantitative laws. Earlier work has focused on one or the other, but has not considered their combination.[7] One ultimate goal of research in machine discovery in the construction of an integrated discovery system that covers many aspects of scientific reasoning, and we believe IDS is an important step in that direction.

---

[7] Falkenhainer and Michalski's [4] ABACUS identifies symbolic conditions on numeric laws, but their system does not discover qualitative laws of the type formulated by GLAUBER (Jones [10]; Langley et al. [17, 21, 22].

## 6. Perspectives on Machine Discovery

Having sampled the evolution of research on data-driven approaches to machine discovery, let us turn to the implications of this research. In any area of study, we find two distinct but complementary views, one concerned with description and the other concerned with prescription. In the study of scientific reasoning, historians of science take the first perspective, while philosophers of science take the second. We close the paper by considering the relevance of machine discovery to these areas, devoting more space to the normative side.

### 6.1. Machine discovery and the history of science

The history of science studies the actual path followed by scientists over the years, attempting to understand the steps taken toward a particular scientific advance, along with the reasons for those steps. Traditionally, historians of science have been content with verbal descriptions of scientific behavior, but the advent of machine discovery systems suggests an alternative: one can view AI discovery systems as computational models of the historical discovery process.

Whether or not they provide *adequate* models is partly a matter of one's goals. In their early work on computational models of human problem solving, Newell and Simon [28] argued for the usefulness of *sufficient* models of behavior. Such models do not account for the details of human behavior on a task, but they do have roughly the same capabilities. Once such models have been developed, they may be replaced with more careful simulations. We would argue that BACON and its successors provide such sufficient models of empirical discovery. On close inspection, we find that the detailed behavior of early scientists like Ohm, Coulomb, Black, and others diverges from that followed by the programs.[8] Nevertheless, these systems have shown themselves capable of discovering the same laws as the scientists, and this provides an excellent starting point for more detailed computational models.

Within both frameworks, one can take two approaches to testing the adequacy of discovery models. The most common technique involves arguing for the model's generality by showing it can discover a wide range of laws with a variety of forms. This is the approach taken with BACON, and Falkenhainer and Michalski [4] have evaluated their ABACUS system along similar lines. The other approach involves running the model on an extended example that consists of a lengthy sequence of discoveries. This is the approach taken by Lenat [23] with his AM system, and Kulkarni and Simon [13] have used a similar strategy in testing their KEKADA system. To the extent that the system's

---

[8] For an example of a more careful model of historical discovery, see Zytkow and Simon's [35] description of STAHL and Kulkarni and Simon's [13] description of KEKADA.

steps follow the same path that was taken historically, one can argue that it constitutes a plausible model of historical discovery.

Although none of the systems that we have described give an acceptable detailed account of historical discoveries, we believe they provide an excellent framework for future work in this direction. Whether such efforts should have high priority is an open question. Clearly, much more remains to be done in developing sufficient models of the discovery process, but this does not exclude the development of detailed models by other researchers. In many ways the latter is more difficult, since it requires intimate familiarity with historical developments. However, this road must ultimately be taken if we hope to formulate complete descriptive theories of scientific discovery.

## 6.2. Validation and discovery

Historically, the nature of induction and discovery have played an important role in the philosophy of science. Early contributors such as Sir Francis Bacon (1620) [1] and John Stuart Mill (1843) [26] proposed "logics of induction" as methods for uncovering scientific laws. However, with the advent of the 20th century this interest passed, and most philosophers turned their attention to the *validation* of scientific laws and theories. Indeed, some researchers even argued that a "logic of discovery" was impossible (Popper [30]). Recently some have regained interest in the topic of discovery (Nickles [29]), but the mainstream has retained its skepticism about the normative study of discovery.

Let us consider more closely what is meant by a normative or prescriptive theory of discovery.[9] Obviously, it suggests a set of methods that one *should* follow in formulating scientific laws. For those with a logical bent, this may translate as "a deductively valid set of methods," and we agree that no such methods are possible; inductive inference is clearly not deductively valid. However, this definition seems overly constraining. We cannot expect inductive techniques to give us *correct* laws, but we might legitimately require them to provide *useful* laws. Let us see what this might mean; the philosophy of science itself provides several responses, as we discuss in the following sections.

## 6.3. Eliminability of theoretical terms

The nature of theoretical terms has occupied a central role in recent philosophy of science. One important result involves the notion of *eliminability*. A theoretical term is said to be *eliminable* if one can replace all of its occurrences in a theory with directly observable terms. A theory containing only eliminable terms can be tested in a straightforward manner, by simply replacing these

---

[9] For a detailed analysis of normative and descriptive systems of discovery and logic of discovery, see Zytkow and Simon [36].

terms with observables and comparing its predictions against the data. In contrast, theories that contain noneliminable terms cannot always be tested, giving them questionable status.

Given this view, one might want a discovery method that introduces noneliminable terms into its law and theories only as a last resort. We have seen the role played by theoretical terms in BACON, FAHRENHEIT, and IDS. Some of these terms, such as the product $PV$ in the ideal gas law, are defined directly using observable variables. Others, such as the intrinsic property of specific heat in Black's law and FAHRENHEIT's limit terms, are defined in a more roundabout manner. However, all such terms can be eliminated from the law and replaced with direct observables. In this sense, the systems we have examined employ normative discovery methods.

## 6.4. Laws and definitions

Another issue involves Glymour's [9] criterion of *bootstrap confirmation*. Many philosophers have made a strong distinction between *definitions* and *laws*, with only the latter having empirical content. Glymour argues against this dichotomy, claiming that it is the combination of laws and definitions that have empirical content, and that these combinations can be tested against the same type of data used in generating them.

This is exactly the situation that occurs when BACON postulates an intrinsic property. In the Black's law example, we saw that when the system initially proposed the property of specific heat, the assigned numeric values were tautologically defined. At this point, the law involving the new term had no empirical content; it was guaranteed to hold. However, as new data were gathered, there was no (deductive) reason to expect it to apply in these cases. Had it failed to describe the new observations, the law would have been disconfirmed. In this case, it successfully covered the data and so was retained, but that is not the issue. Rather, the point is that what begins as a definition with no empirical content can be tested as additional data become available. This is the essence of Glymour's bootstrapping criterion, and to the extent that BACON's methods incorporate this criterion, it can be viewed as a normative theory of discovery.

## 6.5. Optimal laws and heuristic search

The notations of eliminability and bootstrapping place constraints on laws and theories, but they do not specify which laws are optimal for a given set of data. Some proposals have been made for such criteria. For instance, Popper [30] has suggested that more falsifiable theories should be preferred to less easily rejected ones. Other suggestions have invoked the notions of simplicity and fertility. We feel that stating such criteria is a useful task for both machine discovery and philosophers of science, but even if we could agree on such criteria, we would not insist that a normative theory be able to achieve such optimal laws.

One of the central insights of AI is that intelligence involves search through combinatorial spaces, and that one can seldom afford to search these spaces exhaustively. Instead, one must employ heuristic methods that cannot guarantee optimal solutions, but which are reasonably efficient. As Simon [33] has argued, one must often be content with solutions that *satisfice* for a given problem. This means that realistic discovery methods cannot guarantee the generation of optimal laws and theories, even if the criteria for such optimality are clearly defined. Instead, a normative theory of discovery should generate laws that approximate these criteria.

Progress can occur in prescriptive fields just as it can in descriptive ones. The fact that BACON and its successors constitute normative theories of discovery does not mean they are the best such theories. For example, Kokar [12] has argued that his COPER method is superior to the BACON approach along a number of dimensions, and Falkenhainer and Michalski [4] have made similar claims about their ABACUS system. Future work in machine discovery and the philosophy of science may produce improved logics of discovery. Such improvements should be measured by the degree to which a normative theory produces laws that account for existing data and correctly predict new observations.

## 7. Conclusion

In this paper we addressed the task of empirical discovery, focusing on four AI systems that share a common approach to inducing numeric laws. This approach relies on data-driven heuristics, the definition of theoretical terms, and the recursive application of a few basic methods. We saw that Langley, Bradshaw, and Simon's BACON system introduced some important advances over Gerwin's earlier work, including the ability to handle multiple independent terms and to postulate intrinsic properties. We also found that Zytkow's FAHRENHEIT system incorporated some significant methods not present in BACON, such as the ability to determine the scope of laws and the ability to consider different orders of varying independent terms. Finally, we saw that Nordhausen and Langley's IDS is able to embed numeric laws within a qualitative description, providing significantly more context for these laws than earlier systems.

In the last section we examined these systems from two perspectives: as models of historical discovery and as normative theories of discovery. We found that these particular systems do not fare well as detailed historical models, though they provide good starting points for the development of improved models. We also found that the existing systems can be viewed as normative models of how empirical discovery *should* proceed, though we also argued that future systems will provide improved norms for inductive behavior. As we stated at the outset, empirical discovery is only one part of the complex phenomenon that we call science. But we feel that it is an important part, and that the systems we have described constitute a significant step towards understanding the nature of scientific discovery. Recent work has started to address other aspects of the scientific process, including theory formation (Falkenhainer [5]), theory revision (Rose and Langley [31], Shrager [32], Rajamoney [37]), and experimentation (Kulkarni and Simon [13]). We expect future work to extend these promising efforts on isolated aspects of science. However, we also expect researchers to develop *integrated* models that combine many aspects of the discovery process, and we would be surprised if they did not incorporate at least some ideas from the work that we have examined here.

## ACKNOWLEDGMENT

This research was supported in part by Contract N00014-84-K-0345 from the Computer Science Division, Office of Naval Research. We would like to thank the reviewers for useful comments. We would also like to thank Herbert Simon, Gary Bradshaw, Bruce Koehn, and Bernd Nordhausen, who have contributed significantly to the research on BACON, FAHRENHEIT, and IDS.

## REFERENCES

1. Bacon, F., *The New Organon and Related Writings* (edited by F.H. Anderson) (Liberal Arts Press, New York, 1960).
2. Bradshaw, G.L., Langley, P. and Simon, H.A., BACON.4: The discovery of intrinsic properties, in: *Proceedings Third Biennial Conference of the Canadian Society for Computational Studies of Intelligence*, Victoria, BC (1980) 19–25.
3. Dietterich, T.G. and Michalski, R.S., A comparative review of selected methods for learning from examples, in: R.S. Michalski, J.G. Carbonell and T.M. Mitchell (Eds.), *Machine Learning: An Artificial Intelligence Approach* (Tioga, Palo Alto, CA, 1983) 307–330.
4. Falkenhainer, B.C. and Michalski, R.S., Integrating quantitative and qualitative discovery: The ABACUS system, *Machine Learning* **1** (1986) 367–401.
5. Falkenhainer, B.C., Scientific theory formation through analogical inference, in: *Proceedings Fourth International Workshop on Machine Learning*, Irvine, CA (1987) 218–229.
6. Fisher, D., Knowledge acquisition via incremental conceptual clustering, *Machine Learning* **2** (1987) 139–172.
7. Forbus, K.D., Qualitative process theory, *Artificial Intelligence* **24** (1984) 85–168.
8. Gerwin, D.G., Information processing, data inferences, and scientific generalization, *Behav. Sci.* **19** (1974) 314–325.
9. Glymour, C., *Theory and Evidence* (Princeton University Press, Princeton, NJ, 1980).
10. Jones, R., Generating predictions to aid the scientific discovery process, in: *Proceedings AAAI-86*, Philadelphia, PA (1986) 513–517.
11. Koehn, B.W. and Zytkow, J.M., Experimenting and theorizing in theory formation, in: *Proceedings ACM SIGART International Symposium on Methodologies for Intelligent Systems*, Knoxville, TN (1986) 296–307.
12. Kokar, M.M., Determining arguments of invariant functional descriptions, *Machine Learning* **1** (1986) 403–422.
13. Kulkarni, D. and Simon, H.A., The process of scientific discovery: The strategy of experimentation, *Cognitive Sci.* **12** (1988) 139–175.

14. Langley, P., BACON.1: A general discovery system, in: *Proceedings Second Biennial Conference of the Canadian Society for Computational Studies of Intelligence*, Toronto, Ont. (1978) 173–180.
15. Langley, P., Data-driven discovery of physical laws, *Cognitive Sci.* **5** (1981) 31–54.
16. Langley, P., Bradshaw, G.L. and Simon, H.A., Rediscovering chemistry with the BACON system, in: R.S. Michalski, J.G. Carbonell and T.M. Mitchell (Eds.), *Machine Learning: An Artificial Intelligence Approach* (Tioga, Palo Alto, CA, 1983) 307–330.
17. Langley, P., Bradshaw, G.L., Zytkow, J. and Simon, H.A., Three facets of scientific discovery, in: *Proceedings IJCAI-83* Karlsruhe, F.R.G. (1983) 465–468.
18. Langley, P. and Jones, R., A computational model of scientific insight, in: R. Sternberg (Ed.), *The Nature of Creativity* (Cambridge University Press, Cambridge, 1988).
19. Langley, P. and Michalski, R.S., Machine learning and discovery, *Machine Learning* **1** (1986) 363–366.
20. Langley, P. and Nordhausen, B., A framework for empirical discovery, in: *Proceedings International Meeting on Advances in Learning*, Les Arcs, France (1986).
21. Langley, P., Simon, H.A., Bradshaw, G.L. and Zytkow, J.M., *Scientific Discovery: Computational Explorations of the Creative Processes* (MIT Press, Cambridge, MA, 1987).
22. Langley, P., Zytkow, J.M., Simon, H.A. and Bradshaw, G.L., The search for regularity: Four aspects of scientific discovery, in: R.S. Michalski, J.G. Carbonell and T.M. Mitchell (Eds.), *Machine Learning: An Artificial Intelligence Approach* **2** (Morgan Kaufmann, Los Altos, CA, 1986) 425–469.
23. Lenat. D.B., Automated theory formation in mathematics, in: *Proceedings IJCAI-77*, Cambridge, MA (1977) 833–842.
24. Michalski, R.S. and Larson, J.B., Selection of most representative training examples and incremental generation of VL1 hypotheses: The underlying methodology and description of programs ESEL and AQ11, Rept. 867, University of Illinois, Urbana, IL (1978).
25. Michalski, R.S. and Stepp, R., Learning from observation: Conceptual clustering, in: R.S. Michalski, J.G. Carbonell and T.M. Mitchell (Eds.), *Machine Learning: An Artificial Intelligence Approach* (Tioga, Palo. Alto, CA, 1983) 331–364.
26. Mill, J.S., *Philosophy of Scientific Method* (Hafner Press, New York, 1974).
27. Mostow, J.D., Machine transformation of advice into a heuristic search procedure, in: R.S. Michalski, J.G. Carbonell and T.M. Mitchell (Eds.), *Machine Learning: An Artificial Intelligence Approach* (Tioga, Palo Alto, CA, 1983) 367–404.
28. Newell, A. and Simon, H.A., *Human Problem Solving* (Prentice-Hall, Englewood Cliffs, NJ, 1972).
29. Nickles, T. (Ed.), *Scientific Discovery, Logic, and Rationality* (Reidel, Dordrecht, Netherlands 1978).
30. Popper, K., *The Logic of Scientific Discovery* (Science Editions, New York, 1961).
31. Rose, D. and Langley, P., Chemical discovery as belief revision, *Machine Learning* **1** (1986) 423–451.
32. Shrager, J., Theory change via view application in instructionless learning, *Machine Learning* **2** (1987) 247–276.
33. Simon, H.A., Rational choice and the structure of the environment, *Psychol. Rev.* **63** (1956) 129–138.
34. Zytkow, J.M., Combining many searches in the FAHRENHEIT discovery system, in: *Proceedings Fourth International Workshop on Machine Learning*, Irvine, CA (1987) 281–287.
35. Zytkow, J.M. and Simon, H.A., A theory of historical discovery: The construction of componential models, *Machine Learning* **1** (1986) 107–136.
36. Zytkow, J.M. and Simon, H.A., Normative systems of discovery and logic of search, *Synthese* **74** (1988) 65–90.
37. Rajamoney, S.A., Explanation-based theory revision: An approach to the problems of incomplete and incorrect theories, Doctoral Dissertation, Department of Computer Science, University of Illinois, Urbana, IL (1989).

# A Theory of the Origins of Human Knowledge

## John R. Anderson

*Department of Psychology, Carnegie-Mellon University,*
*Pittsburgh, PA 15231, U.S.A.*

ABSTRACT

*The PUPS theory and its ACT\* predecessor are computational embodiments of psychology's effort to develop a theory of the origins of knowledge. The theories contain proposals for extraction of knowledge from the environment, a strength-based prioritization of knowledge, knowledge compilation mechanisms for forming use-specific versions of knowledge, and induction mechanisms for extending knowledge. PUPS differs from ACT\* basically in its principles of induction which include analogy-based generalization, a discrimination mechanism, and principles of making causal inferences. The knowledge in these theories can be classified into the knowledge level, algorithm level, and implementation level. Knowledge at the knowledge level consists of information acquired from the environment and innate principles of induction and problem solving. Knowledge at the algorithm level consists of internal deductions, inductions, and compilation. Knowledge at the implementation level takes the form of setting strengths for the encoding of specific pieces of information*

## 1. Introduction

This paper is an attempt to establish a perspective on the sequence of theories I have been associated with. Anderson and Bower [9] wrote a book about a system called HAM which was a theory of human declarative knowledge. This was succeeded in 1976 by ACT [2] which augmented the declarative knowledge component with a procedural component in the form of a production system. In 1983 [5] ACT evolved into ACT\* which had an elaborate theory of the acquisition of production rules. More recently, Anderson and Thompson [12] have developed the PUPS system which is an attempt to remedy deficits in the ACT\* theory.

These theories have been iterations in an attempt to evolve a theory of the origins of human knowledge. Before going into the claims of these theories it is important to establish the larger historical perspective in which this research takes place. Therefore, I will review the significant issues in the psychological attempts to develop a theory of the origins of human knowledge. The major factor that has caused our work to develop from these historical roots is the emphasis that our theories have a firm computational foundation.

After this historical perspective there will be an analysis of ACT* and PUPS. Finally, I will try to identify where these theories stand on the issue of the origins of knowledge. Despite the considerable technical work that has been done on the theories we have never made them face up to this fundamental issue.

## 2. Origins of Knowledge: A Psychological Perspective

### 2.1. Philosophical origins

Of course, the issue of the origins of human knowledge has been an issue of philosophical debate for centuries. While the philosophical subtleties were many, there were essentially three positions about the origins of any piece of knowledge:

(1) *Nativism*. The person was born with that piece of knowledge or it appeared in the mind according to some predetermined maturational process. A common candidate for innate knowledge is our knowledge about the causal structure of the world. This is the claim that we are born knowing that there are causes and effects in the world even if we have to learn what causes what. Another frequent suggestion in cognitive science is that there is innate knowledge about the syntax of natural language (Chomsky [18]).

(2) *Empiricism*. The knowledge was planted in the mind by experience. A common candidate for such knowledge is our knowledge about what words mean. These word meanings are arbitrary associations we have to commit to memory.

(3) *Rationalism*. The knowledge originated by the person engaging in some reasoning process. More generally, we may think of rationalism as the position that knowledge appears as the result of internal computation, without making the commitment that this computation deserves the categorization of "reasoning." Mathematical knowledge is an example of something that is often thought to arise this way.

These three categories presumably exhaust the plausible sources of knowledge. Therefore, one litmus test for the adequacy of any theory of human knowledge is that it be able to categorize knowledge into these three categories. If it cannot it is not coming to grips with the issue of the origins of knowledge. Philosophers, being philosophers, were inclined to argue that all or most knowledge was of one kind or another. However, even if one takes a less extreme position, the above provides a useful categorization of possible origins of knowledge and one can certainly argue about the origins of any particular piece of knowledge. Fundamentally, such an issue is a scientific issue and not one to be settled by introspection and logical argumentation.

## 2.2. Behaviorism and a science of human knowledge

Psychology started out in the late 1800s as a science with one of its main goals to settle empirically the issue of the origins of knowledge. The field had a great deal of difficulty initially in making any headway on the issue. The problem is that scientists need to have agreed-upon data and it took psychology a while to establish consensus about what its data were. The introspectionists (see Boring [14]) took as their data self-observations of the content of thought. The problem was that different researchers with different theories would observe different things about their internal thoughts that confirmed their different theories. For instance, some introspectionists claim they could have thought devoid of sensory content while others claimed they could not. Because of irresolvable controversies like this, it became clear that a more objective data source was required.

This was one of the stimuli for the behaviorist movement that began around 1920, a movement much misunderstood, particularly by many of the behaviorists who practiced it. The behaviorist movement began with the observation that the prime source of objective data was recordings of the behavior of people. There were other possible sources of objective data such as physiological recordings but these turn out to be much harder to obtain than behavior. There are two essential features that distinguish behavioral data from introspective data. The first is that it is equally available to all scientists and not the private domain of the scientist who is having the introspection. Second, the psychologist is not constrained as to how to theoretically interpret the data. Thus, if a subject of a psychological experiment says "I have a visual image of a cat", the scientist is free to propose any theory that will produce that verbal protocol and is not required to propose visual images as part of the theory. Because of the similarity of verbal protocols to introspective reports, many behaviorists have refused to admit verbal protocol data. However, as Ericsson and Simon [25] correctly argue, verbal protocols are very appropriate and powerful sorts of behavioral data, when treated as behavioral data and not as introspective data.

However, there was a second point of motivation in stressing behavior as the measure by which a theory of knowledge will be assessed. This arose out of an emphasis on the functional nature of human knowledge. There was no point in making distinctions about knowledge that did not have consequences for behavior. If the person behaved the same whether he possessed knowledge $X$ or not, in what sense does he really know $X$? If two pieces of knowledge result in the same behavior in what sense are they really different? Such arguments should be quite familiar to the AI community where we commonly talk about equivalence among different knowledge representation schemes. This point of view also anticipates the Turing-type tests for deciding if a system is intelligent.

The behaviorists frequently argued that there was no such thing as knowledge in the abstract; when we speak of someone having certain knowledge we mean that the person has certain behavioral potentials. This led to prohibitions against discussing mental structures and a claim that an objective science should only talk about behavior. Here we see a basically correct observation being carried to unfortunate extremes.

Behaviorism can be separated into a methodological and a theoretical position:

(1) *Methodological*. Behavioral data is the major data for deciding among theories of knowledge. Different theories that imply no difference for the behavior (including verbal) of the system might as well be regarded as notational variants.

(2) *Theoretical*. The terms of a theory should be behavioral. Since only external behavior counts, a theory should not make reference to underlying mental structures.

The fundamental error in behaviorism comes from extending the methodological prescription to the theoretical prohibition. Given that they were prohibited from theorizing about mental structure it is not surprising that the behaviorist theories tended to take strong empiricist stands and claim all knowledge arose directly from experience. A methodology that denied the existence of a mind denied the possibility of a contribution of the mind to knowledge.

The behaviorists were very fundamentally concerned with issues of learning. The first half-century of American psychology was the era of the grand learning theories (see Bower and Hilgard [15] for a review of these). There were many variations but they all proposed that experience implanted various connections among stimuli and responses which would play themselves out as adaptive behavior under appropriate circumstances. Many of the issues that separated the various theories were really concerned with how motivational variables influenced the acquisition of knowledge and its later appropriate execution.

The behaviorist learning theories of the first half-century, while they were rigorous in their choice of data, were fundamentally sloppy in their theorizing. They never really showed that the mechanisms of their theories could be put together to account for the complexities of human behavior. The advent of more computationally oriented theories in the 1950s provide the basis for exploring the issues of what could actually be computed in these frameworks. It became clear that there were serious inadequacies. Chomsky's [17] criticism of Skinner's [55] account of language was the most dramatic instance of such analysis, but there were many others. The learning theorists had insisted that they could account for behavior with theories whose only terms were objectively observable stimuli and responses. It became apparent that one needed to make reference to non-observable mechanisms to account for human behavior.

## 2.3. Cognitive psychology and computational concerns

Cognitive psychology as a field of endeavor really began with the demise of behaviorism. The development in cognitive psychology has closely paralleled work in artificial intelligence, both contributing to that work and borrowing from it. One of the major contributions of AI work was to provide demonstrations that theories of internal structure and process could be scientifically rigorous. This was constantly used to fend off the behaviorist critics of cognitive psychology.

In the 1960s and 1970s there appeared in cognitive psychology a set of theories that were sufficiently well specified that they could be simulated on a computer. Sometimes these theories even were. These theories tended to focus on the performance of acquired skills. This nonlearning emphasis may have arisen because of the perceived difficulty of addressing learning and because some of the most telling criticisms of behavioristic theories were focused on their inability to perform at adult-level competences, not on the issue of whether these competences could be acquired. The standard remark of the time was that we needed first to understand the system that learning produced before we could try to understand how learning worked. Of course, a similar attitude existed in artificial intelligence about learning research.

The emphasis in psychology became not what we know and how we acquire it but rather how we implement what we know. One of the premier issues of the time was whether various computations are performed in parallel or serial. One domain where this was debated was the Sternberg task [56]. In a prototypical experiment a subject was first told to keep in mind a set of one to six digits and then asked whether a particular probe digit was in the memory set. It is generally found that subjects take about 40 milliseconds longer to make this judgment for each digit that is in the set. The serial model for this task proposed that subjects serially matched the probe digit against each item in the memory set taking about 40 milliseconds to make each comparison. The parallel model for this task proposed that the digit was compared in parallel against all members of the memory set but that there was a fixed capacity for this parallel computation and the more comparisons were being performed the slower any particular comparison was made. It was finally shown that in general such parallel and serial models could be made mathematically equivalent (Townsend [57]). Researchers were forced to make their arguments on vaguer claims such as whether the brain really could perform serial operations at the rate of one per 40 milliseconds (J.A. Anderson [1]).

Another example of a research issue of this type concerned the existence of a separate short-term memory. It was observed that when we are told something we remember it well initially but rapidly forget much of it. So, for instance, we can remember a phone number for a few seconds but an hour later we are lucky to remember any of the number. One model (Atkinson and Shiffrin [13]) proposed that there was an initial short-term memory in which information could be held for a while. However, if the information decayed from short-term memory or was pushed out by interfering information, it would be lost unless it was transferred to long-term memory. The contrary position (e.g., Wickelgren [59]) was that there was just a single long-term memory and this initial rapid decay of information was continuous with the general forgetting curve for long-term memory which is characterized by being quite negatively accelerated. Again, the field reasoned to the conclusion that these positions were essentially indistinguishable (Crowder [20]).

I think these two episodes and many others like them were symptomatic of the fact that the field was theorizing at too concrete a level. It was trying to resolve distinctions which fundamentally could not be resolved on the basis of behavioral data. As a further observation, even if these issues could have been resolved, their resolution would have shed no light on fundamental issues of the origin of human knowledge which is our concern in this paper if not always in cognitive psychology. For instance, these issues said nothing about the nativist-empiricist-rationalist controversy we highlighted at the beginning of this review.

Establishing computational rigor was a major methodological contribution of this era in cognitive psychology. The major theoretical contribution of this era to the issues of the origin of knowledge was the work of Newell and Simon [46] providing a coherent analysis of human problem solving. The basic concepts of this analysis are extremely familiar to the AI community and do not need to be repeated here. However, the essential feature from the point of view of psychology is that it defined a mapping from goals and knowledge to behavior. This provided the kind of computational basis for a theory of human motivation that had not been available to the learning theorists. It was now possible to rigorously address issues about the functional character of human knowledge.

### 2.4. Desiderata for a theory of human knowledge

From this brief survey of how psychology has got to where it is today we see a number of criteria by which to judge a psychological theory if it is to address issues of the origin of knowledge.

(1) That it in fact address the issue of the origin of knowledge. A litmus test of this is that the theory have something to say about the nativist-empiricist-rationalist controversy. This need not mean that it choose among the positions, but it should at least to able to say why a choice would not be meaningful.

(2) That it be cast fundamentally as a scientific theory with testable predictions about human behavior.

(3) That it address not just knowledge in the abstract but the functional consequences of the knowledge for human behavior.

(4) That it be cast with the precision that it can be a runnable simulation of human behavior.

(5) That it be capable of being cast at a level of abstraction that ignores irrelevant and often undecidable issues about how that knowledge is actually implemented in the human head.

The series of theories that I have been associated with were motivated by this agenda, although I must admit that I have only recently articulated to myself the last criterion above. Certainly, my theorizing has not always satisfied the last criterion as will be apparent from the review of that theory to follow. Nonetheless, I will try to focus on the significant abstract claims of the theory.

## 3. The ACT Learning Theory

The goal of this paper is to analyze the knowledge acquisition processes in the PUPS theory (Anderson and Thompson [12]), which is currently our best model of human knowledge acquisition. However, PUPS really is just a revision and embellishment of the ACT theory. Therefore, the next section of the paper will present a development of the ACT theory and the subsequent section will note the modifications involved in the PUPS theory.

### 3.1. The ACT architecture

Figure 1 illustrates the basic ACT production system architecture as developed by Anderson [5]. There are three memories: a working memory, a production memory, and, a declarative memory. Production rules had their conditions matched to the contents of working memory and their actions could add to the contents of working memory. This is the standard production system interpretive cycle of the variety proposed by Newell [44]. Where the ACT series differs

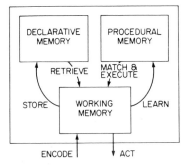

Fig. 1. A representation of the general flow of information in the ACT* architecture.

from Newell is in the postulation of a separate declarative database. Declarative memory consisted of factual knowledge not committed to a particular use. Stored in declarative memory might be an abstract fact of the form, "Two angles whose measure sum to 180 degrees are supplementary angles."

In contrast, in production memory knowledge is encoded in a use-specific way. For instance, we might have the following production rule which is derived from the above definition:

> IF one wants to prove that the measure of angle 1 equals the
>    measure of angle 2
>    and angle 1 is supplementary to angle 3,
> THEN try to prove that angle 2 is supplementary to angle 3.

The procedural-declarative distinction has not had a happy history in artificial intelligence. Therefore, it is important to emphasize that there is a substantial psychological literature pointing to the existence of the two kinds of knowledge in the human case. It also has a somewhat different definition in psychology than artificial intelligence. For psychologists procedural knowledge is distinguished from declarative knowledge by the criteria that it is not reportable and that it is available in a use-specific form rather than in a general form. A number of experiments have been done showing that people can acquire knowledge in procedural form but not declaratively. For instance, Cohen [19] has shown that certain amnesic patients can learn to solve the Tower of Hanoi problem but have no reportable memory of seeing the problem.

As Fig. 1 illustrates, all knowledge from the environment comes into working memory first. The assumption is that various perceptual systems leave descriptions of experience in working memory. A permanent residue of these experiences can be deposited into declarative memory. These memories can be brought back into working memory by a spreading activation process by which associated concepts retrieve these facts. For example, the supplementary angle definition might be brought back into working memory at a later date if the student comes upon a problem that mentions supplementary angles. Thus, working memory contains both encoding from the immediate environment and associated past memories. The contents of working memory result in behavior by means of being matched to the condition side of production rules. Productions can, in their action sides, add goals and facts to working memory. These facts can themselves be stored in long-term memory. We thus remember our past inferences.

An important feature of this architecture is that there is no way by which experience can directly create new productions. Productions are created by a learning system inspecting the trace of past production firings and creating new ones. Thus, procedural learning is a matter of learning by doing.

Another important feature of the ACT architecture was its use of activation-based computations to implement the information processing implied by this architecture. While the details would be a paper in themselves, Anderson [5] went through a concerted effort to establish that the symbolic processing involved in the theory could be implemented in terms that were plausible given what is known about the nature of brain computations on neural activation levels. Working memory is actually the portion of the knowledge structure currently active. Activation has a rapid decay process so that without some source of maintenance any particular piece of knowledge would rapidly decay. Spreading activation, the retrieval process, was a mechanism for making active the related portions of declarative memory. The process of matching production patterns and selecting from among related productions (i.e. conflict resolution) was implemented by excitatory and inhibitory computations taking place on the production rule conditions.

Given this architecture, learning will involve either changes to declarative memory or production memory. There are four basic kinds of learning mechanisms in ACT. We will review them in rough order of increasing complexity.

### 3.2. Declarative recording

Information from the environment is deposited in a declarative form in working memory. Declarative information in working memory may be permanently recorded in a long-term memory. Once in long-term memory the spreading activation process can retrieve the information for later use. In the ACT* theory the recording was a probabilistic process in which information in working memory would only sometimes be permanently recorded. See [5] for a review of the psychological literature that points to such a simple probabilistic encoding process.

This is a particularly simple process but absolutely key to ACT's theory of knowledge acquisition as developed by Anderson [5]. It provides the empiricist component of the theory in that this is the only way for knowledge to enter from the outside into the system.

### 3.3. Strengthening

Both in declarative and production memory, knowledge is stengthened every time it is used. Strengthening a piece of knowledge will make it more likely to be selected at a later point in time. A production is considered to be used whenever it is selected by conflict resolution and fired. A declarative fact is considered to be used whenever it is matched to the condition of a production rule that fires. As developed in [5] these strengths exert their influence primarily through the conflict resolution process, which decides which instantiations of productions to fire. Strengthening is an interesting case of learning in that it in no way changes the knowledge that is encoded in the system but does change what knowledge will actually be manifested in behavior. Thus, the strengthening mechanism is basically a means by which the system concentrates processing resources on knowledge that is frequently used.

There is also a decay process that weakens the strength of knowledge if it is not used for a while. The formula for the strength of a particular item is:

$$S = \sum_{i=1}^{n} t_i^{-d} \, ,$$

where the summation is over the $n$ uses of the item and each $t_i$ is the time since that use of the item. Basically we have a sum of a set of strengthenings each of which is decaying as a power function ($d$ is the exponent) of time. This is a particularly straightforward process and one for which there is an abundance of psychological evidence (for a review read [5]). What is interesting is the amount of "wisdom" built into this equation about what knowledge is likely to prove useful.

(1) The equation has a strong recency component built into it in that it effectively puts recent events into a "cache memory" from which they can be retrieved.

(2) The equation uses frequency of occurrence information and prefers knowledge that has proven useful multiple times in the past.

(3) The equation lets long-term tendencies dominate in the long term. If there are two pieces of knowledge currently equal in strength but one whose strength is based on a recent accumulation of strength and the other whose strength was built up over a longer period, then in the future the more established piece of knowledge will be preferred because its strength is decaying less rapidly.

Anderson [6] has shown that this strengthening function can be derived as an optimal solution to the information retrieval demands facing the human.

### 3.4. Knowledge compilation

In ACT an extended computation can be replaced by a single production rule. Often this new production rule will have built into it knowledge that had been only in declarative memory before. To return to the supplementary angle example given earlier, the definition of supplementary angle might have been used by some general inference productions to come to the conclusion that it would be a good idea to try to prove angles 2 and 3 supplementary. The production given above would then be produced by the knowledge compilation process as a summary of this process. Knowledge compilation is thus the way knowledge can transform declarative to procedural knowledge.

In defining more precisely the knowledge compilation process it is necessary to distinguish between two types of compiling mechanisms, one of which is called composition and the other proceduralization. The description below describes these two components of knowledge compilation as they are implemented in the GRAPES production system (Sauers and Farrell [53]), which is intended to embody certain aspects of the ACT* theory.

### 3.4.1. *Proceduralization*

Proceduralization assumes a separation between goal information and context information in the condition of a production. Consider the following production:

G1    IF the goal is to create a structure
          and there is an operation that creates such a structure,
      THEN use that operation.

This is a classic working-backwards operator, an instance of a general, weak, problem solving method. This production might apply if our goal was to insert an element into a list and we knew that there was a LISP function, CONS, that achieved this goal. In this production, the first line of the condition describes the current goal and the second context line identifies relevant information in declarative memory. Proceduralization eliminates the context lines but gets their effect by building a more specific goal description:

D1    IF the goal is to insert an element into a list,
      THEN use CONS.

The transition from the first production to the second is an example of the transition from a domain-general to a domain-specific production.

To understand in more detail how domain-general productions apply and how proceduralization occurs, one needs to be more precise about the encoding of the production, the goal, and the knowledge about CONS. With respect to the production, we have to identify its variable components. Below is a production more like its GRAPES implementation, where terms prefixed by "=" denote variables:

G1′   IF the goal is to achieve =relation on =arg1 and =arg2
          and =operation achieves =relation on =term1 and =term2,
      THEN use =operation.

When this production applies in the CONS case, the goal is "to achieve insertion of arg1 into arg2," and our knowledge about CONS is represented as "CONS achieves insertion of argument1 into argument2." The production G1′ applies to the situation with the following binding of variables:

|  |  |
|---|---|
| =relation: | insertion |
| =operation: | CONS |
| =arg1: | arg1 |
| =arg2: | arg2 |
| =term1: | argument1 |
| =term2: | argument2 |

The actual execution of the production requires that the definition of CONS be held active in working memory and be matched by the production. This can be eliminated by proceduralization, which builds a new production that has embedded in it the information that was retrieved by matching to the CONS definition. This is achieved by eliminating the parts of the production that matched to the definition (i.e., =operation achieves =relation on =term1 and =term2) and replaces the variables from this part by their bindings (i.e., =relation gets replaced by *insertion* and =operation by CONS). The proceduralized production that would be built in this case is:

D1'   IF the goal is to achieve insertion of =arg1 into =arg2,
      THEN use CONS.

In general, proceduralization operates by eliminating reference to the declarative knowledge of the domain used for problem solution by the weak method productions and building the consequences of the knowledge into domain-specific production rules. In a production system architecture like GRAPES, where this access to the declarative knowledge only occurs through the matching of production conditions, the variable replacement description scheme above is adequate to implement proceduralization. When we talk later about the analogy-based processing in PUPS, it will be necessary to perform different computations to decide how to eliminate reliance on working memory structures. The general concept of proceduralization is to be understood in terms of the elimination of the reliance on declarative, working memory elements.

In ACT* proceduralization would only eliminate matches to declarative knowledge that was permanently encoded in long-term memory. The claim was that, since the knowledge was there, all that proceduralization did was eliminate the need for its retrieval. Proceduralization did not fundamentally change the behavior of the system.

Since 1983 there has been a fair amount of data (e.g., [19, 29, 47]) which suggests that procedural knowledge can be acquired without there being first a long-term declarative representation. The most dramatic data comes from patients who display poor long-term declarative memory for events after the establishment of some neural impairment. Many of these are Korsokof patients who suffer effects of severe alcoholism. However, one of the most impressive patients is HM who had surgical removal of part of his hippocampus. While he can remember events from his childhood, and early adulthood, he has total amnesia for any events after the operation. This patient has been shown nonetheless capable of learning to solve problems such as the Tower of Hanoi puzzle. When presented with the puzzle he will swear he has never seen it before but nonetheless proceeds to solve it perfectly (which he could not do initially). While all these patients do not have such complete declarative impairment many have shown an ability to acquire skills from practicing a task while they cannot remember their experiences on the task.

While these patients have impaired long-term memories they have perfectly functional short-term declarative memories. That is, while solving the problem they can remember the instructions. The memory deficit only shows up when they return to the task. This suggests that ACT* was wrong in the claim that long-term declarative memory was a prerequisite to procedural knowledge. Any declarative representation, even if it is only transient, seems adequate. This is the implementation of proceduralization within PUPS.

### 3.4.2. *Composition*

Composition (Lewis [35]) is the process of collapsing multiple productions into single productions. Whenever a sequence of productions apply in ACT and achieve a goal, a single production can be formed that will achieve the effect of the set.

The original Lewis proposal was to collapse pairs of productions that occurred in sequence. A problem with this is that often contiguous productions have little to do with each other. We use the goal structures in ACT* to decide what productions to compose. Basically, ACT composes productions that generated a sequence of subgoals and actions that led to the satisfaction of a particular goal.

While many times composition applies to sequences of more than two productions, its effect on longer sequences is just the concatenation of its effect on shorter sequences. Thus, if S1, S2 is a sequence of productions to be composed and $C$ is the composition operator, $C(S1,S2) = C(C(S1), C(S2))$. So all we have to do is specify the pairwise compositions.

Let "IF C1 THEN A1" and "IF C2 THEN A2" be a pair of productions to be composed, where C1 and C2 are conditions and A1 and A2 are actions. Then their composition is "IF C1 & (C2 − A1) THEN (A1 − G(C2)) & A2." C2 − A1 denotes the conditions of the second production not satisfied by structures created in the action of the first. All the conditional tests in C1 and (C1 − A2) must be present from the beginning if the pair of productions are to fire. A1 − G(C2) denotes the actions of the first production minus the goals created by the first production that were satisfied by the second.

As an example, consider a situation where we want to insert the first element of one list into a second list. One production would fire and write CONS, setting subgoals to code the two arguments to CONS. Then a second production would fire to code CAR and set a subgoal to code the argument to CAR. Composing these two together would produce the production:

C3     IF the goal is to insert the first element of =arg2 into =arg3,
       THEN code CONS and then code CAR and set as subgoals to
           (1) code =arg2
           (2) code =arg3.

Composition differs from chunking as developed in SOAR (Laird, Rosenbloom and Newell [34]) in that it is defined on the productions involved whereas the SOAR mechanism is defined on the working memory elements involved. In SOAR the same variable is introduced for the same working memory token wherever it appears in the chunk, leading to certain accidental restrictions on the production created because the same variable appears unnecessarily in the same place. Composition, being defined on the production rules themselves can avoid such accidental coincidences of variable bindings. Explanation-based generalization also contrasts with SOAR in this respect (Rosenbloom and Laird [50]).

The weakness of the SOAR variabilization mechanism can be seen in a case of its application to algebraic problem solving (Golding [27]). It tries to chunk the steps that transformed $Y * R = S$ into $Y = S/R$. Note that it is moving $R$ to the *right* of the equation and $R$ appears in the *right* of the expression $Y * R$. It responds to this coincidence of position and builds a rule which has a single variable for these two position descriptors, hence requiring them to be the same. ACT*, by inspecting the actual productions, would recognize this as an accidental coincidence and not build this constraint into the composed rule.

The major effect of composition is to create macro-operators which encode sequences of production rules that frequently follow one another. Again, there is evidence in the human case (McKendree and Anderson [41]) for the existence of such macro-operators. Composition and proceduralization together lead to the development of a rich set of domain-specific operators which encode the special problem structure of that domain.

### 3.5. Generalization and discrimination

The final category of learning mechanism in the ACT theories has been a mechanism concerned with inductive learning—i.e. learning that goes beyond the received knowledge to infer new knowledge. Clearly, such a learning mechanism is absolutely critical in domains such as language acquisition. The major issue in the evolution from ACT* to PUPS has concerned the mechanisms of induction. Generalization and discrimination were the two inductive mechanisms in the 1983 ACT* theory. They were defined on production rules and produced new production rules in response to the history of old production rules.

The mechanisms of generalization and discrimination can be nicely illustrated with respect to language acquisition. Suppose a child has compiled the following two productions from experience with verb forms:

IF the goal is to generate the present tense of KICK,
THEN say KICK + S.

IF the goal is to generate the present tense of HUG,
THEN say HUG + S.

The generalization mechanism would try to extract a more general rule that would cover these cases and others:

IF the goal is to generate the present tense of =X,
THEN say =X + S.

where =X is a variable.

The production rule formed is the maximally specific generalization of the two productions allowed in the description language for the production system. Given that the description language only allows conjunctions of variabilized clauses, generalizations take the form of deleting clauses and replacing constants by variables.

Discrimination deals with the fact that such rules may be overly general and need to be restricted. For instance, the rule above generates the same form independent of whether the subject of the sentence is singular or plural. Thus, it will generate errors. By considering different features in the successful and unsuccessful situations the discrimination mechanisms would generate the following two productions:

IF the goal is to generate the present tense of =X
    and the subject of the sentence is singular,
THEN say =X + S.

IF the goal is to generate to present tense of =X
    and the subject of the sentence is plural,
THEN say =X.

If there are multiple potential discriminating features, one is chosen at random with a probability that is a function of its level of activation. Over multiple opportunities a search is in effect performed over possible discriminations. The strengths of individual production rules serve as evaluations of how well various rules do and successful rules will be strengthened to the point where they come to dominate. These learning mechanisms have proven to be quite powerful, acquiring, for instance, nontrivial subsets of natural language [5].

These discrimination and generalization mechanisms are very much like similar knowledge acquisition mechanisms that have been proposed in the artificial intelligence literature (e.g., [28, 42, 58]). In particular they can be considered syntactic methods, in that they only look at the form of the rule and the form of the contexts in which it succeeds or fails. There is no attempt to use any semantic knowledge about the context to influence the rules that are formed. A consequence of this feature in the ACT theory is that generalization and discrimination are regarded as automatic processes, not subject to strategic influences and not open to conscious inspection. The reports of unconscious learning by Reber [49] seem consistent with this view. He exposed subjects to examples of strings generated by an unknown finite-state grammar. He found that these subjects were able to judge whether new strings were consistent with the rules of the grammar without ever consciously formulating the rules of the grammar.

There are now a number of reasons for questioning whether the ACT* theory is correct in its position that inductive learning is automatic. First, there is evidence that the generalizations people form from experience are subject to strategic control [24, 33]. In a prototype formation experiment, Elio and Anderson [24] showed that subjects could adopt either memorization or hypothesis formation strategies, and the two strategies led them to differential success, depending on what the instances were. Second, Lewis and Anderson [37] found that subjects were able to restrict the application of a problem solving operator (i.e., discriminate a production) only if they could consciously formulate the discrimination rule. Indeed, there is now reason to believe that even in the Reber unconscious learning situation, subjects have conscious access to low-level rules that help them classify the examples (Dulany, Carlson, and Dewey [23]). They do not form hypotheses about finite-state grammars but do notice regularities in the example sentences (e.g., grammatical strings have two Xs in second and third position).

Another interesting problem with the ACT generalization mechanism is that subjects often appear to emerge with generalizations from a single example [24, 32], while the syntactic methods of ACT* are intended to extract the common features of a number of examples. Both of these difficulties with the ACT induction mechanism, conscious access to inductions and single-example generalizations, are dealt with in the PUPS theory.

## 4. The PUPS Learning Theory

The PUPS theory (Anderson and Thompson [12]) basically continues the assumptions of the ACT* learning theory except on three scores:

(a) As noted, proceduralization does not require working memory structures to be permanently recorded in long-term memory in order to delete matching to them in production conditions.

(b) The inductive mechanisms of generalization and discrimination which operated on productions have been replaced by inductive mechanisms of analogy and discrimination which operate on declarative knowledge structures.

(c) There has been the introduction of mechanisms of causal inference.

The most fundamental change has been the development of mechanisms for analogy. The two observations, that subjects seemed to consciously formulate their inductions and that subjects could form inductions from single examples, led to a formulation of analogy-based induction in the new PUPS simulation. The basic idea is that students work from declarative representations of solutions to past problems and try to map these onto new solutions. This example-based learning also fits well with our observations of students learning in domains like LISP and geometry [5, 10, 48] where they seem to place a heavy emphasis on using examples of problem solutions.

## 4.1. Knowledge representation

Analogical problem solving in PUPS makes strong assumptions about the representation of examples. Specifically, it assumes that problems are represented as forms achieving particular functions under certain preconditions. We can encode this information about examples in schema-like structures where function, form, and precondition are three slots among others in the schema-like representation. Below is a representation we might want to impose on the example LISP code (+ 2 3):

```
structure1
    isa: function-call
    function: (add 2 3)
    form: (list + 2 3)
    context: LISP
    medium: CRT-screen
    precondition: context: COMMONLISP
```

It is represented as a function call that adds 2 and 3 in the context of COMMONLISP and which was executed on a CRT screen. The form information states that the example is a list structure consisting of the symbols "+," "2," and "3." The precondition information states that it is essential that the context be COMMONLISP for this form to achieve its function. It would not succeed in INTERLISP, for instance.

## 4.2. The no-function-in-identity principle

There is a basic semantics underlying the relationship among the form, function, and precondition slots. This semantics is basically that jointly the form and the precondition imply the function. We can represent the example above, for instance, by the following implication:

```
IF goal is to achieve the function (add 2 3)
    and the context is COMMONLISP,
THEN use the form (list + 2 3).
```

However, this is a very specific rule. Suppose we wanted to achieve the function of (add 6 8) in the context of COMMONLISP. This production will fail because of the mismatch of the constant 6 to 2 and the constant 8 to 3. Faced with such a mismatch PUPS will try to variabilize the rule embedded in the example so that it will make the current problem. The production rule we want in the current case is:

```
IF the goal is to achieve the function (add x y)
    and the context is COMMONLISP,
THEN use the form (list + x y).
```

PUPS could always variabilize the rule implicit in an example so that it would match in the current context but at the cost of spuriously extending examples. There has to be reason to suppose that the example above can be appropriately variabilized without spuriously extending it. Note that in the example above 2 and 3 appear in both the function and the form. This is critical to the induction that replaced them by $x$ and $y$. The inductive principle underlying this is called *the no-function-in-identity principle*. The basis idea is that it is not an accident that 2 and 3 appear in both function and form. It is merely their *positions* in the form, and not their identities which achieve their positions in the function. The analogous function would be achieved by any elements that appeared in the form. Thus, the "no-function-in-identity" principle allows us to respond to the appearance of a term in both form and function of the example by replacing it everywhere by the same variable.

To summarize, PUPS searches for some substitution of variables for constants such that:

(a) each constant in the substitution must appear both in the condition and the action.

(b) The production rule after the substitution matches in the current context.

(c) No more substitutions are used than is necessary to achieve (b). Thus, if both the example and the problem share a constant a variable is not introduced.

This production rule which PUPS extracts to solve the new problem is stored away for future use—i.e., it becomes an explicit rule unlike the implicit rule in the original example.

In extracting this production rule to apply to the next problem, PUPS has basically computed an analogy from the example to the problem defined by the mapping:

$$2 \rightarrow 6,$$
$$3 \rightarrow 8.$$

All current analogy systems (e.g., [16, 26, 60]) involve putting one structure in correspondence with another such that certain elements map to other elements. These theories differ in terms of their criteria for allowing a correspondence. The "no-function-in-identity principle" is the principle in PUPS. Like all analogical principles it is basically inductive in character.

## 4.3. The principle of functional elaboration

The example above is simple in that it can be achieved by variabilizing terms that appear only in the example. However, in most interesting cases of analogy, the terms that appear in the function do not directly appear in the form. It is necessary to elaborate the form and/or function descriptions to come up with a representation that can be variabilized. For instance, suppose what we wanted to achieve was to multiply 6 and 8. The above variabilized production would have a mismatch between "add" and "multiply." PUPS can get over this hurdle if it has encoded that "+" implements "add" and "*" implements "multiply" encoded in the following PUPS structures:

>  +: isa: LISP function
>      function: (implements add)
>      form: (TEXT +)

>  *: isa: LISP function
>      function: (implements multiply)
>      form: (TEXT *)

One can embellish the representation of the plus example by including this information about the function of the + symbol:

> IF goal is to achieve the function (add 2 3)
>     and the context is COMMONLISP,
> THEN use the form (list =function 2 3)
>     where =function implements add.

Note that the "+" has been replaced by the variable "=function" and "=function" has been given the functional description of "+." This reflects the second inductive principle in PUPS analogy, which we call *the principle of functional elaboration*. The inference is that any term which achieves the function of the replaced symbol will do. There now is a variabilization of this production rule which will extend it to the problem of multiplying 6 by 8:

> IF the goal is to achieve the function $(=op =x =y)$
>     and the context is COMMONLISP,
> THEN use the form (list =function $=x =y$)
>     where =function implements =op.

The constraint "=function implements =op" can be satisfied either by inserting a term which satisfies this function or setting a subgoal to find such a term. PUPS performs a search over functional elaborations of terms in the condition and action side of the original production (implicit in the example) looking for some embellished representation where the no-function-in-identity principle can apply—i.e., where points (a)–(c) specified under that principle can be satisfied.

Note that in extracting this production rule from the example and matching it to the problem we have in fact calculated the following mapping of the example onto the problem:

> add  →  multiply,
> +    →  * ,
> 2    →  6 ,
> 3    →  8 .

Thus, we have performed the analogy defined by this mapping. However, I prefer to talk about rules and not the analogical mapping because PUPS does store the production rule underlying this analogy. These productions are basically proceduralizations in the sense defined earlier. They eliminate the need to make reference to a declarative structure to repeat a computation. In this case, the data structure eliminated is the PUPS encoding of the example. Subjects do show a dramatic improvement in their problem solving after using a single example and tend to drop out reference to an example in the subsequent problem solving episodes [48].

An interesting question concerns how PUPS selects an example from which to make an analogy. If it selects an example which will not work (because it cannot find a variabilization satisfying the no-function-in-identity principle), it simply tries another. Unguided it may have to go through a great many examples before coming up with a successful one. However, PUPS uses a spreading activation scheme and selects the most active example. This means that it will tend to select a recent example and one that overlaps a lot with the features of the current problem. These biases correspond to the biases in human selection of examples for analogy [51].

### 4.4. Form to function analogy

One can use the same analogy mechanism to infer the function of a novel form. The following example, adapted from the dissertation research of Shrager [54], shows analogy operating in this fashion. Subjects were presented with a toy tank that had the keypad in Fig. 2. They determined that the key labelled with the up-arrow moved the tank forward and they had to figure out what the keys with the down-arrow and left-arrow did. Below we have PUPS structures that purport to represent their states of knowledge:

Fig. 2. An example of the device used by Shrager [54].

example
  isa: button
  function: (MOVE forward)
  form: (LABELLED up-arrow)

up-arrow
  isa: symbol
  function: (DENOTE forward)

problem1
  isa: button
  function: ?
  form: (LABELLED down-arrow)

down-arrow
  isa: symbol
  function: (DENOTE backward)

problem2
  isa: button
  function: ?
  form: (LABELLED left-arrow)

left-arrow
  isa: symbol
  function: (DENOTE leftward)

The example is encoded as an up-arrow with the further information that an up-arrow is a symbol which conventionally means forward. The functions of the other two buttons are not represented but we have represented the conventional knowledge that down-arrows symbolize backward and left-arrows left.

We can represent the knowledge encoded by the example by the following variabilized production:

> IF there is a structure with form (LABELLED =symbol)
>   and =symbol denotes =direction,
> THEN the structure has the function (MOVE =direction).

This production can be extracted from the example using the "no-function-in-identity" principle and the principle of "functional elaboration" and just switching the form to the condition and the function to the action side of the production. This production enables us to infer that the function of the problem1 button is to move backwards. Similarly we can infer that the function of the problem2 button is to move left. As it turns out only the first inference was correct. The left-arrow button did not actually move the tank in the left direction but rather only turned it in that direction. This is an example of where the "no-function-in-identity" assumption was violated. Some buttons moved the tank in the specified direction and some turned. One simply had to learn which did which. The actual identity of the direction determined the function of the button. This just proves that analogy has the danger of any inductive inference of coming to conclusions which are not in fact correct. The important observation is that human subjects also made this misanalogy. Later we will discuss discrimination mechanisms in PUPS for avoiding such over-generalizations.

### 4.5. Function to function analogy

Function slots in PUPS can have multiple values corresponding to the basic observation that an object can have multiple functions. The potential for multiple function slots creates a third type of analogy. One can take an example serving two functions and if one of these functions is analogous to the function of a current problem, one can infer that another way to characterize the function of the problem is in analogy to the second function of the example. The following example illustrates this. One might have as a goal to calculate the second element of the list:

> Goal
>     isa: lisp-code
>     function: (second lis)
>     form: ????

Even if one knew what the functions *car* and *cdr* did, one might not see their applicability to this goal because one represented the function of *car* as calculating *first* and *cdr* as calculating *rest* and these relationships do not make immediate contact with the relationship of *second*. However, one might have an example of calculating the second element of a list in some other domain (e.g., the second card in a deck) where that was represented as the first of the rest of the list:

> example
>     isa: card
>     function: (second deck1)
>               (first deck2)
>
> deck2
>     isa: deck
>     function: (rest deck1)

From this example the following rule can be extracted:

> IF there is a structure with function (second =lis1),
> THEN the structure also has function (first =lis2)
>         where =lis2 is the rest of =lis1.

This analogical elaboration then allows one to refine the goal function so that the *car* and *cdr* productions can apply.

### 4.6. Relationship to other work on analogy

There has been a fair amount of research on mechanisms of analogy and it would be useful to relate this current system to other proposals:

#### 4.6.1. *Explanation-based generalization*

Explanation-based learning (DeJong [21], Mitchell, Keller and Kedar-Cabelli, [43]) has some interesting similarities with our analogy mechanisms. Kedar-Cabelli [31] has extended Michell's system to analogy which makes the similarities all the more apparent. In explanation-based learning, the system is given a high-level description of the target concept (the *goal concept*), a single positive instance of the concept (the *training example*), a description of what an acceptable concept definition would be (the *operationality criterion*), and a list of facts about the domain. Included in these facts are abstract rules of inference about the domain. EBG (explanation-based generalization) algorithm tries to find a proof that the training example satisfies the goal concept. To do this it simply expands the terms in high-level description until all the terms in the description meet the operationality criterion. After a proof is generated that the training example satisfies the goal concept, the proof is generalized to form a rule which is capable of matching any instance of the goal concept which meets this same low-level description.

The expansions done by the EBG method are not unlike the functional elaborations done by the PUPS system. The essential difference is that, while the EBG system expands until it either reaches a dead end or the (apparently ad hoc) operational criterion is met, the PUPS system has an implicit operational criterion, which is that the expansion is sufficiently elaborate for the no-function-in-identity principle to apply. A second difference is that PUPS need not be given abstract rules of inference for the domain. It tries to infer these directly from its encoding of examples. Thus, EBG starts out with a strong domain theory and essentially composes new rules; while PUPS discovers the rules hidden in its examples. A third difference is that the EBG method simply characterizes the way in which a single object instantiates a concept, while PUPS draws analogies in order to further problem solving efforts.

#### 4.6.2. *Winston's analogies*

Winston's ANALOGY system [60] is very similar to the work of Mitchell and Kedar-Cabelli discussed above. The major difference is that the rules of inference are stored with the examples and not stored separately and thus the example serves the additional function of providing rules of inference. One of the big differences between ANALOGY and PUPS is that ANALOGY seems only capable of filling in *function* slots (i.e., doing form-to-function mapping). That is, ANALOGY would not be able to generate an example which served a specific function (i.e., do a function-to-form mapping). Indeed, this observation could be made of all the examples we have looked at, except for Carbonell's work (which is only capable of finding form that fills a particular function, and not the reverse). PUPS is the only system we know of that can draw analogies in either direction.

### 4.6.3. *Gentner's structure mapping*

Gentner's [26] structure-mapping approach to analogies distinguishes between various types of features of the model. In particular, there are *attributes*, which are predicates of only one object, and *relations*, which are predicates of two or more arguments. In analogy, one is only concerned with mapping relations. From this assumption, she distinguishes in a natural way those features which should map when comparing the solar system to an atom. The method for selection of what features will map to the target domain involves a causal analysis of the domains. The *systematicity principle* says that those relations which are central to the functional description of the domain are much more likely to get mapped than those which are not. So, for instance, the fact that the sun is more massive than a planet in some way *causes* the planet to orbit the sun. Thus, this relation is more likely to get mapped to the domain of atoms than the assertion that the sun is *hotter* than the planets (which doesn't cause anything). The causal analysis is similar to Winston's model. The central idea is that if you cannot show a reason for a relation to get mapped, then you shouldn't map it.

The PUPS analogy mechanism does not require a commitment to which relationships will be mapped. It will recruit all and only those functional relationships that are required to enable the no-function-in-identity principle to map. However, causal relationships provide an important type of functional link as we will discuss.

### 4.6.4. *Carbonell's derivational analogy*

Carbonell's [16] work is different in kind than the systems so far discussed. His basic strategy is to take a worked-out solution for a problem and convert it to the current task. The problem solution may be represented at any level of abstraction (corresponding to various points along the problem solving continuum) as a list of operators along with an elaborate description of the dependencies among the operators and the parts of the problem domain. These dependencies are then evaluated with respect to the current problem, and various editing operations are performed to convert the solution to one appropriate for the current problem.

A major difference between Carbonell's work and our own is that he represents problem solutions as a whole, and requires that the entire solution be transported (modulo certain possible transformations) into a solution to the current problem. In our work, each operator application is done by a separate step (which may either be a learned rule or an analogy), and our solutions may therefore potentially borrow from many different examples. Also, since the generalizations we learn describe an individual step in a problem solution rather than the entire solution, these generalizations are more widely applicable (our theory predicts more transfer to novel problems). We think this more piecemeal approach is closer to the human use of analogy.

### 4.7. Discrimination

PUPS analogy is meant to replace the ACT* theory of generalization. The compilation of the analogy to produce a production rule amounts to a generalization. As in ACT*, this generalization mechanism needs to be supplemented with a discrimination mechanism which adds appropriate constraints to the generalizations. The precondition slot of a PUPS structure is supposed to encode the constraints on a form achieving its function. When a form fails to achieve its intended function, it is assumed that this is because some critical precondition is missing and an effort is made to find the precondition and encode it within the PUPS structures. Currently, there are two ways such precondition information can be added. Since such precondition information is declarative structure, it can be added by encoding linguistic instruction or by the output of other production actions. Alternatively, PUPS can engage in a comparison of successful and unsuccessful analogies much as ACT* does, looking for critical differences. Applied to the earlier misanalogy in the Shrager situation (Fig. 2) the difference uncovered might be that *left* and *right* require the tank to turn. However, even when PUPS engages in this compare and contrast strategy it differs from ACT* in that the precondition is added to a declarative data structure and so is available for inspection. This produces the phenomenon noted earlier that when subjects make successful discriminations they are able to articulate what the discriminating features are.

### 4.8. Causal induction

PUPS, being a developing theory, does not have a fixed set of learning mechanisms. Recently, influenced by the work of Lewis [36] we have become convinced that we need to work on principles of causal inference to make the theory of learning more complete. The basic idea is that people have a capacity to infer causal relationships among elements in their experience. Basically, in PUPS terms, a causal induction involves encoding as a function of form1 that caused form2. While we have experimented with mechanisms for causal induction in PUPS, there is not a stable implementation as there is in the case of analogy.

Lewis has identified a number of principles for causal induction, including the following two:

(1) *The identity heuristic.* This basically asserts that when two tokens of the same element appear in a sequence, the first token had a role in causing the second token. Thus, if we type (lis) into the computer and we see a message "lis: unknown function object" we can use the identity of lis between what we typed and the message to infer that our action caused the message.

(2) *Previous action.* This basically asserts that if an event has no other apparent cause, ascribe as its cause the immediately preceding action. Thus, if a computer responds immediately with "rubbish" to a symbol we typed we can infer our typing caused the message.

We have built these two mechanisms into PUPS and have been exploring their interaction with analogy. The following is an interesting example of how analogy and causal induction work in concert.

To set the scenario for this example, imagine a learner who neither knew English nor knew LISP, interpreting the following interactions involving an instructor and a computer user. First, an instructor says "Get the first element of (a b c)." Then a computer user, sitting at a terminal, types (car '(a b c)). Finally, the computer responds with just *a*. Figure 3(a) shows PUPS analysis of these three events which turns on these two principles for causal induction. Using the principle of previous action it infers that the first event caused the

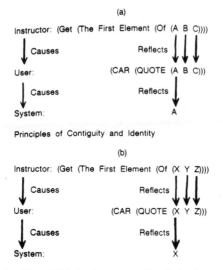

Fig. 3. (a) An example of how PUPS develops a causal analysis of a sequence of three events. (b) An example of how analogy extends to analysis in (a) to interpreting a new utterance.

second and the second caused the third. Using the first principle of identity it assumes that successive tokens of the letters reflect each other. These causal relationships are attached as functional elaborations of the events. For example, the instructor's sentence is represented as having the function of causing the user's input and the computer's *A* is represented as having the function of reflecting the user's *A*.

Suppose the learner now becomes the user and is presented with an example of the instructor saying "Get the first element of (X Y Z)." As can be seen in Fig. 3(b) PUPS fills in what the user will type and how the system will respond by analogy. There are two major steps in making this analogy. First, PUPS tries to figure out the function of the instructor's sentence and extracts the following rule:

IF the instructor utters =structure1 of form
    "GET the first element of (=X =Y =Z),"
THEN the function of =structure1 is to
        get the user to type =structure2 .
        and the function of =structure2 is
        to cause the system to produce =structure3
        and =structure3 reflects =component in
        the user's input
        and =component reflects =X .

Thus, PUPS infers that the sentence will cause the system to type something which will cause the system to produce something to reflect the X in the utterance.

The second major step of analogy by PUPS involves filling in the form of what the user typed. To do this PUPS extracts the following rule:

IF the user types =structure2
    and =structure2 is in response to the
        instructor's =structure1
    and =structure1 has the form
        "GET the first element of (=X =Y =Z),"
THEN the form of =structure2 is
        (CAR (QUOTE =X1 =Y1 =Z1)
        where the function of =X1 is to reflect =X
        the function of =Y1 is to reflect =Y
        the function of =Z1 is to reflect =Z.

Thus, PUPS figures out that the LISP code will be (CAR (QUOTE (X Y Z)) where the elements of list reflect the elements in the instructor's list.

Another principle of causal inference, the principle of minimal contrast, adds more potential to the combination of causal inference and analogy. Suppose our learner observes the following events.

(1) As before, the instructor says, "Get the first of (a b c)" and user types (car '(a b c)) and the system responds *a*.

(2) The instructor says "Get the tail of (a b c)" and the user types (cdr '(a b c)) and the system responds (*b c*).

The principle of minimal contrast will allow the learner to compare these two events and make some further causal inferences. This principle says that if two antecedent events are identical except for one place, and two consequent events are identical except for one place, then the thing in the antecedent place causes the thing in the consequent place. So, from the above the learner can infer "first" leads to *car* and "tail" leads to *cdr*. Also, the learner can infer that *car* causes the computer to respond with the first element of the list and *cdr* causes the computer to respond with the tail of the list. So, indirectly at least, the learner has connected the words "first" and "tail" with their meanings.

Now suppose the learner hears the instructor say "Take (m n o) and find its first element." (Note the form of this sentence is different than in (1) above. The user types (car '(m n o)) and the system responds *m*. Using the link between "first" and "car" it can infer that the "*first*" in this sentence form also caused the *car* to appear in the LISP code.

Now the learner is in a position to predict what will happen when the instructor says "Take (x y z) and find its tail." To do this it will use the analogical mechanisms illustrated in Fig. 3 plus the hooks it has inferred between "tail" and *cdr*, and between *cdr* and the relation "tail." Thus, the combinations of causal inference and analogy enable PUPS to understand a novel sentence form.

I think this example illustrates the tip of the iceberg with respect to the potential for interaction between causal inference and analogy. Analogy can extend established function-form relationships to new examples. However, something like causal inference seems the key to creating the function-form analysis of the initial example. For another example of the joint use of causal induction and analogy see Anderson [7].

## 5. Origins of Knowledge

This then concludes the review of the basic learning mechanisms in the ACT and PUPS theories. For more details and especially for analyses of how they apply to specific situations such as learning LISP, geometry, and language, I refer the reader to publications such as [3, 5, 7, 10, 12]. Now I would like to turn to the original goal of this paper, which is to extract the implications of these learning mechanisms for the issue of the origins of human knowledge. One step in identifying the epistemological claims of the PUPS theory is separating out three levels of analysis in a psychological theory: the knowledge level, the algorithm level, and the implementation level.[1] We need to understand the epistemological claims of ACT of each level.

## 5.1. The knowledge level

Newell [45] is responsible for the term "knowledge level" and Dietterich [22] has argued for its usefulness in analyzing issues of learning. It is the most abstract level and refers to what a person knows independent of how it is actually encoded and how it actually shows up in a piece of behavior. The distinction between what is known and what is represented is easy to make in the domain of logic. Suppose a system has encoded the logical formula $p$ and $p$ implies $q$. Then that system also knows $q$ even though that is not directly represented. A system can be said to know all the entailments of what it has encoded. Two systems with different encoded information can be said to know the same knowledge if the entailments of these two sets of knowledge are identical. So, curiously, a system that has $q$ and $q$ implies $p$ encoded knows the same things as the earlier system because the two sets of premises have identical entailments.

However, given the fundamental behaviorist insight it is a bit strange to talk about human knowledge in terms of its logical entailments. We do not see logical entailments; we see behavior. Therefore, Newell's development of the knowledge level hinges on the *implications* of the knowledge for behavior.[2] He introduces what he terms the "principle of rationality": "If an agent has knowledge that one of its actions will lead to one of its goals, then the agent will select the action." Two encodings of knowledge are equivalent, then, if the principle of rationality maps them onto the same behavior. Thus, it matters not if a child has encoded "mother has baked oatmeal cookies" and "the cookie jar contains what mother has baked" or encoded "the cookie jar contains oatmeal cookies" and "whatever is in the cookie jar mother baked." In either case a polite oatmeal-loving child, who obeys the principle of rationality, should go to the cookie jar and thank mother for the cookies.

Clearly, learning at the knowledge level is critical to the original philosophical discussions mentioned in the introduction of this paper. They were intended to be about the knowledge level, but part of their confusion was that they mixed in issues of learning at the other levels.

---

[1] These three levels bear obvious relationships to Marr's [39] three levels of computational theory representation and algorithm, and hardware implementation. The major difference is that the knowledge level is fashioned somewhat differently to help us address the epistemological issues of concern here. The difference between the knowledge level and the other levels also has a clear similarity to Chomsky's [18] competence-performance distinction.

[2] As we will see there is a distinction between the actual behavior of a system and the implications of knowledge for the behavior. A system may not behave as its knowledge implies it should. The knowledge level is concerned with the implications and not the actual behavior.

It is also an interesting fact that the procedural-declarative distinction is a nondistinction when we talk about learning at the knowledge level. The procedural-declarative distinction turns on whether knowledge is prepared for a particular use (and hence is procedural) or not (and hence is declarative). The knowledge level is defined by the principle of rationality which says that if knowledge is there it will be used appropriately.

## 5.2. The algorithm level

While one might reasonably argue that learning at the knowledge level is the most critical to issues of knowledge, it is by no means the only level nor is the knowledge at this level the only type of knowledge we want to speak about (despite the term Newell gave it). That this is so can be seen by considering chess. One might argue that someone who knows the rules of chess knows how to play a winning game since winning performance follows logically from such knowledge. However, one does not necessarily have the means of turning the knowledge into winning performance. Another example is that the postulates of geometry should imply the ability to do proofs in geometry, but a great deal of learning must occur after students have learned the postulates of geometry before they are facile at generating proofs.

The algorithm level refers to the actual behavioral potentials of the system. The analogy here is to the algorithmic specification of a computer program. This is quite an abstract specification however. Just as a computer algorithm is not committed to the programming language many of the details of the PUPS implementation are irrelevant to understanding human knowledge at the algorithm level. The declarative-procedural distinction is a significant distinction at this level, however. Knowledge that can or cannot be used in a particular way will determine what the system can do.

In ACT* or PUPS, because any procedure must operate on the contents of working memory, there is a close relationship between the algorithm level and working memory. Any algorithm amounts to a specification for a series of transformations of the contents of working memory. Thus, there is also a close relationship between the algorithm level and protocol data because protocol data involves a reporting of the contents of working memory by behavior correlated with these contents. Thus, in addition to verbal protocols [25], protocols can include things like eye movements [30] where the assumption is that the eye is fixated on objects that are represented in working memory.

## 5.3. The implementation level

The program or algorithm for applying the knowledge leaves under-specified the actual performance of the system. This can be seen by analogy to computer programs. The speed with which a program will run depends on how cleverly it is compiled into code and on which machine it runs. The machine and compiler will determine whether the program will fit in memory, whether it will require swapping, and whether it can run at all. Similarly, in the human situation we can inquire as to the speed and efficiency with which the human program can run. There is evidence that the time and attentional costs of a human skill decreases continuously with practice [5]. In the ACT* theory this improvement with practice is a result of its strengthening mechanisms.

Improvement in such resource costs can actually change fundamentally what a person can do. If the resource demands of a particular algorithm are too high a person will simply fail to be able to successfully execute the algorithm. For instance, Anderson and Jeffries [11] argue that most novice errors in LISP programming result from working memory being overwhelmed by the problem demands. They also argue that experts' increased working memory for domain information means that they are able to cope with problem solving demands and so make fewer errors.

## 5.4. The relationship among the three levels

It is worth noting that there is a subset-superset relationship among knowledge at the three levels. Any knowledge at the knowledge level is also knowledge at the algorithm and implementation level and any knowledge at the algorithm level is knowledge at the implementation level. As one goes up the levels one loses distinctions. At the implementation level we have an actual specification of what someone will do including errors and actual timing. Anything that changes the behavior will count as learning at the implementation level. At the algorithm level we ignore differences among behaviors that amount to differences in exact time or differences due to working memory being overloaded. Thus, differences in knowledge states that show up only because of performance considerations are ignored at the algorithm level. On the other hand we do pay attention to differences in behavior that are due to fundamental differences in an algorithm. Thus, someone solving a geometry problem by backward search from what is to be proven knows an algorithm different from that used by someone searching forward from the premises. At the knowledge level however, there might not be a difference in the knowledge of these two people so long as their algorithms implied the same decision about whether the conclusion followed from the premises.

Thus, two systems which yield different behavior may not be distinguishable at the knowledge level but only the algorithm level. For instance, there may be no difference between a knowledge level analysis of a chess expert and a duffer. They may both know the same things about chess but the expert may possess better algorithms for realizing that knowledge and better implementations of those algorithms. Knowledge level refers to what the person in principle should be capable of doing, not what he actually does do—just as a proof system should in principle be capable of recognizing the truth of a theorem even if it cannot find the proof in allotted time. By Newell's own admission the knowledge level is a "radical approximation" to the behavior of most programs, "failing in almost all cases to explore the subtleties of the matter."

## 6. Classification of Knowledge in PUPS

This section will consider the various types of knowledge that PUPS proposes are in the human head and ask the question of how each got there—is it built in (nativism), is it acquired from experience (empiricism), or was it internally computed (rationalism)? To help sharpen the discussion I will consider these questions separately at the three levels of knowledge—the knowledge level, the algorithm level, and the implementation level. Table 1 provides a summary of the conclusions—we have classified knowledge into a three-by-three table according to its three possible origins and the three possible levels of analysis.

### 6.1. Declarative recordings of the environment

In the PUPS theory, declarative recording is closely associated with the knowledge level. Every time there is a declarative recording from the environment there is a change in the knowledge level. The reason that all declarative recordings from the environment constitute learning at the knowledge level is that they constitute some change in the rational behavior of the system—if only to the question "What happened at time $X$?" Thus, the situation stamping of events guarantees that the recording of any event is not redundant in its rational consequences with the current knowledge. Of course, learning at the knowledge level also implies learning at the algorithm and implementation levels because of the subset relationships that exist among the levels.

The only changes that occur at the knowledge level are those that derive from declarative recordings from the environment. One might think that it is possible to have rationalist learning at the knowledge level—that is, to have

Table 1
Classification of knowledge at three levels of abstraction according to the origins of the knowledge

|  | Knowledge | Algorithm | Implementation |
|---|---|---|---|
| Acquired (Empiricist) | Environmental recordings | — | — |
| Computed (Rationalist) | — | Deductions Inductions Compilation | Strengthening |
| Built in (Nativist) | Induction Causal inference Weak methods | — | Principles of operation (?) |

the system compute knowledge that changes its own knowledge state. For instance, consider the cases in Fig. 3 where PUPS first inferred that the speaker's utterance caused the user's command and then later predicted that another utterance would cause a similar command. Why do these causal inference and analogical extensions not constitute rationalist learning at the knowledge level? The reason they are not is that when we dig down into what the system is doing, we see that it at least implicitly possesses knowledge of causation and induction and is just deriving the consequences of this knowledge with respect to the current events. In the case of causation this prior knowledge would include the identity heuristic and the principle of previous action. In the case of analogy this prior knowledge includes the *no-function-in-identity principle* and the *principle of functional elaboration*. It does not really matter whether the system has explicitly represented the knowledge of these principles and is reasoning in terms of this knowledge or if the knowledge is only implicit in the computations. As far as the principle of rationality is concerned, if the system is behaving as if it has the knowledge, then it does have the knowledge.[3]

### 6.2. Deductions and inductions

In PUPS there are three ways declarative facts can be added to memory. These facts can come from the outside which is the just analyzed case of learning at the knowledge level. Second, a production rule can add a declarative fact to memory. In this case we are just making explicit an implication already in the system and we have algorithm level learning. Such declarative learning we refer to as deductions.

The third possibility, is that inductive mechanisms of analogy, discrimination, or causal inference, might apply. By the preceding analysis such inductive learning is really another case of learning at the algorithm level because we are simply deriving the consequences of our principles of induction with respect to the current event. Indeed, it is unclear that inductive learning is any different than deductive learning under this analysis. That is to say, we could embed these inductive principles as production rules and the inductions would just be what is added by production actions.

### 6.3. Knowledge compilation

Knowledge compilation also involves learning at the algorithm level. This might seem peculiar in that knowledge compilation is often thought of as only improving the time or capacity demands of an algorithm. However, in addition

---

[3] Note that this position differs from that of Dietterich who views inductive learning as learning at the knowledge level. The view taken here is that such learning can be deduced from the inductive principles and the existing knowledge.

to these implementation consequences there are two ways in which the behavior of the system changes.

(a) Knowledge compilation in ACT* can actually change the direction of problem solving because of changes in the conflict resolution. In the terminology of Lewis [35] compilation in ACT* is "unsafe" in that it is possible that a compiled production will fire in situations when the production(s) from which it was compiled would be blocked. This is regarded as a feature, not a bug, in the theory because this allows the system to favor the more efficient rules it has formed. Also, when it does lock the system into an overly narrow type of behavior this corresponds to the Einstellung effect noted in human behavior (Luchins [38]) where subjects will produce a learned solution in a new situation when it is no longer optimal.

(b) Compilation will also change the step size of cognition and the contents of working memory. This can result in changes in what people report in concurrent verbal protocols or in other protocol methods of tapping the contents of their working memory such as eye movements.

## 6.4. Strengthening

The strengthening processes constitute learning at the implementation level in that they do not change the behavioral potentials of the system, only the capacity costs of performing these behaviors. Strengthening is a kind of rationalist learning. It is a case of a system mulling over its experience and deciding how to optimize its future processing of knowledge. It is not a case of the system strengthening all of the knowledge which is currently active; rather it is a case of the system deciding to strengthen that subset of the currently active knowledge which it judges to have contributed to the current line of information processing. The insertion of this judgment process is what makes it rationalist learning.

It is interesting to note that strength adjustments are basically the only learning mechanism underlying the connectionist models (e.g., McClelland and Rumelhart [40], Rumelhart and McClelland [52]), and such adjustments are said to produce learning that at least approximates learning at the knowledge and algorithm level. The claim of these connectionists is that our learning that Reagan is President is continuous with growth in the strength of our memory of this fact.

It is also of interest to note that these neural models are fundamentally empiricist in character. These changes in neural connections are thought to be passive reflections of current activation levels set up on the network in response to experience. In contrast, this is not the case in ACT* or PUPS, which provide a much more rationalist characterization of knowledge acquisition.

It is interesting to note that the actual implementation of ACT* is very much a matter of neural computation despite the fact that its epistemological assumptions are very different from connectionist theories. This reinforces a claim I have made elsewhere [8] that the fundamental issue between a "symbolic" theory like ACT and a "connectionistic" model is not the issue of neural implementation, where both basically agree, but rather the issue of learning.

## 6.5. Innate knowledge

To summarize the discussion of the preceding sections, at the knowledge level all learning is a matter of experience, by logical necessity. At the algorithm and implementation level all learning is rationalist, by theoretical choice. What remains to be specified is PUPS's position on innate knowledge.

It is an interesting question what the epistemological status is of innate processes in PUPS, such as those for spreading activation. Since these processes only influence the performance properties of the algorithms people possess, these processes must constitute innate knowledge at the implementation level if they are innate knowledge anywhere. However, even to speak of these as implementation knowledge is a bit strange. Innate knowledge seems only an appropriate concept at the knowledge level.

I think at the knowledge level we can say that there are at least three kinds of important innate knowledge in PUPS: knowledge about causal inference, the inductive knowledge behind analogy and discrimination, and knowledge of a set of weak problem solving methods.

The basic view of human behavior is one of a problem solver who has a set of operators for solving problems and set of methods for applying these operators. Such a system has to start out with a way of extracting operators from experience. In PUPS these are the mechanisms of causal inference, which basically infer that certain things cause certain other things. The actual acquisition of such causal relationships is rationalist learning as we discussed. The principles that underlie this rationalist learning are an important category of innate knowledge about the nature of the world.

In addition to having these operators, we must have some means of deploying them to solve new problems. These mechanisms must include methods which do not have built into them knowledge of the particular problem solving domain to which they apply. These are the so-called weak methods. Analogy, besides being an inductive mechanism, is one weak method which tries to map the solution of one problem to another. Its inductive components enable it to extend the solution to novel contexts but analogy is quite limited in its ability to generate a novel solution. Other weak methods like hill climbing or means-ends analysis do more to concatenate the steps in novel form. In the PUPS framework there is no way to acquire any of the basic weak methods. They have to be built in.

It is interesting to compare PUPS on this score with the SOAR model (Laird, Rosenbloom and Newell [34]) which is said to contain a single universal weak method and that other weak methods emerge in response to encoding of knowledge about a domain. We could do the same thing in PUPS using analogy as the universal weak method. If we encoded a solution to a problem as a means-ends solution we could generate a means-ends solution to an analogous problem. However, this ignores the question of where the original encoding came from. If one traces it back it has to be because the encoding mechanisms knew about means-ends solution. In the PUPS framework, all the weak methods must be traced to innate knowledge. It is not clear the same would not be true if we explored in SOAR where the encodings of domain knowledge came from.

## 7. Summary

In summary, the following are the assertions of the current PUPS theory on knowledge acquisition:

(0) The knowledge acquisition takes place within a production system architecture which assumes a rich enough pattern-matching ability to match operators to situations and to identify differences between goals and current states.

(1) The system begins with
    (a) a set of rules for inferring causal relationships in experience,
    (b) a set of inductive principles for extending or restricting the causal inference,
    (c) a set of weak methods for deploying these causal inferences in problem solving.

(2) Learning at the knowledge level is empiricist and consists of encoding declarative representations of experience as received.

(3) Learning at the algorithm level is rationalist and involves compiling rules that summarize existing computation, storing the declarative structures written into working memory by production actions, and adding the results of inductive procedures for causal inference and analogy.

(4) Learning at the implementation level is rationalist and involves strengthening the procedural and declarative knowledge as a reflection of its frequency of successful use.

### ACKNOWLEDGMENT

I would like to thank Wayne Gray, Claudius Kessler, Clayton Lewis, Jean McKendree, Peter Pirolli, and Kevin Singley for their comments on the paper. Preparation of this paper was supported by contracts MDA903-85-K-0343 from the Army Research Institute and N00014-84-K-0064 from the Office of Naval Research.

### REFERENCES

1. Anderson J.A., A theory for the recognition of items from short memorized lists, *Phychol. Rev.* **80** (1973) 417–438.
2. Anderson, J.R., *Language, Memory, and Thought* (Erlbaum, Hillsdale, NJ, 1976).

3. Anderson, J.R., Tuning of search of the problem space for geometry proofs, in: *Proceedings IJCAI-81*, Vancouver, BC (1981).
4. Anderson, J.R., Acquisition of cognitive skill, *Psychol. Rev.* **89** (1982) 369–406.
5. Anderson, J.R., *The Architecture of Cognition* (Harvard University Press, Cambridge, MA, 1983).
6. Anderson, J.R., A rational analysis of human memory, in: H.L. Roediger III and F.I.M. Craik (Eds.), *Varieties of Memory and Consciousness: Essays in Honor of Endel Tulving* (Erlbaum, Hillsdale, NJ, 1988).
7. Anderson, J.R., Causal analysis and inductive learning, in: *Proceedings Fourth International Workshop of Machine Learning*, Irvine, CA (1987).
8. Anderson, J.R., Methodologies for studying human knowledge, *Behav. Brain Sci.* (to appear).
9. Anderson, J.R. and Bower, G.H., *Human Associative Memory* (Winston and Sons, Washington, DC, 1973).
10. Anderson, J.R., Farrell, R. and Sauers, R., Learning to program in LISP, *Cognitive Sci.* **8** (1984) 87–129.
11. Anderson, J.R. and Jeffries, R., Novice LISP errors: Undetected losses of information from working memory, *Hum.-Comput. Interaction* **22** (1985) 403–423.
12. Anderson, J.R. and Thompson, R., Use of analogy in a production system architecture, in: A. Ortony et al. (Eds.), *Similarity and Analogy* (to appear).
13. Atkinson, R. and Shiffrin, R., Human memory: A proposed system and its control processes, in: K. Spence and J. Spence (Eds.), *The Psychology of Learning and Motivation* (Academic Press, New York, 1968).
14. Boring, E.G., *History of Experimental Psychology* (Appleton-Century-Crofts, New York, 1950).
15. Bower, G.H. and Hilgard, E.R., *Theories of Learning* (Prentice-Hall, Englewood Cliffs, NJ, 1981).
16. Carbonell, J.G., Derivational analogy: A theory of reconstructive problem solving and expertise acquisition, Tech. Rept. 85-115, Department of Computer Science, Carnegie-Mellon University, Pittsburgh, PA (1985).
17. Chomsky, N., Verbal Behavior (A review of Skinner's book), *Language* **35** (1959) 26–58.
18. Chomsky, N., The formal nature of language, in: E.H. Lenneberg (Ed.), *Biological Foundations of Language* (Wiley, New York, 1967) Appendix A.
19. Cohen, N.J., Preserved learning capacity in amnesia: Evidence for multiple memory systems, in: L.R. Squire and N. Ballers (Eds.), *Neuropsychology of Memory* (Guilford, New York, 1984).
20. Crowder, R.G., The demise of short-term memory, *Acta Psychol.* **50** (1982) 291–323.
21. DeJong, G., Generalizations based on explanations, in: *Proceedings IJCAI-81*, Vancouver, BC (1981).
22. Dietterich, T.G., Learning at the knowledge level, *Mach. Learning* **1** (1986) 287–316.
23. Dulany, D.E., Carlson, R.A. and Dewey, G.I., A case of syntactical learning and judgment: How conscious and how abstract?, *J. Experimental Psychol. General* **113** (1984) 541–555.
24. Elio, R. and Anderson, J.R., Effects of category generalizations and instance similarity on schema abstraction, *J. Experimental Psychol. Learning, Memory Cognition* **7** (1983) 397–417.
25. Ericsson, K.A. and Simon, H.A., *Protocol Analysis: Verbal Reports as Data* (MIT Press, Cambridge, MA, 1984).
26. Gentner, D., Structure-mapping: A theoretical framework for analogy, *Cognitive Sci.* **7** (1983) 155–170.
27. Golding, A., Analogical problem solving in SOAR, Unpublished Manuscript, Stanford University, Stanford, CA (1985).
28. Hayes-Roth, F. and McDermott, J., Learning structured patterns from examples, in: *Proceedings Third International Joint Conference on Pattern Recognition*, Coronado, CA (1976) 419–423.

29. Jacoby, L.L. and Witherspoon, D., Remembering without awareness, *Can. J. Psychol.* **36** (1982) 300–324.
30. Just, M.A. and Carpenter, P.A., The computer and eye processing pictures, *Behav. Res. Methods Instrumentation* **11** (1979) 172–176.
31. Kedar-Cabelli, S., Purpose-directed analogy, in: *Proceedings Seventh Annual Conference of the Cognitive Science Society*, Irvine, CA (1985).
32. Kieras, D.E. and Bovair, S., The acquisition of procedures from text: A production-system analysis of transfer of training, *J. Memory Lang.* **25** (1986).
33. Kline, P.J., Computing the similarity of structured objects by means of heuristic search for correspondences, Unpublished Doctoral Dissertation, University of Michigan, Ann Arbor, MI (1983).
34. Laird, J.E., Rosenbloom, P.S. and Newell, A., Chunking in SOAR: The anatomy of a general learning mechanism, *Mach. Learning* **1** (1986) 11–46.
35. Lewis, C.H., Production system model of practice effects, Doctoral Dissertation, University of Michigan, Ann Arbor, MI (1978).
36. Lewis, C.H., Understanding what's happening in system interactions, in: D.A. Norman and S.W. Daper (Eds.), *User Centered System Design: New Perspectives in Human-Computer Interaction* (Erlbaum, Hillsdale, NJ, 1986).
37. Lewis, M.W. and Anderson, J.R., Discrimination of operator schemata in problem solving: Learning from examples, *Cognitive Psychol.* **17** (1985) 26–65.
38. Luchins, A.S., *Mechanization in Problem Solving*, Psychological Monographs **54** (248) (1942).
39. Marr, D., *Vision* (Freeman, San Francisco, CA, 1982).
40. McClelland, J.L., Rumelhart, D.E. and the PDP Research Group, *Parallel Distributed Processing: Explorations in the Microstructure of Cognition*, II: *Applications* (MIT, Cambridge, MA, 1986).
41. McKendree, J.E. and Anderson, J.R., Frequency and practice effects on the composition of knowledge in LISP evaluation, in: J.M. Carroll (Ed.), *Cognitive Aspects of Human-Computer Interaction* (to appear).
42. Mitchell, T.M., Version spaces: An approach to concept learning, Doctoral Dissertation, Department of Electrical Engineering, Stanford University, Stanford, CA (1978).
43. Mitchell, T.M., Keller, R.M. and Kedar-Cabelli, S.T., Explanation-based generalization: A unifying view, *Mach. Learning* **1** (1986) 47–80.
44. Newell, A., A theoretical exploration of mechanisms for coding the stimulus, in: A.W. Melton and E. Martin (Eds.), *Coding Processes in Human Memory* (Winston, Washington, DC, 1972).
45. Newell, A., The knowledge level, *AI Mag.* **2** (1981) 1–20.
46. Newell, A. and Simon, H., *Human Problem Solving* (Prentice-Hall, Englewood Cliffs, NJ, 1972).
47. Nissen, M.J. and Bullemer, P., Attentional requirements of learning: Evidence from performance measures (to appear).
48. Pirolli, P.L., Problem solving by analogy and skill acquisition in the domain of programming, Master's Thesis, Carnegie-Mellon University, Pittsburgh, PA (1985).
49. Reber, A.S., Implicit learning of synthetic languages: The role of instructional set, *J. Experimental Psychol. Hum. Learning Memory* **2** (1976) 88–94.
50. Rosenbloom, P.S. and Laird, J.E., Explanation-based generalization in SOAR, in: *Proceedings AAAI-86*, Philadelphia, PA (1986) 561–567.
51. Ross, B.H., Remindings and their effects in learning in cognitive skill, *Cognitive Psychol.* **16** (1984) 371–416.
52. Rumelhart, D.E., McClelland, J.L. and the PDP Research Group, *Parallel Distributed Processing: Exploration in the Microstructure of Cognition*, I: *Foundations* (MIT, Cambridge, MA, 1986).

53. Sauers, R. and Farrell, R., GRAPES user's manual, Tech. Rept. 1, Department of Psychology, Carnegie-Mellon University, Pittsburgh, PA (1982).
54. Shrager, J.C., Instructionless learning: Discovery of the mental device of a complex model, Doctoral Dissertation, Department of Psychology, Carnegie-Mellon University, Pittsburgh, PA (1985).
55. Skinner, B.F., *Verbal Behavior* (Appleton-Century-Croft, New York, 1957).
56. Sternberg, S., Memory scanning: Mental processes revealed by reaction time experiments, *Am. Sci.* **57** (1969) 421–457.
57. Townsend, J.T., Issues and models concerning the processing of a finite number of inputs, in: B.H. Kantowitz (Ed.), *Human Information Processing: Tutorials in Performance and Cognition* (Erlbaum, Hillsdale, NJ, 1974).
58. Vere, S.A., Induction of relational productions in the presence of background information, in: *Proceedings IJCAI-77*, Cambridge, MA (1977) 349–355.
59. Wickelgren, W.A., Single-trace fragility theory of memory dynamics, *Memory Cognition* **2** (1974) 775–780.
60. Winston, P.H., Binford, T.O., Katz, B. and Lowry, M., Learning physical descriptions from functional definitions, examples, and precedents, in: *Proceedings AAAI-83*, Washington, DC (1983).

# Creativity and Learning in a Case-Based Explainer

**Roger C. Schank and David B. Leake**

*Artificial Intelligence Project, Yale University, P.O. Box 2158, Yale Station, New Haven, CT 06520, U.S.A.*

ABSTRACT

*Explanation-based learning (EBL) is a very powerful method for category formation. Since EBL algorithms depend on having good explanations, it is crucial to have effective ways to build explanations, especially in complex real-world situations where complete causal information is not available.*

*When people encounter new situations, they often explain them by remembering old explanations, and adapting them to fit. We believe that this case-based approach to explanation holds promise for use in AI systems, both for routine explanation and to creatively explain situations quite unlike what the system has encountered before.*

*Building new explanations from old ones relies on having explanations available in memory. We describe explanation patterns (XPs), knowledge structures that package the reasoning underlying explanations. Using the SWALE system as a base, we discuss the retrieval and modification process, and the criteria used when deciding which explanation to accept. We also discuss issues in learning XPs: what generalization strategies are appropriate for real-world explanations, and which indexing strategies are appropriate for XPs. SWALE's explanations allow it to understand nonstandard stories, and the XPs it learns increase its efficiency in dealing with similar anomalies in the future.*

## 1. Introduction

We cannot hope to anticipate every circumstance that a program might encounter. Even if we could, and we built in all the appropriate responses, the changing world would soon make that frozen knowledge base obsolete. Thus learning is essential in programs that deal with the real world.

Explanation-based learning (EBL) offers considerable advantages over traditional inductive methods, and has been the subject of much research (for a discussion of the explanation-based approach, see Mitchell et al. [21] or DeJong and Mooney [4]). But although EBL systems depend on having good explanations available, the problem of building the explanations to use has received surprisingly little attention. Most EBL programs construct explanations from scratch, chaining together basic causal rules. However, this approach is extremely inefficient for explaining complicated situations where many rules might be relevant. Some responses to this problem have been suggested (for example, using inductive generalizations to focus on the features to consider (Lebowitz [19]), or allowing a program to accept externally provided hints that can help it build explanations otherwise beyond its capabilities [4]). But for situations where these aids are not available, an efficient way to construct explanations is still vital.

When people deal with new situations, they seldom reason from first principles. Instead, they start from their memories of experiences in similar situations. Those memories can then be adapted to suggest strategies for dealing with the situation at hand. The case-based approach to planning and problem solving has been advocated by a number of researchers (for example, Schank [25], Carbonell [2], Hammond [10], Kolodner, Simpson and Sycara [16]). We believe that a case-based approach is also a promising way to address the problem of building explanations. Just as people use experience to do planning and problem solving, they often use remindings of old experiences as the starting point for explanation.

Although remindings of old explanations are sometimes applicable in a straightforward way, they may also be hard to apply. When a person is reminded of a seemingly inapplicable episode, and someone else shows how it suggests a good explanation, we may be impressed by his creativity. For programs to do the learning needed to keep abreast of a complex and changing world, they must have the capability for this kind of creativity: programs will need to revise old explanations to explain events that are not very similar to those they've encountered before, even when the explanations they try to apply don't seem to fit. To profit from these creative explanations in the future, systems will also need to remember the explanations they generate, and to index them so that they will be accessible for straightforward or creative application in the future.

The following sections describe an approach to case-based explanation which was developed by the authors, Chris Riesbeck, Alex Kass and Chris Owens during work on the SWALE project (Schank [27], Leake and Owens [17], Schank and Leake [30], Kass [12]). SWALE is a story understander that detects anomalies in the stories it reads, explains them by retrieving and revising old explanations, and installs the new explanations in memory for future use. While work on SWALE is still in progress, the system has already developed a range of novel explanations. Because revision of old cases to fit new situations is creative, case-based explanation offers not only an efficient way to build explanations, but also a framework for investigating creativity as an algorithmic process.

## 2. Overview

Case-based explanation considers explanation as a memory process. We are strongly influenced by previous Yale work on memory organization and the role of failure-driven reminding in learning, and we begin with a sketch of some of that work.

We then consider the representation of explanations in memory. The need for a knowledge structure flexible enough to support the adaptation process prompts us to define *explanation patterns* (XPs) [27], which capture the network of beliefs that underlie explanations. Given this structure, an explainer can directly apply the parts of the old explanation that fit the new case, and can identify and repair the parts of the explanation that do not apply. In this way, many of the results of the original explanation effort can be reused.

We then describe an algorithm for case-based explanation. Our description is in context of understanding stories with novel elements, and learning new XPs by explaining them. We show that our approach generates a range of interesting explanations.

Taking our model as starting point, we argue that creativity is primarily a matter of search and adaptation, and we discuss how our process could be extended to build a more creative system. Two appendices of concrete information follow: a description of the types of beliefs and inference rules represented in the SWALE system, and annotated output from a SWALE run.

### 3. Previous Work on Learning at the Yale AI Lab

Our work on case-based explanation has arisen from a progression of work on memory organization, the integration of events into memory, and the way that information in memory is indexed for retrieval. This perspective strongly influences our view of explanation as a memory-based process.

#### 3.1. Learning and dynamic memory

Establishing the coherence of a story is vital to understanding it. But blindly chaining together inferences to build connections can result in a combinatorial explosion of possibilities (Rieger [22]). One way that people avoid this is by using their knowledge of standard event sequences to guide understanding. Our initial work on the knowledge structures in memory introduced *scripts* (Schank and Abelson [28]). A script is a stereotyped sequence of events within a particular context, such as the standard events involved in having a meal at a restaurant (wait for a table, sit down, order, etc.). Scripts facilitate routine understanding: in familiar situations, people rely on scripts to direct inference of likely events.

People must be able to refine knowledge structures as the world changes, but our formulation of scripts presented an impediment to some types of learning. Each script is completely independent of the others; distinct scripts share no structure. Consequently, learning done in the context of one script has no effect on the others. This conflicts with what we know about how people learn: if someone tries unsuccessfully to use a credit card to pay for a doctor's visit, he'll anticipate that a dentist would refuse it also, even though the scripts for doctor visits and dentist visits are different.

Dynamic memory theory (Schank [24]) responds to the need for knowledge structures that allow cross-contextual learning. It postulates knowledge structures called *memory organization packets* (MOPs). Like scripts, MOPs characterize event sequences; unlike scripts, they allow a sequence to be composed of a number of lower-level components which can be shared by a number of MOPs. The basic components, called *scenes*, describe events which take place in a single location, with a single purpose, and in a single time interval. For example, the act of paying for an office visit to a professional (such as a doctor or dentist) is circumscribed in this way. This PAY scene tends to be standard regardless of the profession involved. Although M-doctor-visit and M-dentist-visit are distinct MOPs, they share a single PAY scene. Because the scene is shared, the learning that people do in our credit card example would also occur in a computer program with a MOP-based memory.

Dynamic memory theory led to two computer experiments. CYRUS (Kolodner [15]) models the organization of episodic memory, integrating new episodes into its previous knowledge, and using a range of retrieval strategies to generate indices for retrieving information. IPP (Lebowitz [18]) uses an inductive approach to learn new MOPs on the basis of newspaper stories.

### 3.2. Learning new MOPs

IPP read newspaper stories about terrorist attacks, using MOPs to provide expectations during the story understanding process. It made inductive generalizations about what it read, and installed them in memory as new MOPs that could guide understanding of later stories. For example, from reading newspaper stories about Italy when the Red Brigades were active, IPP formed the generalization that the usual victims of kidnapping in Italy were businessmen.

#### 3.2.1. *Problems with the inductive approach*

Inductive learning has been used in many AI learning systems (for an overview of some of the methods used, see Dietterich and Michalski [5] or Mitchell [20]). However, because inductive learners have no criterion for importance of features except for their frequency of occurrence, they often make faulty generalizations when they deal with limited sets of data. Some of the conclusions they draw are very unlikely to be considered by people: for example, when IPP read about two bombings in India, each of which resulted in two deaths, IPP generalized that bombings in India always kill two people.

One response to problems dealing with limited data is to restrict a program to considering features that have been preselected as being important. However, this evades the important question of selecting from the many features that are presented by any real-world tasks. In addition, preselecting features would only work in circumscribed domains, since which features are important varies enormously from situation to situation. If a car breaks down, the time of the breakdown is probably insignificant. But the time of a 2:00 AM car accident might be very important, if 2:00 AM is the time when bars close. What determines relevant features is the causal structure of the situation.

Explanation-based generalization allows important features to be selected dynamically, and allows learning systems, like people, to generalize on the basis of single episodes. A discussion of problems of inductive category formation and the need for explanation-based methods appears in [29], and also in EBL work such as [21].

### 3.3. Failure-driven learning

While the construction of new generalizations is important, it is also important to be able to recognize and learn from situations where old generalizations fail to apply. IPP built new knowledge structures on the basis of generalizations, and used them to organize episodes in memory. Thus IPP could recognize a story as commonplace, and could also notice novel aspects of a story. For example, consider the following story from the *New York Times*:

> An Arabic speaking gunman shot his way into the Iraqi Embassy here [Paris] yesterday morning, held hostages through most of the day before surrendering to French policemen, and then was shot by Iraqi security officials as he was led away by French officers.

The beginning of the story is a fairly routine incident of terrorism, but it is startling that the Iraqi officials shot the gunman after he'd surrendered. IPP could recognize from experience that the shooting was exceptional. However, it had no way to account for the deviation from expectations.

When people encounter difficulties, they are often reminded of past problems; thinking about them can help point to the explanation. In a dynamic memory, processing failures are stored under the knowledge structures in which they were encountered. When a subsequent failure is encountered within the same MOP, these cases are accessible.

ALFRED (Riesbeck [23]) presents a model of how failure-driven reminding contributes to incremental learning. In order to understand articles in the domain of economics, the system uses rules that reflect everyday knowledge. If one of these rules of thumb fails, an *exception episode* describing the failure and the recovery procedure is indexed under the faulty rule. When the next failure of the rule is encountered, the original failure is remembered. The previous case provides information to aid in revision of the problematic rule: if it is possible to group the failure episodes into a single class, the rule can be modified to deal correctly with that class.

For example, in one run of the program, ALFRED was given two arguments concerning whether the government should control credit cards as an anti-inflationary measure. The first advocated control, since credit cards account for $55 billion of the credit in the American economy. ALFRED accepted this argument, using the everyday knowledge that $55 billion is probably a significant amount. A subsequent argument said that credit cards accounted for a negligible portion of the $1.23 trillion total credit in the economy. Using this additional information on the relative size of the credit, ALFRED accepted that its old conclusion was wrong.

The program was then given the input that adding a 10 ¢ per gallon gasoline tax would decrease consumption by 100,000 gallons a day. This conflicted with the system's expectation, again based on everyday knowledge of amounts, that the effect of a small tax should not be so large. This reminded the program of its failure judging the size of credit with respect to the total size of the economy. In fact, the explanation of the problem in this instance is quite similar: since gas consumption is over 6 million gallons a day, the change produced by the tax *is* actually quite small. Comparison of the reminding to the current failure could suggest the explanation that sizes are relative, and suggest the new rule that we shouldn't form conclusions about them until we have points of comparison.

### 3.4. Using causal structure to select relevant indices

ALFRED is reminded only when an expectation fails, and only of situations where the failure was attributed to the rule that failed in the original episode. In order to profit fully from experiences, we should be able to be reminded of old cases in a wide range of circumstances. To do this a case should be indexed in such a way that it will be retrieved whenever it is likely to be relevant to current processing.

If the explanation for a failure episode is available at the time of storage, the episode can be indexed to make it available in causally similar situations, in order to warn of likely problems before they occur. Likewise, plans can be indexed in terms of the goals that were active in the original situation, so that remindings will suggest solutions to current problems.

This sort of case-based learning is investigated in CHEF (Hammond [10]). CHEF is a case-based planner that devises recipes in the cooking domain. Instead of basing its planning on a rule library, it relies on its experience: new plans are based on memories of past plans. When a plan fails, or it encounters problems it has previously solved, it is reminded of similar past situations. It then uses them as the basis for dealing with the current situation, and installs the new case in memory for future use. (The use of remindings of past failures to resolve difficulties is also investigated in [31, 32].)

CHEF's learning system uses causal knowledge to focus on important features when integrating plans into memory: when a plan is successful, it is indexed in terms of goals it satisfies and the problems it avoids; when it fails, it is indexed under features that predict the type of failure encountered. Such indexing allows CHEF to anticipate and avoid problems by being reminded of past failures and of plans it has used to deal with them.

Although CHEF uses past cases in its planning, it starts from scratch when it initially explains a plan failure. The following sections show how experience can facilitate explanation.

## 4. Explanations in Memory

If we ask someone why a team lost a game, he won't have to reason from first principles. There are many standard answers for why a team lost, and his answer will probably be one of them, such as:

- They were overconfident and didn't train hard enough.
- They were tired from a previous tough game.
- Key players were injured.
- They couldn't take the pressure.
- The opponents wanted revenge.

As MOPs are fossilized plans, *explanation patterns* (XPs) are fossilized explanations. The explanations they package may come from personal experience, or they may capture culturally shared knowledge. For example, proverbs like *too many cooks spoil the broth* and *pouring oil on the fire is not the way to prevent it* offer explanations of undesirable outcomes.

### 4.1. The structure of XPs

XPs need to include information to support direct application to anomalies, and to have a sufficiently rich internal structure to allow them to be adapted to new situations.

In order for an explainer to recognize when an XP applies directly to a given anomaly, each XP must have a component representing the anomaly it explains. In order for an explainer to preserve and apply the useable portions of a near-miss explanation, XPs must include an explicit representation of the beliefs and belief inter-relationships underlying the packaged explanation.

XPs should also package simple criteria for when the XP is likely to hold. This allows an explainer to avoid re-analyzing each step in the belief support chain when deciding if an XP applies. Also useful are criteria for whether an XP is likely to be useful, even if it doesn't apply directly—that information aids when selecting an XP to try from a set of partially applicable XPs.

The knowledge in an XP can be helpful during planning as well as when recovering from failures. For example, the explanation of an unexpected event may be useful as a trace of a means to bring it about; the explanation of an unusual action may suggest a new way to satisfy particular goals. This planning knowledge is often summarized in a proverb or rule of thumb associated with the XP. Finally, XPs organize in memory the episodes they have been used to explain.

Thus the parts of XPs include:

(1) a representation of the anomaly that the pattern explains,
(2) a set of states of the world under which the pattern is likely to be a valid explanation,
(3) a set of states of the world under which the pattern is likely to be useful, even if it isn't immediately applicable,
(4) a pattern of beliefs, with the relationships between them, that show why the event being explained might have been expected,
(5) a proverb or rule of thumb that summarizes the situation for use in planning,
(6) a set of prior episodes that have been explained by the pattern.

For example, a classic XP is: *killed for the insurance money*. This pattern can be used to explain a premature death. When someone who is heavily insured dies, especially under suspicious circumstances, people sometimes wonder about whether he was killed for his life insurance. The associated XP follows:

*Killed for the insurance money*

(1) An anomaly which the pattern explains: *untimely death*.
(2) A set of states of the world under which the pattern is likely to be a valid explanation: the combination of either *untimely death* or *death heavily insured* with *relatives didn't love him* or *beneficiary is suspicious character*.
(3) A set of states of the world under which the pattern is likely to be useful, even if it isn't immediately applicable: *deceased was rich*; *relatives didn't love him*; *beneficiary is suspicious character*.
(4) A pattern of beliefs, with the relationships between them, that show why the event being explained might have been expected:
  – *beneficiary dislikes policy-holder*,
  – *dislike makes beneficiary want to harm policy-holder*,
  – *beneficiary has goal to get a lot of money*,
  – *inheriting is a plan for getting inheritance*,
  – *insurance means that inheritance will include a lot of money*,
  – *inheriting requires that the policy-holder dies*,
  – *beneficiary kills the insured to harm him and to get money*.
(5) A proverb or rule of thumb that summarizes the situation for use in planning: *a good way to get rich and get rid of someone you don't like at the same time*.
(6) A set of prior episodes that have been explained by the pattern: *deaths seen in movies, mafia killings*.

*Killed for the insurance money* is a *culturally shared* pattern. We learn such patterns from those around us, and have them as a common basis for building explanations. Such an XP is like the restaurant script in that we consider it as a possibility without examining closely the underlying beliefs. Another type of explanation pattern is the *idiosyncratic* pattern. On the basis of their individual experiences and values, people build up a library of explanations. Idiosyncratic patterns may package an incoherent or irrational explanation, yet people use them to guide their behavior. A real-life example follows:

*This generation should fight a war because past ones did*:

> When I was collecting voters for an anti-war candidate, one of the people I contacted began to argue with me about the war. He said that the reason that I was against the war was that I was a coward and was just trying to avoid fighting in it. I argued my point of view but he just ended up saying: I fought in World War II when I was your age and now it is your turn to fight in your war.

This example reiterates that the summary need not be a rational conclusion from the conditions, nor is there any reason that the XP has to have the correct explanation of the situation. Yet even when patterns are idiosyncratic and ill-formed, they may be useful to the people who devised them: this is clear from people's reliance on them.

## 5. An Algorithm for Case-Based Explanation

Our model of understanding is the integration of new facts into the knowledge in memory. If an input conflicts with memory, an explanation must be generated to show why previous knowledge or expectations failed to apply, and to generate correct expectations. We propose the following understanding/explanation cycle:

*Step* 1. *Anomaly detection.* Attempt to fit a new fact into memory.
– If successful, processing of the fact is complete.
– Otherwise, an anomaly has been detected. The anomaly is characterized according to a classification of anomaly types.

*Step* 2. *XP search.* Using the failure type as an index, try to retrieve an XP that responds to the anomaly type. If none are retrieved, generate other indices to retrieve potential XPs.

*Step* 3. *XP accepting.* Attempt to apply the XPs.
– If successful, and the XP could be accepted without revision, memory is updated with the beliefs in the XP. Processing of the fact is complete.
– If a revised explanation was accepted, update memory with the beliefs it involves, and skip to Step 5 (XP integration).
Otherwise, characterize the problems of the inapplicable XPs.

*Step* 4. *XP tweaking.* On the basis of the anomaly characterization generated in Step 3 (XP accepting), select strategies for revising the XP to repair the problem. New XPs that are generated are sent back to Step 3 to be evaluated.

*Step* 5. *XP integration*. If a new XP is accepted, store it in memory, making appropriate generalizations.

This cycle is implemented in preliminary form in the SWALE system, which has three modules: the main program (by Leake) handling anomaly detection, XP accepting, and XP integration, and modules handling XP search (by Owens) and XP tweaking (by Kass). The following sections will discuss the issues involved in each of these processes, and the ways we address them.

As a continuing example, we will show the role of each phase of the process as SWALE built explanations for a story that surprised many people when it originally happened. In 1984, Swale was the best 3-year-old racehorse, and he was winning all the most important races. A few days after a major victory he was found dead in his stall. The shocked racing community tried to figure out why. Many hypotheses appeared, but the actual cause was never discovered.

The SWALE system detects the anomaly in Swale's premature death, and builds explanations of the death by tweaking remindings of XPs for other episodes of death. It picks the best of these candidate explanations, and adds it to its XP library for future use.

### 5.1. Anomaly detection

When SWALE reads a story, it tries to connect the input to its existing knowledge; a fact is anomalous if it cannot be integrated into memory. Part of our effort is developing a small number of anomaly classes for categorizing the problems found. The description of an anomaly in terms of this categorization can then be used as an index into explanations relevant to that anomaly class.

On the basis of a list of more than 170 anomalies and explanations collected at Yale (Kass and Leake [13]), and on the basis of the types of tests required to detect and repair different types of problems, we have grouped anomalies into a small number of classes (currently, 14 types). When SWALE detects an anomaly, it categorizes it according to these types. The anomaly classes include:

- *Role-filler of wrong category*.
  Example: A horse jogging, since joggers are usually human.
- *Premature event*.
  Example: A premature death.
- *Planning problems*.
  Example: A plan to drug a horse to improve his performance before a big race, since the horse would be tested and disqualified.
- *Novel causal connection*.
  Example: A suggestion that the market crash was caused by sunspots.

SWALE detects anomalies when new facts cannot be reconciled with its model of the world. To reconcile facts with its model, the system tries to integrate them into memory in terms of previous expectations, known patterns, and prior knowledge of specific facts; anomalies are failures of the understanding process. Whether a fact is acceptable or problematic is determined by the following questions, which guide SWALE as it attempts to understand an input fact:

*Is the input fact already in memory?*
If the fact is already known to the system, no more integration needs to be done.

*Does the input satisfy an active expectation?*
Routine understanding in SWALE is done with a MOP application process modeled on [3]. Input facts are checked to see whether they satisfy the expectations provided by active MOPs. If so, they are stored in memory, organized by the accepting MOPs [15, 18, 24]. Installing a fact in a MOP activates expectations for future actions. For example, the fact that Swale races at Belmont places Swale in the racing phase of the MOP M-racehorse-life, and generates the expectation that he will race for a few years, live at the stud farm for a few years, and then die.

When an input only partially matches an expectation, the conflicts are detected as anomalous. For example, when SWALE installs the event of Swale's death in Swale's M-racehorse-life, the time of the death (during the racing phase of Swale's life) conflicts with the expectations from M-racehorse-life that the death of a racehorse normally happens a few years after the end of its racing career.

By checking the temporal separation of events as it integrates new facts into a MOP, the program detects *premature event, delayed event,* and *premature termination of event sequence.*

*If the fact was not expected, can an accepting knowledge structure be instantiated, or can the input fact be accepted in terms of other known patterns?*
When an input fact is irrelevant to its active expectations, SWALE attempts to instantiate a new MOP to accept it. For example, when the system begins to process the story of Swale, it accepts the new fact that Swale was a racehorse by instantiating the MOP M-racehorse-life for him.

SWALE also tries to account for facts in terms of standard plans, and by using patterns associated with *role themes* [28]. For example, if SWALE is given the input that someone is a jogger, and then is given input about a specific instance of that person jogging, it uses the jogger's role theme to account for the specific instance.

Trying to accept a fact in terms of plans and goals can lead to detection of *planning problems.*

*Do other circumstances make the fact more likely?*
Even if a fact cannot be accounted for by an existing knowledge structure,

circumstances may make it plausible. SWALE's MOPs include information about factors that make occurrence of the MOPs more likely. For example, its MOP M-heart-attack includes the information that a predisposing circumstance is for the actor to be high-strung.

For all new facts, another question is considered:

*Are the fact's role-fillers reasonable?*
Each input fact is checked for whether its role-fillers are reasonable. Associated with each MOP in memory is information on the normative role-fillers (e.g., the filler of the diner role in M-restaurant is usually human, though not necessarily: a recent newspaper story described a restaurant for dogs). One of the wild explanations the system generates is that Swale might have eaten something poisonous at a restaurant. The system rejects the explanation both because horses normally don't eat in restaurants, and because restaurant food is normally wholesome. This check detects the anomaly class *role-filler of wrong category*.

## 5.2. XP search

A number of studies have shown that people often fail to retrieve relevant analogies (e.g. Gick and Holyoak [8, 9] and Gentner and Landers [7]). If relevant experiences are not retrieved efficiently, much of the advantage of case-based reasoning is nullified. Consequently, a key question in case-based or analogical reasoning is how to select indices for storing and retrieving cases from memory. If a case-based system can usually retrieve the appropriate cases from its memory of cases, even as the number of cases grows, increases in the size of its knowledge base will make its processing more efficient: a system with a large library of cases is more likely to have similar experiences to draw on.

### 5.2.1. *Using the anomaly characterization as an index*

For an explainer, a natural choice of index is a characterization of the anomaly that needs to be resolved. In straightforward cases, an XP will be indexed directly under the observed anomaly. If we learn of the murder of someone heavily insured, we easily retrieve the pattern *killed for the insurance money*.

SWALE's first approach to retrieval of XPs is to try to retrieve an XP that explained a similar problem. XPs are organized both by the anomaly class they involve, and by the role-fillers for slots of the anomaly; for a given anomaly type, the XPs dealing with anomalies whose fillers are closest in the abstraction hierarchy to the new problem are retrieved first. For example, given an instance of premature death of a beagle, the program would first retrieve any XPs for premature deaths of beagles, than of dogs in general, and then of other animals. (SWALE's abstraction information is actually a net rather than a tree;

any node may have multiple abstractions. The search for XPs of events with the closest-possible fillers is done breadth-first up this abstraction net.)

When SWALE tries to explain Swale's death, the system first retrieves its XPs of premature death in animals. For example, animals are sometimes accidentally run over. However, this XP does not apply to Swale, since he would have been carefully supervised.

### 5.2.2. Unusual feature search

If no XP that deals with the anomaly is available, other strategies must be used to retrieve XPs. Although the causal structure of the episode is not yet available, it is possible to select features likely to be relevant.

One heuristic people often use when explaining is *coordination of anomalies* [26]: if a situation has two anomalous features, a useful strategy for explaining them is to try to connect them. For example, if we see an unknown person in a nearby office, and then hear that a computer disappeared from the building, we may connect them by conjecturing that the person we saw was a thief.

The basic principle of coordination of anomalies underlies another search strategy used by SWALE. When an anomaly occurs and the system cannot retrieve an explanation for the anomaly, it examines other unusual features of the situation, and sees if any XPs indexed under them can account for the anomaly. The system determines features to check by comparing features of objects in the anomaly with normative expectations for their abstractions. For example, Swale is compared against normative expectations for star racehorses (compared to that class he has no unusual features that index XPs), and then to racehorses in general (compared to which class he is in exceptionally good physical condition). Using the indices of death and outstanding physical condition, the system retrieves a possible explanation: the explanation of the death of Jim Fixx, who died because exertion over-taxed a hereditary heart defect.

### 5.2.3. Search for folkloric explanations

When people have no experience to fall back on, they sometimes try to explain by using proverbs, even though they must work to select an appropriate one and to figure out how it applies to the specific case at hand. One index for retrieving proverbs is the class of event they explain. For example, for an anomalous death, we might retrieve *dead men tell no tales*. While this does not apply immediately to the death of an animal, it might be possible to revise it to apply. *Dead men tell no tales* involves killing to keep from being incriminated. This might explain the death of a racehorse who had been stolen, and was killed to destroy the evidence when the people who stole him thought police were closing in. When SWALE exhausts its library of experiences, it attempts to retrieve proverbs that account for events of the type that was anomalous.

## 5.3. XP accepting

Once an XP has been retrieved, the anomaly explained by the XP is matched with the anomaly to be explained, binding variables of the XP. In some cases this instantiated XP will apply immediately. In the above example of the team's loss, any of the explanations might apply without modification. The XP accepting phase must determine whether the explanation is acceptable and identify any problems that need repair. Since the system may generate a number of explanations, none of which is completely certain, it also must weigh the relative merits of competing explanations.

Evaluation cannot be done in the abstract: it must be influenced by what the explainer knows and needs to learn. Thus an explanation should be judged on the basis of three criteria: whether it answers the explainer's underlying question, whether it substantiates its answer, and whether its answer gives the explainer the supplementary information needed to respond in accordance with the explainer's active goals.

### 5.3.1. *Relevance of an explanation*

An explanation is relevant if it addresses the underlying question that prompts the explanation attempt. Many EBL systems explain situations that cannot be accounted for by existing schemas. For them, the underlying question is *what caused this event to occur?* Another class of situations needing explanation, which has received less attention, is those where an active expectation is contradicted. To explain the mistaken expectation, an explainer must answer *why did my expectation go wrong?*

As an example of the difference between these questions, and of the reason that addressing expectation failures is important, suppose we expect a restaurant to be good because a restaurant guide recommended it. If we have a bad meal there, an explanation of the *event* of the bad meal might be that the chef is incompetent. EBL systems could generalize this to learn that restaurants with incompetent chefs serve bad meals. However, we could also learn from explaining why we predicted incorrectly. Since our prediction was based on the review, a relevant explanation might show why we shouldn't have trusted the guide. If we found that the guide always gives favorable reviews to places that advertise in it, we would know to avoid similar problems by discounting its praise of advertisers. In general, a system confronting an expectation failure must try to explain *both* why the surprising event happened, and why it shouldn't have formed the expectation.

What constitutes a relevant explanation of an event is well understood: it is simply a causal chain leading to the event. Since SWALE explains expectation failures, it needs explanations that address them as well. An explanation of an expectation failure must show a flaw in the reasoning that led to the expectation. For example, an explanation that is relevant to the expectation failure underlying a *premature event* is one that shows why normal temporal delays were superceded: either by catalyst (e.g., bread might have risen quickly because a room was unusually warm), or by an independent cause that brought the event about earlier than expected (e.g., someone died prematurely because he was hit by a car). SWALE has procedures, indexed by anomaly types, to check whether an XP's belief support chain gives a reason that the original expectation does not apply.

### 5.3.2. *Judging believability*

SWALE judges believability of an XP's hypotheses by integrating them into its model of the world, and seeing if they generate anomalies. Thus this phase of evaluation is simply trying to understand the facts of the explanation in light of its other knowledge.

To check the believability of an XP's causal links, SWALE first tries to retrieve the rule used from the system's rule library. If the rule is known to the system, templates for its antecedent and consequent are matched with the belief nodes linked in the XP, and any restrictions on role-fillers of the rule are checked. If the rule is unknown, the XP is returned to the tweaker for elaboration of the connection.

### 5.3.3. *Evaluating detail*

Even if an explanation is believable, it is unsatisfying unless it is adequately detailed. The level of detail needed depends on the explainer's goals. For example, when a car owner has car trouble, all he needs to know is whether the problem is transient (such as getting a bad tank of gas) or needs to be repaired. A mechanic requires a more detailed explanation, since he must trace the problem to a faulty part or a needed adjustment.

As a first step towards evaluating detail in terms of explainer needs, SWALE has a library that associates role themes [28] with tests for the detail that theme-driven actors need in different situations. For each theme, the information has two parts:

(1) *A list of types of anomalies whose resolution is important to the theme.* For example, two types of anomalies important to a veterinarian are animals' physical changes (e.g., weight loss) and behavioral changes (such as loss of appetite), since they might be signs of a health problem. A detective would investigate anomalies such as premature deaths and violent acts.

(2) *For each relevant anomaly, a test to judge whether the explanation provides enough information for a theme-driven actor to respond.* For example, a detective would need to trace the cause of a premature death until he found whether it was due to natural causes or foul play.

The program applies this knowledge to judge the elaboration of explanations. Its criteria need to be expanded so that in addition to standard theme-based requirements, requirements for detail could be dynamically determined on the basis of active goals and plans of the system.

SWALE now has only simple criteria for comparing explanations. Relevant explanations are divided into three classes of believability: *confirmed* (all assumptions verified or accounted for by expectations), *assumed* (some hypotheses couldn't be verified, but there are no problems reconciling memory with the hypotheses), and *unacceptable* (problems have been found). Out of the most believable explanations, the system tries to elaborate those with insufficient detail, and the evaluator finally accepts any resultant explanation that is relevant, believable and adequately detailed. If no explanation is acceptable, the explanation and a description of its problems are passed to the tweaking phase of the process, which attempts to repair the problems.

## 5.4. XP tweaking

The goal of the tweaking process is to make it possible to use an XP in a wide range of circumstances. Even when a new situation shares few features with the one explained by an XP, the XP can give a starting point for generating hypotheses.

### 5.4.1. *Applying explanations to new situations*

For any analogical reasoning, a key issue is how to map old knowledge to a situation. Work on analogy has presented a number of approaches. Gentner's *structure-mapping theory* [6] assumes that specific objects from a source domain have been previously identified with objects in a target domain, and gives criteria for exporting some relationships from the source domain to the target domain. The relationships chosen to map are those that have high systematicity (i.e., that belong to coherent sets of mutually consistent relationships). For example, in the analogy "the hydrogen atom is like the solar system," the relationship more-massive-than is preserved, because it is related to other relations such as distance and attractive-force, while the relationship hotter-than is not.

However, as Holyoak [11] points out, it is possible to imagine many relationships that hotter-than *is* related to, so syntactic criteria alone are not sufficient to determine which relationships to preserve. Also, Gentner's approach implies that for a given source domain, the same relationship with a target should always be favored, regardless of the circumstances. This conflicts with our experience: the aspects of an analog that people notice depend on context.

Holyoak [11] suggests that pragmatic context, such as goals of a problem solver, focuses analogical mapping. When a previously solved problem is applied to a new situation, the first step is to generate an abstraction of the old problem's statement that is sufficiently general to apply to the new case. This mapping of goals, constraints and operators is extended to include an abstraction of the old solution, which is then mapped to the new problem.

SWALE's mapping between cases is also determined by the problem the system needs to resolve, but is formed directly. SWALE retrieves an XP that explains a similar anomaly, and matches the old anomaly with the one to be explained. This match establishes the correspondence between the two cases; on the basis of the variable bindings it determines, SWALE instantiates the old XP.

Whenever transfer of a previous case is attempted, the mapping may break down: the mapped case may need to be adapted to deal with aspects that have no direct analog in the source case. For example, someone who knows how to drive a car with automatic transmission will not be able to use a manual transmission without adding shifting gears to the driving procedure. Because SWALE maps XPs without any further abstraction of their structure, the ability to repair such problems is especially important. To do such repairs, the system maintains a set of revision rules. The flavor of this approach is similar to that of Carbonell [1], who transforms a solution applicable to an old problem into one for a new problem; SWALE's *tweaking strategies* are similar to Carbonell's analogy transformation operators.

### 5.4.2. SWALE's *tweaking algorithm*

Tweaking strategies are procedures for revising or repairing parts of XPs that are inapplicable to the situation being explained. The types of revisions suggested by SWALE's strategies range from quite abstract to highly specific. Some strategies call for operations such as splicing in new steps to provide support for unsupported links; these may require considerable search to be applied. Others give a highly constrained way of patching a specific problem.

Which tweaking strategies are applied to a problem depends on the problem characterization generated by the XP accepting process. SWALE's method of selecting tweaks is similar to that used in CHEF [10] to repair plan failures: CHEF's goal failure configurations are used as indices for retrieving plan repair strategies; SWALE's anomaly types are used as indices into its library of repair strategies. The basic tweaking cycle is:

*Step* 1. Index from a failure description to a tweaking strategy.
*Step* 2. If strategy is found, attempt to apply it.
*Step* 3. If no tweak applies to the problem, abandon the belief that caused the failure.

### 5.4.3. *Examples of* SWALE's *tweaking strategies*

SWALE uses tweaking strategies at varying levels of specificity. If a failure description gives a very general characterization of a problem, the tweaks indexed under that description can only give general repair suggestions. For example, to repair the problem *novel causal connection*, which occurs when an XP linking two facts does not substantiate the connection between them, SWALE uses the strategy:

*Find connecting XP*
If the causal connection between beliefs in an XP cannot be substantiated, splice in the reasoning of another XP that substantiates the connection.

However, for tweaking to be efficient, it is important whenever possible to constrain the alternatives considered. Our approach to repairing *role-filler of wrong category*, when the role being filled is actor of an action, shows the types of restrictions that are useful. For an action with a problematic actor, the system attempts two types of tweaks. The first tries to retain the actor, but substitute another action for the problematic one. If possible, it uses information about the actor to guide selection of a substitute action that is likely for him. The second type of strategy retains the basic action, and tries to use characteristics of that action to suggest likely substitute actors.

### 5.4.4. *Strategies for substituting an alternative action*

*Substitute alternate theme*
If an XP depends on an actor having a particular role theme [28], but the actor in the current situation doesn't have that theme, try to substitute a role theme of the current actor that has causally equivalent effects.

For example, the XP for Jim Fixx's death depends on Jim Fixx's jogger role theme to support the belief that Fixx was running, but that theme does not apply to Swale since Swale is not human. Using *substitute alternate theme*, SWALE examines the themes of Swale to see if any support the belief that he was running. Since Swale's horse-racing theme is a support, the tweaker generates the explanation that Swale's racing caused him to run, which caused exertion, which over-taxed a heart defect and caused his death.

*Substitute related action*
When an action doesn't apply, it may be possible to obtain the desired effects by substituting a similar action that is applicable.

For example, when someone visiting New York is late for a meeting, we might remember that he was late once before because he took the wrong subway train. If we remember that there is a subway strike, we might use *substitute related action* to generate the hypothesis that this time he got on the wrong bus.

To hypothesize related actions, the system uses its abstraction hierarchy: it selects abstractions of the problem action that fit the causal structure, and looks at their specifications to find other possibilities. Thus although one abstraction of subway could be "dangerous place," the system would not attempt to splice dangerous places into the explanation, but would consider other modes of transportation.

### 5.4.5. *A strategy for substituting an alternative actor*

Tweaks to substitute an alternative actor have not been implemented, but an example of such a tweak is:

*Substitute an actor who could benefit*
When the hypothesized actor is unlikely, consider actors with goals satisfied by the action. For example, if we investigated the explanation that Swale's owners killed him to collect his insurance, we would rule it out because Swale was under-insured. But this might make us look at who might have had reasons to kill him, suggesting possibilities like *killed by a competitor's owner*.

SWALE currently has a small set of tweaking strategies. When a problem is encountered, all applicable ones are tried, and the resultant set of new XPs is evaluated. However, we anticipate that there will be many more strategies; heuristics will be needed to guide more selective retrieval.

## 5.5. XP integration

Once SWALE has accepted a new XP, the XP is integrated into its library of explanations. This allows it to efficiently explain similar anomalies in the future. In order to integrate the XP into memory, SWALE performs two tasks: generalization of the new XP, and indexing it in memory.

### 5.5.1. *Generalization*

The traditional assumption in systems using explanation-based methods is that they have access to perfect causal knowledge of their domains. Given this assumption, it is reasonable for them to generalize their explanations to the greatest extent licensed by their rules. However, knowledge of situations in the real world is usually approximate, and too many factors are involved in events to explain them completely. Consequently, people rarely make explanations that are deductively valid.

In response to the incompleteness of domain theories for real-world events, the only generalization SWALE always does is variabilizing of the belief support chain of an XP. Further generalization is only done to the extent necessary to accommodate examples the system has seen. When the system has retrieved an explanation that doesn't fit, but successfully tweaked it to apply, the system compares the two. For segments of the belief support chains that do not match, the system tries to produce the most conservative generalization that subsumes the original explanations. (Generalization based on the comparison of two explanations' causal structure is also suggested by Kedar-Cabelli [14].)

For example, when the system accepts that Swale's death was caused by exertion caused by running in races, combined with a heart defect, it compares the new XP to the explanation of Jim Fixx's death that it tweaked to generate the Swale explanation. Both explanations share the same structure, except that

Swale's death was supported by the role theme of running in horse races, and Jim Fixx's death by the role theme of jogging. The system uses its abstraction net to look for a shared abstraction of horse racing and jogging that could substitute for an initial segment of nodes in the belief support chain. It finds that having a role theme of physical exertion supports the basic chain, and it generalizes the two explanations to form the generalized explanation *performing physical exertion raised the actor's exertion level, which over-taxed a heart defect, causing a heart attack, which led to death.*

Once the generalized explanation of Swale's death has been installed in memory, a new class of anomalies can be explained efficiently by retrieving and directly applying the XP. For example, even though the form of a plow horse's exertion is different from that of Swale and Jim Fixx, the generalized XP could be retrieved to explain his premature death. The new XP is also available for tweaking to fit more distantly related situations.

## 5.5.2. *Indexing*

Initial work on explanation-based methods focused on using explanations for generalization [21]. A wider view is suggested by DeJong and Mooney [4], who propose that explanation is important not just for generalization, but for specialization of concepts. We believe that EBL includes another important task: the selection of indices for storing cases or generalizations in memory.

For real-world situations, the problem of applying old cases to new events is best approached by concentrating on indexing an episode so that it will be retrieved in relevant cases, rather than doing all generalization when the episode is stored. (Our perspective is similar to that of Hammond [10], who argues that a case-based planner does not generalize the plan itself, but instead generalizes the indices under which the plan is stored.) When a new case cannot be accounted for by an existing XP, the retrieved cases can be modified to fit the situation, and generalization can then be done to form a new XP that explains both cases.

In addition to avoiding overgeneralization when causal knowledge is uncertain, modifying cases when necessary gives more flexibility: old cases can contribute to dealing with situations that may not be subsumed by any obvious generalization of the explanation.

For this approach to be effective, we need to index cases so that similar cases will be retrieved first, but apparently dissimilar cases will be available when there are no direct solutions. While surface features have a large effect on people's retrieval of analogies [7], we believe that indexing with deeper features, such as causal factors, is very important [24]. SWALE uses two classes of features to index XPs:

– *The anomaly categorization.* As was discussed in the section on XP search, the XPs that explain a particular type of anomaly are organized first by the anomaly type, and then hierarchically on the basis of their primary role-fillers.

For example, XPs considered for premature death of a racehorse would first be premature deaths of racehorses, then of horses, and then of animals.

– *Causal preconditions of the situation*. The system uses the explanation to identify features that are causally relevant, and indexes new XPs under the event type and the causally relevant features. For example, the generalized XP for Swale's death is indexed under *death + exertion*.

We believe that the following types of features are also important, even though they are not directly implicated in the explanation. While we have not implemented indexing of new XPs under these types of features, they are used to index XPs in SWALE's initial XP library:

– *Features participating in anomalous aspects of the situation described by the XP*. One reason that Jim Fixx's early death was anomalous was that he was in excellent physical condition. The Jim Fixx XP is indexed under the combination *death + good physical condition*.

– *Membership in stereotyped groups*. Death of a rock star, for example, might remind us of the deaths of Jimi Hendrix or Janis Joplin. In SWALE, the explanation of Janis Joplin's death from a drug overdose is indexed under *death + star performer*.

## 6. Creative Explanation

Creativity is sometimes thought of as an almost mystical process, where a creative act produces something out of nothing. However, there is a fundamental flaw in any attempt to consider creativity as something that transcends our knowledge. No human discovery occurs in a vacuum: If we really accepted that creative acts must build something out of nothing, we would be hard-pressed to argue that human creativity exists.

It seems obvious that to come up with new ideas, we must start with old ideas. Creativity comes from retrieving knowledge that is not routinely applied to a situation, and using it in a new way. Thus the key issues of explanation by XPs, search and adaptation, are also the key issues for creativity.

Creativity is not an all-or-nothing thing: there is a spectrum of creativity, going from minor revisions of old knowledge all the way to a totally new world view. Application of XPs can take place at any point along the spectrum of creativity, from the completely noncreative application of a perfectly appropriate XP, to the very novel use of an inappropriate XP that must be totally revised to be useable. This section presents some of the explanations that SWALE generates along that spectrum, and considers what is necessary to extend such a system's creativity.

### 6.1. The range of explanations generated by SWALE

In order to give an idea of the range of explanations that a system using our approach can generate, below are some reminders that the SWALE system has, and a few of the explanations it generates from them. Some are reasonable explanations; others are quite fanciful or can be ruled out on the basis of other knowledge. However, they show that a memory-based explanation system, even if it has a limited range of XPs and of retrieval and tweaking strategies, can come up with a variety of interesting explanations.

*Reminding.* Thinking of other deaths of those in peak physical condition causes the system to be reminded of the death of the runner Jim Fixx, who died when his running over-taxed a hereditary heart defect.

*Explanation.* Swale might have had a heart defect that caused his racing to prompt a heart attack.

*Reminding.* Thinking about other deaths of young stars, the system is reminded of Janis Joplin's death from a drug overdose.

*Explanation* 1. The pressure of being a superstar was too much for Swale, and he turned to drugs to escape. He died of an overdose.

*Explanation* 2. Swale might have been given performance-enhancing drugs by a trainer, and died of an accidental overdose.

*Reminding.* Thinking of folkloric causes of death causes the system to recall the old wives' tale *too much sex will kill you.*

*Explanation* 1. Although racehorses are prohibited from sex during their racing careers, Swale might have died of a heart attack from the excitement of just *thinking* about life on the stud farm.

*Explanation* 2. Swale might have committed suicide because he became depressed when thinking about sex.

*Explanation* 3. Swale might have died in an accident when he was distracted by thinking about sex.

### 6.2. Requirements for creative explanation

The above examples show that interesting explanations arise when we try to use an XP that doesn't quite apply. In order to obtain creative explanations, an explainer might try to *intentionally misapply* XPs. Interesting ideas can arise from using old explanations to deal with situations where those explanations were never intended to be used.

While using an XP that doesn't apply gives a fresh perspective on a situation, the idea of building a system to intentionally misapply XPs raises many issues: Which XPs do you retrieve? Which tweaks should be applied? How long should the tweaking process be continued? As our research progresses, we hope to be able to answer these questions. However, we can now suggest some of the things that are needed to build creative case-based explainers:

*We need heuristics for the intentional reminding of explanation patterns*
XP retrieval is the process of formulating questions to memory: we characterize an anomalous situation in terms of a set of indices, and ask what XPs in memory explain similar situations. When no answer is available, we must

reformulate the question into one that we can answer [15, 27]. When no solution is directly available, people often fall back on asking standard questions that give background information. Answers to *explanation questions* like *what physical causes underlie this event?*, *what special circumstances made the event happen now?*, *what motivates the actor of this surprising action?*, *how did the victim enable this bad event?*, or *what groups might the actor be trying to serve?*, may suggest relevant factors that can be used as indices for XP retrieval. Though the XPs accessed in this way might not be directly applicable, it may be possible to adapt them. A creative system needs a set of explanation questions for gathering information, rules for selecting which questions to apply in a given situation, and rules for transforming them to fit.

*We need tweaking strategies that can do significant revisions*
Tweaking must also be able to make significant revisions. Rather than requiring tweaks to always maintain causal structure, we should allow them to make broad changes. Their revisions will not always be successful, but failures produce new possibilities for still more revision.

*We need heuristics for knowing when to keep alive seemingly useless hypotheses*
In addition to choosing between explanations generated by the system, the evaluation process also has a more direct part in the creative process. We cannot tweak a candidate explanation indefinitely; the evaluator must decide whether a hypothesis is worth pursuing. This estimation will always be imperfect, but the better it is, the more resources the system will be able to devote to fruitful revision of XPs. One heuristic would be to continue tweaking an explanation as long as each tweak generates a better explanation. But the decision whether to continue tweaking should also depend on the availability of competing candidate XPs, and on an estimate of how important the final explanation is to goals of the system (since that affects how many resources should be expended explaining).

*We need a system with a rich memory of explanations*
Finally, a creative case-based explainer must have access to a wide range of explanation patterns. There are two ways that people or machines might learn new XPs: by being taught them directly (as children are given explanation patterns by parents, teachers, or friends), or by learning new ones through creative misapplication. One step towards making a computer creative would be to collect an extensive list of XPs that it could use as the starting point for adaptation. Many interesting explanations might be constructed starting with a collection of culturally shared XPs, such as proverbs.

## 7. Conclusion

Machine learning will be successful when computers are able to learn interesting things. Because of the importance of explanation-based learning, constructing interesting explanations is important.

We have argued for a case-based approach to building explanations: that just as people use experience to explain, so should computers. For this approach to be successful, systems will need an extensive library of explained episodes, in a form that is flexible enough to permit revision. We have defined the *explanation pattern* knowledge structure to package the information needed to support revision.

Case-based explanation requires heuristics for retrieving and revising XPs to deal with new situations, and we have sketched the algorithms SWALE uses to generate new XPs. In order for a system to improve future performance on the basis of experience, learning the XPs it generates is also important. While we believe that XPs must be indexed under a wide range of features, our current implementation of SWALE indexes them under two main types of indices. One is a categorization of the anomaly being explained: XPs can be used most efficiently when they are retrieved for anomalies similar to those they were built to explain. The other major class of indices is causally relevant features; we suggest that *explanation-based indexing* is an important type of explanation-based learning.

SWALE deals with incomplete and uncertain knowledge, which is unavoidable in real-world domains. Consequently, our generalization strategies for XPs are very conservative. We believe that the flexibility necessary to deal with a range of events should be maintained by indexing cases under a wide range of indices and modifying the case to fit once it is retrieved, rather than by trying to generalize as much as possible when it is generated.

The SWALE project shows that a memory-based explanation system, even if it has a limited range of XPs and of retrieval and tweaking strategies, can come up with interesting explanations. We have sketched issues that will have to be confronted to attack creative explanation more thoroughly: the key problems of creative explanation are the problems of retrieving and tweaking existing explanations. Each is a major problem in its own right, but they are problems on which we can make progress.

## Appendix A. SWALE's Representation of Beliefs and Belief Supports

Input to SWALE, and the beliefs and links in XPs, are represented in terms of a limited number of belief types. In the current implementation of the system, the following classes of facts are represented:

– *Action description.* The fact that an action occurred. For example, that Swale raced at Belmont.

– *Theme description.* The fact that an actor frequently performs a certain class of action. (This is part of the information in *role themes* [28].) For example, a jogger tends to go jogging frequently.

– *Value description.* That fact that a given attribute of an object has a given value. For example, that Swale's color was brown.

– *Packaging description*. The fact that an object or event fills a role in a MOP. For example, that Swale filled the role of actor in the MOP representing racehorse-life.

– *Goal description*. The fact that an actor holds a certain goal. For example, the fact that Swale's owner had the goal for Swale to win races.

In the belief support structure of an XP, assertions of the above types are linked by nodes representing the inferences by which acceptance of one fact would support acceptance of another.

As described above, the rules used by the system are not deductive rules; a reasonable belief support chain cannot be considered a proof that an inference is true. Because the correctness of a rule's conclusion depends on many factors, people sometimes require a number of independent supports before they believe an event occurred. In *killed for the insurance money*, either the beneficiary wanting to hurt the policy-holder or wanting to inherit money is support for the belief that he killed the policy-holder. Even though we wouldn't normally believe that either one alone resulted in a murder, the two together are fairly convincing evidence.

The types of rules used by the program include:

– *Physical causation*. Effects accounted for by physical or biological laws. For example, that running raises exertion level.

– *Social causation*. Effects we expect because of custom or social patterns. For example, that a Frenchman will like wine.

– *Economic causation*. Effects that we expect because of economic principles. For example, that a decrease in supply will cause prices to increase.

– *MOP sequence*. That in a given context, certain events tend to follow others. For example, that in a fast-food restaurant, customers pay immediately after ordering.

– *Specification*. That an object or event belonging to a certain category can be inferred to belong to a more specific subcategory if it has certain features. For example, that a successful rock performer belongs to the category of rock star (which carries with it default assumptions about his life style, etc.).

– *Preservation goal activation*. That a threat to a desired state prompts a goal to neutralize the threat. For example, that working in a high pressure environment causes people to want to decrease stress.

### Appendix B. Output from SWALE

The annotated output below demonstrates our case-based explanation process for a few of the explanations the system generates. (The trace generated by the program is more complete; some output has been deleted.)

### B.1. Detecting that Swale's death is premature

The following output is generated by the program as it instantiates the MOP

racehorse-life to accept input about Swale's Belmont victory. On the basis of its
representation of racehorse-life, the program generates the expectation that he
will go to the stud farm in a few years, and die a few years later. When the
program is given the input that he died a week after the race, it detects that his
death is premature.

*Input.* The fact *Swale won the Belmont Stakes*, represented as:

    [HORSE-RACE
      ACTOR: SWALE
      LOCATION: BELMONT
      TIME: TIME-TOK-1
      OUTCOME: WIN]

Output from processing:

> Integrating SWALE's HORSE-RACE into memory.
>
> Trying to link SWALE's HORSE-RACE to SWALE's active MOPs.
>
> The fact SWALE's HORSE-RACE will be stored as the HORSE-RACE scene
> in SWALE's RACEHORSE-LIFE.

*Input.* The fact *Swale died a week later*, represented as:

    [DEATH
      ACTOR: SWALE
      TIME: TIME-TOK-2]

(TIME-TOK-2 represents a time a few weeks after TIME-TOK-1 above.)
Output from processing:

> Integrating SWALE's DEATH into memory.
>
> Trying to link SWALE's DEATH to SWALE's active MOPs.
>
> The fact SWALE's DEATH will be stored as the SWALE's DEATH scene in
> SWALE's RACEHORSE-LIFE.
>
> Temporal anomaly detected:
>    SWALE'S DEATH occurs abnormally early in RACEHORSE-LIFE.

## B.2. Explaining an anomaly by tweaking existing XPs

To resolve the anomaly, the system first tries to retrieve XPs indexed under
similar anomalies. None of the XPs it retrieves are applicable, so the program

tries to retrieve XPs indexed under other features. To retrieve XPs indexed by unusual features of Swale, the search module climbs the abstraction hierarchy, starting with the node representing Swale, and attempts to retrieve XPs indexed under any features of his that are unusual with respect to the given category. The following output traces the search process:

> Asking explorer to find possible explanation.
>
> Considering SWALE's DEATH as an instance of a generalized DEATH.
>
> SWALE's NAME is SWALE, while
>   a generalized SUCCESSFUL-RACEHORSE's NAME is UNKNOWN.
>   Nothing found connecting (NAME SWALE)
>   with DEATH.
>
> A generalized SUCCESSFUL-RACEHORSE's HEALTH is HIGH, while
>   a generalized RACEHORSE's HEALTH is UNKNOWN.
>   Nothing found connecting (HEALTH HIGH)
>   with DEATH.
>
> A generalized SUCCESSFUL-RACEHORSE's PHYSICAL-CONDITION is
> HIGH, while
>   a generalized RACEHORSE's PHYSICAL-CONDITION is UNKNOWN.
>   Found JIM-FIXX-XP-263 indexed under DEATH
>   with index: (PHYSICAL-CONDITION HIGH).          ·

The Jim Fixx XP (that his jogging role theme caused him to run, which caused exertion that combined with a heart defect to cause a heart attack) is retrieved, and the XP is evaluated. In the following output, the program detects that Swale is not a suitable role-filler for the ACTOR role in jogging, since the actor is normally a human. The program then uses the tweaking strategy *substitute alternate theme* to find another support for the belief that Swale was running.

> Checking #{EXPLANATION 183 FIXX-XP}.
>
> Found problem:
>   [XP-FAILURE
>     TYPE: INAPPLICABLE-THEME
>     ROLE: ACTOR
>     PROBLEM-DESCRIPTION:
>       [TYPE-MISMATCH
>         DESIRED-ATTRIBUTE: #{TYPE-NODE 140 HUMAN}]
>     BELIEF-LABEL: JOG]
>
> Attempting to tweak XP titled FIXX-XP.
>
> Searching for appropriate modification strategies . . .
> One strategy retrieved.

Attempting to apply a modification strategy:
"Substitute a theme that is associated with the actor"
to XP: FIXX-XP.

The belief labeled JOG is a support in the following way(s):
It supports the belief RUN via support type MOP-SCENE.
Asking memory for other life-themes for SWALE.
Associated themes:
SWALE often has the ACTOR role in the HORSE-RACE theme.
SWALE often has the ACTOR role in the EAT-OATS theme.

Seeing whether any of these themes can substitute . . .

Swale's horse-racing theme is successfully substituted for the jogging theme in the XP. The system then checks whether Swale's other known theme, eating oats, could provide support for RUN. That tweak fails.

The explanation that Swale had a heart defect, and died when exertion of horse racing over-taxed his heart, is evaluated. The explanation does not conflict with the system's beliefs, but the premise that Swale had a heart defect cannot be substantiated.

The explanation #{EXPLANATION 187 FIXX-XP-1} may be OK,
but requires some assumptions.

Since the explanation cannot be confirmed, the program seeks alternative explanations. No more XPs are indexed under unusual features of Swale, so the program looks for folkloric XPs.

Looking for folkloric explanations of DEATH . . .
The explorer has returned #{EXPLANATION 189 TOO-MUCH-SEX}.

The explanation retrieved is the old wives' tale *too much sex will kill you.*

The program's representation of the MOP for a racehorse's life includes that he is prevented from breeding during his racing days, and then is sent to the stud farm to be bred. Thus the old wives' tale might have applied later in his career, but doesn't apply during his racing days. When an XP hypothesizes that an event took place, but that event could not have happened early enough to contribute to the explanation, one of SWALE's tweaking strategies is *substitute anticipation*: see if effects of *anticipation* of the event could have been similar to those of the hypothesized event itself. (This rule is reasonable in a number of domains. For example, if the rise in a company's stock is explained by the XP *new product introduction makes stock rise*, but the introduction actually didn't take place before the rise, people's anticipation of the new product is a possible explanation.)

The problem, and the attempt to repair it by tweaking, are reflected in the following output:

> Checking #{EXPLANATION 189 TOO-MUCH-SEX}.
>
> Due to being a SUCCESSFUL-RACEHORSE, SWALE might be prevented from SEX.
>
> Misorder found: SWALE hasn't yet reached SWALE's STUD-FARM.
>
> Found problem:
>   [XP-FAILURE
>     TYPE: INAPPLICABLE-THEME
>     ROLE: ACTOR
>     PROBLEM-DESCRIPTION:
>     [MOP-SCHEDULING-FAULT
>       POSITIONING-PROBLEM: [ACTION-TOO-EARLY]
>       MOP-NAME: RACEHORSE-LIFE
>       LAST-SUCCESSFULLY-PROCESSED-SCENE: 4
>       MATCHING-SCENE: 3]
>     BELIEF-LABEL: SEX]
>
> Attempting to tweak XP titled TOO-MUCH-SEX.
>
> Searching for appropriate modification strategies . . .
> 2 strategies retrieved. Will try each in turn.
>
> Attempting to apply a modification strategy:
>   "Try substituting anticipating action for action itself"
>   to XP: TOO-MUCH-SEX.

This tweak generates the explanation that Swale's death was caused by thinking of future sex. The other tweaking strategy tried, *substitute a theme that is associated with the actor* for the XP's theme of sex, fails to yield possible causes of death.

The XP *death caused by thinking of sex* is then evaluated. The connection between thinking of sex and death is not substantiated:

> Checking #{EXPLANATION 190 TOO-MUCH-SEX-1}.
>
> Explanation has unconvincing support.
>
> Attempting to tweak XP titled TOO-MUCH-SEX-1.
>
> Searching for appropriate modification strategies . . .
> One strategy retrieved.
>
> Attempting to apply a modification strategy:

"Splice in another explanation pattern to explain a connection"
to XP: TOO-MUCH-SEX-1.

To construct a link, the program chains forward one step from sex to its effects, and tries to retrieve XPs linking them to death. One effect of thinking of sex is depression (if you're thinking about problems in your love life):

Looking for an XP to connect:
?X?'s VERY-LOW EMOTIONAL-STATE ... with ... ?X?'s DEATH

Found an XP to connect ?X?'s VERY-LOW EMOTIONAL-STATE to ?X?'s DEATH:
XP is #{XP 194 DISTRAUGHT-SUICIDE}

The resultant XP is that Swale was depressed because of thinking about sex, and he committed suicide.

From distraction and excitement, two other possible effects of thinking of sex, the program generates the explanations that Swale might have died from an accident caused by his being distracted, or that he might have died from a heart attack caused by excitement. The three new XPs are then evaluated. Although none of the new XPs can be confirmed, the attempt to retrieve more potential XPs is unsuccessful, so the program selects the best of the candidate XPs.

All of the XPs are judged relevant to Swale's death, since each suggests a new factor intervening to cause death before old age. When the system judges believability, death from suicide is ruled out (suicide is motivated by anticipating good effects from death, while the program assumes that animals are only aware of the effects of events they have already experienced). Accidental death is ruled out because racehorses are carefully supervised.

Death from being excited and having a heart attack is possible. But since Swale's becoming excited is an unsubstantiated hypothesis, while his running can be confirmed on the basis of his racing role theme, the explanation *heart attack caused by running and a heart defect* is preferred.

Finally, detail must be evaluated. In the output below, the program evaluates detail with respect to the detective's role theme:

Checking sufficiency of explanation for detective's role theme.

Anomaly is a negative health change, so adequate detail is important to detective.

Checking whether the explanation traces SWALE's DEAD HEALTH to natural causes, to an accident, or to a crime and suspect.

Explanation hypothesizes ORGAN-FAILURE as a natural cause:

HEART-1078's M-HEART-ATTACK. It also shows a physical-result chain between this cause and SWALE's DEAD HEALTH. Consequently, level of detail is acceptable.

Conclusion: the explanation is ACCEPTABLE.

After the explanation is accepted, the old and new XPs are generalized:

Looking at possible generalization of original and tweaked XPs.

Looking for a generalization of JOG and HORSE-RACE which will support the same causal chains.

The theme of actor in PHYSICAL-EXERTION accounts for all necessary facts.

Installing generalized XP.

Indexing the XP under the anomaly class it explains.

Installing a class of specializations of DEATH explainable by FIXX-XP-1.

Adding to memory the facts implicit in #{EXPLANATION 187 FIXX-XP-1}.

## B.3. Using the new XP

Since the new XP has been installed in memory, SWALE can retrieve it and apply it without modification to another story in which it detects a similar anomaly. The following output was generated in processing the story of a racehorse named Last Chance Louie, who died a few weeks after the Kentucky Derby.

When the anomaly of Louie's premature death is detected, three XPs of similar anomalies are retrieved from the program's XP library. *Death from exertion combined with heart defect* is indexed under premature death of an actor with a role theme of exertion, while *death by being run over* explains the premature death of an animal, and *death from illness* explains the death of any living thing. Since the exertion theme gives a more specific characterization of a racehorse than animal or living thing, the first XP SWALE tries is *death from exertion combined with heart defect*. This XP applies without revision.

Temporal anomaly detected:
LAST-CHANCE-LOUIE'S DEATH occurs abnormally early in RACEHORSE-LIFE

Trying to pull up XPs indexed by the anomaly.

Seeing if one of these XPs is relevant:
FIXX-XP-1

XP-EARLY-DEATH-FROM-RUN-OVER
XP-EARLY-DEATH-FROM-ILLNESS

Checking #{EXPLANATION 209 FIXX-XP-1}.

The XP is accepted.

## ACKNOWLEDGMENT

We would like to thank Chris Riesbeck and Alex Kass for helpful comments on a draft of this paper.

This work is supported in part by the Air Force Office of Scientific Research, under grant 85-0343, and by the Defense Advanced Research Projects Agency, monitored by the Office of Naval Research under contract N00014-82-K-0149.

## REFERENCES

1. Carbonell, J.G., Learning by analogy: Formulating and generalizing plans from past experience, in: R.S. Michalski, J.G. Carbonell and T.M. Mitchell (Eds.), *Machine Learning: An Artificial Intelligence Approach* (Tioga, Palo Alto, CA, 1983).
2. Carbonell, J.G., Derivational analogy: A theory of reconstructive problem solving and expertise acquisition, in: R.S. Michalski, J.G. Carbonell and T.M. Mitchell (Eds.), *Machine Learning: An Artificial Intelligence Approach* 2 (Morgan Kaufmann, Los Altos, CA, 1986) 371–392.
3. Cullingford, R., Script application: Computer understanding of newspaper stories, Ph.D. Thesis, Tech. Rept. 116, Yale University, New Haven, CT (1978).
4. DeJong, J. and Mooney, R., Explanation-based learning: An alternative view, *Mach. Learning* 1 (1986) 145–176.
5. Dietterich, T. and Michalski, R., A comparative review of selected methods for learning from examples, in: R.S. Michalski, J.G. Carbonell and T.M. Mitchell (Eds.), *Machine Learning: An Artificial Intelligence Approach* (Tioga, Palo Alto, CA, 1983) 41–81.
6. Gentner, D., Structure-mapping: A theoretical framework for analogy, *Cognitive Psychol.* 7 (1983) 155–170.
7. Gentner, D. and Landers, R., Analogical reminding: A good match is hard to find, in: *Proceedings IEEE 1985 International Conference on Systems, Man and Cybernetics* (1985) 607ff.
8. Gick, M.L. and Holyoak, K.J., Analogical problem solving, *Cognitive Psychol.* 12 (1980) 306–355.
9. Gick, M.L. and Holyoak, K.J., Schema induction and analogical transfer, *Cognitive Psychol.* 15 (1983) 1–38.
10. Hammond, K.J., Case-based planning: An integrated theory of planning, learning and memory, Ph.D. Thesis, Tech. Rept. 488, Yale University, New Haven, CT (1986).
11. Holyoak, K.J., The pragmatics of analogical transfer, in: G.H. Bower (Ed.), *The Psychology of Learning and Motivation* (Academic Press, Orlando, FL, 1985).
12. Kass, A., Modifying explanations to understand stories, in: *Proceedings Eighth Annual Conference of the Cognitive Science Society*, Amherst, MA (1986).
13. Kass, A. and Leake, D.B., Types of explanations, Tech. Rept. 523, Yale University, Department of Computer Science, New Haven, CT (1987).
14. Kedar-Cabelli, S.T., Purpose-directed analogy, in: *Proceedings Seventh Annual Conference of the Cognitive Science Society*, Irvine, CA (1985).
15. Kolodner, J.L., Retrieval and organizational strategies in conceptual memory: A computer model, Ph.D. Thesis, Tech. Rept. 187, Yale University, New Haven, CT (1980).

16. Kolodner, J., Simpson, R. and Sycara, K., A process model of case-based reasoning in problem solving, in: A. Joshi (Ed.), *Proceedings IJCAI-85*, Los Angeles, CA (1985) 284–290.
17. Leake, D.B. and Owens, C., Organizing memory for explanation, in: *Proceedings Eighth Annual Conference of the Cognitive Science Society*, Amherst, MA (1986).
18. Lebowitz, M., Generalization and memory in an integrated understanding system, Ph.D. Thesis, Tech. Rept. 186, Yale University, New Haven, CT (1980).
19. Lebowitz, M., Integrated learning: Controlling explanation, *Cognitive Sci.* **10** (1986) 219–240.
20. Mitchell, T.M., Generalization as search, *Artificial Intelligence* **18** (1982) 203–226.
21. Mitchell, T.M., Keller, R.M. and Kedar-Cabelli, S.T., Explanation-based generalization: A unifying view, *Mach. Learning* **1** (1986) 47–80.
22. Rieger, C., Conceptual memory and inference, in: R.C. Schank (Ed.), *Conceptual Information Processing* (North-Holland, Amsterdam, 1975).
23. Riesbeck, C.K., Failure-driven reminding for incremental learning, in: *Proceedings IJCAI-81*, Vancouver, BC (1981) 115–120.
24. Schank, R.C., *Dynamic Memory: A Theory of Learning in Computers and People* (Cambridge University Press, Cambridge, 1982).
25. Schank, R.C., The current state of AI: One man's opinion, *AI Mag.* **4** (1) (1983) 3–8.
26. Schank, R.C., Explanation: A first pass, Tech. Rept. 330, Yale University, Department of Computer Science, New Haven, CT (1984).
27. Schank, R.C., *Explanation Patterns: Understanding Mechanically and Creatively* (Erlbaum, Hillsdale, NJ, 1986).
28. Schank, R.C. and Abelson, R., *Scripts, Plans, Goals and Understanding* (Erlbaum, Hillsdale, NJ, 1977).
29. Schank, R.C., Collins, G. and Hunter, L., Transcending inductive category formation in learning, *Behav. Brain Sci.* **9** (4) (1986).
30. Schank, R.C. and Leake, D.B., Computer understanding and creativity, in: H.-J. Kugler (Ed.), *Information Processing 86* (Elsevier Science Publishers B.V. (North-Holland), Amsterdam, 1986) 335–341.
31. Simpson, R.L., A computer model of case-based reasoning in problem-solving: An investigation in the domain of dispute mediation, Ph.D. Thesis, School of Information and Computer Science, Georgia Institute of Technology, Atlanta, GA (1985).
32. Sycara, E.P., Resolving adversarial conflicts: An approach integrating case-based and analytic methods, Ph.D. Thesis, School of Information and Computer Science, Georgia Institute of Technology, Atlanta, GA (1987).

# AUTHOR INDEX

# SUBJECT INDEX